Poverty, Crisis and Resilience

NEW HORIZONS IN SOCIAL POLICY

Series Editors: Patricia Kennett and Misa Izuhara, *University of Bristol, UK*

The New Horizons in Social Policy series captures contemporary issues and debates in social policy and encourages critical, innovative and thought-provoking approaches to understanding and explaining current trends and developments in the field. With its emphasis on original contributions from established and emerging researchers on a diverse range of topics, books in the series are essential reading for keeping up to date with the latest research and developments in the area.

Titles in the series include:

Housing Wealth and Welfare
Edited by Caroline Dewilde and Richard Ronald

Social Investment and Social Welfare
International and Critical Perspectives
Edited by James Midgley, Espen Dahl and Amy Conley Wright

Social Services Disrupted
Changes, Challenges and Policy Implications for Europe in Times of Austerity
Edited by Flavia Martinelli, Anneli Anttonen and Margitta Mätzke

Social Policy After the Financial Crisis
A Progressive Response
Ian Greener

Social Policy in the Middle East and North Africa
From Social Assistance to Universal Social Protection
Edited by Rana Jawad, Nicola Jones and Mahmood Messkoub

The Small Welfare State
Rethinking Welfare in the US, Japan, and South Korea
Edited by Jae-jin Yang

Poverty, Crisis and Resilience
Edited by Marie Boost, Jennifer Dagg, Jane Gray and Markus Promberger

Poverty, Crisis and Resilience

Edited by

Marie Boost

Department of Joblessness and Social Inclusion, Institute for Employment Research (IAB), Federal Employment Agency, Germany

Jennifer Dagg

Centre for Disability Law and Policy, National University of Ireland, Galway, Ireland

Jane Gray

Department of Sociology, Maynooth University, Ireland

Markus Promberger

Head, Department of Joblessness and Social Inclusion, Institute for Employment Research (IAB), Federal Employment Agency, Germany and Institute for Sociology, University of Erlangen, Germany

NEW HORIZONS IN SOCIAL POLICY

Edward Elgar
PUBLISHING

Cheltenham, UK • Northampton, MA, USA

Published by
Edward Elgar Publishing Limited
The Lypiatts
15 Lansdown Road
Cheltenham
Glos GL50 2JA
UK

Edward Elgar Publishing, Inc.
William Pratt House
9 Dewey Court
Northampton
Massachusetts 01060
USA

A catalogue record for this book
is available from the British Library

Library of Congress Control Number: 2020948589

This book is available electronically in the **Elgar**online
Social and Political Science subject collection
http://dx.doi.org/10.4337/9781788973205

MIX
Paper from
responsible sources
FSC
www.fsc.org   FSC® C013604

ISBN 978 1 78897 319 9 (cased)
ISBN 978 1 78897 320 5 (eBook)

Printed and bound by CPI Group (UK) Ltd, Croydon, CR0 4YY

Contents

Figures

Tables

Contributors

María Arnal, PhD, is a lecturer in Sociology at Complutense University of Madrid, Spain. Her main research interests include precarious labour and its relations to new poverty and social exclusion. She has also published on international migration and changes in labour identities. María Arnal is a member of the Employment, Gender and Regimes of Social Cohesion (EGECO) research team and TRANSOC institute at Complutense University.

E. Attila Aytekin holds degrees in political science and public administration, and a PhD in history. He has published on Ottoman working class and peasantry, Turkish political history, deindustrialization and poverty in contemporary Turkey, and Ottoman urban history. Currently he is an associate professor at Middle East Technical University, Ankara, Turkey and a fellow at Kulturwissenschaftliches Institut, Essen, Germany.

Marie Boost, diploma in Sociology from Dresden Technical University, is a junior researcher in the department 'Joblessness and social inclusion' at the Institute for Employment Research, Nuremberg, and a doctorate student at Friedrich-Alexander-University, Erlangen, Germany. Her research fields are poverty, social exclusion, unemployment and precarious labour, with a special focus on socioeconomic practices at household level, qualitative and mixed methodologies.

Aida Bosch, DPhil., is Professor of Sociology at Friedrich-Alexander-University, Erlangen, Germany, where she teaches cultural sociology, social theory and interpretive methodologies. Her research and publications include the sociology of objects, social exclusion, the challenge of human biology and materialities for social thinking, philosophical anthropology and visual hermeneutics. Aida Bosch was an advisor in visual methodologies for the 'RESCuE: Citizens' Resilience in Times of Crisis' project and is leading editor of the book series 'Visuelle Soziologie', together with Hans-Georg Soeffner, Roswitha Breckner, Michael M. Müller and Jürgen Raab.

Alexandre Calado, PhD student in Sociology, is working on the topic of the debt crisis, the transformation of the welfare states in Europe and the politics of resilience. Currently he is a Researcher at the Centre for Research and Studies in Sociology (CIES-IUL) in Lisbon, Portugal. His main fields of interest are political sociology and welfare state studies. He has participated in research studies on the evaluation of public policies oriented towards decreasing poverty and increasing qualifications among disadvantaged social groups.

Luís Capucha, PhD in Sociology, is head of the Department of Social Sciences and Public Policies at the Lisbon University Institute (ISCTE-IUL) and senior researcher at the Centre for Research and Studies in Sociology (CIES-IUL). His main research and publishing interests are poverty and education, and he co-developed the concept of 'poverty ways of life'. Luís Capucha is advisor to the Portuguese government in social policy issues and was General Director in the Portuguese Ministry of Labour and Social Solidarity from 1999 to 2002 and in the Portuguese Ministry of Education from 2007 to 2011.

Concepción Castrillo is a researcher in the Department of Social Psychology and Social Anthropology at the Complutense University of Madrid, Spain. She obtained her PhD in Sociology from the same university, with an extraordinary doctorate award. Her research interests include gender, care, emotions and social inequalities; currently she participates in several research projects on care and vulnerability.

Carlos de Castro, Dr, Lecturer at the Department of Sociology, Universidad Autónoma de Madrid, Spain. His research focuses on the political and institutional configuration of work and workers in the context of global production networks in several sectors. He has published on the role of workers in the global agricultural production chain.

Hulya Dagdeviren is a Professor of Economic Development at University of Hertfordshire, UK, and the Editor-in-Chief of the journal *Competition and Change*. Her research focuses on social consequences of economic structure and policy for the poorer sections of society. Recent publications include topics like low income household indebtedness and the impacts of privatization of essential services on the welfare of low income groups. She worked as an advisor for international institutions such as the United Nations Development Programme and coordinated the UK 'RESCuE: Citizens' Resilience in Times of Crisis' project.

Jennifer Dagg holds a PhD in Sociology from the National University of Ireland, Galway. Currently, she is a postdoctoral researcher at the Centre for Disability Law and Policy at the National University of Ireland, Galway, exploring reproductive justice for persons with disabilities. Her research interests are the intersection of sociology and politics with particular interest in the dynamics of power, agency and subjectivity, exclusion and marginalization, along with qualitative research methods. She has published in the areas of migration and poverty, and on qualitative research methods.

Matthew Donoghue is Lecturer in Comparative Social Policy at the University of Oxford, UK. His research is concerned with social and economic integration, the role of social citizenship in these processes, and the political conditions in which they take place. He has expertise on social cohesion, critical approaches to resilience and the politics of welfare. He is on the editorial board of 'Palgrave Communications', on the politics and social policy panels.

Pedro Estêvão is a PhD student in Sociology on the topic of firm and workers' strategies regarding education and training in the context of economic and social crisis. He is a researcher at the Centre for Research and Studies in Sociology (CIES-IUL). His main research interests are economic sociology and public policy analysis. He has participated in projects evaluating the impact of educational reforms to promote school success amongst disadvantaged social groups and also on studying phenomena such as early school leaving and school underachievement.

Monika Gnieciak is Associate Professor at the Institute of Sociology, University of Silesia, Katowice, Poland. Her areas of interest include sociology of literature, sociology of culture and culture studies, social anthropology, and social communication.

Jane Gray is Professor of Sociology at Maynooth University, Ireland. Her scholarship centres on questions relating to families, households and social change, with a particular focus on biographical life course analysis. She was national co-ordinator for Ireland on the recently completed FP7 funded project 'RESCuE: Citizens' Resilience in Times of Crisis', and has a longstanding interest in sharing and re-using qualitative social science data.

Nelli Kambouri has worked since 2015 as a senior research fellow at the Centre for Gender Studies, Panteion University of Social and Political Sciences, Athens, Greece. Her work and publications focus on gender theory, violence, migration, precarity, social movements and new media. In the past, she has worked on several European Union (EU) funded projects, taught at the Department of Social Policy of Panteion University and held scientific advisory posts in the Greek General Secretariat of Gender Equality and the International Labour Organization.

Witold Mandrysz, PhD in Sociology, is a teacher and researcher in the Social Work Unit, Institute of Sociology, University of Silesia, Katowice, Poland. He has been involved in various international, national and regional research projects. His main research fields are: social work, social economy, community work, participation and civic dialogue, and local governance.

Soula Marinoudi obtained her PhD from the Department of Social and Cultural Anthropology, Panteion University, Athens, Greece in 2014. She has taught as an adjunct lecturer at the University of Thessaly and the National and Kapodistrian University of Athens. Her research and publications are concerned with anthropology of health and disability studies with an emphasis on autism and the formation of autistic subjectivities, as well as queer approaches to gender and sexuality.

Mª Paz Martín, Dr, researcher in the Department of Sociology: Methodology and Theory, Complutense University of Madrid, Spain. Her research interests are social policies in a cross-national comparative perspective, the development of qualitative comparative research frameworks, welfare state reforms, social governance and the influence of European institutions in social policy-making. She is also interested in studies of citizenship representation, gender orders and political and community participation in the context of the recent recession. She has published several abstracts and chapters related to these topics.

Lars Meier, Dr, sociologist and geographer, is Professor of Sociology, Johann-Wolfgang-Goethe University in Frankfurt, Germany. His main focus is on social/spatial inequalities and diversity, cultural studies, migration, urban studies and qualitative methods. Meier has been working at the Institute for Employment Research in Nuremberg, where he was involved in the EU project 'SPHERE' and 'RESCuE: Citizens' Resilience in Times of Crisis'.

Janina Müller holds a BA and an MA in social sciences, literature and media studies. From 2016 to 2018 she worked at the Institute for Employment studies in Germany, first as a junior researcher in the research unit for Joblessness and Social Inclusion, then in the institute's press office. Presently she works in the central administration of the German Federal Labour Agency in Nuremberg.

Georgia Petraki is Professor of Sociology in the Department of Social Policy at Panteion University of Political and Social Science, Greece, and since 2015 has been director at the Center of Gender Studies, Panteion University. She teaches qualitative methodology, sociology of labour and social stratification. She has published several books and articles about segregation in the labour market, work organization and class structure. She has participated in different European Research Programs. Petraki's research interests include work organization, working conditions, social stratification and social movements.

Markus Promberger, DPhil., is Professor of Sociology at Friedrich-Alexander-University and head of the research unit Joblessness and Social Inclusion at the Institute for Employment Research (IAB) in Nuremberg, Germany. His background is labour sociology and history, social theory, economic anthropology, and his research fields include precarious labour, flexible organizations, social policy evaluation, poverty, social inequality and the

Poverty, crisis and resilience

logics of action at the low end of developed societies. Promberger is advisor to the German Parliament, Federal Ministry of Labour, the German Trade Union Federation, and the Federal Labour Agency. He was the international coordinator of the 'RESCuE: Citizens' Resilience in Times of Crisis' project.

Juan Carlos Revilla, Dr, is Professor and Head of the Department of Social Anthropology and Social Psychology at Complutense University of Madrid, Spain. His main research interests are identity processes, critical management studies and youth studies. He has been national coordinator of two EU 7th Research Framework Programme projects, 'RESCuE: Citizens' Resilience in Times of Crisis' and 'SPHERE'.

H. Tarık Şengül holds degrees from Middle East Technical University (BCP, City Planning and MS, Political Science) in Ankara, Turkey, and the University of Kent (PhD in Urban Studies), UK. He has published mainly in the fields of urban studies, local government and geography. He is currently a Professor of Urban Studies in the Political Science Department and head of the interdisciplinary postgraduate programme on Urban Policy Planning and Local Government at Middle East Technical University in Ankara. Şengül is a policy advisor in the field of spatial and social development and urban planning to various public bodies in Turkey, and was the National Coordinator of the 'RESCuE: Citizens' Resilience in Times of Crisis' project for Turkey.

Araceli Serrano, Dr, is a researcher in the Department of Sociology: Methodology and Theory, Complutense, University of Madrid, Spain. She specializes in Social Science Methodology, the Analysis of Discourse, visual analysis and mixed methods. Her research activities focus on poverty, social exclusion and social policy. She currently investigates and publishes on care work, ways of representing poverty and social exclusion, collective representation of economic crisis of vulnerable people and the multidimensional effects of crisis in households.

Frank Sowa is Professor of Sociology at Nuremberg Tech Georg Simon Ohm, Germany. He received his PhD degree from the University Erlangen-Nuremberg and worked as researcher at the Nuremberg Institute for Employment Research for many years. His areas of research include the changing welfare state, street-level bureaucracy, poverty, deviance and homelessness, including ethnographic and cross-cultural perspectives.

Monica Tennberg is a research professor and leader of the Northern Political Economy research group at the Arctic Centre, University of Lapland, Rovaniemi, Finland. She is a political scientist who has worked with Arctic issues since the late 1980s. Her current research focuses on politics of everyday life in the Arctic in the midst of complex, intertwined changes due to warming climate and globalization and their implications for local peoples, communities and livelihoods.

Joonas Vola is a junior researcher in the Culture Based Service Design doctoral programme at the Faculty of Social Sciences, and a member of the Northern Political Economy research group in the Arctic Centre, University of Lapland, Finland. He received a master's degree in social sciences, International Relations, from the University of Lapland in 2012 and has worked since then in the field of Arctic research and political science.

Terhi Vuojala-Magga is an anthropologist who specializes in Arctic issues, such as climate change, reindeer husbandry, Arctic skills and knowledge. She lives in Kuttura, which is a tiny reindeer herders' wilderness village in Finnish Lapland. At the moment she runs a wilderness company called Wildernesslife Kuttura.

Kazimiera Wódz has an MA in psychology, a PhD in Humanities and a habilitation in Sociology. She has been Professor of Sociology since 1994, and is head of the Cultural Studies department and head of the Social Work Unit at the University of Silesia, Katowice. Her scientific experience covers cultural studies, European studies, urban and regional studies, political sociology, social work and social policy. She has worked on several international projects dealing with different aspects of regional transformations, such as 'Social History of Poverty in Central Europe, The Polish Case', 'SPHERE' and 'RESCuE: Citizens' Resilience in Times of Crisis'.

Acknowledgements

Both this book and the underlying project would not have been possible without numerous people who were extremely helpful, sometimes without even knowing. We would not have come across the 2012 European Union (EU) call for tenders on 'citizens' resilience in times of crisis' without Dionyssis Balourdos, when he and Markus Promberger searched for interesting calls and funding options for research in the field of households' and institutions' behaviour in the European financial crisis of 2007 and later. It was also crucial for the later success of the 'RESCuE: Citizens' Resilience in Times of Crisis' project proposal that we had had a complete test run with a (narrowly) rejected research proposal on poverty biographies only a few months before – thanks to Almut Wietholz and Anna Koniotaki who were part there but had moved to other issues when it came to finally develop RESCuE. Gratitude goes also to Robert Miller, who brought in the Irish team almost at the last minute, and to the Spanish team, who brought in the Portuguese team likewise – a tough quick-notice networking exercise of a kind which is only possible in a well-working scientific community, driven by the fascination of sharing and producing knowledge. From the earliest stage of the project, Ursula Huws played an invaluable role in co-developing the concept and the proposal, contributing a blueprint to the extensive management section of the proposal, establishing contacts to other project partners and supporters, co-interviewing poor households in the UK case study interviews, and freely giving advice from her rich EU project experience to Markus Promberger who took the task of coordinating the project.

The initial 2013 proposal group then included Athena Athanasiou, Attila Aytekin, Luis Capucha, Hulya Dagdeviren, Jane Gray, Ursula Huws, Witold Mandrysz, Lars Meier, Georgia Petraki, Markus Promberger (coordinator), Juan Carlos Revilla, Tarık Şengül, Monica Tennberg and Kazimiera Wódz. Other researchers joined in 2014 or later: Maria Arnal, Marie Boost, Alexandre Calado, Daniel Calderon, Carlos de Castro, Jennifer Dagg, Matt Donoghue, Pedro Estêvão, Krystyna Faliszek, Monica Gnieczak, Krysztof Łęcki, Lukas Kerschbaumer, Soula Marinoudi, Paz Martín, Janina Müller, Anna Schneider, Araceli Serrano, Barbara Slania, Kiko Tovar, Joonas Vola, Terhi Vuojala-Magga and Aggeliki Yfanti. Many of them have been involved in this book – thank you to all co-authors for your efforts and perseverance!

Our gratitude furthermore goes to Yuri Borgmann-Prebil who, as the EU project officer in charge, saw the potentials and risks of the project and of the resilience concept very clearly, and provided tremendous support. Extremely valuable contributions in terms of critical comments and support came from Selçuk Candansayar, Jane Millar and the late Elżbieta Tarkowska (deceased 2016), as the RESCuE scientific advisory board, and Peter Ester, who chaired this board in his usual manner as relaxed, challenging and precise. Many thanks also go to our visual methodology advisers, Aida Bosch from Erlangen University and Roswitha Breckner from Vienna University, for their methodological inspirations. Visual hermeneutics are certainly a huge effort but have a tremendously deep impact on understanding hard-to-access groups and situations.

Every project has periods where work is just going on like a buzzing beehive, but also periods where the house is close to being on fire. It was great to find supportive people in such critical phases, joining the local teams for a certain while – Cansu Civelek, Pawel Ćwikła, Andreas Dounis, Daniela Dzienniak-Pulina, Ruth Gerraghty, Andreas Hirseland, Lukas Kerschbaumer, Maciej Klimek, Jolanta Klimczak, Sheila Luz, Janina Müller, Dorota Nowalska-Kapuścik, Sabina Pawlas-Czyż, Ufuk Poyraz, Marta Romero, Anna Schneider, Frank Sowa, Monika Szpoczek, Zofia Trzeszkowska-Nowak, Mariano Urraco and Alexis Wearmouth. Others were eminently involved in the project since quite early, but could not contribute to this publication because they had moved on in the meantime to other tasks, such as Athena Athanasiou, Aggeliki Yfanti, Francisco José Tovar, Krystyna Faliszek, Krysztof Łęcki and Barbara Slania.

There are more people who contributed to the success of both the project and the book, who cannot be named here for obvious reasons. Gratitude goes to three anonymous referees for evaluating the project proposal, another two anonymous reviewers of the book proposal, to more than 20 anonymous referees evaluating the single book chapters and, last but not least, to our more than 250 respondents, who freely shared their experiences and openly revealed their way of life to us – and from which we have learned a tremendous amount!

For infrastructural support, flexibility and hospitality, in some cases also for additional funding, we wish to thank our chapter authors' home institutions: Panteion University Athens, University of Hertfordshire Business School, Maynooth University, Silesian University Katowice, University of Lapland in Rovaniemi, Universidad Complutense in Madrid, Lisbon University Institute, and the Technical University of the Middle East in Ankara. Special thanks also go to the coordinator's institutional affiliations: to the Institute for Employment Research (IAB) in Nuremberg and its director at that time, Joachim Möller, to the IAB administrators Mike Kindley, Holk Stobbe and Kerstin Hurnik for their early and ongoing support, and to the Berlin Science Centre (WZB), namely its President Jutta Allmendinger for very generous and flexible support in January 2017. Although the EU project funding period ended soon thereafter, analysis and co-authorships are continuing still, with new researchers and co-authors joining in – such as Concepción Castrillo, Juliane Achatz and Anton Nivorozhkin. We are happy that the publication output of the project is growing, as well as the literature on resilience in general, and the results of this project are beginning to be discussed in the policy field.

As editors, we wish to express our gratitude to the chapter authors as well as to all those who have made the book possible in a technical sense: Catherine Elgar, Harry Fabian, Emily Mew, Saffron Watts, Sue Sharp, Conor Byrne and Sarah Price from Edward Elgar Publishing, Melitta Matthias and Melanie Meier from the IAB. Nevertheless, authors and editors are solely responsible for any content, errors and incompleteness, and you, the readers, have the final judgement. We hope you appreciate our way of thinking about poverty and resilience and can benefit for your own study and practice.

Nuremberg, Maynooth and Galway, June 2020

The editors

PART I

Introducing poverty, crisis and household
resilience

1. Introduction: poverty, resilience and the European crisis

Markus Promberger, Marie Boost, Jennifer Dagg and Jane Gray

RESILIENCE: A THREEFOLD QUESTION

This book is about those few households which are in poverty, or close to it, but manage to get by relatively and sometimes unexpectedly well. Not necessarily in the sense of standard understandings of a decent life, but in terms of getting-by-better than most of their peers, despite the range of adversities and crises that they face. This book explores what makes them, or how they make themselves, resilient. It seeks to know how they, and we, can learn from resilient processes and practices. As a result, this book develops new concepts for poverty research in order to broaden the analytical lens (poverty is not only an income problem) and overcome the important, but often dominant deficit approach. This is achieved by exploring various dimensions of how families and households in, or close to poverty actually get by, as well as how and why some of them do so better than others under similar circumstances.

There are three main questions explored in this book: is there social resilience among households at the brink of poverty? How does it work (or not), and what are its respective resources, conditions, restraints, limits and risks? And, what can social policy learn from these findings to aid crisis?

In part, this book reflects the social effects in Europe of the global economic crisis of 2007, or the 2008 Great Recession, and beyond. It refers to the period in which the global financial market was in turmoil (the 'subprime crisis'), caused by shifting speculative risks, post-democratic elite formations, dis-information, irresponsibility and specific decouplings (see Sennett 2012; Jackson 2009; Crouch 2011) that resulted in state budgets having to support the financial sector in order to maintain economic stability. This shift of risk overburdened many state budgets with some states forced to apply for international support. In many cases, this support was conditional upon national governments implementing fiscal reforms and introducing austerity policies, most prominent in Greece and Spain. Such conditions resulted in increased privatization of state properties, drastic cuts in expenditure related to social investment and employment policy, public services including health, public sector labour, and even education. This period saw tremendous wealth redistribution in favour of the international financial sector, ultimately compensating them for moral and economic failures at the cost of ordinary middle- and low-income people.

This book is in part also a response to the fact that European anti-poverty policies have not been able to reduce poverty substantially. Even since the Lisbon 2002 anti-poverty goals and the implementation of 'activating' social policies – which increased work pressure, reduced transfer payments and public expenditures and increased thresholds for eligibility into social programmes – there has not been much change in overall poverty rates (see Chapter 7). There has been little effect apart from turning some unemployment into precarious labour, often without the intended budget savings (see Promberger 2015 for the German case). There is still considerable poverty in European welfare states (see Chapter 3). Indeed, poverty research needs some fresh answers. We know quite a lot about poverty thresholds, income poverty, and the size and dynamics of poor populations. There is some evidence of the efficiency and effectiveness of anti-poverty programmes. However, there is still just a small thread of research on how living conditions are transformed as a result of life processes and practices, and the differences between coping or transforming poverty situations.

To describe getting by under adversity, terms like coping or adapting have been introduced. Yet one specific concept specifically targets getting-by-better, and this is the concept of resilience. It has just recently crossd the borders of science and entered the socio-political discourse, mainly in the UK and partly at EU level. The genealogy of the 'resilience' concept will be discussed more broadly in Chapters 4 and 5. However, it has to be emphasized here that the concept poses both potentials and drawbacks when it becomes a discursive register within the political realm. Simplistically, it can mean that some units of observation are successfully beating the odds while others are not. It promises to restore belief in human nature and survival ability, in the 'ordinary magic' (Masten 2001) and inherent powers of human individuals, groups and families, and to provide a general solution to crises of various kinds, including natural disasters, economic downturns, or deprived childhoods. All the while, the concept poses a drawback – as an argument misused to blame vulnerable people for not being resilient, and distracting observers from the institutional failures surrounding crises. By entering the political discourse, and being exposed to political rhetoric, it shares the fate of many scientific concepts like class, identity, or even society. At the beginning of the project underlying this book, we encountered criticisms and warnings of various kinds on the concept of resilience, nevertheless, we decided not to abandon it but to stick to the scientific use of the concept and develop its social scientific explanatory power. Similar to psychology, where resilience has been attributed to empirically identifiable dimensions, such as salutogenetic factors (Antonovsky 1996; Lösel and Bender 2003), social resilience – as we conceive it – is specifically related to the observable practices and resources used by the resilient households observed. These observations structure the discussion throughout the chapters in this book.

DEVELOPMENT OF THE BOOK AND THE UNDERLYING RESEARCH

Given the European crisis, the European Commission issued a call for research proposals in 2013 under its 7th Framework Programme (FP7) entitled 'Citizens' Resilience in Times of Crisis'. This was inspired by developments in different research fields such as disaster recovery, terrorism, ecosystems and disadvantaged communities. A group of researchers from nine European countries, of which the editors of this book were part, successfully applied for three years funding, which was granted from early 2014 to early 2017 under the project title 'Patterns of resilience during socioeconomic crises among households in Europe' (RESCuE). The chapters in this book contain results from six years of collaborative research on the resilience of households in or close to poverty, completed by more than 30 researchers from nine European countries.

The research, development and transference of the concept of resilience for use within the discipline of sociology, along with its application for sociological poverty research has been one of the ground breaking achievements of this book.

The main hypothesis of the project was that resilience in poverty, where it existed at all, was based on the practical mobilization of social, economic and cultural resources. These practices or resources are not necessarily obvious, they are not on the radar of standard poverty administration and research, they are not easy to mobilize nor are they available to many households. Resilient households are able to identify, access and mobilize such resources when paid labour – the standard resource of non-propertied households – is lost, unavailable or insufficient for the household's livelihood. It has to be said that this approach of exploring household practices has been an issue in social history (Malcolmson 1989), labour and economic anthropology (Wallman 1979), and in development research approaches like the livelihood concept. Despite this, studying household or other small-scale socioeconomic practices has seldom been associated with resilience (except by a few, namely Béné et al. 2011), and is more commonly associated with similar concepts like sustainability or livelihood. These not only share a mixed field of meaning with the resilience concept, but also comprise analytical, teleological and political aspects, as resilience does. Resilience itself, already well established in psychology and ecosystems research, has become a hot topic in disaster research and social geography. To begin to transfer resilience into a sociological approach, one needs to understand it in a more sociological than psychological way (see Chapter 4), that is, in a way that mostly investigates social, cultural or economic resources or affordances at hand that are mobilized and utilized within certain patterns of practice (Haslanger 2018).

The research teams focused on studying resilient (and some non-resilient) households, but not larger communities, social groups or individuals, for various reasons. First, most individuals do not live alone but in a shared household, which normally centres on family relationships. Within that household, they usually share their lives and resources and take decisions together, no matter how equal or asymmetric this may be. Thus, it does not make sense to investigate the resilience of individuals only and treat their households and families as external conditions when we actually have an interactive co-production of living patterns and conditions within the household. The second reason is a substantial theoretical and practical problem: if the level of observation moves beyond individuals and families, into larger communities, the validation of outcome – like surviving or beating the odds – will also move to an elevated level. This shift may hide cases where communities may well survive or even thrive, but at the cost of selected members or sub-groups. The third reason is that social policy usually addresses individuals, families and households and not larger communities, although there might be political agendas in that direction. Looking at larger groups or wider social aggregates can make some limited sense for considering changes in ecosystems of plants and animals, but certainly does not make sense in the ethical framework of equality, social justice, and civil and human rights within which European social policy acts (see also Chapter 4).

Accordingly, the household is the economic or institutional framework for observing resilience as we understand it. A private household is a basic socioeconomic unit with a local centre of at least partial or temporal cohabitation. It is involved in external relations to markets and institutions with the relative absence of market relations internally. Households are conceived as the basic economic units of consumption and reproduction. For most of human history, and still for most people around the world, they also are the basic unit of production. Family relationships form the kernel of most households. As implied in the RESCuE project, family is defined as close interpersonal ties, often involving cohabitation and resource sharing on the basis of non-market intimate and/or genealogical relations. This can include couples married or unmarried, hetero-, homo- or non-sexual, with or without children, three or more generation families, patchwork families, single parent families, wider kin and affective peer cohabitation. Family may include members which are temporarily or permanently absent, but still related. Further, under certain circumstances we can even talk about family when people interviewed just call themselves a family.[1]

Concerning poverty, the RESCuE project uses a multilayered definition. This starts with the double definition of poverty by Georg Simmel (1992[1908]): first, being poor means having significantly lower means of living than one's respective peers. Second, being poor means being identified as such by wider society. The latter, at least, is quite complex. Simmel explicitly thought of the early roots of the welfare state defining the poor and creating institutions to support them. Being poor from the perspective of society can occur through being registered for welfare or receiving donations, but also by public begging, being homeless, living in an area which is perceived to be inhabited by poor people, working in jobs known to be badly paid, becoming evicted or something else. But being socially identified as poor can also happen differently, like having an income below the – socially defined – poverty line or showing signs of deprivation without seeing oneself as poor in the strict sense. And, certainly, being poor does not necessarily mean receiving welfare benefits, nor to be jobless. The working definition of poverty for the project researchers and authors of this book was a pragmatic and conventional one – having a monetary income of up to 60 per cent of the national median needs-based net household income. This definition is used as a standard by national governments and supranational authorities around the world. Nevertheless, as this definition is stricter than lived experience, it needs to be amended by two considerations. First, two households with the same monetary income may have very different assets or may experience different degrees of undersupply or deprivation. This is the reason why quantitative poverty researchers often prefer to talk about income poverty, material deprivation or welfare recipiency instead of poverty in general, and increasingly include non-monetary indicators in measures of poverty (Nolan and Whelan 2018). Second, a very small difference in income may make one household count as poor in terms of income, and the other one not, although there may not be any remarkable difference in their situation. Third, there are households below the income poverty line who manage to live on their own income and do not claim benefits, and households with the same monetary income but from welfare state sources. This gives reason to talk about socioeconomic vulnerability in low-income situations instead of talking about poverty in the strict sense. Pragmatically, most contributions in this book nevertheless talk about poverty, where the concern is about living on an income, self-provided or not, above but close to, on or below the poverty line.[2]

It has to be noted that these working definitions used by the project team are intended to be precise only in so far as is necessary to become operable, to still keep a certain openness at the 'fringes', instead of being so precise that they are completely free of logical contradictions and ambiguities. Concepts are the main element of giving structure to and speaking about observations, and they refer to inherent characteristics of the observed elements as well as to the perspective of the observers. Empirical operability of a concept means that it includes a certain level (neither maximum nor minimum) of variation and is sharp enough to draw distinctions, although not perfectly distinctive to shed any similarities between observed units.

METHODOLOGY AND DESIGN OF THE PROJECT

As there has not been much research on poverty and resilience, and even less so at household level, an explorative qualitative approach was taken. Nevertheless, in order to enable a certain level of generalizability – in terms of saturation (Glaser and Strauss 1967) and coverage of varieties, not in terms of statistical representativeness – a substantial number of case studies were included and a contrastive pattern of sampling was implemented. The ex-ante contrasting dimensions were:

- Contrastive country selection in order to cover different types of welfare states according to an expanded Esping-Andersen model (Esping-Andersen 1989), including a Mediterranean and a post-socialist type of welfare state alongside the liberal, conservative and social-democratic models. The United Kingdom and Ireland have been selected to represent the liberal welfare state, Finland for the Scandinavian or social-democratic model, Poland for the post-socialist type and Germany as a conservative welfare state. Spain, Portugal, Greece and Turkey represent the Mediterranean type, intendedly represented by four countries, with Turkey also standing for what could be called a kind of 'tiger economy' or emerging welfare state in crisis, as well as a non-EU welfare state.
- Both urban versus rural settings were observed, with rural meaning not a prevalence of agricultural life, but rather distance to urban agglomerations and expected variations in access to land and nature, density of settlements, self-owned housing, community relations and so on.
- Country and area selection were moreover considered to cover different degrees of socioeconomic impact of the crisis. For instance, Poland, Germany, Finland and Turkey were chosen to represent countries which have not been affected as severely in terms of their national economy and labour market developments. Nevertheless, they have areas or social groups affected by the crisis of 2007 and after, or group-specific crises, or structural crises. In those countries, areas with increased poverty rates, above average labour market problems or similar symptoms were chosen for the case studies. In Finland, the Finnish Lapland was chosen as an

economically and environmentally critical region – the relative decline of wood-related industries, an increasing vulnerability of traditional reindeer herding due to climate change (Vuojala-Magga et al. 2011), and the generally harder living conditions of the far North. In Turkey, a region in a Kurdish populated area was selected according to ongoing ethnic and political tensions imposing an increasing framework of risk, while in the other selected area a huge migrant inflow from Syria resulted in an above average vulnerable population. Poland and Germany, relatively unscathed in the Great Recession of 2008 and after, nevertheless had poverty populations, those left behind by the speed of transformation and modernization in Poland, and by German unification and its economic perturbances at a regional level. Ireland, Spain and Portugal, although they belong to different welfare state types, shared a relatively quick macroeconomic recovery at the expense (to varying degrees) of the welfare state and social policy budgets and thus the socioeconomically vulnerable population. While Germany and the UK shared a relatively low crisis impact, and a poor population of similar and persistent size, welfare state activities and intensities differed considerably (see Lohmann and Andreß 2008; Taylor-Gooby et al. 2017). Last but not least, Greece was chosen as having suffered the heaviest impact of the crisis, including the meltdown of public employment and welfare state provisions to minimal levels, and – like Ireland for a short time – exposing state budget control to the EU 'troika' in order to obtain budget creditability.

• Gender was included as a criterion, not only in terms of having roughly the same proportion of female and male persons interviewed as representative of the household, but also to assess broader socioeconomic shifts related to the financial crisis on the dynamics, patterns and practices of men and women, within and outside the family.

More contrasting dimensions were included where they emerged through the sampling process, which was organized to coincide with interviewing and the first tentative analysis. During sampling, different sampling ways had to be employed to achieve a variation of cases as wide as possible. The fieldwork began by contacting local experts from welfare authorities, charities and civil society organizations, asking them to suggest cases which match a first-order concept approximating the concept of resilience – like getting by well in poverty. Then, the number and kind of such experts were varied at later stages of the fieldwork – through snowballing of interviewed household members and local experts – for collecting more and different cases.

Not only were sampling and ways of access deliberately varied and contrasted, but also the methods of data collection. Data collection took place at four levels with different, yet simultaneously, overlapping methods: (1) Macro data at macro level (Europe and country); (2) expert information and open observation at regional and local level; (3) qualitative biographical interviewing (Schütze 1983); (4) interviewees' self-taken photographs (Noland 2006; Kolb 2008) and photo elicitation interviews (Harper 2002; Wuggenig 1990) at household level, but with individual components, as well as participant observation at household level. Triangulation (Flick 2011) or a multi-method approach would be an appropriate label for the procedures applied to collect information. These consisted of analysis of documents and statistics, expert knowledge, household narratives of representative members, and non-verbal information gathered and composed by the interviewees and their families including photographic fieldwork and researchers' participant observations.

Many of the areas where we did our research were well known to us beforehand, yet not all of them, thus, we did actually share the lives of our respondents for longer periods in some cases, and short periods in other cases. Furthermore, we had to apply some loose structures such as choice of methods, development of thematic checklists, and the use of ex-ante and second-order concepts (like resilience) in order to achieve a framework as open and consistent as possible in order to allow for cross-national (and cross-language/cultural) comparison.

Under these presumptions, considerations and conditions, it was decided to do interviews with local experts in the case study areas, and, after doing 'ethnographic walks' (Flick et al. 2018) to explore the surroundings and localities, conduct a first wave of narrative interviews in 24 households in each country. These were divided between rural and urban case study regions. Country wise, 12 of these households were selected to participate in the photographic fieldwork and subsequent photo elicitation interviews. Criteria included interviewees' consent to participate in this second step, a certain minimum level of responsiveness, mutual trust relations in the foregoing interview situation, and making sure to involve different and contrasting constellations and observations.

Interviewing in the first wave was based on a thematic checklist but was also open to issues raised by the interviewee. This was achieved by commencing with a narrative phase, and when the narrative potential was exhausted, shifting to tackle the topics of the checklist which had not already been addressed. The photographic fieldwork (see Chapter 13) was done with simple digital cameras provided by the research teams and gifted to the participants together with an inspirational guideline developed by the research team. This inspirational guide provided open topics that could be photographed by the participants, formulated in everyday language – *my home, family and friends, work, my neighbourhood, what I like, what I dislike, leisure, a day of feast, an everyday meal, a source of strength* and similar topics. The guideline was distributed with encouragement to the photographers to address other or different topics of their own choice as well as, or instead of, the ones provided on the guide. The number of photographs per family/household was not limited by the interviewers and free to choose by the participants. After four to six weeks, a photo elicitation interview followed, mainly structured by the interviewees' explanations of their photographs to the interviewer. Most interviews took place in the households of the study participants, a small number in other places suggested by the interviewees – the latter not only in order to avoid bringing the interviewer into bad housing conditions or other open signs of poverty, but also to be seen together with strangers in reputable public places like cafes or community cultural centres. All thematic checklists, inspirational guidelines, selection of places, or choice of incentives were 'localized' – which means they were translated into the respective language, adapted to local cultural conditions to a certain extent, walking the thin line between keeping up homogeneity to ensure comparability, and allowing for heterogeneity to adapt to local conditions. Complete verbal transcriptions of the interviews were done in the original language by or under the control of the local research teams.

During these procedures, between 2014 and 2015, a body of more than 70 expert interviews and more than 330 first and second wave interviews were conducted and recorded in 220 households, leading to almost 10,000 pages of transcripts with more than 1,000 photographs contributed by participants. A small number of households investigated turned out to lack signs of resilience and served as comparative cases, while the majority of the selected households indeed showed resilience, albeit in very different manners and degrees. In some countries this comparison of non-resilient and resilient households was expanded by including cases from preceeding research projects with similar designs, like the IAB (Institute for Employment Research) qualitative poverty studies in Germany (Hirseland and Ramos Lobato 2010, p. 41) or other foregoing work like the FP7 project 'SPHERE' on identities in areas of industrial decline in Poland, Germany, Turkey and Spain (see Kirk et al. 2011).

Area, local and expert information, interviews and photographs were then analysed in two parallel processes. The first process was a dimensional analysis that investigated the collated cases for the thematic fields considered relevant ex ante for theoretical reasons, like the three families of resources (social, cultural, economic), with gender and ethnicity as the main intersectionalities, together with a spatial dimension, and the relation to welfare state institutions. The second process was a typological analysis. This was based on case profiles comprising visual and interview materials, organizing the cases along inductive and dimensional heterogeneities and homogeneities. The dimensional analysis was largely a collaboration between research teams, as cases were compared and drawn together jointly and interactively, in copresence or through correspondence of the project consortium, organized along the thematic or dimensional structure of macro developments and crisis impact such as socioeconomic practices (Chapter 6), cultural and community patterns (Chapters 7 and 11), biographical dimension (Chapter 8), spatial dimension (Chapter 10), the relations to welfare state and social economy activities (Chapters 12 and 15), and intersections with gender, ethnicity and migration issues (for gender see Chapter 9). As a first step, work consisted of local teams collecting, analysing and reporting relevant dimensional findings of their respective country. This process enabled analysis, synthesis, explanation and translation of findings into English. Following this, one or two commissioned lead teams further analysed and synthesized the national reports produced by each country to create an international report on a particular dimension. Furthermore, classificatory and typological analysis was mainly undertaken by the UK team where socioeconomic practices are concerned (see Chapter 6), and by the German team, who created a tentative multidimensional typology of resilience (see Chapter 14). Furthermore, classificatory and typological analysis has been undertaken on several topics like community, household practices, household types, welfare state change and forms of social economy.

OUTLINE OF THE BOOK

The book is divided into four parts. Part I begins with this introduction. Chapter 2, by Promberger and Vuojala-Magga, provides a microsociological and cultural anthropological perspective to explore concepts that enable a study of household resilience. It suggests conceiving of resilient practices of poor households as being economic, cultural and social at the same time, and identifies their usually non- or low-commodified nature, such as in sharing and gift exchange, or mutual help. The chapter emphasizes the affordances and enskilment of small-scale routinized habits and practices that are embedded in cultural and social patterns, which in turn produce social and cultural outcomes aside the economic one. Chapter 3, written by Estêvão, Calado and Capucha, investigates the impact of the global financial crisis, meanwhile called the Great Recession, in Europe and offers a macro European perspective. It uses statistical indicators to compare the effects of the crisis on private households in the nine countries investigated – Finland, Portugal, Ireland, Greece, Poland, United Kingdom, Spain, Turkey and Germany.

Part II of the book focuses on different perspectives on the concept of household resilience. Chapter 4, by Boost, Promberger, Meier and Sowa, examines the genealogy and concept of resilience and the potential to transfer it from fields like psychology, cultural geography or ecosystems research into sociology and social policy research in general, as well as to poverty research in particular. Chapter 5, written by Calado, Capucha, Dagdeviren, Donoghue and Estêvão, adds another critical perspective to resilience by rejecting heroic uses of the concept and emphasizing the limitations and risks of resilience.

Part III brings together different empirical dimensions of resilience. First, Chapter 6 by Dagdeviren and Donoghue examines and classifies the observed socioeconomic practices of resilient and less resilient households in order to develop the thesis that resilience of poor households is mainly coping and adaption to adverse living conditions, with little transformation. Chapter 7, by Gnieciak and Wódz, explores cultural practices and resources involved in the life of resilient households, from knowledge and skills to cultural affiliations, norms and values. Chapter 8, by Dagg and Gray, develops a comparative biographical analysis of resilience in the lives of Europeans experiencing hardship after the economic crisis, using concepts from the life course perspective in social science. It shows how some participants sought to recover a sense of agency and positive anticipation through the reconfiguration of their biographical projects, often in ways that involved the adoption of new ethical frameworks. Chapter 9, by Castrillo, Martín, Arnal and Serrano, focuses on the intersecting dimension of gender and inequality in resilient households. Chapter 10, by Aytekin and Şengül, discusses the spatial aspects of resilience using three analytical levels from the body to the global. Chapter 11, by Serrano, Revilla, Martín and de Castro, questions whether or how communities play a role in resilience formation. Chapter 12, by Mandrysz and Wódz, likewise questions the role of social economy organizations; given the multifacetedness of both concepts and field which deserved a research project of its own, they decided on a descriptive analysis. Lastly, Chapter 13, by Bosch and Promberger, discusses how the aesthetic practices of participants reveal a level of self-reliance that can assist with coping, or even transforming, critical situations and circumstances towards a resilient way of life.

Part IV of the book provides the conclusions and implications of the research findings. Chapter 14, by Promberger, Boost and Müller, synthesizes the empirical analysis into a multidimensional typology of resilient low-income households. It shows that resilience may consist of very different clusters of practices, habits and resources which accumulate for different types of household resilience, which show different forms and levels of outcomes – some of them including more transformative capacities than others. This can lead to remarkable differences in terms of availability of resources, quality of life, welfare dependency and life satisfaction. Chapter 15, by Kambouri, Marinoudi and Petraki, asks whether the impact of the crisis and the resilience patterns shown in Greece, Spain and Portugal indicate an erosive pattern characteristic of the Mediterranean or Southern European type of welfare state. Chapter 16, by Tennberg and Vola, shows how the resilience concept and findings relate to the European policy discourse. This leads into a set of tentative yet insightful policy implications. Finally, in Chapter 17, the editors draw conclusions in both scientific terms and from a social policy perspective.

It may be important for the reader to know that international comparative projects with a qualitative empirical approach require a certain empirical openness not only in terms of concepts, methodology and theory, but also in the interpretations made and the conclusions drawn. This counts even more when there are more than 30 researchers from different countries and disciplinary backgrounds taking part in the research. This variance necessarily develops different perspectives, but luckily, in the case of RESCuE, with a large overlap. Saying that, differences should not be neglected. Controversies existed, primarily about the concept of resilience itself. For instance, resilience usually is a clear second-order concept in the terminology of Alfred Schütz, thus limited to the sphere of scientific observation and interpretation and not part of the knowledge of the observed. But, particularly within the liberal countries, resilience is a political concept operational in a neoliberal context, such as the UK 'Big Society' programme. These tensions may be identified in Chapters 3 and 4 and are also ongoing in publications outside the book (see Dagdeviren et al. 2016, 2017; Promberger 2017; Revilla et al. 2018). Nevertheless, most of the researchers shared the opinion that using the concept of resilience can bring forward new aspects and shed new light on poverty and social policy.

The second difference was a philosophical one with empirical implications: is resilience an inherent quality in most human beings, but manifesting at different times in different biographies, being hindered or ameliorated by socio-historical forces and structures? This is an implicit understanding in youth psychology, educational studies (e.g. Ungar and Liebenberg 2005; Dolan, 2012) and more broadly within the life course perspective in social science (see Elder 1998, p. 9). Or should we think of resilience as rare, especially under extreme adversities, like Viktor Frankl (1985[1946]) did? Although fundamental in its anthropological meaning, this difference did not prove too relevant in the empirical realm of limited data and observations when both positions observed that resilience manifested itself in different degrees, differently across cases within different periods of time and under different conditions. However, the difference between these two perspectives does have significant implications when it comes to establishing empirical criteria for evaluating whether and how any individual household or individual may be deemed 'resilient'. Two of the editors of this volume (Boost and Promberger) subscribe to the second perspective, assuming that resilience always presents itself differently depending on varying contextual and processual conditions, but usually occurs rarely, likely to be true of only a small minority of poor households in Europe. Dagg and Gray subscribe to the first perspective, treating resilience as a *process* with identifiably 'better' or 'worse' outcomes for individuals, households and communities, depending on biographical and historical timing, and on variations in enabling and constraining social contexts. According to this perspective, resilience is likely to be more common than not – albeit at a price – over extended periods of time. Promberger and Boost nevertheless think that, beyond the mentioned etiological difference, this dissent is less about the undoubted procedural nature of resilience and more about scaling and thresholds – and their representation. Do we talk about little, less or more resilience in a certain case and at a certain point of time, or do we use an implicit or explicit context-dependent threshold above which we talk and below which we don't talk about resilience?

The third difference was how to estimate and interpret the power of socio-economic structures and frameworks executed on vulnerable households – like class, gender, ethnicity – and the degree of freedom and the options for acting outside, beneath or below these structures, as well as on the chances and attempts of success of such unorthodox practices. Is it only the state which can mend the detrimental effect of a crisis on low-income households? What exactly is and should be the role of the welfare state? Are neoliberal agendas inevitably ruling every inch and corner of a society, or can those policies be juggled to a certain extent at an individual or household level? What do we researchers expect and hypothesize, and what are our own personal and professional frameworks for interpretation? In the end, is a glass half empty or half full? This may seem quite abstract – but it comes to life very early and quickly in an internationally comparative qualitative research project. Is a small garden with vegetables just a hobby or a budget release, a resource for gift exchange and nutritional improvement? We might tend to judge it a hobby, or check for cultural and social effects of, say, plot gardening, urban gardening or residual farming, and decide not to follow that track when trying to understand the economy of resilient or non-resilient families. On the other hand, we might overestimate the yields and underestimate the risks of firewood collecting to combat fuel poverty, ignoring the fact that the families observed seldom use dry wood from the forest but prefer destroyed furniture, cardboard and broken plastic items? Are any escapes possible at all from the logics and structures of having just two alternatives, paid labour or living badly from little or no welfare? Is the only way out a meagre life from small wages? Yes, mostly – that's the answer from one part of the research team. No, the second part of the team says. Often there is barely a way out, but under certain conditions it can be possible to stay around the poverty line and get by relatively well. Dagdeviren et al. (2016) give an early account of how those difficulties may turn into a theoretical framework, but there is no final solution in sight, either in the social sciences in general, or among the research teams and authors of this book. Chapters 2 and 14 are strongly influenced by the second perspective, and Chapters 5 and 6 by the first one. Nevertheless, of course, this is not only a matter of structure versus action or constraints versus degrees of freedom, Foucault (1977) versus Thompson (1978), structural sociology versus ethnography and anthropology, but a matter of data. On the one hand, the nature of the project did not allow for in-depth quantitative case studies on household budget and income development, and, on the other hand, the project could not go further into generalization, such as through a representative survey, but had to stick to just identifying practices, action patterns, and their functional relations (also in symbolic and cultural terms). Quantitative household case studies and representative surveying on socioeconomic resilience will have to be done by other researchers or at another time.

Thus, the question partly has to remain open, calling for further research, and we have to live with a kind of ambiguity. It is possible to do better than others in poverty and crisis, but the conditions and resources are difficult to obtain. Many of the few resilient households observed do just cope better, few of them improve by transforming their conditions, and even fewer of them manage to leave the poverty zone. But where a good level of common goods, networks, cultural 'capital' exists, people may indeed develop resilient patterns of living in or around poverty, and reduce the need for welfare-provided income support.

When finishing the work on this book's manuscript in mid-2020, we found ourselves in the midst of the next European and worldwide crisis caused by the Covid-19 virus. In responding to this crisis, the question of resilience has arisen frequently and loudly. The resilience of cities and regions, healthcare provision and infrastructure, decision-making systems and procedures – such critical infrastructures in this crisis – are determining the level of suffering and loss that we are encountering. And poverty and social inequality seem to highly determine exposure and harm levels of people and families confronted with Covid-19. We dare say that some of the findings in the chapters of this book, which we identify as relevant for poor households, can apply to exploring resilience for a greater diversity of groups confronted by, and responding to, Covid-19 (see Chapter 17). We hope that resilient and non-resilient poor households, the practitioners who support them, as well as scientists and policy makers concerned with poverty issues will benefit from the findings and discussions contained in this book.

NOTES

1. As a consequence, the concept of family as used here excludes all kinds of institutional cohabitation or residential living, like in a prison, a hospital, a nursing home, a shelter, a flat shared for mere economic reasons, or a boarding school, no matter if the inmates talk about themselves as a family. As one main difference to companies and economic establishments, the primary outcome of a family is the life and wellbeing of the family itself. See also the EU definition of family, https://ec.europa.eu/eurostat/statistics-explained/index.php/Glossary:Household_-_social_statistics (accessed 19 August 2020).

2.   For a recent overview of research on the prevalence of poverty in Europe and its quantitative measurement, see Nolan (2018).

REFERENCES

Antonovsky, A. (1996), 'The salutogenic model as a theory to guide health promotion', *Health promotion international* 11(1): 11–18.

Béné, C., Mills, D. J., Raji, A., Kodio A., Morand, P., Andrew, N., Evans, L., Ovie, S., Tafida, A., Sinaba, F. and Lemoalle, J. (2011), 'Testing resilience thinking in a poverty context: experience from the Niger River basin', *Global Environmental Change* 21(4): 1173–84.

Crouch, C. (2011), *The strange non-death of neo-liberalism*, Cambridge: Polity Press.

Dagdeviren, H., Donoghue, M. and Promberger, M. (2016), 'Resilience, hardship and social conditions', *Journal of Social Policy* 45(1):1–20.

Dagdeviren, H., Donoghue, M. and Meier, L. (2017), 'The narratives of hardship: the new and the old poor in the aftermath of the 2008 crisis in Europe', *The Sociological Review* 65(2): 369–85.

Dolan, P. (2012), 'Travelling through social support and youth civic action on a journey towards resilience', in Ungar, M. (ed.), *The social ecology of resilience*, New York, NY: Springer, pp. 357–66.

Elder, G. H. (1998), 'The life course as developmental theory', *Child Development* 69(1): 1–12.

Esping-Andersen, G. (1989), *The three worlds of welfare capitalism*, Cambridge: Polity Press.

Flick, U. (2011), *Triangulation. Eine Einführung*, 3. aktualisierte Auflage, Wiesbaden: VS-Verlag.

Flick, U., Hirseland, A. and Hans, B. (2018), 'Walking and talking integration: Triangulation of data from interviews and go-alongs for exploring immigrant welfare recipients' sense(s) of belonging', *Qualitative Inquiry* 25(8): 799–810.

Foucault, M. (1977), *Discipline and punish: the birth of the prison*, New York: Pantheon Books.

Frankl, V. E. (1985[1946]), *Man's search for meaning*, New York: Simon and Schuster.

Glaser, B. G. and Strauss, A. L. (1967), *The discovery of grounded theory: Strategies for qualitative research*, Chicago: Aldine Pub. Co.

Harper, D. (2002), 'Talking about pictures: A case for photo elicitation', *Visual studies* 17(1): 13–26.

Haslanger, S. (2018), 'What is a social practice?', *Royal Institute of Philosophy Supplements* 82: 31–47.

Hirseland, A. and Ramos Lobato, P. (2010), *Armutsdynamik und Arbeitsmarkt: Entstehung, Verfestigung und Überwindung von Hilfebedürftigkeit bei Erwerbsfähigen*, Nürnberg: IAB-research report, 03/2010.

Jackson, T. (2009), *Prosperity without growth: Economics for a finite planet*, London: Routledge.

Kirk, J., Contrepois, S. and Jefferys, S. (2011), *Changing work and community identities in European regions*, Basingstoke: Palgrave Macmillan.

Kolb, B. (2008), 'Involving, sharing, analysing – potential of the participatory photo interview', *Forum Qualitative Social Research* 9(3): 12.

Lohmann, H. and Andreß, H.-J. (2008), 'Explaining in-work poverty within and across countries', in H. J. Andreß and H. Lohmann (eds.), *The Working Poor in Europe*,

Employment, Poverty and Globalization, Cheltenham, UK and Northampton, MA, USA: Edward Elgar Publishing, pp. 293–314.

Lösel, F. and Bender, D. (2003), ' Resilience and protective factors', in D. P. Farrington and J. W. Coid (eds.), *Prevention of adult antisocial behavior*, Cambridge: Cambridge University Press, pp. 130–204.

Malcolmson, J. M. (1989), 'Ways of getting a living in eighteenth-century England', in R. E. Pahl (ed.), *On work. Historical, comparative and theoretical approaches*, Reprint, Oxford: Blackwell, pp. 48–60.

Masten, A. S. (2001), 'Ordinary magic: Resilience processes in development', *American Psychologist* 56(3): 227.

Nolan, B. (2018), 'Poverty and social exclusion in the European Union', in P. Kennett and N. Lendvai-Bainton (eds.), *Handbook of European Social Policy*, Cheltenham, UK and Northampton, MA, USA: Edward Elgar Publishing, pp. 97–114.

Nolan, B. and Whelan, C. T. (2018), 'Poverty and social exclusion indicators in the European Union: The role of non-monetary deprivation indicators', in R. Carmo, C. Rio and M. Medgyesi (eds.), *Reducing Inequalities: A Challenge for the European Union?*, Cham: Palgrave Macmillan, pp. 97–114.

Noland, C. M. (2006), 'Auto-photography as research practice: Identity and self-esteem research', *Journal of Research Practice* 2(1): M1.

Promberger, M. (2015), 'Nine years of Hartz IV – a welfare reform under scrutiny', *Cuadernos de relaciones laborales* 33(1): 35–63.

Promberger, M. (2017), *Resilience among vulnerable households in Europe. Questions, concept, findings and implications*, Nuremberg: Institute for Employment Research, IAB Discussion Paper No 12/2017.

Revilla, J. C., Martín, P. and de Castro, C. (2018), 'The reconstruction of resilience as a social and collective phenomenon: poverty and coping capacity during the economic crisis', *European Societies* 20(1): 89–110.

Sachße, C. and Tennstedt, F. (1992), *Geschichte der Armenfürsorge in Deutschland. Der Wohlfahrtsstaat im Nationalsozialismus*, Bd. 3, Stuttgart: Kohlhammer.

Schütze, F. (1983), 'Biographieforschung und narratives Interview', *Neue Praxis*, 13(3): 283–93.

Sennett, R. (2012), *Together: The rituals, pleasures and politics of cooperation*, New Haven, CT: Yale University Press.

Simmel, G. (1992[1908]), 'Der Arme', in G. Simmel (ed.), *Soziologie. Untersuchungen über die Formen der Vergesellschaftung*, Gesamtausgabe Band II, Frankfurt/M.: Suhrkamp, pp. 512–55.

Taylor-Gooby, P., Leruth B. and Chung, H. (eds.) (2017), *After austerity: Welfare state transformation in Europe after the Great Recession*, New York: Oxford University Press.

Thompson, E. P. (1978), *The poverty of theory and other essays*, London: Merlin Press.

Ungar, M. and Liebenberg, L. (2005), 'The International Resilience project, a mixed methods approach to the study of resilience across cultures', in M. Ungar (ed.), *Handbook for working with children and youth: Pathways to resilience across cultures and contexts*, Thousand Oaks, CA: Sage, pp. 211–29.

Vuojala-Magga, T., Turunen, M., Ryyppö, T. and Tennberg, M. (2011), 'Resonance strategies of Sámi reindeer herders in northernmost Finland during climatically extreme years', *Arctic* 64(2): 227–41.

Wallman, S. (1979), *Social anthropology of work*, London: Academic Press.

Wuggenig, U. (1990), 'Die Photobefragung als projektives Verfahren', *Angewandte Sozialforschung* 16: 109–29.

2. Household economy as cultural and social practice: towards a framework for investigating poverty and resilience

Markus Promberger and Terhi Vuojala-Magga

INTRODUCTION

Empirical research is a process of discovery (Abbott 2004). This requires leaving one's personal comfort zone and immersing oneself in an unknown living world through sharing conditions, materiality and life-and-time practices of the researched, in order to physically and cognitively conceive of their life patterns and their functionality, rationality, rituals, rules and structures of relevance. Collecting information or 'data' does necessarily include developing a body of concepts that connects the lifeworld of the observed with the lifeworld of research, in order to reduce or make productive use of differences between both – which is the purpose of this chapter.

How can some people survive better under adverse conditions than others? Where does that resilience come from and what are its outcomes? What dimensions are important in resilience? How is resilience produced and reproduced? How do people's everyday economic practices and social relations work – and how are they embedded within cultural patterns? What are suitable concepts to understand problems of poverty and survival in affluent societies under critical conditions?

MAKING USE OF NATURE'S AFFORDANCES: OYSTER PICKERS IN CENTRAL LONDON

At a very early stage in our comparative European study (see Chapter 1) it became apparent that among those few households doing relatively well under adverse conditions, there was more use of land and natural resources than expected. From Poland, Finland, Germany and Spain, there were reports of gardening and of breeding small animals, gathering fruit and mushrooms, collecting firewood in the forests, fishing, even herding. From Spain, Greece and Portugal, there was some evidence of families actually returning to small agriculture. The subsequent comparison revealed a variety of functions performed by those practices:

- Improving family nourishment beyond the level feasible on the families' monetary income alone.
- Reducing food expenditure and being able to save the household budget for other issues.
- Gaining goods which can be shared within or outside the family, fed into gift exchange relations, traded in kind and sometimes sold for money.
- Giving structure and sense to daily life.
- Strengthening family and neighbourhood relations through gift exchange and cooperation.
- Reproducing practical knowledge and skills through practice and sharing.

As Western European consumers and labour market participants we tend to underestimate the extent to which activities like gardening, small agriculture or foraging can contribute economically to a family's living, beyond just providing meaningful activities for their daily lives. There are quite a lot of examples in the past and present that prove this – like the highly productive Datcha economy in Eastern Europe (Caskie 2000; Gerry and Li 2010), or the Matsutake mushroom foragers in Northern America, whose work not only pays for them, but forms the basis of a global luxury trade chain (Tsing 2015).

Of course, those practices have a lot to do with availability, accessibility and purposeful use of land or nature, whether self-owned, tolerated or public, and the related knowledge and skills. This can certainly not be assumed for the living context of every poor family – it might seem at least that these are just facilities of a rural population with access to natural resources. But although there may be such a tendency, there is counter-evidence, such as modern urban gardening (Corcoran and Kettle 2015) and the persistence of older working-class allotments, and even foraging in one of the biggest European cities – London, as described below.

Crossing the River Thames at Tower Bridge in autumn 2013, at low tide, the bank reinforcements were now footed by previously unseen sandbanks, on which seagulls and other birds stood. But they weren't alone in their business. Looking from the north embankment to the south, I, Markus Promberger, suddenly recognized a man slowly moving forward downstream, just above waterline of a huge sandbank. Aged well beyond 60 and wearing scruffy clothes, he was holding a small shovel, a stick, and a pale green plastic bucket.

He paced along, stood still again, poking the stick into the ground, dug a bit with his shovel, and then threw a small lump of sand and something else into his bucket, which he then dived into the water and pulled out again, letting the water rinse through holes in the bucket's bottom. He repeated this procedure every few steps until he came to the end of the sandbank, turned the bend and disappeared from my sight. His prey was unrecognizable, but his behaviour was exactly like that of the shellfish gatherers searching the sandy firths of Spain's northern coast. No wonder, as the London authorities have similar classes of shellfish to those in Northern Spain inhabiting the Thames estuary between West London and the North Sea, such as oysters, mussels and crabs of various kinds.[1]

Observing and comparing nature-related livelihood practices gives a general first impression that there is a certain **hidden richness** in such small-scale activities that supply more to life than expected. Although they might be called residual (Williams 1977), or be mistaken for mere hobbies, for resilient households they seem to be re-emerging and regaining economic meaning under conditions of hardship – or just becoming more visible when we remove the reference framework of economic modernity. Using natural resources at such a small level is not limited to the countryside, and it may occur in a cultural reference frame of a hobby or tradition that has positive economic side effects. The practices are as surprisingly diverse as natural conditions, resources and human skills, techniques and habits are. Thus, when we look for resources that low-income households might practically draw upon, nature, knowledge and skills might be successfully combined by some of them. And we must include this for our attention.

Nevertheless, it is not just one lonesome male or female foraging or hunting. Humans' ability to survive and get by depends largely on social relations and cultural embeddedness. Humans are social beings and, as such, cooperation, social divisions of labour and social organization of distribution arise everywhere as part of the social and cultural nature of humans, which forms a kind of environment or ecology of human life. The following examples illustrate how this works below the levels of the modern market and working society.

APPLE PICKERS: THE MORAL ECONOMY OF FRUIT

The village of Abersdorf lies half an hour by car north of a large city in Bavaria, a southern province of Germany. It is inhabited by about 100 families with few full-time farmers left, yet many people are involved in extensive gardening, growing fruit trees, pond fishery, hunting and breeding small herds of cattle or poultry on patches of farmland. There is a rather broad set of informal and formal small-scale economic practices, which support not only the livelihood of the Abersdorf inhabitants, but also reach out to nearby cities. Those economic practices are strongly related to cultural patterns, like the collective identity of the village and its symbolic expressions or the cultural embedding of economic activities below market production. Let us take a closer look.

Primarily, fruit is evidently something to eat, to make domestic foodstuffs and drinks from, and to feed domestic animals. The climate in Abersdorf is on the cold end of commercial fruit growing, but not bad, as the incidence of endemic plum varieties shows. There are cherries, which were a cash crop for centuries, and countless varieties of apples, ancient and modern. Fruit trees require not much more than just land and skilled labour. They have to be planted, pruned, taken care of, cut and harvested, and there are interrelations with other kinds of agricultural activities, as the land between the trees can be used for gardening, as a pasture or a meadow, or for bees. The simplest model of the economy of fruit is to *produce it and to consume it in one single family* household. Nevertheless, this simple model neglects some special characteristics of fruit growing – which may apply to other types of small-scale agriculture as well.

First, most fruit cannot be kept for long without preservation. Cherries in Abersdorf ripen within a few weeks in late June and have to be consumed or preserved within just a few days. Plums ripen between August and September and must be processed quickly. Apples ripen between August and November; some varieties are kept for just a few days before they rot, while others are stored for up to six months.

Second, fruit trees of the traditional type tend not to produce their yield continuously from year to year, but in an alternating way. They might richly produce fruit one year, and then give you just a handful the next year. Coping with this requires skill and equipment for food preservation, for reducing the difference between annual yields, and for distributing lack and surpluses of fruit to a wider community. This means that fruit growing and use tends to involve more than just one family, as it implies making use of techniques, premises, knowledge, skills and (mostly) local co-production and distribution networks. Fruit are a key object in village societies from a practical, economic, social and cultural view. As Karl Polanyi (1944) states, economies are embedded in certain settings or cultural frameworks. And cultural anthropologists know that there is no economic practice which is not at the same time a cultural one, as knowledge transforms into skills through representations, customs, symbols and artefacts when human beings interact with each other (Pálsson 1994; Williams 1977) and their natural surroundings in which non-human life forms play a crucial role, not just as objects of human action, but also as actors themselves (Ingold 2013; Münster 2012; Tsing 2015). Thus, a wide concept of culture is required, and we need to imply a wide concept of economy as well, to include how people not only interact with each other, but also with landscape, nature and other living forms about their means of living and their symbolic representations, and how they reproduce as a group or society through history, within a complete ecosystem of which humans are just a part, understood as the ecology of life.

Thus, there is a need to expand the simple model of producing and using the fruit in just one household by the concept of *sharing*. Sharing is not only a scientific concept from anthropology, therefore 'second order' in the terminology of Alfred Schuetz (2013), but also a first order concept existing in the minds and languages of participants – just as Jesus *shared* the bread with his followers, as the local Christian priests in Bavaria would say. Thus, fruit could be shared with others, and this is done extensively in Abersdorf. It is relatively common for older people from Abersdorf and similar villages to share their fruit harvest with their children living in the cities, with visitors like friends or wider kinship, or with their colleagues in their city workplaces. An important issue for this kind of fruit growing village is that families also share their fruit harvest – sometimes excluding the cash crops – with other families' children. Typically, when some children come by to visit a family's own children, they might be given a bag of fruit when leaving again, with words like 'take some plums with you and give greetings to your parents'. Another example is the informal right for children to sample a handful of fruits from the ground below any (unfenced) tree at any time when they come by. Giving fruit away to children is quite common and would also be done similarly with homemade baking products, or with purchased sweets, especially around seasonal feasts, weddings, birthdays. The idea behind it is multilayered: it is regarded as respect for nature not to throw away a surplus which is threatened by decay; it is the half-conscious remembrance of periods of scarcity, like 1942–1955. And it is the common understanding that raising kids is expensive and requires solidarity, and feeding them is everybody's business in a village, not only the nuclear family, and fruit is a healthy way to do this. It is about strengthening social ties through sharing food by giving away some of the surplus, or having common meals. It is almost impossible to enter someone's house in Abersdorf without being invited to have a drink at any time, or to share a meal at mealtimes. Giving fruit away to children is the easiest way, as it avoids the necessity of reverse gifts or other obligations (see Mauss 2002 on the potlatch) and therefore does not burden the gifted side beyond saying thank you.

As we see, we are moving from intra-family production and consumption through cross-family sharing into gift exchange – which of course is generally far from being avoided in Abersdorf. If a family has a big fruit harvest, they would certainly invite neighbours (especially, again, those with younger children) to come over and collect fallen fruits or pick them from the trees. This would stimulate reverse gifts like giving back some products made from the given fruit, such as marmalade, dried fruit, juice or a pie. Other reverse gifts would range from one's own different harvest surplus, helping out with small household items like sugar or a light bulb, or lending a tool or a hand if required. Or, just come by, sit a bit on the outside bench and have a chat, which is highly valued by elderly neighbours. Technology from equipment to recipes is also involved, shared and exchanged even at those simple stages of the economy. The same counts for knowledge and skills, such as how to treat plants and fruit during growth and harvest, or about the respective properties of apple varieties, processing fruit by drying, preparing marmalade and other preserves, cooking, making juice or distilling the remainder into spirits and liquors – or feeding it to animals.

Although the Abersdorf inhabitants' fruit growing differs in scale and extent, and their socioeconomic situation is quite heterogeneous, most of them are involved in sharing and exchanging networks. Nevertheless, the kind of involvement seems to depend on social, local and personal characteristics as well as on economic ones – such as the nature and kind of fruit: the cherry economy quickly tends towards producing for sales on larger well-organized markets, as cherries are best if eaten fresh and cannot be stored very long. Plums go either the same way or are distilled into spirits. But apples are special, covering the full range from self-production via sharing and gift exchange to being sold for money, thus giving the economic substance for a moral economy sustaining local culture and community ties and providing chances for non-market gains in nourishment, knowledge, social relations – and all the while improving local living conditions.[2]

SOCIETY, COMMUNITY AND THE SOCIAL DIVISION OF LABOUR

Emile Durkheim (1933[1893]) addressed the fact that societies and the social division of labour are becoming more and more complex. Many of his contemporaries thought that this increasing complexity was associated with technological and social progress, although Durkheim himself and other thinkers of that time already recognized the dark sides to this progress. Nevertheless, the idea of – at least in the long term – steady progress and growing complexity became part of the paradigm of modernity. But in the beginning of the 21st century and after four decades of austerity policies, it is obviously no law of nature that a crisis has to be followed by a socially inclusive recovery period like post-1945. Moreover, it is historically evident that economic progress may harm not only working classes or certain locales, but also complete countries, natural environments and the global climate (see Tsing 2015).

Crises enable us to rethink this issue of economic progress by looking at poor households during such times. Evidently, complex modes of production (exchange, consumption and social integration), like paid work beyond the home in a modern labour and market society framed by a welfare state, are vulnerable if exposed to a crisis. Could it be possible that, in a crisis, some people are re-actualizing older, residual layers or patterns of production, consumption and social integration? In some cases of vulnerable households which get by relatively well (see the typology in Chapter 14), a huge part of productive work which had been done as formal labour in offices, companies and factories, now moves to the home, extensifying housework, and returning to direct use of nature and informal work in networks. Labour, exchange and consumption may – for such households – become less 'societal' in terms of losing formal markets under a Smithian (1976[1776]) expression of 'the social', but are now increasingly being allocated alongside patterns of acquaintance, like family, kinship, neighbourhood, subculture and informal communities. Exchange for money gets supplemented by older systems like barter, gift exchange, sharing and subsistence economy, keeping production and consumption more within the own 'oikos'. Ferdinand Toennies (1957) held society to be a rather precarious and abstract accomplishment, requiring deliberate action of citizens who do not necessarily know each other, while communities come into existence naturally, based on similarity of life situations, co-presence, kinship or co-locality. Toennies' thoughts also expressed that society might historically take over tasks from communities – which is evident in the case of the welfare state. For both Durkheim and Toennies, a very regular price to pay for the increasing growth of society, the growing complexity of the social division of labour and the decline of community may be anomie in the case of failure, and a lack of affective inclusion even if working well. Symptoms of this, throughout Europe post-2000, may be persistent poverty, growing unemployment, as well as a growth in crime, rising social protest not only from the left and a lack of social belonging. All the while it seems that few people are able to turn the tables and develop strategies to buffer or cope with the crisis and develop resilience.

Why so few? This is where the inherent complexity growth argument of Durkheim, less visible but also crucial for Toennies, might have another weak point. It might well be a liberal modernist misunderstanding that only markets (including financial markets), a highly developed global division of labour and modern institutions and organizations could be complex at all. Why should older layers and practices be thought of as less complex? Change is always a game of gains and losses. On average, we Western citizens may have won professional skills throughout the twentieth century, but lost the knowledge of seasons, places, properties of the non-human world and skills of foraging, growing, caring, harvesting and using which are required to get an outcome from nature, without talking about repair and construction skills, not lost so far but unevenly distributed. Moreover, not everyone has the skills to build and keep up informal networks and ties for mutual help in a poor and deprived neighbourhood.

KNIFE: FROM KNOWLEDGE TO ENSKILMENT

Reporting from her research from the Northern European Arctic wilderness, Vuojala-Magga turns to deepening our understanding of experiences and practical skills within one's lifeworld, or an ecology of life, in the context of resilience against hardship.

Certain tools are compulsory in the everyday life of the Arctic wilderness because they are vital for individual survival. One will never go to the forest without a box of matches wrapped in plastic; naturally, it has to be watertight in case one falls through the ice into the cold water. A warm fire will save a person from freezing to death. In order to start a fire, one needs at least to have dry matches and a knife with one. Finally, the knife as well as the small axe give the surest chance of survival in the wilderness – if one knows how to use them.

More than 20 years ago, I, Terhi Vuojala-Magga, started to live in a small Sámi reindeer herding community in Lapland, some 100 kilometres north of the Arctic Polar Circle. One of my very first observations was the fact that everyone was carrying one or two knives on their belt; of course it was as natural as having their shoes on. There is not a single thing that is not done by using a knife. I wrote about my first experiences of knives in 2009: 'The knife is the one of the most profound tools in the forest. It can help the human being in various situations; it can be used for slicing, cutting, killing, opening, eating, taking out or putting in, breaking ice, making earmarks or fur marks on reindeer, getting dry wood and branches' (Vuojala-Magga 2009, p. 167).

The knives can be beautiful pieces of handicraft or they can be just cheap ordinary knives with a plastic handle brought from the hardware store. If it is good and handy for everyday use, it makes no difference where it comes from. Despite the different outlooks, good knives share similar features: the blade has to be easy to sharpen and the handle has to fit into the hand and palm without sliding.

When I started to live with the Sámi people, I hardly knew anything about knives. For me it was just a kitchen tool, that's all. My very first experience was to learn to open up a beer bottle with the knife and, surely, it took some time to get this practice done smoothly. I also understood that while learning to use the knife I was also observed. Those skilful Sámi reindeer herders can draw different kind of conclusions about the knife user – those conclusions tell them about the person's survival capacities in the Arctic wilderness. I guess, my clumsy beginning with the knife use gave them a clear message about my poor basic skills of coping in the Arctic wilderness; no words were needed (Vuojala-Magga 2009, p. 167).

As the years passed on, I became more advanced in using the knife; meta-phorically, the knife and my hand grew together. Today I know what kind of knife I prefer to use and I feel comfortable in using them. One evening my neighbour brought a pike weighing 3 kilograms. He sat down by the table and looked at me intently while I was cutting the pike and slicing out the fillet by using a medium sized knife. Eventually he commented: 'Yes, it is not the first time you are cutting the fish, the knife slides smoothly though the fish meat even though the blade is rather small for that size of a fish.' I guess, I have learned something about a knife, and yet there is still a lot to learn.

Gisli Pálsson in his beautiful article of Enskilment at Sea (Pálsson 1994) writes about the concept of enskilment in the context of the Icelandic fishery. Most of his fieldwork happened onshore until one skipper invited Pálsson to join him on one of his fishing trips by commenting: 'If you really want to know what the fishing industry is all about, you must go fishing'. For Pálsson it was a journey of being seasick and he was far out of his comfort zone. Finally, the weather improved and Pálsson gained his sea legs, which means he was able to get on with his research work on the boat. While working on that fishing ship he was able to understand the complexity of various individual skills and collective skills of the crew as a whole. He came to realize that to engage in anthropology is not just to 'observe' and record but to participate in the lives of other people (Pálsson 1994, 1996).

ENSKILMENT, AFFORDANCES AND THE ECOLOGY OF LIFE

Tim Ingold argues that individual skills are not only techniques of the body itself but also 'the capabilities of action and perception of the whole organic being situated in a richly structured environment' (Ingold 2000, p. 5). In that sense, individual skills are not transmitted from one generation to another but they are incorporated into the modus operandi of a developing human organ-ism through training and experiencing the performance of a particular task (Ingold 2000, 2011).

Gisli Pálsson (1996) points out that enskilment connected to the richly struc-tured marine environment is crucial for the everyday life world of individuals in the fishing industry, and it does not happen through formal schooling but by active practice in interaction with the surrounding environment. This also applies in learning the basic skills in the Arctic wilderness. One learns those unique abilities to perceive and respond in an environment by taking part in everyday tasks, by imitating the people mastering the skills and by simply practising and training in the needed skills with the guidance of the members of a skilled community. Learning to use a knife is an everyday action among other things in the wilderness. The knife is a tool for individual unique practices, and it is a tool of social actions too. Enjoying lunch by the fire is a social event. There are no forks or spoons, only a knife from one's belt, and instead of using fingers the knife functions as a fork and knife at the same time. The elders use the knife as they have always done and younger ones imitate the elders with all the rich variation of using this tool. To understand this, one does not have to look at something as an observer, instead one has to attend and participate in this joint action – as a function of operation (Polanyi 1969, p. 153).

However, when learning to use a knife, we have to make ourselves aware of it as well as of our bodily actions. We internalize this tool and make ourselves dwell in it. Eventually we can rely on our own subsidiaries and the knife becomes a part of ourselves (see Polanyi 1969, pp. 134, 148). For example:

> 'we can rely on our sensations or our hand and fingers holding the knife within our movements of a hand and thumb when we cut for example a delicate earmark on an ear of a newborn reindeer calf. Our focus is on the ear and on the cut itself but we do not need to think about the hand and the knife – it becomes a trained delicacy of a skilful herder's eye, ear and touch.' (Vuojala-Magga 2009, p. 167)

Enskilment is one of the common denominators among the resilient families and individuals of practice-emphasizing societies in the Arctic. The concept of enskilment is twofold: on the one hand, it encompasses the system of situated learning and locality (Lave and Wegner 1991). Coming to be skilful means that the social settings, community and its rich structure environment enables the individual's development and learning – an individual becomes attuned and engaged to their own environment. On the other hand, it is personal, thus no skill is handed down as heritage of the past generation, instead to become skilled one needs to train, practise and develop to the stage where one is enskilled. Once having mastered the stage of basic skills, one will reach the state of creativity – for example, a knife can be used in various other contexts, like in carving or replacing a missing tool with imaginative ways of using a knife, then it truly becomes a part of one's identity.

Not only the knife but also **fur shoes** are an important part of my life in the Arctic. Each winter when the snow starts to fall, we start wearing the fur shoes made out of reindeer skin. The material comes from the legs of adult male reindeer. The shoes are soft because the fur skin is flexible and they are light to wear. Eventually when one puts ordinary leather or plastic shoes on at -30 degrees Celsius, it feels like putting one's feet in an iron cage.

The reindeer-fur shoe has many names in the Sámi language according to its shape and function or the seasonal state of the fur and its colour. Here I concentrate only on forest fur shoes, which are commonly worn in winter throughout the reindeer herding region in Finnish Lapland. Forest fur shoes are warm and very practical in cold weather and on dry snow. Originally, forest shoes were designed not only for walking but also for skiing. Therefore, the shoes still have a turned-up tip, but they have developed in a number of ways and now vary from artisan to artisan and their locality and traditions. The particular shape of the tip is one part of the artisan's signature and the reindeer herders who wear the shoes know which artisan made them by looking at the curl of the tip. Forest shoes also have a decorative trim around the ankle, made of woven laces, which prevents snow backing up inside the shoe.

There are three important affordances one must have around oneself before becoming an artisan in fur shoe making: first, one has to have an opportunity to learn the skills; second, there have to be good possibilities to get the material (reindeer leg skins); and, finally, there have to be professionals who will use the shoes.

To acquire the requisite skills, that is, to gain the necessary enskilment, one has to have a 'will of fire' to enter what is a lifelong process of learning. In the stage of final enskilment, the artisan enters the world of cutting and sewing; the professional dwells in the actions and material. Before getting to the work of cutting the shoe components, one has to know what size the shoes have to be and the functions required of them. The skin and the knowledge of making shoes from it are all connected to the hands and eyes of the artisan. Enskilment and craftsmanship give rise to creative processes. For example, there are common sayings that the leg skin itself guides the fur shoemaker, the sculptor reveals what is already inside the stone, the wood leads the woodworker.

Eventually, making fur shoes becomes an individual skill, ending up as part of an individual's knowledge. 'The cutting and the sewing, however, is each duojár's [artisan who makes fur shoes] individual knowledge that must be mastered in order for that product to be successful at all, and a duojár passes on what he/she has learned and puts his/her own design and understanding into the work' (Guttorm 2007, p. 73). Heterogeneity and locality can be found in the techniques used to make artefacts in their particular shapes. 'Subsequently, the Sámi in the different regions have developed their own cutting methods, sewing techniques and skaller shapes' (Guttorm 2007, p. 72).

One of the most important phases in shoe making is receiving feedback from the users, that is, reindeer herders. This means that the people who wear the shoes in the forest provide valuable comments about them. Each person has his or her personal preferences and special demands, and every foot is unique in shape. A professional artisan has to know these variables, and has to make the most comfortable and best-fitting shoes for the personal use of the reindeer herder/customer.

In the art of sewing the fur shoes there are numerous **affordances** that make the shoe production possible. In the broadest sense, the affordances can be understood as a frame of context in terms of J. J. Gibson's theory of perception of ecological psychology. In his work, James Gibson studied the direct perceptions without cognitive processing, which was a rather new thing in psychology at the time. He argued that organisms *directly* perceive the value of one's own environment through affordances. In its simplest case an affordance of an object is what the infant begins by noticing. The meaning is observed (Gibson 1986).

These can be various kinds of possibilities of nature or built environment, which can be perceived or acted upon. Gibson continues, 'It is a mistake to separate the natural from the artificial as if there were two environments; artefacts have to be manufactured from natural substances. It is also a mistake to separate the cultural environment from the natural environment' (Gibson 1986, p. 129; see also Greeno 1998).

According to Gibson (1986), the affordances of the environment are what it offers an animal or human being, what it provides or furnishes, for good or ill. They can be terrain, shelter, water, fire, objects, tools or other animals. Both the human being and the animal can perceive an affordance in a similar way; for example, a cloudberry marsh attracts people and bears. The affordance can be perceived in a different way; for example, weak river ice is a good surface for a fox but it is deadly dangerous for a person. As such, affordances are something that refer to both the environment and the animal or human being and imply the complementarity of the animal and the environment (Gibson 1986, p. 127).

There are affordances of the medium, that is, of substances and surfaces and their layouts. As said before, they can be either good or ill or there can be constraints and possibilities. The Arctic is known for its harsh cold winter, the medium is known as the air. In some cases, the air can be bright and good to breathe, or foggy without any vision. Cold air gives constraints or challenges for all the living creatures in the Arctic. For surviving the wintertime, warm fur or fire are the best affordances for living creatures. However, the lifesaving value of the skin or fur lies in the way it is produced for human use.

Here we come to the concept of enskilment again – the life world and environment transfer means of coping as long as a person also has the needs and skills to produce and maintain those goods and items. Reindeer skin and sealskin are the warmest and most resistant hides of the Arctic. Reindeer, for the person of craftsman, can see the animal not only as a member of a herd, or the value of income, but from the perspective of the condition and fitness of the animal, its skin and fur. Furthermore, one has to know how to process and soften the skin so the fur will not wear out. As Gibson states:

> 'An affordance is not a process of perceiving a value-free physical object to which meaning is somehow added in a way that no one has been able to agree upon; it is a process of perceiving a value-rich ecological object. Any substance, any surface,

any layout has some affordance for benefit or injury to someone. Physics may be value-free, but ecology is not' (Gibson 1986, pp. 127–44).

Value-richness means a high potentiality in offering affordances, or polyfunc-tionality in other words. The actual value of affordance emerges on the level of individual enskilment, which defines the human part of the interface.

In this respect, an affordance reflects the environment and behaviour. It is both physical and psychical, yet neither. An affordance is a resource or support that the environment offers for living creatures (human/animal) which again, in turn, one must possess the abilities to perceive and to use. As such, affordances are meaningful to human beings, they provide opportunity for particular kinds of behaviour depending on the level of enskilment of the individual (Gibson 2002).

The main idea of affordances is that those characteristics of objects and arrangements in the environment provide potential support to various activities and, therefore, the characteristics of the environment that agents need to per-ceive (Greeno 1998, p. 341), or as Stoffregen (2003) asserts, that 'affordances are properties of the animal–environment system ... The dynamics of the animal–environment system are an emergent property and, as such, cannot be identified in the dynamics of the animal or in the dynamics of the environ-ment' (Stoffregen 2003, p. 124). Furthermore, the animal–human relationship is not one way. Human beings in the shared life world with reindeer produce man-made affordances for reindeer. For example, during summertime when reindeer suffer from mosquitoes, there are man-made cool and dark shelters where reindeer can rest without the irritation of blood sucking insects.

RESILIENCE FROM A LIFE–ECOLOGICAL PERSPECTIVE

Conceptualizing resilience beyond psychological questions requires improved integration with other spheres of life and understandings of complex systems, like small-scale economies of production, distribution and consumption embedded in a cultural framework of norms, values and practices, along market and non-market networks and relations. These cultural and social frameworks are themselves embedded in an ecology of life, including non-human life as well as material objects from whatever origin. In the classic socio-ecological framework, resilience is understood as the capacity of a dynamic system to adapt successfully to disturbances that threaten the viability, the function, or the development of that system (Southwick et al. 2014; Masten 2014). In the contemporary studies of resilience of socio-ecological systems it is tightly con-nected to the processes of adaptive transformations (Keskitalo 2008, p. 19). In this respect, the concepts of adaptation, vulnerability and resilience share the same epistemology. On the one hand, adaptation is understood as an optimal solution to outside forces and, on the other hand, resilience indicates a process of bouncing back or a process for future adaptation. Ontologically there is a kind of outside force, for example, economic depression or climate change that is posing a problem and the individual/community posits the solution either by being resilient or adapting (see also Lewontin 2001, p. 60).

There are alternative approaches for understanding the resilient systems of Arctic people such as NCT (niche construction theory), the developmental systems theory of Oyama (2000) and Ingold's ecology of life. Each of these approaches share a similar ontology and epistemology of holism, in which the living organism is seen-in-its-environment (Dewey 1896). Ingold (2000) expresses the ecology of life as follows: first, people's environment is the world as it exists and takes meaning in relation to the people and, in that sense, it comes into existence and develops with and around the people. Second, the environment is never complete but, as long as life goes on, it is continuously under construction. Third, this process of modifying the life world within one's environment will be exposed to the next generation. Finally, each generation inherits the meaning and legacy of the life world by practice and attention to learning.

The forms of life of the entire matrix of relations (human or non-human) emerge and are held in place, and these forms are neither genetically nor culturally configured but have to be seen as an emergent outcome of the dynamic self-organization of developmental systems that can be regarded as an open process. Ontologically, human beings can be thought of '…in terms not of what they are but what they do' (Ingold 2013, p. 8).

A concept of affordance applies at the same time to the environment and to behaviour. It is both physical and psychical, yet neither. An affordance is a resource or support that the environment offers for living creatures (human/animal) which again, in turn, must possess the abilities to perceive and to use it. Thus, it includes resources, and resource perception and mobilization, and includes non-human beings as well as other materialities. As such, affordances are meaningful to human beings: they provide opportunity for particular kinds of behaviour depending on the level of enskilment of the individual (Gibson 2002). Affordances can be berry places, a safe place to rest in the wilderness, an accessible patch of arable land, ice as a means of travel, apple trees, life signs of an oyster in the mud, a tool to use in need, etc. Both the human being and animal can perceive an affordance in a similar way; for example a cloudberry marsh attracts people and bears. The affordance can be perceived in a different way, too – for example, weak ice is a good surface for a fox but deadly dangerous for a person – or the affordance might be contested, like a cloudberry marsh between humans and bears, or a garden between gardeners and voles.

How to define Arctic resilience in a framework of ecology of life? According to this alternative approach resilience is not a coping system or option for the emerging challenges like economic depression. For example, climate change is not happening outside us but is a part of our global world. In Arctic surroundings, resilience is emerging in the practice of everyday life. There is a simple answer to this: the harsh times are continually present. The extreme weather conditions such as cold and snow storms connected to the polar night are a part of everyday life in the north. On a daily basis people face problems with cars, water pipes and water pumps. Snowstorms make travelling difficult and dangerous.

Arctic people have learned that the life world is never stable – weather changes, the environment changes, as do the food resources. One year can be good for berries, while the next one is a bad berry year. After a successful reindeer year, there can be two difficult years with less income. There is a good year for fishing but the next rainy summer makes fishing impossible. This also applies to the global monetary system: the tourist industry follows the global markets – after good years there will be bad years. The global system makes no difference to the local system. Tim Ingold (2013) asks about the difference in being or becoming. In the Arctic life cycle, with all different variations, life is in a continuous process – each day comes to be different. Beside the irregularity and harshness of the Arctic conditions, the northern residents have learned to live on irregular incomes. The reindeer herders get their yearly income during the autumn months, the seasonal workers in the tourist industry earn their salaries during the winter months, fishermen earn nothing during the months of weak ice, construction workers get their income mainly during summer. The rest of the year, people have to lean on other means of living. The salary from 'the real work' is just one stream among several streams of getting along with a mixed livelihood. But this is not just the case in the Arctic wilderness: the few resilient households in other European countries may show similar features: some intensify their gardening, fishing or foraging activities when they have no proper job, some work for mutual support or wages in kind when they are not in paid labour, some of them spin and knit wool that others consider not economically relevant and give away for free, some move to holding multiple small jobs, make money out of other people's leftovers or increase their self-sustainability and turn their labourers' household into a self-producing oikos, realizing new or hidden affordances of their life ecology.

What do those resilient people do eventually? First, Arctic people have learned to keep their nerves calm; no energy should be wasted in vain. This is the most important human resource especially in extreme weather conditions. Second, each individual has to acquire specific skills to live in all the conditions that emerge and each one should be able to make a living from surrounding affordances. Since childhood, the skills are learned in practice in the guidance of other people. Young people learn reindeer herding, berry harvesting, fishing, processing meat, cooking, baking, knitting and sewing fur shoes. Though it is a time-consuming practice, this type of learning is important. The Arctic resilience is hidden in skills of this everyday work, tasks and social settings – it can be tacit knowledge (Polanyi 1969). Some resilient households in East Germany learn to turn bad conditions into chances: the fact that a house in the river area is flooded every few years decreases the price dramatically but enables a poor family to buy it and live in a self-owned house without any debts – they just have to use their craftsperson skills to keep the house in a good state in spite of the floods. Being an active member of an extended family or community enables other families to have rich access to social and economic networks without investing money, by sharing or social exchange of fruit, support labour, knowledge, values and beliefs, be it in Spain, Poland, Finland, Germany or another country. Others, experiencing hardship but developing resilience, decide on certain practices using the criteria of their plurifunctionality. A family day out in the forest, collecting berries and mush-rooms, not only improves the family's diet for free, but is also meaningful time spent together as a family, has recreational qualities, fosters the enskilment of the children and does not require any money for costly leisure activities. But to be able to realize such affordances, the level and diversity of enskilment is of major importance for resilience, as it is understood here. You need to sensually and physically know what to do with a patch of land in Lisbon or Ukraine, a damp little house in East Germany, apples in Northern Bavaria, the wild leek in the Andalusian mountains, a sandbank in the River Thames, thrift objects from flat clearances, a knife, a fishing rod or some reindeer leg fur in Lapland to make them help you survive. Practical skills – and this also includes skills of communication and organization – are a crucial element of resilience anywhere, as they open up and mobilize affordances or resources of the ecology people live in, beyond the standard affordances of a (post)modern market and labour society. But, other than in the Arctic, where such practices are rather common, acting in a resilient way in other parts of Europe requires a certain distance towards norms and values of the market and labour societies. We may not wonder whether resilient households take a stand for traditional craftsmanship, residual knowledge and skills, values like solidarity, reciproc-ity or mutuality, parsimony, and family, sharing, self-sustainability, self-help, neighbourhood and community, eco-friendliness and do-it-yourself.

Enskilment means that only well-practised people can act flexibly when challenged, which again is a vital part of resilience. When one line of liveli-hood is facing hard times, the other line replaces the loss. The art of utilizing various affordances and replacing them is a part of Arctic sustainability. For example, if there is a bad lingonberry year, people harvest more blueberry. If there is less reindeer meat in a household, the family members eat more moose meat. If there is less fish in the river, people go to fish from the lake. In the same way people perceive the global economic system, if there is no work with income, they can centralize their activity to those of traditional works.

Affordances are there – both in the social settings and in one's environment. Affordances can be seen as preconditions for activity and indicate possible action. The presence in a situation of a system that provides an affordance for some activity does not imply that the activity will occur. Activity occurs if the person knows how to deal with one's life world, for example being skilful. In the Arctic, among the people of subsistence economies, the concept of resilience cannot be regarded as a coping system, which is handed down to the people. Rather, these self-sufficient peoples' skills and a success in making a livelihood is supporting their activity. All the practice emerges within the life world of the person.

To conclude, if we want to gain new insights on poverty and poverty allevi-ation by studying resilience, we have to open out our perspective. We have to use a wider concept of economy than that of the formal market-and-paid-labour economies. There are potentially more resources or affordances involved than just commodities, money and formal skills, and more patterns of gaining a living than paid labour on other people's premises. This includes small-scale and subsistence economies, multiple livelihoods, non-monetary, non-market and non-formal practices like sharing, bartering, gift exchange, many of them multi-purpose practices which not only are meant to give material yields but also to establish and strengthen social ties and enable cultural reproduction. We have to take into account that economic practices are embedded in cultural and social patterns as well as having social and cultural outcomes. And we have to take a life–ecological perspective, where the economic, the cultural and the social are not only interrelated through 'mechanisms' of enskilment and resource mobilization, social exchange, sharing and cultural reproduction, but are also embedded in a dynamic ecology involving other lifeforms and non-living materialities.

NOTES

1. London authorities warn against eating shellfish from the Thames estuary due to environmental pollution.
2. It has to be noted that the moral economy of Abersdorf includes at least three other powerful and even formally organized networks with similar functions: the voluntary fire brigade, the sports club and the singers' association.

REFERENCES

Abbott, A. (2004), *Methods of discovery: Heuristics for the social sciences*, Contemporary Societies Series, Oxford: Claredon Press.

Caskie, Paul (2000), 'Back to basics: Household food production in Russia', *Journal for Agricultural Economics* 51(2): 196–209.

Corcoran, M. P. and Kettle, P. C. (2015), 'Urban agriculture, civil interfaces and moving beyond difference: the experiences of plot holders in Dublin and Belfast', *Local Environment* 20(10): 1215–30.

Dewey, J. (1896), 'The reflex arc concept in psychology', *Psychological Review* 3(4): 357–70.

Durkheim, E. (1933[1893]), *The division of labor in society*, Illinois: The Free Press Of Glencoe.

Gerry, C. J. and Li, C. A. (2010), 'Consumption smoothing and vulnerability in Russia', *Applied Economics* 42(16): 1995–2007.

Gibson, J. J. (1986), *The ecological approach to visual perception*, New Jersey: Lawrence Erlbaum Associates.

Gibson, J. J. (2002), 'A theory of direct visual perception', in A. Noë and E. Thompson (eds.), *Vision and mind: Selected readings in the philosophy of perception*, Cambridge, MA: MIT Press, pp. 77–91.

Greeno, J. G. (1998), 'The situativity of knowing, learning, and research', *American Psychologist* 53(1): 5–26.

Guttorm, G. (2007), 'Duodji – hvem eier kunnshapen og verkene?', in J. T. Solbakk (ed.), *Tradisjonell kunnshap og oppkavsrett*, Karasjok: Callidlagadus and Samikopiia (online). Available at: www.samikopiia.org/web/index.php?sladja=7&giella1=nor (accessed November 2017).

Ingold, T. (2000), 'Culture, nature, environment: steps to an ecology of life', in T. Ingold (ed.), *The perception of the environment: Essays on livelihood, dwelling & skill,* London, New York: Routledge, pp. 13–26.

Ingold, T. (2011), *Being alive: Essays on movement, knowledge and description*, Abingdon: Routledge.

Ingold, T. (2013), 'Prospect', in T. Ingold and Pálsson, G. (eds.), *Biosocial Becomings*, New York: Cambridge University Press, pp. 1–21.

Keskitalo, E. C. H. (2008), 'Vulnerability and adaptive capacity in forestry in northern Europe: A Swedish case study', *Climatic Change* 87(1–2): 219–34.

Lave, J. and Wegner, E. (1991), *Situated learning: Legitimate peripheral participation*, New York: Cambridge University Press.

Lewontin, R. C. (2001), *The triple helix: Gene, organism, and environment*, Cambridge: Harvard University Press.

Masten, A. S. (2014), *Ordinary magic: Resilience in development*, New York.

Mauss, M. (2002), *The gift: The form and reason for exchange in archaic societies*, London: Routledge.

Münster, D. (2012), 'Farmers' suicides and the state in India: Conceptual and ethno-graphic notes from Wayanad, Kerala', *Contributions to Indian Sociology* 46(1–2): 181–208.

Oyama, S. (2000), *The ontogeny of information: Developmental systems and evolution*, Durham, NC: Duke University Press.

Pálsson, G. (1994), 'Enskilment at sea', *Man* 29(4): 901–27.

Pálsson, G. (1996), 'Commodity fiction and cod fishing', *Nordic Journal of Political Economy* 23: 75–86.

Polanyi, K. (1944), *The great transformation,* Boston, MA: Beacon Press.

Polanyi, M. (1969), 'On body and mind', *The New Scholasticism* 43(2): 195–204.

Schuetz, A. (2013), *Der sinnhafte Aufbau der sozialen Welt: Eine Einleitung in die verstehende Soziologie*, Berlin: Springer.

Smith, A. (1976 [1776]), *An inquiry into the nature and causes of the wealth of nations*, Oxford: Oxford University Press.

Southwick, S. M., Bonanno, G. A., Masten, A. S., Panter-Brick, C., and Yehuda, R. (2014), 'Resilience definitions, theory, and challenges: Interdisciplinary perspectives', *European Journal of Psychotraumatology* 5(1): 253–38.

Stoffregen, T. A. (2003), 'Affordances as properties of the animal–environment system', *Ecological Psychology* 15(2): 115–34.

Toennies, F. (1957), *Community and society (Gemeinschaft und Gesellschaft)*, Michigan: Michigan State University Press.

Tsing, A. L. (2015), *The mushroom at the end of the world: On the possibility of life in capitalist ruins*, New Jersey: Princeton University Press.

Vuojala-Magga, T. (2009), 'Simple things but complicated skills: Sámi skills and tacit knowledge in the context of climatic change', in T. Äikäs (ed.), *Mattut Maddagat: The roots of Saami ethnicities, societies and spaces/places*, Oulu: Publications of the Giellagas Institute, pp. 164–73.

Vuojala-Magga, T. (2010), 'Knowing, training, learning: The importance of reindeer character and temperament for individuals and communities of humans and animals. Good to eat, good to live with: Nomads and animals in northern Eurasia and Africa', *Northeast Asian Study Series* 11: 43–62.

Williams, R. (1977), 'Dominant, residual, and emergent', in R. Williams (ed.), *Marxism and Literature*, Oxford: Oxford University Press, pp. 121–27.

3. The impact of the European crisis in vulnerable households in Europe

Pedro Estêvão, Alexandre Calado and Luís Capucha

ECONOMIC CRISIS AND STAGNATION IN EUROPE

The 2007–08 global financial crash triggered a major recession in Europe, followed by a prolonged and ongoing period of economic stagnation. European gross domestic product (GDP) fell by 4.4% in 2009 alone and would fall again by 0.5% in 2012, while the years of 2010 and 2015 were the only recent years when European GDP grew at all, and did so barely above 2.0%.

Yet not all the countries discussed and compared in this volume suffered the effects of this crisis on the same measure or over the same timeframe (see Tables 3.1 and 3.2). The study countries situated in the outer periphery of the European Union (EU) and of the Eurozone – Greece, Ireland, Portugal, Spain and Finland – bore the harshest and longest of the recessions that followed the crisis.

Owing to its close economic ties with the United States of America and the large weight of the financial sector in its national economy, Ireland was the first of the study countries to plunge into recession: amid a large-scale banking crisis associated with the bursting of a real estate bubble, Irish GDP fell by 4.4% in 2008 – by far the deepest slump in our study countries for that year – and would plunge a further 4.6% in 2009. Between 2010 and 2013, the Irish GDP more or less stagnated; and although registering a hike of 8.5% in 2014, this was still 2.1% below the immediate pre-crisis level of 2007.[1]

Greece is another country on the frontline of the financial and economic crisis in Europe – and arguably the one that has suffered the most from it. As early as 2008, Greek GDP had already declined by 0.3%. It would continue to drop continuously until 2013, at annual rates as high as 9.1% in 2011 and 7.3% in 2012. By 2015, Greek GDP still registered an annual decline of 0.2% and was a massive 24.5% below the pre-crisis level.

Spain has also been heavily hit by the crisis. High growth rates came to a halt with the bursting of a real estate bubble and a banking crisis that bore

Poverty, crisis and resilience

Table 3.1   *Real GDP growth, in percentage from previous year*

	2004	2005	2006	2007	2008	2009	2010	2011	2012	2013	2014	2015
EU28	+2.5	+2.1	+3.3	+3.1	+0.4	−4.4	+2.1	+1.7	−0.5	+0.2	+1.6	+2.2
Finland	+3.9	+2.8	+4.1	+5.2	+0.7	−8.3	+3.0	+2.6	−1.4	−0.8	−0.7	+0.2
Germany	+1.2	+0.7	+3.7	+3.3	+1.1	−5.6	+4.1	+3.7	+0.5	+0.5	+1.6	+1.7
Greece	+5.1	+0.6	+5.7	+3.3	−0.3	−4.3	−5.5	−9.1	−7.3	−3.2	+0.4	−0.2
Ireland	+6.7	+5.8	+5.9	+3.8	−4.4	−4.6	+2.0	+0.0	−1.1	+1.1	+8.5	+26.3
Poland	+5.1	+3.5	+6.2	+7.0	+4.2	+2.8	+3.6	+5.0	+1.6	+1.4	+3.3	+3.9
Portugal	+1.8	+0.8	+1.6	+2.5	+0.2	−3.0	+1.9	−1.8	−4.0	−1.1	+0.9	+1.6
Spain	+3.2	+3.7	+4.2	+3.8	+1.1	−3.6	+0.0	−1.0	−2.9	−1.7	+1.4	+3.2
UK	+2.5	+3.0	+2.5	+2.6	−0.6	−4.3	+1.9	+1.5	+1.3	+1.9	+3.1	+2.2
Turkey*	+9.4	+8.4	+6.9	+4.7	+0.7	−4.8	+9.2	+8.8	+2.1	+4.2	+3.0	+4.0

Sources: Eurostat (2017). Real GDP Growth – volume [tec00115]. Available at: http://appsso
.eurostat.ec.europa.eu/nui/show.do?dataset=tec00115&lang=en (accessed 12 January 2017).
* For Turkey, World Bank (2017). GDP growth (% annual). Available at: https://data.worldbank
.org/indicator/NY.GDP.MKTP.KD.ZG (accessed 12 January 2017).

some similarities to Ireland's. Spain registered negative GDP growth rates for
every year between 2009 and 2013 – with the single exception of a zero growth
year in 2010. By 2015, despite recovered growth, GDP was still 0.5% below
its pre-crisis level.

Portugal was another major casualty of the crisis. Unlike Ireland, Spain or
Greece, Portugal had already been experiencing slow GDP growth rates in
the early to mid-2000s. This owed much to a loss of competitiveness of the
Portuguese economy, still struggling from the impacts of the EU opening to
international markets in mid-to-low added value production and the lack of
the option of currency devaluation following the adoption of the euro. Yet
Portugal's trajectory in the crisis would be very much the same as its periphery
European partners. An initial annual drop of 3.0% in GDP in 2009 was followed by a short rebound to 1.9% growth in 2010, before the country plunged
into negative growth for three consecutive years. Low growth rates afterwards
meant that it took until 2015 for GDP to return to pre-crisis levels.

Finland was also hard hit by the crisis. The immediate impact was extremely
hard, with Finnish GDP declining by 8.3% in 2009 alone – the worst slump for
that year in the RESCuE sample. Quick recovery ensued, with GDP growing
by 3.0% in 2010 and 2.6% in 2011. However, such recovery was short-lived.
With an economy struggling with loss of competitiveness and hit by considerable industrial delocalization phenomena, the Finnish economy again entered
recession, with slight annual GDP reductions.

A second group of countries in the study is composed of the traditional
European industrial powerhouses such as Germany and the UK. Although

Table 3.2   *GDP, current prices, 2007 = 100*

	2004	2005	2006	2007	2008	2009	2010	2011	2012	2013	2014	2015
EU27	85.5	89.3	94.4	100.0	100.5	94.7	98.7	101.6	103.6	104.4	107.8	113.3
Germany	90.3	91.5	95.2	100.0	101.9	97.9	102.7	107.6	109.7	112.5	116.3	120.7
Ireland	79.1	86.3	93.8	100.0	95.1	86.0	84.7	87.7	89.1	91.3	97.9	129.7
Greece	83.2	85.6	93.6	100.0	104.0	102.1	97.1	89.0	82.2	77.6	76.5	75.5
Spain	79.7	86.1	93.3	100.0	103.3	99.8	100.0	99.0	96.2	94.9	95.9	99.5
Poland	65.7	78.4	87.5	100.0	116.7	101.0	115.3	121.1	124.1	125.8	130.9	136.9
Portugal	86.8	90.4	94.7	100.0	101.9	100.0	102.5	100.4	96.0	97.0	98.6	102.3
Finland	84.9	88.1	92.5	100.0	103.8	97.0	100.3	105.5	107.1	109.0	110.1	112.1
UK	85.9	90.2	95.4	100.0	87.8	76.2	81.9	83.9	92.3	91.6	101.1	115.3
Turkey	65.9	81.5	88.5	100.0	105.9	93.7	117.9	121.0	137.7	144.9	142.7	156.8

Note: Own calculations.
Source: Eurostat (2017). GDP and main aggregates – selected international annual data [naida_10_gdp]. Available at: http://appsso.eurostat.ec.europa.eu/nui/show.do?dataset=naida_10_gdp&lang=en (accessed 26 January 2017).

recovering much more quickly from the crisis than the periphery, these countries have been dogged by slow growth rates afterwards.

Like Ireland, the UK became one of the first countries in the sample to enter recession after the global crisis, in large part due to the importance of the financial sector in the British economy. British GDP dropped by 0.6% immediately in 2008 and proceeded to fall by a further 4.3% in 2009. Despite returning to positive annual rates from 2010 onwards, it also showed a pattern of relatively slow growth until 2013.

Germany presents a somewhat different picture. After falling by 5.6% in 2009 alone, German GDP not only recovered quickly but recorded its highest growth rates of the decade in the two following years – 4.1% in 2010 and 3.7% in 2011 – which suggested at the time that Germany could be seen as a sort of a "winner" of the crisis. Yet this relative economic boom was short-lived and Germany quickly entered a path close to stagnation in the years after.

Finally, Turkey and Poland are the two countries that more strongly contrast with the general trend of the study countries regarding economic growth. Turkish GDP did fall by 4.8% in 2009 but, by 2010 and 2011, GDP was growing at the spectacular rates of 9.2% and 8.8% respectively – by far the largest growth levels in the entire sample. Even if at a somewhat more moderate pace, Turkish GDP continued to grow at strong rates until 2015.

Poland is the country in the comparative study sample that seems to have been spared the aftershocks of the 2007–08 global financial crisis. Despite strong speculative pressure on the zloty and high levels of public debt, Polish GDP continued to grow even in 2009 – by 2.8% – making Poland the only study country not to have technically experienced recession at the height of the global financial crisis. By 2010, Polish GDP growth was back at 3.6% and would even peak at 5.0% in 2011. Although these rates became more moderate afterwards they are still well above the EU average, which leads to the term "economic downturn" rather than "economic crisis" being drawn upon in domestic debates on the economic situation.

UNEMPLOYMENT AND DEGRADATION OF LABOUR CONDITIONS

One of the more visible and immediate impacts of the economic crisis was a massive hike in unemployment – from which Europe was arguably still to recover at the time of writing. The unemployment rate in the EU rose continuously between 2008 and 2013, when it peaked at 10.9%. Even if 2014 and 2015 witnessed a significant reduction, unemployment in the latter year was still 2.4 percentage points (p.p.) higher than in 2008. Thus, not only did the initial impact of the crisis run very deep in the labour market but its effects were acutely felt for a very long period afterwards. In some of the study coun-

Table 3.3   Unemployment rate – annual average

	2004	2005	2006	2007	2008	2009	2010	2011	2012	2013	2014	2015
EU28	9.3	9.0	8.2	7.2	7.0	9.0	9.6	9.7	10.5	10.9	10.2	9.4
Finland	8.8	8.4	7.7	6.9	6.4	8.2	8.4	7.8	7.7	8.2	8.7	9.4
Germany	10.4	11.2	10.1	8.5	7.4	7.6	7.0	5.8	5.4	5.2	5.0	4.6
Greece	10.6	10.0	9.0	8.4	7.8	9.6	12.7	17.9	24.5	27.5	26.5	24.9
Ireland	4.5	4.4	4.5	4.7	6.4	12.0	13.9	14.7	14.7	13.1	11.3	9.4
Poland	19.1	17.9	13.9	9.6	7.1	8.1	9.7	9.7	10.1	10.3	9.0	7.5
Portugal	7.8	8.8	8.9	9.1	8.8	10.7	12.0	12.9	15.8	16.4	14.1	12.6
Spain	11.0	9.2	8.5	8.2	11.3	17.9	19.9	21.4	24.8	26.1	24.5	22.1
Turkey	–	9.5	9.0	9.1	10.0	13.0	11.1	9.1	8.4	9.0	9.9	10.3
UK	4.7	4.8	5.4	5.3	5.6	7.6	7.8	8.1	7.9	7.6	6.1	5.3

Source: Eurostat. Unemployment by age and sex, annual average (ut_rt_a). Available at: https://appsso.eurostat.ec.europa.eu/nui/show.do?dataset=une_rt_a&lang=en (accessed 12 January 2017).

tries, mass unemployment became a harrowing feature of economic life for several years.

The peripheral countries of the Eurozone – Greece, Ireland, Portugal and Spain – saw the most dramatic increases in total, long-term and youth unemployment rates in the wake of the crisis (see Table 3.3). Greece and Spain are the two most emphatic cases of resurgence of mass unemployment. In both cases, unemployment rates reached staggering figures at the height of the crisis. By 2013, unemployment rates had spiked to 27.5% in the case of Greece and 26.1% in the case of Spain – more than triple the homologous 2008 figures. The same year also saw the Portuguese unemployment rate reaching 16.4%, representing an almost twofold increase on 2008. In turn, the Irish unemployment rate reached the high plateau of 14.7% in 2011 and 2012 – nearly three times the reference level of 2008. Unemployment would proceed to decline slowly over the following years. Yet, by 2015, rates were still considerably high when compared to the 2008 levels: 3.2 times higher in Greece, 1.9 times in the case of Spain, 1.5 times in the case of Ireland and 1.4 times in the case of Portugal.

Other study countries registered significant – even if not so dramatic – growth of unemployment rates in the wake of the crisis. This was the case in Finland, the UK, Poland and Turkey. Of these, Finland saw the smallest of the surges, with a 1.8 p.p. increase between 2008 and 2009. However, it is also the only one of the four countries where unemployment had not returned to 2008 levels by 2015. On the contrary, the Finnish unemployment rate has been creeping up since 2012, reaching 9.4% in 2015. The Polish case is more puzzling, as GDP growth only suffered a minor slowdown in the period of the crisis. Yet there is no denying that a trend in unemployment was reversed in the crisis years. Unemployment rates fell rapidly after the country joined the EU, from 19.1% in 2004 to just 7.1% in 2008. However, they would grow almost continuously to a maximum of 10.3% in 2013, before finally starting to decline, reaching 7.5% in 2015.

In turn, the UK suffered a gradual increase in unemployment after 2008, peaking at 8.1% in 2011 – 1.5 times the 2007 figure – and declining slowly afterwards. Only in 2015 did unemployment return to pre-crisis levels. Turkey experienced a sharper rise in unemployment, with the corresponding rate jumping from 9.1% in 2007 to 13.0% in 2009. Yet a return to pre-crisis levels was far quicker: by 2011 unemployment was back to 9.1%.

The remarkable exception to the trend of rising unemployment within the country cases is Germany. With the exception of the immediate rebound in 2010 and 2011, German GDP has featured low growth rates since the start of the crisis. Yet, not only is the early shock of the crisis barely noticeable in terms of unemployment (a mere 0.2 p.p. increase between 2008 and 2009), this slight increase is the single exception in a decade of continuous decline – culminating in an unemployment rate of 4.6% in 2015, the lowest in the entire sample for that year.

Rising unemployment tells an important part of the story of the transforma-tions in the labour market in some of the study countries before and after the global financial crisis. But it is by no means an exhaustive account of it. There are also signs of a tendency towards an increasing precarity of labour relations which, while not being a new phenomenon stemming from the crisis, may have been intensified by it. For instance, the share of temporary and part-time contracts in Britain has been steadily growing since the crisis. Extremely pre-carious labour relations such as "zero-hour contracts" – where the employer does not have to guarantee any specific weekly number of working hours to the employee – experienced a sharp rise after 2008. By 2016, a total of 903 000 workers were under zero-hour contracts, representing 2.9% of the total British workforce – although this is likely to be a severe underestimation (ONS 2016).

In the peripheral countries of the EU, this problem is even more evident. In Greece and Portugal, for instance, deregulation of labour markets was a key point in the Memorandum of Understanding that accompanied the International Monetary Fund (IMF) and EU financial intervention during the debt crisis (Karamessini 2015; Lima 2016). In the Greek case, this seems to have resulted in a fully-fledged phenomenon of conversion of full-time and permanent contracts into part-time and ad-hoc ones in the private sector, with firms frequently firing employees, and re-hiring them afterwards at lower wages and on a precarious basis (Petraki 2014).

AUSTERITY

Given that eight of the nine country cases are EU members and six of them are Eurozone members, it should not come as a surprise that national economic and social policy responses to the 2007–08 global financial crisis and its aftershocks were heavily influenced by the EU. As it turned out, however, EU action did not stem from a single coherent approach for tackling the crisis, but rather resulted in a hesitant and improvised course with several u-turns along the way. Indeed, it is possible to identify three very distinct phases in the European approach to the crisis between 2008 and 2010 alone (Costa and Caldas 2014; Pedroso 2014).

The first was a *financial* phase, running during late 2007 and early 2008. In this early phase, the crisis was seen by European institutions as purely a matter of the financial system. As such, it was to be tackled through regulatory action and later direct financial support to ailing financial institutions by national governments.

The second was an *expansionist* phase, running from late 2008 until mid-2010. As the effects of the banking crisis began to be felt over the real economy, the European Commission launched a European Economic Recovery Programme to stimulate aggregate demand and also to "lessen the human cost of the economic downturn and its impact on the most vulnerable" (European Commission 2008, p. 3). This set the tone for national governments to launch public investment programmes and/or increases in public spending levels.

The third was an *austerity* phase, which arguably has lasted from mid-2010 until the time of writing. In the context of the Greek debt crisis, priorities were suddenly reversed. Deficit and sovereign debt reduction now took centre stage. "Restoring macroeconomic stability and returning public finances on a sustainable path" were now to be regarded as the "prerequisites for growth and jobs" (European Council 2010, p. 1). Also, from 2010 onwards, peripheral Eurozone countries began to fall prey one after the other to mounting levels of interest on their sovereign debt. Three of the study countries – Greece, Ireland and Portugal – were pressed to call for international loans in order to avoid both national bankruptcy and an eventual collapse of the euro. The loans by the IMF and the European Central Bank involved the adoption and implementation of heavy austerity programmes. Even though not suffering this fate, other cases, such as Spain, were the target of heavy pressure to adopt austerity packages.

Looking at social expenditure levels, as in Table 3.4, one can detect signs of both the expansionist and austerity phases that were described above. With the exception of Greece, in all the study countries for which there is registered data available, 2009 brought the highest growth in social expenditure in the period considered, ranging from 11.6% in Ireland to 5.2% in Finland. This was reflected in measures such as increasing child allowance in the UK (HM Treasury, 2008), prolonging unemployment benefit coverage in Portugal (Pedroso 2014) or simply resisting the urge to roll back existing social policies in Spain (Laparra and Pérez 2010).

Yet, by 2011, social expenditure per inhabitant declined even in countries where GDP growth was negative, such as Portugal, Spain or Greece. A similar behaviour can be observed for Ireland in 2012. Cuts in social expenditure were typically achieved through: lowering the amount of transfers, as with pensions in Greece (Petmezidou 2011); release of public servants, as with social workers in Spain (Fundación 1º de Mayo, 2014); and also through more indirect measures such as lowering the maximum threshold for accessing transfers, as with child allowance and minimum guaranteed income in Portugal (Pedroso 2014).

It is worth noting again, however, that there is considerable diversity in the study sample in this regard. Indeed, social expenditure in Finland kept increasing throughout the country's 2012–14 recession, while Germany's low growth period from 2012 to 2015 was also accompanied by moderate increases in this regard.

Public services were also affected by the turn to austerity, in some cases deepening the previous retraction trend and in other cases (like Spain and Portugal) joining it. One example at hand is health care (see Table 3.5). There is little trace of an increase in health expenditure corresponding to the expansionist phase – which is not surprising given that, unlike education and even social transfers, spending on health was not specifically encouraged by the EU at that point in time. However, declines in government expenditure in health occurred in Greece and Portugal after 2010, in Spain after 2009, in the UK between 2010 and 2012 and in Ireland after 2012. Again, Finland appears to be a major exception as the only country in the sample that did not register annual negative growth rates after 2009.

Families' capacity for coping with the effects of economic crisis is affected not only by the evolution of social transfers and the quality of public services but also by taxation policies. Indeed, changes in taxation can have a direct impact on family income and the regressive or progressive nature of these changes can influence inequality levels.

The crisis period was marked by a general increase in the weight of household taxes wthin total taxation in the EU peripheral countries (see Table 3.6). By 2015, the importance of taxes on individual and household gains within total taxation had grown by 5.4 p.p. in Ireland, 4.6 p.p. in Portugal, 0.6 p.p. in Finland and 0.2 p.p. in Greece – in the latter case, despite the huge impact of the crisis on employment and labour conditions. This increase took different forms such as direct creation of new taxes – as in an extra income levy in Ireland for example – or reduction of the number of tax brackets, thus

Table 3.4   *Total social expenditure per inhabitant (in euros, 2010 constant prices)*

	2004	2005	2006	2007	2008	2009	2010	2011	2012	2013	2014
Germany	8 610	8 575	8 490	8 483	8 627	9 344	9 400	9 453	9 513	9 684	9 877
Ireland	6 461	6 748	7 028	7 297	7 705	8 601	8 794	8 798	8 649	8 423	8 262
Greece	4 014	4 325	4 605	4 892	5 202	5 495	5 324	5 086	4 801	4 426	4 374
Spain	4 604	4 789	4 910	5 059	5 252	5 769	5 716	5 693	n.a.	n.a.	n.a.
Poland	1 465	1 496	1 561	1 581	1 724	1 879	1 874	1 833	1 864	1 956	n.a.
Portugal	3 832	3 919	3 953	3 941	3 971	4 344	4 386	4 260	4 171	4 389	4 339
Finland	8 856	9 010	9 181	9 313	9 506	9 999	10 223	10 196	10 404	10 644	10 814
UK	7 257	7 648	7 745	7 752	7 909	8 336	8 491	8 493	8 571	8 434	8 351

Source: Eurostat. Expenditure: main results [spr_exp_sum]. Available at: https://appsso.eurostat.ec.europa.eu/nui/show.do?dataset=spr_exp_sum&lang=en (accessed 25 January 2017).

Table 3.5   Government expenditure in health as a percentage of GDP

	2004	2005	2006	2007	2008	2009	2010	2011	2012	2013	2014
EU27	–	–	6.6	6.5	6.7	7.3	7.2	7.1	7.1	7.2	7.2
Germany	6.4	6.5	6.4	6.3	6.4	7.1	7	6.8	6.8	7.1	7.2
Greece	–	–	5.9	6.0	6.4	6.8	6.8	6.4	5.8	5.1	4.7
Spain	5.4	5.6	5.6	5.7	6.0	6.8	6.6	6.5	6.2	6.1	6.1
Finland	6.6	6.8	6.8	6.6	7.0	7.9	7.9	7.8	8.2	8.3	8.3
Ireland	6.7	6.7	6.6	6.9	7.7	8.5	8.1	8.1	8.2	7.9	7.6
Poland	4.2	4.4	4.6	4.5	5.0	5.0	5.0	4.7	4.6	4.6	4.6
Portugal	7.2	7.3	7.0	7.0	7.2	7.9	7.3	6.8	6.5	6.4	6.2
UK	6.5	6.6	6.8	6.8	7.2	8.0	7.8	7.6	7.5	7.5	7.6

Source: Eurostat. General government expenditure by function (COFOG) [gov_10a_exp]).
Available at: https://appsso.eurostat.ec.europa.eu/nui/show.do?dataset=gov_10a_exp&lang=en
(accessed on 26 January 2017).

*Table 3.6   Taxes on individual and household gains, excluding holding
                  gains, as percentage of total taxation*

	2004	2005	2006	2007	2008	2009	2010	2011	2012	2013	2014	2015
Ireland	26.4	25.7	24.5	25.1	27.4	29.8	30.1	30.8	32.2	31.3	30.9	30.5
Greece	12.7	13.0	13.3	13.5	13.5	13.5	11.6	13.1	18.0	15.5	15.1	13.7
Poland	12.1	12.6	13.3	14.6	15.1	14.1	13.5	13.2	13.5	13.6	13.9	14.0
Portugal	14.7	14.6	14.6	15.1	15.4	16.4	15.9	16.8	16.9	20.7	20.8	19.7
Finland	29.5	29.5	28.9	28.5	29.8	30.4	28.5	28.2	28.6	28.2	29.4	29.1
UK	27.3	27.7	27.4	28.2	27.0	27.7	27.1	26.5	25.5	25.6	25.4	25.4

Source: Eurostat (2016). Main national accounts tax aggregates [gov_10a_taxag]. https://appsso
.eurostat.ec.europa.eu/nui/show.do?dataset=gov_10a_taxag&lang=en
(accessed 26 January 2017).

decreasing its progressive character and enlarging the tax base by lowering the
thresholds of exemption, as in Portugal. Only in Poland, barely touched by the
crisis, and the UK, was the share of household gains in total taxation in 2015
smaller compared to 2007 – 0.6 p.p. and 2.8 p.p. respectively.

By contrast, taxation on capital and business income in most of the study
countries follows a tendency to decline during the period of analysis, suggesting that austerity actually resulted in a shift in taxation from capital to labour
during the crisis years in most RESCuE countries. As Table 3.7 shows, the
proportion of taxes on income or profits of corporations as a share of total
taxation fell by 5.9 p.p. in Spain, 4.1 p.p. in Finland, 1.9 p.p. in the UK, 1.5
p.p. in Portugal, 1.3 p.p. in Germany and Greece between 2007 and 2015. Of
these, only Greece had in 2015 a GDP value significantly inferior to that of

Table 3.7   *Taxes on the income or profits of corporations including holding gains as percentage of total taxation*

	2004	2005	2006	2007	2008	2009	2010	2011	2012	2013	2014	2015
EU27	6.6	7.2	8.1	8.2	7.5	5.7	6.1	6.3	6.2	6.2	6.0	6.2
Germany	5.3	6.0	7.1	7.2	6.4	4.7	5.4	6.2	6.5	6.1	6.0	5.9
Ireland	11.4	10.7	11.6	10.6	9.1	8.0	8.4	7.7	7.8	8.1	8.1	11.1
Greece	8.5	9.7	7.8	6.8	6.4	7.6	7.4	5.7	2.8	3.0	4.8	5.5
Spain	10.0	10.9	11.4	12.9	8.8	7.8	6.2	6.0	6.8	6.4	6.1	7.0
Poland	5.9	6.3	6.9	7.7	7.7	7.0	6.0	6.2	6.3	5.4	5.3	5.5
Portugal	8.4	7.6	8.1	9.9	10.1	8.2	8.1	8.8	8.0	8.8	7.6	8.4
Finland	8.1	7.6	7.7	9.0	8.1	4.7	6.0	6.2	4.9	5.4	4.4	4.9
UK	7.7	8.8	10.2	9.0	9.1	7.5	8.2	8.1	7.7	7.3	7.0	7.1

Source: Eurostat (2016). Main national accounts tax aggregates [gov_10a_taxag]. Available at: https://appsso.eurostat.ec.europa.eu/nui/show.do?dataset=gov_10a_taxag&lang=en (accessed 26 January 2017).

2007. Ireland and Poland are the exceptions in this regard. However, it should be noted that both countries already had very low business taxation in place before the crisis. At 12.5% and 19.0% respectively, Ireland and Poland were the two countries from the sample with the lowest combined corporate income tax in 2008 (OECD.stat 2017).

INCOME AND POVERTY

Although with varying intensity in the nine country cases, unemployment growth and increasing labour precariousness seem to be key features in a transformation of European labour markets that accelerated with the global financial crisis. At the same time, dwindling social expenditure and public services funding, as well as increased taxation on labour, were part of austerity policy packages in several of these countries. It is thus important to assess how these changes are reflected in household income (see Table 3.8).

Table 3.8 illustrates how deep and prolonged was the impact of the crisis and of its aftershocks over European households' financial resources. By 2015, median equivalent net income was still inferior to pre-crisis levels in Greece, Ireland and the UK. Greece displays the more emphatic transformation in this regard, with median income falling continuously between 2011 and 2015 by a total of €4 436 – representing a staggering drop of 37.1% in relation to 2010 levels. Ireland registered annual declines in median income in all years between 2009 and 2013, totalling €3 930 (a 17.3% drop in relation to 2008). Continuous declines were also felt in Spain (€1 526 between 2010 and 2014, representing a 10.3% drop in relation to 2009), Portugal (€501 between 2011

Poverty, crisis and resilience

Table 3.8   *Median equivalized net income (euros)*

	2004	2005	2006	2007	2008	2009	2010	2011	2012	2013	2014	2015
EU27	–	12 626	12 919	13 898	14 607	14 815	14 958	15 082	15 571	15 554	15 914	16 269
Germany	–	16 395	15 646	17 774	18 304	18 586	18 795	19 043	19 592	19 545	19 712	20 644
Ireland	18 075	18 798	19 757	22 065	22 995	22 445	20 512	19 726	19 078	19 065	19 477	–
Greece	8 857	9 400	9 833	10 080	10 800	11 530	11 963	10 985	9 460	8 377	7 680	7 527
Spain	10 200	10 417	11 111	11 644	13 963	14 795	14 605	13 929	13 864	13 523	13 269	13 352
Poland	–	2 531	3 111	3 502	4 154	5 090	4 402	5 032	5 057	5 174	5 339	5 560
Portugal	6 921	7 200	7 311	7 576	8 152	8 267	8 678	8 410	8 323	8 177	8 229	8 435
Finland	16 679	17 481	18 304	18 703	19 794	20 962	21 349	21 826	22 699	23 272	23 702	23 763
UK	–	18 546	19 403	21 139	18 766	16 266	17 106	17 136	19 168	18 694	20 528	20 947
Turkey	–	–	2 353	2 693	2 903	3 049	2 752	3 326	3 220	3 438	–	–

Source: Eurostat (2017). Mean and median income [ilc_di04]. Available at: https://appsso.eurostat.ec.europa.eu/nui/show.do?dataset=ilc_di04&lang=en (accessed 24 January 2017).

Table 3.9   *At-risk-of-poverty rate before social transfers (pensions included in social transfers) (60% of median income)*

	2004	2005	2006	2007	2008	2009	2010	2011	2012	2013	2014	2015
EU28	–	43.1	43.2	42.7	42	42.4	43.5	44.1	43.9	44.4	44.7	44.6
Germany	–	43.3	46.2	43.2	43.5	43.5	43.9	44.6	43.3	43.7	44.0	43.9
Ireland	38.9	39.6	40.1	40.1	41.8	46.2	50.1	50.5	50.4	49.8	48.8	–
Greece	39.7	39.2	40.5	41.9	41.5	42.0	42.8	44.9	49.8	53.4	52.2	52.9
Spain	41.3	39.1	39.1	38.6	37.8	39.3	42.1	43.8	43.8	45.5	47.5	47.0
Poland	–	50.8	49.1	47.1	44.1	42.6	43.3	43.4	42.7	43.0	43.7	43.6
Portugal	41.3	40.8	40.2	40.0	41.5	41.5	43.4	42.5	45.4	46.9	47.8	47.8
Finland	41.5	40.4	40.6	41.1	39.5	38.6	40.7	41.3	41.3	41.7	43.3	43.4
UK	–	42.7	42.0	41.7	40.7	43.2	44.1	43.4	44.5	45.2	43.6	44.2
Turkey	–	–	39.4	38.2	39.0	39.9	40.5	38.7	38.8	39.5	–	–

Source: Eurostat (2017). At-risk-of-poverty rate before social transfers (pensions included in social transfers) by poverty threshold, age and sex. Table code: [ilc_li09]. Available at: http:// appsso.eurostat.ec.europa.eu/nui/show.do?dataset=ilc_li09&lang=en (accessed 6 February 2017).

and 2013, representing a 5.8% in relation to 2010). In the UK decline was concentrated in a shorter time span, but was no less brutal: after declines in 2008 and 2009, median income was €4 873 lower than in 2007 – representing a 23.1% drop.

Only Finland and Germany escaped this prolonged trend of decline. In Finland, median income kept increasing despite years of negative growth, which can be seen partly as a demonstration of the capacity of the Finnish welfare state to protect most of the recession shocks from households.

Such drops in household income necessarily translated into increased exposure to poverty. Indeed, Table 3.9 confirms the extent of decline on households' living conditions in several of the study countries. By 2012, all countries in the sample apart from Poland recorded higher poverty rates before social transfers than in 2007. Rates jumped dramatically in this period in Ireland (more 10.3 p.p.), Greece, (7.9 p.p.), Portugal (5.4 p.p.), Spain (5.2 p.p.) and the UK (2.8 p.p.). By 2015, and despite signs of economic recovery in most of these countries, the situation had failed to improve. Poverty rates before social transfers remained higher than in the yardstick year of 2007 in all of these countries with the distance even increasing in the case of Greece (now 11.0 p.p. higher than in 2007), Spain (8.4 p.p.) and Portugal (7.8 p.p.).

However, as indicated in Table 3.9, the rise in the poverty rate before social transfers was much more muted in Finland – despite being 2.3 p.p. higher in 2015 than in 2007 – and Turkey and almost non-existent in Germany. In

Poland, too, there were no significant hikes, although a fast-declining trend evident since 2005 halted in 2010, and stagnated afterwards.

The intensity of poverty increase during the crisis can also be grasped from the evolution of the poverty gap – that is, the distance of the average household income of poor households from the poverty threshold. Again, the same pattern of differentiated evolution among the countries emerges. In Portugal, Spain and Greece, the poverty gap increased rapidly between 2007 and 2014 (by 6.0 p.p., 5.7 p.p. and 5.3 p.p. respectively) while Ireland also recorded a significant increase in this regard (1.3 p.p.).

By contrast, no changes and even slight decreases between 2007 and 2014 were recorded in Germany, Finland, Turkey and Poland (0.0 p.p., 0.2 p.p., 0.5 p.p., 0.8 p.p.), while the UK even recorded a substantial decrease during this period (−3.0 p.p).

This panorama becomes somewhat more complex when social transfers are brought into the equation. Comparing before and after social transfers rates in each country illustrates how the welfare state acts as a powerful buffer to economic crisis. Across the sample, poverty rates after social transfers feature much lower values and also much milder fluctuations than before social transfer rates. This exercise also reveals how different countries adopted different approaches to the crisis and different welfare state regimes can mitigate or enhance the impact of the crisis.

Not surprisingly given the magnitude of the losses of income in these countries, Greece and Spain are the countries where a negative evolution regarding poverty rates after social transfers was most pronounced, as Table 3.11 shows. By 2012, the at-risk-of-poverty rate after social transfers was up by 2.8 p.p. in Greece and by 1.1 p.p. in Spain in relation to 2007. But in other countries the hike was barely visible, if visible at all. To be sure, at-risk-of-poverty after social transfers had increased in Germany by 0.9 p.p. in this period and in Finland by 0.2 p.p. in this period. But in other countries, the rate in 2012 was either close to or inferior to 2007 values. This was the case of Poland (−0.2 p.p.), Portugal (−0.2 p.p.), Turkey (−1.0 p.p.), Ireland (−1.5 p.p.) and the UK (−2.4 p.p.)

Yet two caveats ought to be taken into account when analysing the latter figures. On the one hand, one must consider the fall in median income in some of these countries – such as Portugal, the UK or Ireland – in relation to which the at-risk-of-poverty rates are calculated. On the other hand, it is worth pointing out that, by 2015, five out of the seven study countries for which there was data available had higher at-risk-of-poverty rates than in 2007: Spain (more than 2.4 p.p.), Germany (1.5 p.p.), Greece (1.1 p.p.), Portugal (1.4 p.p.) and Poland (0.3 p.p.). That is, once the median income began to rise again with economic recovery, the extent of the impact of economic hardship and austerity-inspired social policy over income inequality became more apparent.

Table 3.10   Relative poverty gap (cut-off point: 60% of median equivalized income)

	2004	2005	2006	2007	2008	2009	2010	2011	2012	2013	2014	2015	2016	2017
EU28	–	–	–	–	–	–	22.9	23.0	23.4	23.8	24.6	24.8	25.0	–
Germany	–	18.9	20.4	23.2	22.2	21.5	20.7	21.4	21.1	20.4	23.2	22.0	20.7	–
Ireland	19.2	20.2	16.6	17.6	17.7	16.2	15.5	17.5	20.0	17.5	18.9	18.5	18.1	–
Greece	24.6	23.9	25.8	26.0	24.7	24.1	23.4	26.1	29.9	32.7	31.3	30.6	31.9	30.3
Spain	24.8	25.6	26.4	25.9	25.6	25.7	26.8	27.4	30.6	30.9	31.6	33.8	31.4	32.4
Poland	–	30.1	25.0	24.0	20.6	22.7	22.2	21.4	22.2	22.6	23.2	22.3	24.4	23.6
Portugal	24.7	26.0	23.5	24.3	23.2	23.6	22.7	23.2	24.1	27.4	30.3	29.0	26.7	27.0
Finland	14.3	13.8	14.5	14.1	15.7	15.1	13.8	13.5	15.0	15.0	13.9	13.2	13.9	13.7
UK	–	22.3	22.8	22.4	21.0	20.6	21.4	21.3	20.9	19.6	19.4	20.4	22.4	–
Turkey	–	–	36.5	28.9	30.0	32.1	32.3	31.9	30.3	27.9	28.4	27.8	–	–

Source: Eurostat. Relative median at-risk-of-poverty gap. Code: [sdg_10_30]. Available at: http://appsso.eurostat.ec.europa.eu/nui/show.do?dataset=sdg_10_30&lang=en (accessed 6 February 2017).

Table 3.11   *At-risk-of-poverty rate (cut-off point: 60% of median equivalized income after social transfers)*

	2004	2005	2006	2007	2008	2009	2010	2011	2012	2013	2014	2015
EU27	–	16.5	16.5	16.6	16.5	16.4	16.5	16.8	16.8	16.7	17.2	17.3
Germany	–	12.2	12.5	15.2	15.2	15.5	15.6	15.8	16.1	16.1	16.7	16.7
Ireland	20.9	19.7	18.5	17.2	15.5	15.0	15.2	15.2	15.7	14.1	15.6	
Greece	19.9	19.6	20.5	20.3	20.1	19.7	20.1	21.4	23.1	23.1	22.1	21.4
Spain	20.1	20.1	20.3	19.7	19.8	20.4	20.7	20.6	20.8	20.4	22.2	22.1
Poland	–	20.5	19.1	17.3	16.9	17.1	17.6	17.7	17.1	17.3	17.0	17.6
Portugal	20.4	19.4	18.5	18.1	18.5	17.9	17.9	18.0	17.9	18.7	19.5	19.5
Finland	11.0	11.7	12.6	13	13.6	13.8	13.1	13.7	13.2	11.8	12.8	12.4
UK	–	19.0	19.0	18.6	18.7	17.3	17.1	16.2	16.0	15.9	16.8	16.7
Turkey	–	–	26.7	24.7	24.7	25.3	24.4	23.5	23.7	23.1	–	–

Source: Eurostat. At-risk-of-poverty rate by poverty threshold, age and sex – EU-SILC survey (code: [ilc_li02]). Available at: http://appsso.eurostat.ec.europa.eu/nui/show.do?dataset=ilc_li02 (accessed 24 January 2017).

Also, the relative mildness of the general trend regarding poverty rates after social transfers masks how specific groups suffered sharp increases in their vulnerability to poverty during the crisis years. Table 3.12 shows how distinctly the trends evolved between age groups. Between 2007 and 2015, only in two countries – Germany and Poland – did the risk of poverty after social transfers for over 64-year-olds increase. Falls in this age group range from 7.8 p.p. in Finland to 17.4 p.p. in Ireland. But the reverse of the coin is that the risk of poverty after social transfers for 18–64 year-olds increased in all countries, with Turkey being the only exception. In several cases, these increases were very significant: 6.4 p.p. in Spain, 3.8 p.p. in Greece, 3.6 p.p. in Portugal and 2.1 p.p. in Germany. The at-risk-of-poverty rate after social transfers for 18–64 year-olds grew even in Ireland and the UK – by 1.7 p.p. and 0.6 p.p. respectively – two countries in which the overall rate declined.

Considering that these age groups greatly overlap with the active age and retired populations, two effects can be discerned here: on the one hand, the welfare state acting as a buffer for crisis impacts on the elderly population, through redistribution mechanisms such as pensions; on the other hand, unemployment and deterioration of labour conditions take their toll on the active population.

Table 3.12   *At-risk-of-poverty rate (cut-off point: 60% of median equivalized income after social transfers) in 2015 by age group and difference in relation to 2007*

	< 18 years		18–64 years		> 64 years	
	2015	Δ2015–07	2015	Δ2015–07	2015	Δ2015–07
EU27	21.1	1.0	17.1	2.2	17.1	−5.1
Germany	14.6	0.5	17.3	2.1	17.3	0.3
Ireland*	17.0	−2.2	16.1	1.7	16.1	−17.4
Greece	26.6	3.3	22.5	3.8	22.5	−9.2
Spain	29.6	3.4	22.8	6.4	22.8	−13.8
Poland	22.4	−1.8	17.6	0.4	17.6	4.3
Portugal	24.8	3.9	18.8	3.6	18.8	−8.5
Finland	10.0	−0.9	12.7	1.2	12.7	−7.8
UK	19.8	−3.2	15.7	0.6	15.7	−10.1
Turkey**	33.7	−0.6	18.5	−1.9	18.5	0.0

Note: Own calculations.
Data source: Eurostat, At-risk-of-poverty rate by poverty threshold, age and sex – EU-SILC survey [ilc_li02]. Available at: http://appsso.eurostat.ec.europa.eu/nui/show.do?dataset=ilc_li02 (accessed 24 January 2017).

CONCLUSION

The 2007–08 global financial crisis generated an economic shockwave that engulfed most of Europe. In the immediate wake of the crisis, severe dips in economic activity were recorded in almost all of the countries discussed and compared in this volume. The aftershocks of the crisis were prolonged and particularly acute in the periphery of the EU, afflicting not only its Southern rim – Portugal, Spain and Greece – but also its Northern one – Ireland and Finland. But even the centre was, in the case of the UK, suffering a lasting recession and, in that of Germany, facing a long economic stagnation after 2011. Within the study sample, only in the cases of Poland or Turkey did the crisis leave few long-term traces.

Rising unemployment followed in the footsteps of recession, with the Northern and Southern peripheries again being particularly negatively affected. Portugal, Spain, Greece and Ireland suffered major hikes in unemployment rates in the years after the crisis while Finland has witnessed a slower creeping up of unemployment since 2012. But other countries in the study sample also fell prey to unemployment problems. The UK suffered a continual increase until 2011 with the subsequent fall taking place very gradually while Poland and Turkey, which had recovered very quickly from the crisis, still witnessed significant increases in unemployment in subsequent years. Among the study countries, only Germany was spared in this regard.

There is, however, a strong case for seeing the European crisis not only as the result of an exogenous economic shock but also – if not decisively – as the product of political and policy choices that either predated it or were devised to respond to it. This chapter focused on three of these policy trends: deregulation of the labour market; cutbacks in social transfers and public services; and transfer of the fiscal burden from capital to labour.

A general trend for deregulation of the labour market has surely predated the crisis. The cases of Portugal and Greece are particularly notable in this regard. Within the financial rescue interventions led by the European Commission and the IMF in these two countries, deregulation of the labour market was an explicit objective.

Social policy responses to the crisis were affected by the oscillation of EU economic policy – which went through a financial and then a fiscal expansionist phase before settling on an austerity framework from mid-2010 onwards. Partly following this oscillation, but also owing to differences in national policy agendas and domestic political equilibria, policy responses at national level varied considerably within the study sample. While countries such as Ireland, Finland and Germany resisted cutbacks in social transfers, others such as Spain, Portugal and Greece engaged in a severe reduction of social expenditure at the height of the crisis. Likewise, investment in public health provision declined after 2010 in countries such as Spain, Portugal and Greece.

The crisis period was also marked by a general increase in the weight of household taxes in total taxation in the EU peripheral countries that are part of the sample – Ireland, Portugal, Finland and Greece – which took place despite the impact of the crisis on employment and labour conditions. By contrast, capital and business share on overall taxation fell – apart from those that already had very low corporate taxes. This suggests that austerity policies actually resulted in the shifting of the tax burden from capital to labour.

In conclusion, in most countries – and particularly Portugal, Spain, Greece and even the UK – families were clearly caught in a pincer movement between, on one side, the degradation of the labour market – including fast-rising unemployment, precaritization and wage reductions – and, on the other side, cuts in social transfers and public services and increases in taxation of labour incomes. This has led to significant drops in household income from pre-crisis levels and severely increased exposure to poverty for large tracts of the population. Nevertheless, it should be stressed that some study countries such as Germany, Finland, and even Ireland, kept social expenditure levels at pre-crisis levels, thus offering a contrasting background within the sample in this regard.

It was against this general – though not homogeneous – harsh socioeconomic backdrop and also counting on different levels of resources made available by the welfare state in different countries, that resilience processes examined and reported on in this volume were shaped and took place.

NOTE

1. While statistics for 2015 show a staggering Irish GDP growth of 26.3% in Ireland, this figure seems to have little relation to the performance of the Irish real economy. Indeed, Eurostat clarified that this apparently huge growth was in fact "primarily due to the relocation to Ireland of a limited number of big economic operators" (EUROSTAT, 2016).

BIBLIOGRAPHY

Aytekin, E. A. and Sengül, H. T. (2014), *National report, Turkey. Work package 2: State of the art*, unpublished RESCuE project report.

Buğra, A. and Keyder, Ç. (2006), *New poverty and the changing welfare regime in Turkey*, Ankara: United Nations Development Programme in Turkey.

Capucha, L., Calado, A. and Estêvão, P. (2014), *National report, Portugal. Work package 2: State of the art*, unpublished RESCuE project report. Available at : https://repositorio-iul.iscte.pt/handle/10071/11406?mode=full (accessed 10 January 2017).

Castro, C., Serrano, A. and Tovar, F. (2014), *National report, Spain. Work package 2: State of the art*, unpublished RESCuE project report.

Costa, A. and Caldas, J. C. (2014), 'A União Europeia e Portugal entre os Resgates Bancários e a Austeridade. Um mapa das políticas e das medidas', in J. Reis (ed.), *A Economia Política do Retrocesso: Crise, Causas e Objetivos, observatório sobre crises e alternativas*, Coimbra: Almedina, pp. 87–126.

Dagdeviren, H., Donoghue, M. and Huws, U. (2014), *The UK state of the art report. Work package 2*, unpublished RESCuE project report.

Dagg, J. and Gray, J. (2014), *Ireland State of the art Report. Work package 2*, unpublished RESCuE project report.

Deeke, A. (2009), 'Konjunkturelle Kurzarbeit: was kann bei vorübergehendem Arbeitsausfall bewirkt werden?' *WSI Mitteilungen* 62(8): 446–52.

European Commission (2008), *Communication from the European Commission to the European Council: A European Economic Recovery Programme*, Brussels: European Commission.

European Council (2010), *European Council 25/26 March – Conclusions*, Brussels: European Council.

EUROSTAT (2016), *Irish GDP revision*. Available at: http://ec.europa.eu/eurostat/documents/24987/6390465/Irish_GDP_communication.pdf (accessed 18 January 2017).

Fundación 1º de Mayo. (2014), *La situación social en España: Informe anual de Política Social*, Madrid: Fundación 1º de Mayo. Available at: http://www.1mayo.ccoo.es/nova/files/1018/Informe76.pdf (accessed 15 January 2017).

HM Treasury (2008), *Facing global challenges: Supporting people in difficult times. Pre-budget report 2008*. London: HM Treasury.

INE (2011), *Estatísticas do Emprego 2010 – 4º trimestre*. Lisboa: Instituto Nacional de Estatística.

Kambouri, H., Marinoudi, T. and Yfanti, A. (2014), *National report, Greece. Work package 2: State of the art*, unpublished RESCuE project report.

Karamessini, M. (2015), 'The Greek social model: Towards a deregulated labour market and residual social protection', in D. Vaughan-Whitehead (ed.), *The European social model in crisis: Is Europe losing its soul?*, Cheltenham, UK and Northampton, MA, USA: Edward Elgar Publishing, pp. 230–88.

Keller, C., Tucci, I., Jossin, A. and Groh-Samberg, O. (2012), 'Prekäre Verläufe von Jugendlichen mit Migrationshintergrund in Deutschland und Frankreich', in J. Mansel and K. Speck (eds.), *Jugend und Arbeit: Empirische Bestandaufnahme und Analysen,* Weinheim: Juventa, pp. 135–56.

Koller, L., Neder, N., Rudolph, H. and Trappmann, M. (2012), *Selbständige in der Grudsicherung: Viel Arbeit für wenig Geld*, IAB – Kurzbericht 22/2012, Nuremberg: Institut für Arbeitsmarkt- und Berufsforschung.

Laparra, M. and Pérez, E. (2010), *El primer impacto de la crisis en la cohesión social en España*, Madrid: Cáritas Española/ Fundación FOESSA.

Lima, M. P. C. (2016), *O desmantelamento do regime de negociação coletiva em Portugal, os desafios e as alternativas*, Coimbra: Observatório sobre Crises e Alternativas. Available at: https://www.ces.uc.pt/observatorios/crisalt/documentos/cadernos/CadernoObserv_VIII_N8_VERSAO_REFORMULADA.pdf (accessed 10 January 2017).

Meier, L. and Promberger, M. (2014), *National report, Germany. Work package 2: State of the art*, unpublished RESCuE project report.

Möller, J. (2010), 'The German labour market reform in the world recession: Demystifying a miracle', *Zeitschrift für Arbeitsmarkt Forschung* 42(4): 325–36.

OECD.stat (2017), Table II.1. Statutory corporate income tax rate. Available at: https://stats.oecd.org/index.aspx?DataSetCode=TABLE_II1 (accessed 18 January 2017).

ONS (2016), *Contracts that do not guarantee a minimum number of hours: September 2016*, Office of National Statistics. Available at: https://www.ons.gov.uk/employmentandlabourmarket/peopleinwork/earningsandworkinghours/articles/contractsthatdonotguaranteeaminimumnumberofhours/september2016 (accessed 18 January 2017).

Pedroso, P. (2014), *Portugal and the global crisis: The impact of austerity on the economy, the social model and the performance of the state*, Berlin: Friedrich-Ebert Siftung, Available at: http://library.fes.de/pdf-files/id/10722.pdf (accessed 12 January 2017).

Petmezidou, M. (2011), *Is the EU-IMF 'Rescue Plan' dealing a blow to the Greek welfare state? CROP Poverty Brief 4*, Bergen: University of Bergen, Available at: www.crop.org/viewfile.aspx?id=225 (accessed 15 January 2017).

Petraki, G. (2014), 'Le Travail Intérimaire en Gréce: Certains Cas de Travail Inteérimaire dans la Fontion Publique. Les Marges du Travail et de l'Emploi: Formes, Enjeux et Processus', paper presented at 14éme Journées Internationales the Sociologie du Travail, Lille, France, 17–19 June 2014.

Tennberg, M., Vuojala-Magga, T. and Vola, J. (2014), *National report, Finland. Work package 2: State of the art*, unpublished RESCuE project report.

Wódz, K., Faliszek, K., Łęcki, K., Mandrysz, W. and Słania, B. (2014), *National report, Poland. Work package 2: State of the art*, unpublished RESCuE project report.

PART II

Perspectives on household resilience

4. Developing the concept of poverty and resilience

Marie Boost, Markus Promberger, Lars Meier and Frank Sowa

THE CONTRIBUTION OF RESILIENCE TO POVERTY RESEARCH AND SOCIAL POLICY

When investigating poverty and methods of fighting poverty in Europe today, three general observations stand out. First, despite radical reforms and ambitious political goals, poverty is neither substantially nor permanently on the decline in European welfare states – at least, not in the last two decades. Although the population at risk of poverty and social exclusion declined slightly from 24.8% in 2012 to 22.4% in 2017, still 112.9 million people suffer income poverty, material deprivation, unemployment or low work intensity (Eurostat 2019). Second, the substantive side of anti-poverty policies at best consists of paying transfer income (sometimes insufficient for a life with less deprivation), of maintaining job search pressure and providing advice and support in terms of a limited accessible and comprehensive infrastructure of social, health and labour market services. Third, almost everywhere in Europe, we found a small number of low-income households managing their lives better than others: be it that they succeed to rise out of poverty again, or stay living on or close to the poverty line but managing on a low amount of transfer benefits, or none at all. Many of them make use of small-scale and non-market practices contributing to the household's well-being.

Not all poor households actually feel ashamed or not fully informed by the responsible institutions, or have no relevant claim to benefits. Some manage instead to get by, to limit or avoid poverty or the drawing of benefits, or even to rise out of poverty again off their own bat. Heuristically, these can be described as resilient. From the dominant scientific positions, poverty is mostly seen as a situation or development regarding income, consumption, health status, assets, employment or education deviating deficiently from a social aggregate state or standard development. Those social aggregate states or standard progressions, although being defined in different ways, are usually described in statistical and quantitative terms. Qualitative poverty studies deepen those statistical insights by focussing on lifestyles and habits, cultural conditions of poverty or examples of social exclusion, so far with little regard to processes of coping, transformation and resilience. Unlike in psychology or health research, poverty research shows little attention to non-standard or extraordinary potentials for action, coping patterns and processes in problematic social situations and contexts, although a gradual increase in research interest and an attempt to expand methodology and concepts has begun (Narayan et al. 2009; Solga et al. 2013).

From a social policy perspective, the question arises whether the 'poverty of the anti-poverty policies' is not simply a question of distribution and management; it may also be connected to the limited spectrum of means and approaches. This is where the term 'resilience' comes into play from a practical point of view: in this way, anti-poverty politics could learn from resilient households and extend the range and nature of institutional support due to their actual needs, but also change the widespread view of poverty as an individual deficit.

CONCEPTUAL HISTORY OF RESILIENCE[1]

With regard to the history of the term, four sources of the concept of resilience can be identified: psychology, ecosystem research, a socio-spatial perspective in geography and related disciplines, and the earlier but obsolete concept from solid-state mechanics of an object to bounce back into shape after a mechanical impact. The meaning of the term initially oscillated between a return to the original state after an external shock, and an above-average capacity for inner adjustment, coping and survival. In arts, humanities and social sciences, the term was initially used in the field of psychology, based on Viktor Frankl's studies of concentration camp survivors (2010[1959]). These studies were followed by research in development and education psychology of children from deprived backgrounds, with the concept still in use today (Werner 1977, 1999). Since the late 1980s, social factors have become more clearly outlined in concepts of resilience with similar approaches in the fields of medical research, psychology and social psychology (Nuber 1995; Zander 2011; Schumacher et al. 2005). Here, resilience is always a rare phenomenon in circumstances and events which normally provoke trauma and severe suffering in those affected; it is connected to an extraordinary capacity of individuals and communities to adapt, and to protective factors within them (Lösel et al. 1992; Zander 2011). The concept of resilience shifts the analytical focus away from deficits and disorders towards powers of resilience, strengths and capacities, which also include social factors. According to this, resilience is to be understood as an antonym of vulnerability (Glavovic et al. 2003); such studies on resilience are already relevant in the field of child, youth and family welfare (e.g. Alicke 2012; Messer 2012; Uslucan 2010).

In ecosystems research, resilience has been understood as a possible system attribute; and from here the term was transferred to disaster research, human geography and the spatial sciences. Within that, resilience is defined as an attribute that enables a system to regain its former state after suffering a shock or to maintain (Walker et al. 2004; Holling 1973, 1996) a specific state (function, structure, identity and feedback) after such a shock and possibly to regenerate itself (Folke 2006). In many approaches in the fields of human ecology and cultural anthropology, ecological resilience is associated with human action. Therefore, the aim is to develop an analytical relationship between social and ecological resilience (Adger 2000). Adger defines social resilience as the ability of communities to withstand external shocks to their social infrastructure, and focusses on both ecological and social developments as a trigger for both vulnerability and resilience. There is a similar grasp of resilience in disaster research (Lorenz 2013). Here – to a certain extent as a spill-over from ecosystem research – resilience appears as a phenomenon that describes specific human reactions to natural disasters that have occurred (McCarthy and Martello 2005) and enables precautions to be taken (Kaufmann and Blum 2012, 2013; Manyena 2006). The field of study increasingly includes human-made crises like terrorism (Coaffee et al. 2009) and economic setbacks (e.g. Lukesch et al. 2010; Okech et al. 2012; Batty and Cole 2010).

More recent approaches in resilience research are increasingly taking a socio-spatial perspective (e.g. Raco and Street 2012), which understands the subject's perception and possibilities for action as being socially and spatially limited (Balgar and Mahlkow 2013; Christmann and Ibert 2012). The focus of analysis is ever-expanding – from the individual to households, groups, communities (Amundsen 2012; Batty and Cole 2010), indigenous peoples (Posey 1999; Turunen et al. 2014) and on a global scale (Glavovic et al. 2003). Even if some critics warn of the term 'resilience' becoming de-socialized and biologized (Lidskog 2001; Cannon and Müller-Mahn 2010), it seems impossible to ignore the overall tendency for the term to be absorbed by the field of social sciences – which, for many authors, also incidentally precludes the return to an original state once and for all (Hall and Lamont 2013).

Likewise, from the standpoint of many researchers, resilience exceeds the concepts of merely coping and adapting and embraces transformative potentials: it 'not only enables people to cope with change but also creates the potential to translate adversity into opportunity' (Glavovic et al. 2003, p. 291). Focussing on the capacities of social resilience, Keck and Sakdapolrak (2013) summarized the theoretical debate by providing three different types of social resilience: coping, adaption and transformation (Keck and Sakdapolrak 2013; Lorenz 2013; Béné et al. 2012, p. 405). While coping means an immediate 'ex-post' reaction to a crisis, adaption and transformation mean ex-ante measures, behaviours or responses to anticipated crises in a long-term temporal horizon. While adaptive capacities 'secure the present status of people's well-being in the face of future risks' (Keck and Sakdapolrak 2013, p. 11), transformation aims to improve future well-being by applying strong changes. One line of social science resilience research to which little attention has been paid so far deals with social problems, social policy and the welfare state. It has begun to attract more attention since 2007 due to the effects of the European financial and economic crisis (see overview in Promberger et al. 2019). Accordingly, it is important to focus on the shape of resilience and to note that it is not a sole individual attribute but rather a dynamic process shaped and embedded in structures, processes and institutions (Revilla et al. 2018; Dagdeviren et al. 2016). It is further strongly influenced by the specific way family history, biography and the social environment are interwoven (Gray and Dagg 2019; Promberger 2017). Hence, the 'heroic' connotation of resilience, meaning a 'positive attribute of individuals or families' brought in from medical research and psychology has to be rejected for a sociological use of resilience (see Chapter 5 in this volume; Calado et al. 2018).

RESILIENCE IN SOCIOLOGICAL POVERTY AND SOCIAL POLICY RESEARCH: ELEMENTS OF A DEFINITION

In order to render the concept of resilience fruitful for poverty research and social policy, further understanding and detailed definitions are required (Promberger 2017, pp. 6–8).

First of all, it is necessary to reject the mechanical definition, including the classic mechanical definition of resilience as the return to the original state after an external mechanical shock. As processes of sense making, construction of meaning, interpretation and reflection always accompany human action, the actors change when they go through a crisis at least because of their experiences and reflections of the crisis. A return to the original state is therefore impossible. Heraclitus's conclusion that we cannot step into the same river twice also applies here, at least to individuals and families. Nevertheless, for functionalist anthropology or ecosystem research a return to the original 'balance' does not pose a theoretical problem – individual survival is not an issue for those approaches, as long as the ecosystem stays in balance.

Resilience, if applied to poverty and social policy, needs to be understood as a social phenomenon. Psychological resilience research greatly emphasizes the inner strength and abilities of those affected, while social research, which by definition looks for social factors to explain resilience, has to understand resilience – and poverty as well – as a social phenomenon. In social sciences, the term 'resilience' would therefore be understood in a way that was complementary and not contrary to the psychological concept. Just as the medical psychological term 'salutogenesis' (Antonovsky 1987) includes social components, resilience as a socio-scientific term can also incorporate psychological components.

Social resilience has a history and does not happen suddenly, or randomly. Two dimensions can be distinguished concerning the relevance of time. First, practices of resilience occur in a certain historical context with specific structures, knowledge systems and institutions, as described above, for instance as part of a specific regulation regime. Accordingly, practices of resilience have time-related specifics and are only to be understood in this context. Second, individual practices of resilience have a history. They can be based on biographical knowledge and experience which is related to the knowledge of our ancestors (or a collective, identity-related store of knowledge) and their economic, cultural and social capital. This can be reflected in today's practices in the sense of the historical perspective in Bourdieu's concept of habitus (Bourdieu 1982). From a sociological point of view, the practices of resilience by individual people are therefore to be seen not only as biographically based but also as part of the specific historical tradition of a social group or a (real or imagined) community.

Resilience is not a stable state but a process. It can develop and be achieved (Promberger et al. 2019), but it can also be lost again. Thus, a process of descent from the middle class, observed in Spain or Great Britain during and after the Great Recession (Dagdeviren et al. 2017), can also be interpreted as a loss of individual or household resilience.

Social resilience is not something that one has or not; it is a gradual phenomenon. Regarding how far the strain on the household budget is relieved or how large one income component becomes, similar patterns of practice can lead to different results in different households and under different combinations of conditions (Promberger et al. 2019). Resilient and less-resilient households can apply similar practices with gradual different results.

Social resilience consists of specific resources and patterns of action of individuals and groups under certain specifiable conditions. Analytically speaking, it is a question of resources from the natural, cultural and socio-economic environment. This includes resources that have been personalized by the individuals in processes related to their history, their socialization and their experience, and have developed in part into knowledge, capacities and patterns of action, and in any case have developed to equip the person or group. External resources and conditions in the actual situation, which are identified and mobilized while coping with or transforming the adverse circumstances, are not less important. The parallels to Bourdieu's forms of capital (2011[1986]) are obvious (see Promberger 2017 for more detail), but we suggest rejecting the 'capital' part of the approach for the reason that the concept of capital includes commodification – which, as we know, is not necessarily a given among poor households and the items of their living.

Resilience can only be described in comparison to non-resilience, for if everyone or all those with a low income were declared resilient, the concept would no longer have any power of distinction required for comparative analysis.

Social resilience requires a rejection of concepts of 'heroic' resilience. With regard to poor households, social resilience can include not only individual and social risks and costs, but also deviant behaviour. This may mean health risks and overwork, and in a few cases damage to the community as well due to illegal behaviour or behaviour that damages resources. Hence, despite all empathy for the 'ordinary magic' which has been found in some resilience research (Masten 2001), it is recommended to use a concept of non-heroic resilience (Estêvão et al. 2017).

The appropriate level of investigation for resilience in social policy research is the household. Independent of the number of persons and the family constellation, private households are the fundamental unit of consumption, reproduction, sharing and mutual support alongside non-market-related, direct personal relationships. This is where the markets end and give way to sharing, trust relations or gift exchange. Individuals do not generally make socio-economic decisions alone, but for, or together with, the persons living with them in the common household. Even if capacities, resources and risks can be individually assigned, in everyday life they are regulated, communicated and included at the level of the household.

There are at least two reasons against the idea of studying the socio-economic resilience of larger collectives such as communities in the context of social policy, and the policies concerning the fight against poverty which is currently emerging in the English-speaking world (Joseph 2013). For one thing, it is the closeness of such a community approach to system and ecosystem research, which – notwithstanding its other scientific merits – is not very interested in the life opportunities and welfare of particular individuals or small groups as long as the overall system being studied continues to exist and function. In contrast, social policy is concerned with the well-being of individuals and their direct reference groups. Likewise, communities or collectives beyond families in modern societies can scarcely be meaningfully understood as direct, practical units of consumption and income generation alongside non-market-related domestic relationships. In poverty research, however, this is the prerequisite for identifying suitable analytical units.

In connections and discussions relating to social policy and development policy, the concept of resilience shows the potential to broaden perspectives and capacitate and empower vulnerable groups, a concept which can override deficit approaches in poverty research and anti-poverty policies. However, there are certain reservations against the use of the term 'resilience', particularly in the United Kingdom (Dean 2015; Dagdeviren et al. 2017). One reason is that Conservative governments have begun to propagate resilience at municipality level as a means of coping with and managing public hazard or disaster control for the time being, but, implicitly, this concept of resilience may also include social problems and conflicts as well (Bulley 2013). Dealing with the resilience concept in such a way, it shifts social questions back to the responsibility of municipalities, local authorities, communities and families. On the other hand, for critics from the political left the idea of resilience contradicts certain understandings of the inescapable and complete social determination of causes and states of poverty. Where structural social factors such as power asymmetry, unfavourable relationships of distribution, neo-liberal welfare state concepts, exclusion from employment and deterioration in the conditions of employment and remuneration lead to poverty, there can be no individual way out. Or, if so, such a way out is not considered interesting for this kind of analysis and politics.

On the other hand, the first objection to be made is that empirical results regarding the resilience of vulnerable households tend to support the social and political necessity of a redistributive welfare state (Canvin et al. 2009; Promberger 2017), rather than reject it. Moreover, there is evidence (see Chapter 5 of this volume) emphasizing the welfare state's substantial contribution to resilience as a guarantor for common goods. Second, the findings of dynamic poverty research show enough changes through time in what poverty is and how it intersects with biography and time to reject any deterministic notion of 'poverty as a fate', replacing it by the image of a dynamic and far reaching risk (Bane and Ellwood 1986; Leibfried et al. 1995). Third, from an epistemological viewpoint, the objection has to be made that statements regarding the structure–action nexus do not permit a deterministic prediction of the empirical fates of individuals, particularly as certain degrees of freedom and inconsistencies indisputably exist within structural restrictions of any kind (Giddens 1988; Dagdeviren et al. 2016; Promberger 2017). Otherwise, it would be very difficult to explain resilient practices which actually stand alongside, or even in conflict with, institutional structures: informal employment, barter deals, or the unauthorized but tolerated private use of common goods. Beyond that, concerning social policy terminology as a contested terrain, it would be purist to reject the concept of resilience just because an opponent in the discourse attempts to instrumentalize it. In fact, ambiguity and controversy are constitutive for socio-scientific terms, particularly where they enter political language. However, the criticism of resilience aspects of the conservative Big Society programme is justified to the extent that the welfare situation of poor and vulnerable households and families is hidden in a 'community', which is defined vaguely in any case or is defined alongside political interests, or in a 'human ecological system' as formulated above.

SOURCES OF RESILIENCE IN POVERTY

First of all, it must be established that, according to existing findings, resilience is rare in households that are close to the poverty line and that can hardly survive without welfare state structures (Canvin et al. 2009). These structures include far more than direct social transfers. Moreover, there is evidence that resilience decreases with increasing economic pressure (Okech et al. 2012) and can take on different forms, whether with respect to strategies practised (Dagdeviren et al. 2017; Boost and Meier 2017) or with respect to complex, typical patterns of daily living, value systems, and internal and external resources (Promberger et al. 2019). Furthermore, it has been shown that the resilience of poor households in economic crises depends significantly on the degree to which those affected have access to economic opportunities. However, it also particularly depends on social resources, which allow them to cushion the blow of negative consequences of a crisis, even if these are worse than average locally (Batty and Cole 2010). Resilient practices of households around the poverty line can be distinguished by their plurifunctionality, diversity, interlacement and creativity (Dagdeviren et al. 2017; Bosch and Promberger 2017; Boost and Meier 2017). In the research presented in this book, an absence of the households' own significant assets or paid work is partly compensated by applying various practices and resources to secure their livelihood (see Chapters 6 and 7 of this volume). Resilient households often show numerous, simultaneously practised, highly diversified strategies of economic relevance. Informal self-employment, subsidized employment, practices of saving foodstuff as well as energy (especially in winter times), self-provision, barter trade and mutual help are combined to form a mixed economy (Malcolmson 1988; Chapter 6, this volume). Many practices are plurifunctional themselves. For example, a family's Sunday excursion to the nearby forest is a key example as there are – compared to alternatives – not only no costs associated with it but also mushrooms or berries to be collected, enriching the family's diet, slightly relieving the family budget.

Thus, in contrast to non- or less-resilient households in a similar position, resilient households often have some small economically relevant property at their disposal to a greater extent. This can be self-owned housing, a second-hand car, tools, or a garden, for instance. In some constellations, direct welfare state transfers are not used as much as in non- or less-resilient cases, but resilient families participate in collective and common goods more frequently and, to a considerable extent, not only as users but also as co-producers. These common and collective goods include the access to cultivated or uncultivated nature, whether for leisure and recreation purposes, or to collect foodstuff or firewood. Common goods also include public infrastructures which have not been subject to much commodification, such as the water and energy supply in some countries, education and information, data networks, advice bureaus, charitable facilities such as soup kitchens, food banks and clothing distribution centres, employment agencies and cheap local public transport. Further, the wide range of common or collective goods used by resilient low-income families comprises access **to civil society organizations and facilities** (Promberger et al. 2016), club activities, neighbourhood facilities and social services. Several of those structures would hardly be able to function without public financing and the commitment of a developed civil society.

Moreover, differently from other low-income households, resilient households often have outstanding and multiple social networks. Following Bourdieu's terminology, this social capital can be described as a social resource which is mobilized and used by resilient individuals. These networks usually are economically supportive and are neither socially homogeneous nor just restricted to the local area. They can include extended family even if they are living in other parts of the country, as well as neighbours, work colleagues and bosses from former workplaces, fellow club members, networks of informal workers, service providers and small tradesmen, friends, purchasers, customers, decision-makers and employees from municipal or social service facilities, colleagues from the trade – to name just a few typical combinations. The network relationships of resilient families and households are intensively cultivated and maintained through the sharing and exchange of information, material gifts, mutual support and cooperation. Culture repeatedly comes into play as a resource in resilient households. On the one hand, culture presents itself as knowledge and skills from professional qualifications or other qualifications which can be exploited for economic gain, to an implicit body of knowledge, via the art of economical household budgeting, folk psychology and folk pedagogy and embodied practical skills (see Chapters 2 and 7 of this volume). On the other hand – particularly in the few households with very marked resilience – culture comes into play in terms of headstrong or self-reliant standards, values and aesthetic elements of practice, which make it possible to imagine and live an existence outside the commodified patterns of action and experience inherent to market societies (see Chapter 7 of this volume). The welfare state also plays an important role in the life of resilient households, either as a final fall-back system whose benefits can be claimed if their own resilience strategies do not work, or as a guarantor for common goods and social infrastructure, or to help resilient households whose life is stable, but whose income is not sufficient for them to live without direct income transfers (see Chapters 15 and 16 of this volume).

FIRST CONCLUSIONS FOR SOCIAL POLICY AND POVERTY RESEARCH

As empirical results show, resilient low-income households are in need of welfare state and charitable support and infrastructures with suitable income transfers or offers of support, so that any existing economic, social and cultural resources (such as knowledge, experience and skills, and values and attitudes) can actually be mobilized and used for resilience. However, these resources are spread across the poor population in a decidedly selective fashion and can in no way be multiplied ubiquitously or by means of conventional social programmes. Hence, resilience is no cure-all in the fight against poverty or even a 'communitarian' substitute for a functioning welfare state. On the other hand, however, the targeted support of resilience through social and welfare state activities and some more progress in research could enrich poverty alleviation policies concerning the fight against poverty (see Chapter 16 of this volume).

In order to do this, where and how should one start? First of all, as addressed in Chapter 16, the concept of resilience as developed within the study that forms the basis for this book should be adopted in European Union (EU) policy frameworks and action plans. Subsequently, this would enable states at national and local level to maintain and, if necessary, build up the conventional welfare state by providing or increasing transfer benefits, social insurance, labour market services and offers of education and advice. Moreover, in a comparison of European welfare state structures, there seem to be considerable differences regarding coverage, support levels, and horizontal differentiation. The same applies to the maintenance and development of common and collective goods in times of tight state budgets and the ongoing privatization of state property. Many findings of the present research indicate that transfer dependency becomes reduced where resilience is increased, and that deeper resilience reaches into the economic behaviour of households. In those cases, conventional poverty alleviation policies just play the role of warranting basic income support in the case of employment interruptions, or failure of other economic activities. At the same time, case studies indicate that especially resilient low-income households make extensive use of common and collective goods in comparison to non- or less-resilient cases. Local social workers and other experts are often well aware of the great significance of many common and collective goods for the life of low-income households, but as common goods hardly play a role in the social policy discourse in society as a whole, local experts, activists and non-governmental organizations (NGOs) are often lone warriors in the bitter fight against rising fares on local public transport, the gentrification of residential areas, the privatization of communal water and energy supply or the closure of public libraries, or they fight for the right to use buildings that are standing empty, inner-city scrubland or parkland, or local recreation areas.

The social integration which is eminently important for resilience (Revilla et al. 2018) can be promoted on two levels: first, aspects of self-help and self-organization have only played a small role in social policy to date – at least in Germany – but it is a role that has the potential for development. Second, empirical findings (Promberger et al. 2016) show that self-organization and integration require points of intersection and crystallization. These primarily arise at the interface between the welfare state, civil society and the lives of those affected who seek support. The scope of options runs from self-help groups initialized by welfare offices or charities, network building leisure activities, free meeting space in community centres, church parishes, and opening charities for voluntary work of beneficiaries, to subsidized labour. As such, we reiterate the suggestions in Chapter 16, that EU actions should re-invest in the welfare state to expand and target activation policies towards the social realm. Promoting resilience, moreover, opens the perspective towards education, information and culture offers, their accessibility, their supply by civil society and public actors, and their integration into the living world of low-income households and families. Furthermore, the concern of supporting resilience directs attention to the offerings related to education, knowledge and culture, and to providing and integrating them in the lives of low-income households and families.

In this context, supporting resilience can probably not be expected to result in a more rapid reduction in public spending. But, instead, it could increase opportunities for a social policy that is geared towards creating a better life, one with greater proactivity and social cohesion while reducing or ending situations of poverty.

NOTE

1.   This chapter intends to transfer the concept of resilience into poverty research. An extended debate on critical aspects of resilience is given in Chapter 5.

REFERENCES

Adger, W. N. (2000), 'Social and ecological resilience: are they related?' *Progress in Human Geography* 24(3): 347–64.
Alicke, T. (2012), 'Resilienz und Lebensbewältigung bei Kindern und Jugendlichen mit Migrationshintergrund', *Jugendhilfe* 50(6): 347–51.
Amundsen, H. (2012), 'Illusions of resilience? An analysis of community responses to change in northern Norway', *Ecology and Society* 17(4): 46.
Antonovsky, A. (1987), *Unraveling the mystery of health: How people manage stress and stay well*, San Francisco: Jossey-Bass.

Balgar, K. and Mahlkow, N. (2013), *Lokalkulturelle Konstruktionen von Vulnerabilität und Resilienz im Kontext des Klimawandels*, Erkner: IRS Working Paper 47.

Bane, M. and Ellwood, D. (1986), 'Slipping in and out of poverty', *Journal of Human Resources* 21: 1–23.

Batty, E., and Cole, I. (2010), *Resilience and the recession in six deprived communities. Preparing the worse to come?*, York: Joseph Rowntree Foundation Programme Paper.

Béné, C., Wood, R. G., Newsham, A. and Davies, M. (2012), *Resilience: New utopia or new tyranny? Reflection about the potential and limits of the concept of social resilience in relation to vulnerability reduction programmes*, Brighton: IDS working paper 2012.

Boost, M. and Meier, L. (2017), 'Resilient practices of consumption in times of crisis – Biographical interviews with members of vulnerable households in Germany', *International Journal of Consumer Studies* 41(4): 363–70.

Bosch, A. and Promberger, M. (2017), 'Ästhetischer Eigensinn und Resilienz in vulnerablen Lebenszusammenhängen', in A. Bosch and H. Pfütze (eds.), *Ästhetischer Widerstand gegen Zerstörung und Selbstzerstörung,* Wiesbaden: VS Verlag pp. 489–504.

Bourdieu, P. (1982), *Die feinen Unterschiede. Kritik der gesellschaftlichen Urteilskraft*, Suhrkamp: Frankfurt am Main.

Bourdieu, P. (2011[1986]), 'The forms of capital', in I. Szeman and T. Kaposy (eds.), *Cultural theory: An anthology*, pp. 81–93.

Bulley, D. (2013), 'Producing and governing community (through) resilience', *Politics* 33(4): 265–75.

Calado, A., Estêvão, P. and Capucha, L. (2018), Crise e Pobreza em Portugal: resiliência ou proteção social? Available at: https://ciencia.iscte-iul.pt/publications/crise-e-pobreza-em-portugalresiliencia-ou-protecao-social/49173 (accessed 19 August 2020).

Cannon, T. and Müller-Mahn, D. (2010), 'Vulnerability, resilience and development discourses in context of climate change', *Natural Hazards* 55(3): 621–35.

Canvin, K., Marttila, A., Burström, B. and Whitehead, M. (2009), 'Tales of the unexpected? Hidden resilience in poor households in Britain', *Social Science and Medicine* 69: 238–45.

Christmann, G. and Ibert, O. (2012), 'Vulnerability and resilience in a socio-spatial perspective', *Raumforschung und Raumordnung* 70: 259–72.

Coaffee, J., Wood, D. M., and P. Rogers (2009), *The Everyday Resilience of the City: How cities respond to terrorism and disaster*, Basingstoke: Palgrave.

Dagdeviren, H., Donoghue, M. and Promberger, M. (2016), 'Resilience, hardship and social conditions', *Journal of Social Policy* 45(1): 1–20.

Dagdeviren, H., Donoghue, M. and Meier, L. (2017), 'The narratives of hardship: The new and the old poor in the aftermath of the 2008 crisis in Europe', *The Sociological Review* 65(2): 369–85.

Dean, H. (2015), 'Resilience or resistance: Crisis, hardship and a critical engagement with the resilience approach', paper presented at Resilience in Times of Crisis (RESCuE) project meeting, Hertfordshire Business School, UK, 25 June.

Estêvão, P., Calado, A. and Capucha, L. (2017), 'Resilience: Moving from a "heroic" notion to a sociological concept', *Sociologia, Problemas e Práticas* I: 9–25.

Eurostat (2019), People at risk of poverty or social exclusion (t2020_50) [dataset]. Available at: https://ec.europa.eu/eurostat/statistics-explained/index.php?title=

Archive:People_at_risk_of_poverty_or_social_exclusion#Number_of_people_at
_risk_of_poverty_or_social_exclusion (accessed 19 August 2020).
Folke, C. (2006), 'Resilience: The emergence of a perspective for social–ecological
systems analyses', *Global Environmental Change* 16: 253–67.
Frankl, V. (2010[1959]), *Man's search for meaning*, New York: Simon and Schuster.
Giddens, A. (1988), 'Die "Theorie der Strukturierung", Ein Interview mit Anthony
Giddens', *Zeitschrift für Soziologie* 17(4): 286–95.
Glavovic, B. C., Scheyvens, R. and Overton, J. (2003), 'Waves of adversity, layers
of resilience: Exploring the sustainable livelihoods approach', in D. Storey, J.
Overton and B. Nowak (eds.), *Contesting development: Pathways to better prac-
tice, proceedings of the Third Biennial Conference of the Aotearoa New Zealand
International Development Studies Network (DevNet)*, Massey University, Institute
of Development Studies, pp. 289–93.
Gray, J. and Dagg, J. (2019), 'Using reflexive lifelines in biographical interviews to
aid the collection, visualisation and analysis of resilience', *Contemporary Social
Science* 14(3/4): 407–22.
Hall, P. A., and Lamont, M. (2013), *Social resilience in the neoliberal era*, Cambridge:
Cambridge University Press.
Holling, C. S. (1973), 'Resilience and stability in ecological systems', *Annual Review
of Ecology and Systematics* 4: 1–23.
Holling, C. S. (1996), 'Engineering resilience versus ecological resilience', in P.
Schulze (ed.), *Engineering within ecological constraints*, Washington, DC: National
Academy Press, pp. 31–44.
Joseph, J. (2013), 'Resilience as embedded neoliberalism: A governmentality approach',
Resilience 1(1): 38–52.
Kaufmann, S., and Blum, S. (2012), 'Governing (in)security: The rise of resilience',
in H.-H. Gander, W. Perron, R. Poscher, G. Riescher and T. Würtenberger (eds.),
*Resilienz in der offenen Gesellschaft. Symposium des Centre for Security and
Society*, Baden-Baden: Nomos, pp. 235–57.
Kaufmann, S. and Blum, S. (2013), 'Vulnerabilität und Resilienz. Zum Wandern von
Ideen in der Umwelt- und Sicherheitsdiskussion', in R. v. Detten, F. Faber and M.
Bemmann (eds.), *Unberechenbare Umwelt. Zum Umgang mit Unsicherheit und
Nicht-Wissen*, Wiesbaden: Springer, pp. 91–120.
Keck, M. and Sakdapolrak, P. (2013), 'What is social resilience? Lessons learned and
ways forward', *Erdkunde* 67(1): 5–19.
Leibfried, S., Leisering, L., Buhr, P., Ludwig, M., Mädje, E., Olk, T., Voges, W.
and Zwick, M. (1995), *Zeit der Armut, Lebensläufe im Sozialstaat*, Frankfurt a.M:
Suhrkamp.
Lidskog, R. (2001), 'The re-naturalization of society? Environmental challenges for
sociology', *Current Sociology* 49(1): 113–36.
Lorenz, D. (2013), 'The diversity of resilience: Contributions from a social science
perspective', *Natural Hazards* 67(1): 7–24.
Lösel, F., Kolip, P. and Bender, D. (1992), 'Stress-Resistenz im Multiproblem-Milieu:
Sind seelisch widerstandsfähige Jugendliche "Superkids"?', *Zeitschrift für Klinische
Psychologie* 21(1): 48–63.
Lukesch, R., Payer, H. and Winkler-Rieder, W. (2010), *Wie gehen Regionen mit
Krisen um? Eine explorative Studie über die Resilienz von Regionen*, Wien: ÖAR
Regionalberatung GmbH.

Malcolmson, R. W. (1988), 'Ways of getting a living in eighteenth-century England', in R. Pahl (ed.), *On work: Historical, comparative and theoretical approaches*, Oxford: Basil Blackwell, pp. 48–60.

Manyena, S. B. (2006), 'The concept of resilience revisited', *Disasters* 30(4): 433–50.

Masten, A. (2001), 'Ordinary magic: Resilience processes in development', *American Psychologist* 56(3): 227–38.

McCarthy, J. J. and Martello, M. L. (2005), 'Climate change in the context of multiple stressors and resilience', in C. Symon, L. Arris and B. Heal (eds.), *Arctic Climate Impact Assessment*, Cambridge: Cambridge University Press, pp. 945–88.

Messer, H. (2012), 'Resilienzförderung in der Kindertagesbetreuung', *Jugendhilfe* 50(6): 338–42.

Narayan, D., Pritchett, L. and Kapoor, S. (2009), *Moving out of poverty Volume 2: Success from the bottom up*, Washington, DC: World Bank Publications.

Nuber, U. (1995), *Der Mythos vom frühen Trauma. Über Macht und Einfluß der Kindheit*, Frankfurt am Main: S. Fischer Verlag.

Okech, D., Howard, W. J., Mauldin, T., Mimura, Y. and Kim, J. (2012), 'The effects of economic pressure on the resilience and strengths of individuals living in extreme poverty', *Journal of Poverty* 16: 429–46.

Posey, D. A. (1999), *Cultural and spiritual values of biodiversity*, London: United Nations Environment Programme.

Promberger, M., Marinoudi, T. and Martín, P. (2016), 'Unter der erschütterten Oberfläche. Sozioökonomische Praktiken, Zivilgesellschaft und Resilienz in der europäischen Krise', *Forschungsjournal Soziale Bewegungen* 29(3): 86–97.

Promberger, M. (2017), *Resilience among vulnerable households in Europe: Questions, concept, findings and implications*, Nuremberg: Institute for Employment Research, IAB Discussion Paper No 12/2017.

Promberger, M., Meier, L., Sowa, F. and Boost, M. (2019), 'Chances of 'resilience' as a concept for sociological poverty research', in B. Rampp, M. Endreß and M. Naumann (eds.), *Resilience in Social, Cultural and Political Spheres*, Wiesbaden: VS Verlag, pp. 249–78.

Raco, M. and Street, E. (2012), 'Resilience planning, economic change and the politics of post-recession development in London and Hong Kong', *Urban Studies* 49(5): 1065–87.

Revilla, J. C., Martín, P. and de Castro, C. (2018), 'The reconstruction of resilience as a social and collective phenomenon: Poverty and coping capacity during the economic crisis', *European Societies* 20(1): 89–110.

Schumacher, J., Leppert, K., Gunzelmann, T., Strauß, B. and Brähler, E. (2005), 'Die Resilienzskala – Ein Fragebogen zur Erfassung der psychischen Widerstandsfähigkeit als Personmerkmal', *Zeitschrift für Klinische Psychologie, Psychiatrie und Psychotherapie* 53(1): 16–39.

Solga, H., Brzinsky-Fay, C., Graf, L., Gresch, C. and Protsch, P. (2013), *Vergleiche innerhalb von Gruppen und institutionelle Gelingensbedingungen: Vielversprechende Perspektiven für die Ungleichheitsforschung*, Berlin: Berlin Social Science Center, Discussion Paper No 501.

Turunen, M., Vuojala-Magga, T. and Giguère, N. (2014), 'Past and present winter feeding of reindeer in Finland: Herders' adaptive learning of feeding practices', *Arctic* 67(2): 173–88.

Uslucan, H.-H. (2010), 'Resilienz oder was macht Jugendliche mit Zuwanderungsgeschichte stark?', *Unsere Jugend* 62(4): 151–59.

Walker, B., Holling, C. S., Carpenter, S. R. and Kinzig, A. (2004), 'Resilience, adapt-
    ability and transformability in social–ecological systems', *Ecology and Society* 9(2):
    5.
Werner, E. E. (1977), *The Children of Kauai: A longitudinal study from the prenatal
    period to age of ten*, Honolulu: University of Hawai'i Press.
Werner, E. E. (1999), 'Entwicklung zwischen Risiko und Resilienz', in G. Opp, M.
    Fingerle and A. Freytag (eds.), *Was Kinder stärkt. Erziehung zwischen Risiko und
    Resilienz*, München: Reinhardt, pp. 25–36.
Zander, M. (2011), *Handbuch Resilienzförderung*, Wiesbaden: VS Verlag für
    Sozialwissenschaften.

5. Critical perspectives on resilience

Alexandre Calado, Luís Capucha, Hulya Dagdeviren, Matthew Donoghue and Pedro Estêvão

INTRODUCTION

Resilience is a relatively new addition to the social sciences (e.g. Rose 2007; Akter and Mallick 2013; Sapountzaki 2012; Martin and Sunley 2015). It has been transposed into the field from the natural sciences to help describe and explain how subjects respond to major and unexpected negative events, such as (natural) disasters, various trauma, hazards and crises. It has a long history in physics (Gordon 1979), psychology (Eitinger 1964; Werner 1977), and ecosystems research (Holling 1973). Most recently it has begun to be used in an attempt to explain how individuals and families can withstand and over-come hardship, and in some cases even thrive despite the adversity they face (Hoggett 2001; Mitchell 2013). Central to these literatures is the importance of positivity and agency; the notion that the individual is capable of taking control of their situation and overcoming the odds through employing multiple practices, such as savvy use of resources, networks and support structures.

The concept is still embryonic in the social sciences, and conceptual development is ongoing. Nevertheless, the notion of resilience has been adopted enthusiastically by a number of policy organizations, institutions and political actors. Billions of dollars have been invested into deploying the concept in a development context (Béné et al. 2015). It has found favour with governments, think tanks and I(N)GOs (international non-governmental organizations) because of its focus on individual agency as a response to various crises and shocks (e.g. ODI 2016). The UK's Department for International Development defines resilience as 'the ability of countries, communities and households to manage change, by maintaining or transforming living standards in the face of shocks or stresses … without compromising their long-term prospects' (DFID 2011, p. 6). The OECD uses a similar definition of resilience, understanding it as 'the ability of households, communities and nations to absorb and recover from shocks, while positively adapting and transforming their structures and means for living in the face of long-term stresses, change and uncertainty' (OECD 2014, p. 6).

The central theme, then, is the ability to take control of one's circumstances and excel with limited resources, in terms of moving beyond simply surviving. This clearly aims to afford significant agency to those in hardship, rather than seeing them as passive victims (e.g. Royce 2009; Lister 2002). However, as a concept in its infancy in social science, it requires critical appraisal and further development. This chapter contributes to that critical process by focusing on current understandings as exhibited in the existing literature (the next section), exploring what is necessary for resilience and the contexts in which resilience flourishes or flounders (third section), and outlines a tentative concept of resilience that answers these concerns (fourth section).

A CRITICAL ENGAGEMENT WITH THE RELATED LITERATURE

The use of the notion of resilience for the study of poor households in times of crisis requires a revision of the vast research and theoretical development produced in the poverty research literature. The pertinence of this task is made clear when one considers, on the one hand, the growing tendency in the social sciences to use the notion of resilience to characterize and/or explain the behaviour of poor households and groups and, on the other hand, the growing literature on resilience approaches studying the effects of large-scale economic shocks on poor communities and populations (Rose 2007), such as the Great Recession that followed the 2007–08 global financial crisis.

Resilience approaches have tried to gain their place in poverty studies by defining themselves in opposition to what they deem as the 'traditional approaches' to poverty. According to this criticism, poverty studies define individuals and communities mostly according to the 'deficit model', by assuming that individuals are passive victims of the hardship they face, proving impotent to change the structural forces that condition their agency (Canvin et al. 2009). In sharp contrast, resilience approaches focus their attention on individuals and practices that turn external constraints into opportunities. In accordance, they engage in the collection and analysis of narratives of overcoming setbacks or of coping with poverty in a better way than expected (e.g. Harrow 2009).

Such criticism of poverty studies requires closer scrutiny. For starters, the claim that poverty studies concentrate solely on the vulnerable dimensions of social actors is highly disputable. Indeed, we can safely argue that these studies looked at poverty as a sociological problem that can be identified, measured and understood in its relation to other institutions and social structures. These include, for instance, concepts such as absolute poverty (Rowntree 2000[1901]) and relative poverty (Townsend 1962). Models of analysis have also been developed to capture the multidimensionality of the phenomenon. These were first put forward by Walker (1897), when discussing the relation between industrialization, law and some behaviours of the working classes. Later on, Room (1989) developed a definition of poverty as the deprivation of access to income, work, education, health and housing, while Sen (1999) proposed the inclusion of non-monetary indicators to offset their predominance in the construction of poverty indices and, more than this, proposed an approach based on the notion of 'capacities' that focused on people's agency.

In fact, it is possible to turn this criticism on its head. The resilience literature tries to set itself apart by bringing back agency into the study of poverty. Yet, such effort often results in a tendency to overemphasize the individual while suppressing a range of structural forces that act upon him/her and constrain agency. In this vein, resilience approaches seek to collect strategies and practices for the construction of a repertoire of attributes and capacities to respond positively to hardship and shocks (Batty and Cole 2010), while showing little concern for the material and structural conditions required for the positive use of these resources. This is also the case with the natural and social risks involved in these strategies or practices (Sapountzaki 2012) or the outcomes of coping strategies that do not result in positive wellbeing (Arnal 2015).

This is particularly marked when we analyse the conditions, status and objectives of individuals' involvement in social networks and other contexts of collective participation. Poverty studies explore how deprivation of material resources has negative consequences for people's ability to engage in participatory and citizenship institutions, producing social exclusion (Paugam 1991), which reduces the quality of life and affects the social cohesion of societies (Levitas et al. 2007). In contrast, resilience approaches, while looking to social networks as one of the main resources that individuals must activate when they face hardship to overcome it, reduce the analysis of the conditions for participation to the development of positive attitudes and behaviours (Batty and Cole 2010). To be sure, there have been calls to incorporate issues of social power and rights more concretely into frameworks of resilience (Walsh-Dilley et al. 2016); for some this is directly related to politics, participation and power relations (e.g. Keck and Sakdapolrak 2013). But this still remains a severely underdeveloped aspect in resilience approaches.

Many of the resilience approaches, particularly those which take on the 'heroic' meaning of resilience (Estêvão et al. 2017), have promoted an interpretation of poverty in which the burden of responsiveness is centred on the individual agency (Hickman 2018), implicitly eschewing the role of society and the state in solving or mitigating the phenomenon. Poverty studies, by contrast, have developed theoretical models that consider the conditions of existence of individuals and families in relation to their position in the class structure, which in turn relate to the modes of economic production of societies (Bourdieu 1993; Sen 2009). Thus, to understand the set of objective and subjective constraints that produce poverty, one needs not only to understand the place of poor individuals and households on the class structure, but also to understand the socioeconomic model that sets the conditions for said social structure. It was by following this perspective that the welfare state has developed mechanisms and instruments to combat poverty, attacking what is considered to be the main areas of vulnerability of individuals and households (e.g. illness, unemployment, physical or mental incapacity and ageing), thus reducing their exposure to hardship (Ranci 2009).

Neglecting to sufficiently account for social and structural factors in the development and analysis of resilience leads to four major problems, as outlined by Dagdeviren et al. (2016). The first is an *identification problem*. What may appear as a lack of resilience for certain individuals may instead be the result of a number of interacting factors such as social exclusion, the efficacy of social support, various prejudices and biases, and different social and personal problems. Conversely, for some what comes across as resilience may more accurately reflect privilege. The second is the *intermittence of hardship*. Escaping poverty does not guarantee a life free of poverty (Seccombe 2002, p. 386). People can 'move on, but they fall back' (Canvin et al. 2009, p. 241), which can only be explained if resilience is *not* understood as a permanent personal attribute, but rather as a process dependent upon social as well as individual factors. The third problem is the *masking of the detrimental effects* of the practices involved in the processes of resilience. Focus on individual agency in resilience can lean towards understandings of resilience as 'ordinary magic' (Masten 2010) and mask the potential various detrimental effects of responses to hardship, such as burnout (Harrison 2013), mental and physical health, and social exclusion. In addition, some households thought of as resilient have to make detrimental decisions, such as forgoing heating or food in order to save money – neither of which are sustainable practices. The fourth problem is the potential for the *legitimization of an ideological agenda*. Significant focus on the individual when combined disregard for social and structural factors can help fulfil an ideological agenda that 'depoliticises and shifts responsibility … away from those in power' (Harrison 2013, p. 99). In this sense, emphasizing the ordinary magic of individuals removes focus on the central role played by social and institutional support structures in developing and maintaining resilience, justifying regressive social policies (MacLeavy 2011; Klein 2007). Resilience approaches, while increasingly recognizing the links between institutions and individuals or social structures and social practices, still fail to actually integrate them into the models of analysis (Dagdeviren et al. 2016).

This is not to say that resilience approaches – particularly the more recent ones, which integrate the role of structures and do not disconnect the individual from his/her conditions of existence (Dagdeviren et al. 2016) – may not provide a contribution both to the poverty and to the welfare state debate, insofar as they can go beyond approaches of vulnerability (Béné et al. 2015). Recently, increasing academic research has been dedicated to analysing how subjects and families use and manage their resources in contexts of hardship and economic contraction, allowing us to understand, for example, what resources individuals use to support themselves, which social networks they have access and turn to and which constraints they face while trying strategies for survival and/or to turn their situation into a positive one (Patrick 2017).

Such strategies are, thus, much more than individual. 'Because of its institutional context, social resilience is defined at the community level' (Adger 2000, p. 349). By highlighting the community, Adger establishes space, which is composed by 'the diversity of the ecosystem as well as the institutional rules which govern the social systems' (Adger 2000, p. 354), as a core dimension for social resilience, together with the social and economic dimensions. Also, as Milne and Rankine (2013) argue, resilience is an explicitly social phenomenon as well as having economic elements. It incorporates interaction and integration, the development of strong social networks, and processes for acquiring and deploying relevant skills, resources, and support.

Theoretical development on resilience opens the space for the usefulness of these approaches in the understanding of the effects and responses to social and economic shocks on societies. The concept of resilience has proved to be useful for understanding the immediate effects, reactions and consequences of unexpected and sudden shocks on the living conditions of individuals, families and communities, and also the strategies and practices put in place by those social actors to cope and overcome their altering situation, contrasting with the long-term structural approaches of poverty studies. In this sense, the concept of resilience should not be used for studying more long-term hardship – even if it must take into account longer-term trajectories of poverty and hardship. Its focus should be, rather, the major natural, social, personal, economic or political adversities that affect people's livelihoods, and how, under these conditions, individuals and families adjust their ways of living and their practices to cope and/or transform their living conditions and opportunities.

The concept of resilience should be designed to provide a framework for responding to shocks, rather than incremental change. It is also important to differentiate large-scale systemic crises from individual shocks and traumatic events. Events such as illness, death or separation affecting only individuals are significant, but their impact largely remain contained to the individual and immediate networks and can be dealt with through individual action and intervention or through the existing regular social welfare mechanisms. Larger social crises inevitably require action at the social and political level, since the existing individual assets, common or public resources and/or welfare mechanisms are not able to provide answers in the same way or scope they previously did, at least in a way that changes positively the long-term living conditions of individuals, households or communities.

In sum, resilience approaches find a rather new object of study: the analysis of the survival and adaptation processes of individuals and households in contexts of unexpected adversity. By integrating the social and multidimensional nature of the phenomenon of poverty, these approaches can foster a deeper understanding of the relations that are established between the structural forces and agency capacities in these contexts.

In this regard, resilience should thus not be understood as a personality trait of individuals that allows them to thrive when the odds are against them or an individual attribute of survival and heroism – not least, because this lends itself towards identifying people as resilient and non-resilient. This would bring with it a series of normative claims that are not productive for improving households' and families' ability to withstand socioeconomic shock and long-term sustainability and prosperity. In addition, such an essentialist take on resilience is not very helpful analytically, as people may be resilient in one domain, but not in another, in a particular occasion and not always.

WHAT ARE THE INGREDIENTS OF A SOCIALLY AND STRUCTURALLY INFORMED RESILIENCE ANALYSIS?

We claim that resilience has strong social foundations. In many cases, trajectories of resilience can be seen to exert a level of path dependence (Dagdeviren et al. 2016). There are three interrelated structural factors where this can be clearly seen. The first is the *political foundations of resilience*, which are dependent on how power relations, participation and representation enable and constrain, generate or diminish households' resilience during and after various shocks. European austerity programmes act as a prime example. There is an overwhelming amount of literature that argues austerity was counterproductive in the post-crisis period and did more harm than good, particularly to those on low and middle incomes (e.g. Blyth 2015; Skidelsky 2014). Austerity in fact increased poverty and stalled recovery in countries such as Greece, Portugal and Spain (Matsaganis and Leventi 2014). As shown in the analysis of the impacts of the European Crisis among households, significant numbers suffered widespread job loss or increasing insecurity, and a rising cost of living, in order to contribute towards stabilizing macro-level financial and banking systems.

Austerity has been demonstrated to be a political choice rather than a necessary measure. It is, in the words of Blyth (2015), a 'dangerous idea'. Its ascendency can be attributed to the strength of neoliberal thought, as manifested through the strength of corporate interests relative to union influence, for example. The hegemony of this ideology (Capucha et al. 2014) furthered the interests of capital at the cost of the wellbeing of labour, organized or otherwise. This has important implications for the path dependency of resilience. As previously discussed in Chapter 3 of this volume, in many cases vulnerable groups need to become resilient due to systemic shocks that come about as a result of the actions of capital, such as in the recent financial crisis. In attempting to negate systemic shock, responses that stabilize capital are prioritized over ensuring the wellbeing of vulnerable citizens, justified usually through arguing that, if the current system is allowed to fail, the wellbeing of all citizens will be even more damaged (e.g. Aalbers 2013).

Resilience requires well-functioning and responsive support mechanisms that ensure those in vulnerable situations have the resources and wherewithal to prepare for crisis before-the-shock or withstand it after-the-shock. More broadly than this, it requires policies that help counter power structures that favour heavily those already in privileged positions.

The second element is the *institutional foundations of resilience*. This includes markets, law, regulatory bodies, social, economic and political freedoms, social protection, public services, and even the media, and their role in supporting or constraining resilience in times of crisis. The institutional framework of labour markets and financial markets can both create and counteract shocks. By extension they also weaken or strengthen resilience. A well-regulated financial system can provide an essential service through responsible and productive lending, enabling households to prepare for or weather shocks. This sits in contrast to recent lending practices that have prioritized profit and (almost) completely dismissed social and economic responsibility. Yet the mechanisms involved in stabilizing financial instability and crisis had a significant individual impact, particularly for those whose homes were repossessed.

Likewise, labour markets are usually a main factor in defence against economic shock, while also being the cause of many household shocks. Unemployment insurance schemes, as well as other benefits (particularly regarding disability, caring and pensions) are crucial in counteracting some of these uncertainties. In less universal or developed welfare states for example, where access to essential services such as quality healthcare and education is mediated and policed by one's consumer power, households can become increasingly more vulnerable in less prosperous times. This is particularly so when attention is drawn away from addressing crises in order to focus on gaining or maintaining access to these essentials. Therefore, such systems of social protection and development should be seen as essential and crucial elements of any programme of resilience (e.g. Béné et al. 2015).

The third element concerns the *economic foundations of resilience*, which interact strongly with its political and institutional dimensions. Here the focus is on the distribution of assets, resources, wealth and income and the implications of this for resilience. The current market model favours heavily top earners (Piketty 2014). Indeed, rising inequality can be seen as contributing to the financial crisis (e.g. Wisman 2013). The crisis caused the wealth share of middle-income groups to collapse, while wealth continued to be further concentrated within an ever-smaller elite group. This implies that in times of crisis those who are more at risk of facing hardship and deprivation are competing for an ever-smaller pool of resources with which to build resilience. Economic resources can include financial systems such as credit and savings, non-mercantile assets like gift and redistribution networks and self-production of goods or services; or technical means of production, such as agricultural tools or computers (Estêvão et al. 2017).

The importance afforded to these elements and their interrelation does not negate the fact that resilience, although systemic, is experienced and enacted at the individual level. To capture this adequately there needs to be an appropriate theoretical framework that is able to locate this individual experience of resilience within and in relation to broader structural and social forces. Bourdieu (1984, 1993) can provide a heuristic framework. For Bourdieu, individuals' trajectories and life experiences have strong influences on personal and social action. These practices are (re)produced on the basis of objective and subjective conditions in the space in which they are located. The distribution of various forms of capital (economic, social, cultural) shape the conditions of this social space, which are played out through social, economic and cultural interaction and socialization. These processes produce the *habitus* (internalized structures generating structural dispositions for action) of actors. Habitus involves relatively stable and robust ways of thinking and acting, and largely shared among people of similar social, economic and cultural standing. This creates a distribution of resources, risks and power differentiated by social group (e.g. class).

These differentiations can be seen, for example, through the narratives and experiences of the 'old' and 'new' poor during and after the financial crisis (Dagdeviren et al. 2017). This study demonstrates that access to cultural, social and economic resources allows those with higher incomes to largely avoid and overcome increased risk of hardship in crisis situations. However, transitions do still occur between socioeconomic groups in times of crisis, especially when previously well-off families are ill prepared for the pace of the increase in cost of living, for example, or the growing instability of the labour market, which can lead to rapidly deteriorating living conditions. A central point is that the 'new' and 'old' poor have different experiences of hardship and different strategies to deal with it. A 'crisis' will look different for the former and the latter. For example, as evidenced in Chapter 8 of this volume, seeking formal assistance is difficult if one has no prior experience with the system and procedures, or even feels ashamed by the dependent situation. Those who have, for whatever reason, had more contact with the system will have caches of knowledge, experience and support networks to draw upon in order to help with their situation.

Actions therefore tend to follow particular routines. These impacts upon social processes can influence one's conditions, depending on whether these actions tend toward conformism or action that is more likely to disrupt circumstances. Social stratification, class and social rules generally are experienced as objectively existing and provide 'appropriate' ways of acting in different situations. At critical junctures, such as when a crisis hits, individuals and households will respond based on their dispositions alongside their position within the broader social structure. This involves the family, social networks, social and political organizations, social and political participation, and varying access to social transfers and essential services.

According to Dagdeviren and Donoghue (2019), for example, cutting back on expenditure has been particularly prevalent amongst low- and some middle-income households across Europe. In cases where social protection systems were inadequate, support from family and faith-based organizations became more important. Stigma was apparent in participants' experiences of the welfare system, but was also apparent in some of the cases involving faith-based and family networks. The major difference was that for the former the stigma was externalized and formalized, and used as a disincentive, whereas the stigma felt in relation to family, charities such as foodbanks, and faith-based networks in some cases created a sense of failure on the part of those seeking help. In some cases, participants would cut back on food to the point of causing hunger, or would forgo necessary medical treatment, clearly reflecting severely constrained agency. Participants' limited options for increasing income, particularly during the downturn, led to unsustainable but unavoidable levels of debt for many.

OUTLINE OF A CRITICAL CONCEPT OF RESILIENCE

Benefitting from this theoretical framework, we can put forward a critical notion of resilience. Resilience should be understood as a social process by which individuals, institutions or societies respond to sudden adverse shocks in a way directed at reducing damages, keeping or achieving basic standards of quality of life. Thus, resilience should not be understood as a characteristic that is innate and prevalent in some chosen individuals, nor as operating in a social or environmental void. Instead, resilience is a social phenomenon shaped by both social structure and the natural environment.

The existence of a shock, irrespective of the size and duration, is a distinctive feature of resilience processes. These processes are activated either when individuals, institutions or societies undergo a shock which alters and constrains their objective conditions of existence, or when this shock causes the reconfiguration of social structures. Shocks may come from localized or biographical events, such as an accident that leads to some incapacitation, a death in the family or a loss of a job. But often shocks originate from – or at least occur in the context of – wider changes in the social structures, namely on macroeconomic structures, in the cohesion of social systems and in cultural norms and standards. We are thinking here of events such as economic crises, natural or man-made disasters or wars, which have the potential to seriously affect the living conditions, routines and dispositions of people, households and groups.

Shocks may also motivate the processes of institutional (re)structuring, such as those associated with labour market regulation policies, redistribution of income, education and training, health and housing policies, all of which affect the scope of opportunities for individuals and households. Thus, shocks and their consequent effects have the potential to affect social structures, creating a new and unique social and economic context for individuals and institutions alike.

In these types of contexts, individuals and social groups devise strategies and practices to react to the new situation by mobilizing resources and attempting to shift (or share) risks and losses in time, space and across social structures (Estêvão et al. 2017). The household dynamics provide an example of this. As evidenced by the empirical collection under the research reported on in this volume[1] and the analysis of socioeconomic strategies, in the contexts of mass unemployment, such as those occurring in Southern Europe during the post-2008 Great Recession, pensioners become the mainstay of their families through money transfers, food gifts and payment of bills for children who have either lost their jobs or suffered significant wage cuts, increasing their available material resources. However, the risks of hunger, lack of housing and indebtedness of children (and grandchildren) are being shifted to parents and grandparents, and converted into another risk of poverty for the elderly.

Unlike living organisms and their environments, or inert materials, whose resilience is a consequence of attributes determined by their physical and biological constitution, social resilience processes result from choices made by reflexive actors with different dispositions, which shape the choices they make when confronted with situations of hardship. These processes are not included in this or that individual, household or social group, but are instead variables depending on the capacities and powers possessed, which include the perception of available resources and the evaluation of the consequences of their alternative use. Access to resources that allow recovery from crisis situations or living with them in order to maintain or improve living conditions is a central issue.

Thus, the devising of such responses will be decisively framed by two closely related factors: on the one hand, the experiences, capabilities and resources incorporated by the agents (for example formal education, professional experience, informal knowledge and competences); on the other hand, the framework of institutions and policies in which the individual is embedded (that is family, networks of friends, local governments and the welfare state). The interplay between these two kinds of factors will either boost or hamper the availability of and access to social and personal resources and the ability to transfer or share risks and losses associated with the shock.

Yet the relationship between resilience processes on the one side, and social structure and the environment on the other side is a double-edged sword. Resilience processes actively contribute to the reproduction and transformation of the social structure and environment. On the one hand, resilience processes draw on finite stocks of resources that may not be easily (or not at all) replenished or whose exploitation may imply significant personal, social and/or environmental damage. On the other hand, they can make use of power relations and mechanisms of social inequality, thus contributing to their reinforcement.

This can be illustrated with a few examples related to households' dynamics derived from empirical data from our shared research. A family's home budget adjustment efforts may result in a less varied diet – such as switching from fresh food items, like fruit and vegetables, to ready-made meals or 'junk food', or in parents, mostly mothers, reducing their food intake in favour of their children. This may have the undesired consequence of declining health among family members. Increased reliance on extended family networks to provide services hitherto supported by paid or state-provided services – for instance, childcare – may lead to burdening extended family members and result in increased tensions and eventual breakdowns in family relations.

In sum, the development of a critical perspective of resilience, moving away from heroic perspectives, aims to shift the resilience debate from a narrow perspective focusing solely on the individual and individual actions to the social and politics, more specifically to the creation of conditions that allow individuals and families to transform their way of life, in a manner that lessens their hardship and reduces their social vulnerability. Thus, resilience is unavoidably related to certain types of outcomes. Adaptation processes lead to resilience when they lead to an outcome where individuals or social groups find a new balance of acceptable objective and subjective conditions of life and dignity, not succumbing to poverty and/or social exclusion, nor worsening them. This means coping, overcoming, struggling and changing between alternative life strategies and solving problems. It is not just about surviving. Surviving, in this sense, means being the subject of hardship and accommodating oneself to it in a passive manner. Resilience implies a process of mobilization of energies and power incorporated in personal and group previous experience and accessing resources inscribed in social structures and institutions (ranging from family and community to welfare state and labour markets) to overcome in some fashion the impacts of the shock, invest in alternative ways to achieve standards of wellbeing, cope with the new constraints, or, at least, deal with new risks and to adopt an active relation with them.

NOTE

1. For more information about the RESCuE project please see Chapter 1.

REFERENCES

Aalbers, M. (2013), 'Neoliberalism is dead … Long live neoliberalism!', *International Journal of Urban and Regional Research* 37: 1083–90.

Adger, W. N. (2000), 'Social and ecological resilience: Are they related?', *Progress in Human Geography* 24: 347–64.

Akter, S. and Mallick, B. (2013), *An empirical investigation of socio-economic resilience to natural disasters*, Munich: Munich Personal RePEc Archive, MPRA Paper No. 50375.

Arnal, A. (2015), 'Resilience as transformative capacity', *Geoforum* 66: 26–36.

Batty, E. and Cole, I. (2010), *Resilience and the recession in six deprived communities?* York: JRF Programme Paper – Poverty and Place Programme.

Béné, C., Frankenberger, T. and Nelson, S. (2015), *Design, monitoring and evaluation of resilience intervention*, London: Institute of Development Studies Working Paper No 459.

Blyth, M. (2015), *Austerity: The history of a dangerous idea*, Oxford: Oxford University Press.

Bourdieu, P. (1984), *Distinction: A social critique of the judgement of taste*, London: Routledge.

Bourdieu, P. (1993), *La misére du monde*, Paris: Seuil.

Canvin, K., Marttila, A., Burstrom, B. and Whitehead, M. (2009), 'Tales of the unexpected? Hidden resilience in poor households in Britain', *Social Science and Medicine* 69: 238–45.

Capucha, L., Estêvão, P., Calado, A. and Capucha, R. (2014), 'The role of stereotyping in public legitimation: The case of the PIGS label', *Comparative Sociology* 13: 482–502.

Dagdeviren, H., Donoghue, M. and Promberger, M. (2016), 'Resilience, hardship and social conditions', *Journal of Social Policy* 45: 1–20.

Dagdeviren, H., Donoghue, M. and Meier, L. (2017), 'The narratives of hardship: The new & the old poor in the aftermath of the 2008 crisis in Europe', *Sociological Review* 65: 369–85.

Dagdeviren, H. and Donoghue, M. (2019), 'Resilience, agency and coping with hardship: Evidence from Europe during the Great Recession', *Journal of Social Policy* 48(3): 547–67.

DFID (2011), *Defining disaster resilience: A DFID Approach Paper*, London: DFID Publishing.

Eitinger, L. (1964), *Concentration camp survivors in Norway and Israel*, Oslo: Universitetsforlaget.

Estêvão, P., Calado, A. and Capucha, L. (2017), 'Resilience: Moving from a "heroic" notion to a sociological concept', *Sociologia Problemas e Práticas* 85: 9–25.

Gordon, J. E. (1979), *Structures*, Harmondsworth: Penguin.

Harrison, E. (2013), 'Bouncing back? Recession, resilience and everyday lives', *Critical Social Policy* 33: 97–113.

Harrow, J. (2009), 'Leadership and resilience – Local communities and service in a time of fragmentation. Are there reasons to be cheerful?' Paper presented to the public policy seminar 'Leadership and Resilience', University of Edinburgh Business School, Edinburgh, Scotland, 30 October.

Hickman, P. (2018), 'A flawed construct? Understanding and unpicking the concept of resilience in the context of economic hardship', *Social Policy and Society* 17: 409–24.

Hoggett, P. (2001), 'Agency, rationality and social policy', *Journal of Social Policy* 30: 37–56.

Holling, C. S. (1973), 'Resilience and stability of economic systems', *Annual Review of Ecology and Systematics* 4: 1–23.

Keck, M. and Sakdapolrak, P. (2013), 'What is social resilience?', *Erdkunde* 67: 5–19.

Klein, N. (2007), *The shock doctrine: The rise of disaster capitalism*, New York: Henry Holt and Co.

Levitas, R., Pantazis, C., Fahmy, E., Gordon, D., Lloyd, E. and Patsios, D. (2007), *The multi-dimensional analysis of social exclusion – project report*, Bristol: University of Bristol.

Lister, R. (2002), 'A politics of recognition and respect: Involving people with experience of poverty in decision making that affects their lives', *Social Policy and Society* 1: 37–46.

MacLeavy, J. (2011), 'A "new politics" of austerity, workfare and gender?', *Cambridge Journal of Regions, Economy and Society* 4: 355–67.

Martin, R. and Sunley, P. (2015), 'On the notion of regional economic resilience: conceptualization and explanation', *Journal of Economic Geography* 15: 1–42.

Masten, A. (2010), 'Ordinary magic: Lessons from research on resilience in human development', *Education Canada* 49: 28–32.

Matsaganis, M. and Leventi, C. (2014), 'The distributional impact of austerity and the recession in Southern Europe', *South European Society and Politics* 19: 393–412.

Milne, A., and Rankine, D. (2013), *Reality, resources, resilience: regeneration in a recession*, York: JRF Programme Paper.

Mitchell, A. (2013), *Risk and resilience: From good idea to good practice*, Paris: OECD Development Co-operation Working Papers, No. 13.

ODI (2016), *Unlocking resilience through autonomous innovation*, London: Overseas Development Institute.

OECD (2014), *Guidelines for Resilience System Analysis*, Paris: OECD Publishing.

Patrick, R. (2017), *For whose benefit? The everyday realities of welfare reform*, Bristol: Bristol University Press.

Paugam, S. (1991), *La disqualification social: Essai sur la nouvelle pauvreté*, Paris: Presses Universitaires de France.

Piketty, T. (2014), *Capital in the twenty-first century*, Cambridge, MA: Harvard University Press.

Ranci, C. (2009), *Social vulnerability in Europe*, Basingstoke: Palgrave MacMillan.

Room, G. (1989), *Poverty and the Single European Market*, Bath: Centre for Analysis of Social Policy – University of Bath.

Rose, A. (2007), 'Economic resilience to natural and man-made disasters: Multidisciplinary origins and contextual dimensions', *Environmental Hazards* 7: 383–98.

Rowntree, B. S. (2000[1901]), *Poverty, a study of town life*, Bristol: Policy Press.

Royce, E. (2009), *Poverty and power: The problem of structural inequality*, Lanham, MD: Rowman & Littlefield.

Sapountzaki, K. (2012), 'Vulnerability management by means of resilience', *Natural Hazards* 60: 1267–85.

Seccombe, K. (2002), '"Beating the odds" versus "changing the odds": Poverty, resilience, and family policy', *Journal of Marriage and Family* 64: 384–94.

Sen, A. (1999), *Development as freedom*, Oxford: Oxford University Press.

Sen, A. (2009), *The idea of justice*, New York: Penguin.

Skidelsky, R. (2014), 'Austerity: The wrong story', *The Economic and Labour Relations Review* 26: 377–83.

Townsend, P. (1962), *Poverty in the United Kingdom. A survey of household resources and standards of living*, Berkeley: University of California Press.

Walker, F. A. (1897), 'The causes of poverty', *The Century Magazine* LV: 210–16.

Walsh-Dilley, M., Wolford, W. and McCarthy J. (2016), 'Rights for resilience: Bringing power, rights and agency into the resilience framework', *Ecology and Society* 21: 11.

Werner, E. (1977), *The children of Kauai: A longitudinal study from the prenatal period to the age of ten*, Honolulu: University of Hawai'i Press.

Wisman, J. (2013), 'Wage stagnation, rising inequality and the financial crisis of 2008', *Cambridge Journal of Economics* 37: 921–45.

PART III

Dimensions of household resilience

6. Socio-economic practices of households coping with hardship

Hulya Dagdeviren and Matthew Donoghue

INTRODUCTION

The 2008 crisis and austerity policies have directly affected mostly low- and middle-income households, especially in countries that were heavily impacted, such as Greece, Spain, Ireland and Portugal. In some cases it intensified existing hardship, while in other cases it pushed previously well-off people into poverty as discussed by Dagdeviren et al. (2017) in an article comparing 'the new and the old poor in Europe'. Experiences of hardship, however, were not always directly related to the 2008 financial crisis and the austerity policies. Crises were sometimes linked to political conflict, as demonstrated in the case of Turkey. The forced migration of Kurds in the 1990s and more recent years was a factor that compelled hundreds of thousands of people to leave their villages and move to large cities in different parts of Turkey. The Syrian conflict caused a similar humanitarian crisis in Turkey as the largest recipients of Syrian refugees (Şengül and Aytekin 2015). The Greek case also contained stories of migration and hardship, particularly concerning refugees from the Middle East (Kambouri et al. 2015). Crises can also strike through homelessness or redundancy, putting pressure on families, creating emotional, financial and social instability, lack of direction and uncertainty (see Chapter 9 of this volume).

This chapter deals specifically with the socio-economic practices of vulnerable households in the face of crises and hardship with a view to reflect on 'resilience' as detailed in Chapters 4 and 5 of this volume. The analysis is based on the data obtained from nine European countries through semi-structured interviews that were conducted as part of a European comparative study (see Chapter 1 of this volume). The households[1] that participated in the study were predominantly from low-income backgrounds. Within this there was a mix of households with at least one member in work, and others which were more dependent on the state for assistance. However, the duration of employment, whether it was full or part time, and the quality of employment (for example in terms of salary, benefits and available hours) varied dramatically across sites and countries. For example, casual and temporary work was prominent for the investigated households in most countries sampled, reflecting the continuing shift away from permanent or long-term employment within lower-income households. It was common for participants to be in low-paid and insecure employment with variable hours and little job security.

There was a significant variation in terms of levels and duration of educational experience across the countries sampled. Greece's sample, for example, contained a high number of university graduates. Spain's sample, in comparison, contained only one household with a member who had a university education. That being said, almost all participants had at least primary and secondary level education, to some level. Family size varied across all countries, ranging from couples with children, single parent households, and childless households. The majority of participants across all samples were of working age, with a very small number approaching or having just reached retirement age. Across all countries there was significant representation from migrants. Some countries, such as the UK and Greece, had almost 50/50 splits in terms of migrant and native participants, although in the UK this was due overwhelmingly to the urban sample. Finally, in some households one or more members suffered from a disability or impairment. In the UK, for example, several participants suffered from mental health problems such as depression, which in many cases was related to their experiences of and difficulties with hardship. A small number experienced substance abuse issues, while others had experienced physical disabilities which made working difficult.

In this chapter, socio-economic practices employed in times of crises and hardship have been classified into three categories. The first is related to the practices and efforts to generate and/or prevent major falls in family income. The second concerns the efforts of households to lower the quantity and/or cost of consumption (or the cost of living) in order to remain within often reduced means. The third is linked to the ways families re-arrange the use of their own assets and resources as well as those around them to survive and overcome hardship. In what follows, we discuss these three forms of socio-economic practices and then reflect on the implications of these findings to further develop our understanding of the notion of 'resilience', and its strengths and weaknesses in the light of specific findings presented in this chapter. The chapter ends with a brief conclusion.

LITERATURE REVIEW

There is considerable research in Social Policy, Development Studies, Human Geography and Urban Studies that is relevant to the topic of discussion in this chapter. Perhaps it would be useful to start with a description of socio-economic practices. Jones and Murphy offer a useful definition of socio-economic practices: 'The stabilized, routinized, or improvised social actions that constitute and reproduce economic space, and through and within which diverse actors (for example entrepreneurs, workers, caregivers, consumers, firms) and communities (for example industries, places, markets, cultural groups) organize materials, produce, consume, and/or derive meaning from the economic world' (Jones and Murphy 2011, p. 367). While aspects of stability and routinisation are important, our interest in this study is to understand how families and individuals react to shocks and crises which imply a change rather than stability, routine and reproduction.

Studies that investigate how families respond to major instability and societal transformation are plentiful. Investigations of family coping during the Great Depression, or periods of capitalist restructuring or transition from socialist systems are all relevant for our purposes here. Studies of socio-economic practices that emerged in the course of transition were conceptualised in a slightly different way, partly reflecting the institutional differences among countries. Piirainen (1997), for example, studied post-socialist Russia at a time when social structure was in state of flux. He argued that households that pursued a 'market oriented' strategy emerged as the middle class, those with traditional defensive strategies (relying on state help and informal economy) ended up as a static working class and those with 'the proletarian strategy' (relying on official state economy) formed the poverty stricken 'underclass'. Other research by Lokshin and Yemtsov (2004) looked at family strategies after the 1998 financial crisis, and classified them as active (home production, supplementary work, renting rooms and so on), social network based (help from family and friends) and passive strategies (cutting spending).

For capitalist economies, a landmark contribution to the literature on socio-economic practices of families is by Elder (1974). He identifies two distinct family strategies during the Great Depression in response to change in their needs and resources: reducing expenditures and/or generating alternative/extra sources of income. Many other studies follow this categorisation with some modification. For example, Datta et al. (2007) discuss the contributions to the new economy literature, highlighting how flexibilisation and privatisation have forced people to find new ways of 'coping'. These included expenditure minimising and income maximising strategies supplemented by reorganisation of the household (for example extension/nuclearisation) as well as use of social networks and self-provisioning.

An interesting dimension of these discussions is related to temporality of the socio-economic responses that emerge during and after the change (for more discussion on this see Dagdeviren and Donoghue 2019). Wallace (2002) also discussed post-Fordist transformations (flexible employment, informality, female entry to workforce, privatisation) and how they lead people to take on multiple jobs, part-time work and rely on their own resources rather than on the welfare state. Similar findings are reported by Baek and DeVaney (2010). Sherman (2006) finds in a rural community in the USA that subsistence food production, hunting, fishing and raising livestock and living rent free with family and friends are some of the strategies people used to deal with change.

Part of the socio-economic responses households employ are usually conceptualised as asset (and resource) based strategies, following Mingione (1987) and Rakodi (1999). This reflects the extent to which individuals or households can make better or more intensified use of their own as well as external resources in times of adversity, including income from formal or non-formal employment or self-provisioning, and resources from state, family, friends and social networks.

More recent studies identify cuts made to spending as an important response by households in difficult times. In Anderson et al. (2012) the primary house-hold strategy to cope in pressing times was to reduce spending, including on essentials such as heating and food in order to keep up with core payments. This tendency is confirmed by Hossain et al. (2011), although in their study most cutting back was from non-essential spending. Another recent study by Heflin et al. (2011) classifies households' socio-economic practices in times of major change into work-based (reported, unreported, legal, illegal), network based (help from family and friends) and agency based (help from charities) strategies. They argue that families would face hardship in multiple domains including housing, utility and food hardships.

Most studies in this literature accept that the socio-economic status of families affects the choice of strategies, as well as the perceived control over circumstances (Caplan and Schooler 2007). For example, Henly et al. (2005) explain how assistance from poor families' social networks helps with coping without significantly improving their economic status because the gifts and transfers are usually small.

Our reading of this literature leads us to conclude that socio-economic practices of households can be discussed in different ways depending on the context, nature of shock experienced and the circumstances of the families. However, the studies reviewed above also suggest that it is possible to draw a common framework that may encompass a multitude of socio-economic practices in any context and under any circumstances. Drawing on the liter-ature discussed above, we suggest that the key elements of this framework involve the highlights presented in Table 6.1.

In what follows, we utilise this framework to make sense of the socio-economic practices of resilience, emerging from our data and research.

Table 6.1   *Socio-economic practices of households*

Key objectives of household practices	Major practices
Stabilising household income to prevent further falls	• Paid, unpaid, formal and informal work • Migration • Acting on capabilities (for example, going back/ continuing education)
Efforts to cut cost of living to contain the effects of the crisis and to protect the standard of living	• Reducing quantity or the monetary value of consumption • Bargain hunting • Prioritising spending • Self-provision
Re-organising assets and resources in and around the household	• Support from family, friends, community • Running down savings • Borrowing from formal/informal lenders • Using public/communal resources

HOW FAMILIES TRY TO STABILISE THEIR INCOME

In this research, work, welfare benefits and migration to other countries for work have emerged as major routes for families to stabilise the potential falls in their income. Of these, work was found to be the most important contributor to the incomes of households, followed by social welfare in most countries included in this project. What stands out almost without exception is that non-permanent, low-paid employment is sometimes more common than formal, permanent employment. Pointedly, there is a lack of decent employment across vulnerable households in all of the nine countries under investigation. Many participants in this research relied either upon insecure jobs to scrape a living or resorted to them in order to complement other sources of income, as exemplified in Table 6.2. These involved a variety of arrangements (Şengül and Aytekin 2015; Capucha et al. 2015; Dagdeviren and Donoghue 2015; Wódz et al. 2015), including:

• Formal but successive short-term contracts.
• Cash-in hand, sequential, sporadic or occasional work.
• Regular work with 'zero-hours contracts'.
• Semi-formal work as in Poland, Turkey and Portugal, where full-time work often reported as part time or as self-employed as a way for the employer to avoid tax and social security contributions. For example, Baluta[2] was

working on the basis of 'green receipts' – that is, as a false independent worker – which meant that her employer not only transferred the social security obligations to Baluta but also made her unable to eventually claim unemployment benefit (Portugal/F/migrant/part-time worker).

Such deterioration in the conditions of employment, resulting in low and/ or erratic earnings and income uncertainty, has to be ultimately harmful for resilience in the long run as insecurity obliges households to focus on their most urgent needs for the day without having any ability to plan and act to improve their conditions for the future (see Chapter 9 of this volume). Lack of contribution to social protection (for example social insurance) schemes in casual jobs not only implies extension of current insecurities into old age (for example pensions) but in some cases also a lack of access to various services (for example health) in the present time.

Table 6.2   Varieties of informal market activities cited in selected Case Studies*

Greece: Working in bars, coffee shops and restaurants during the tourism season, giving private lessons, hairdressing, cleaning and street vending.
Poland: Repairing or cleaning other people's houses, making and selling handicrafts (for example crochets, dolls, flowers) at local markets or through the internet.
Turkey: Working as an unregistered shop keeper, scrap paper collector, betting agent, porter.
Finland: Gathering and selling wild berries, marketing items (for example Tupperware, stamps), taking on odd jobs (for example sports referee in local games), making and selling handmade garments, collecting recycled goods and selling at flea markets.
The UK: Painting neighbours' houses, working in bars, distributing leaflets or magazines, construction work, cooking or waiting in restaurants.

Note: * While these emerged as key informal activities in household interviews, note that these activities can also involve formal work.

Some participants applied for jobs they were overqualified for as exemplified by cases from Greece, Portugal and the UK. Others tried further education and retraining as a way to improve their chances of employment, but this aspiration remained unrealised in all cases because of the decline in labour market opportunities. In some cases, young people seem to be making an early exit from education in order to work and contribute to the family budget.

Ups and downs in the economy also affected the fortunes of micro and small businesses.

'We started as textile workers and we met in a textile workshop and got married. Then we decided to open our own workshop. We've had so many up and downs.

> When the economy was doing well we made some savings and then when the textile sector got into crisis [twice – in 2001 and 2009] we lost our savings. We closed our workshop a couple of times and put our machines in storage to wait for the right times.' (Turkey/F/40s)

This is clearly a story of resilience but one that is defeated for periods of time by wider economic forces. To improve their living conditions, the couple showed an entrepreneurial spirit, used their acquired knowledge and skills in the textile sector, and took some risks in order to transform their lives by becoming self-employed and an employer of others. The downturns in the market, which were beyond their control, counteracted their initiatives and led to the closure of their workshop and loss of savings.

State transfers have been an important barrier against poverty and destitution across the European Union (EU). These were the second most important source of income and of social resilience for our participants, protecting them when they are unemployed or employed, but on low incomes. In-work benefits (compensating low wages or part-time/temporary work) as well as child benefits have been important in supporting working participants. Quite often households combined wages from formal or informal employment with welfare benefits, help from family members with pensions and assistance from charities.

The comparative strengths of the welfare state, its history of development and evolution of citizens' rights and entitlements (cf. Esping-Andersen 1990) has made a significant difference to vulnerable households' socio-economic position and social resilience in individual countries. In this respect, Finland, Germany, the UK and Ireland, despite variations amongst them, clearly provided better safety nets in terms of value and/or coverage with various forms of welfare support, particularly in comparison to the more traditionally, residual or developing welfare systems (for example Turkey, Greece, Portugal, Spain, Poland). The degrees of exposure to the recent financial crisis and the associated policy changes have also impacted welfare protection and therefore the foundations of social resilience. Austerity implied significant cuts and, in some cases, complete abandonment of various social protection payments. In Greece, these cuts were more severe as part of the conditionality imposed on the country by the lenders. 'Welfare support is limited since the structural adjustment programs have abolished most family benefits, as well as tax exemptions for children. The only benefits that still exist are those given to families with more than two children.' (Kambouri et al. 2015:18).

Reverse migration from urban to rural areas in Greece raised the migrants' chances of employment in addition to helping them to lower the cost of living due to lower housing and food costs (Kambouri et al. 2015). Findings in Lapland provide examples of both reverse migration and short-term international migration – in particular to Norway, during periods when work in reindeer farms is relatively light (Vuojala-Magga et al. 2015).

FAMILY ENDEAVOURS TO LOWER THE COST OF LIVING

Going without was a prominent theme in the narratives of participants in all case study countries, reflecting the material deprivations of families. Some of the sacrifices were from non-essential goods and services while others were from essential consumption goods, threatening the health and survival of participants. The choice they made between these, as well as the severity of deprivations, signified the degree of hardship they lived in, on a spectrum ranging from getting by to destitution.

Cutting down from essential consumption often involved energy, food and medical necessities. Switching off heating for a period of time, using public spaces such as libraries (for example for doing homework), going to bed early to save heating costs, were common. Some participants in the UK, Ireland, Poland and Spain admitted limiting the number of meals or reducing expensive food items such as meat from the diet. In Greece, Poland and Germany some participants reported delaying or giving up some of the medical expenses that they needed such as medicines, spectacles and dental treatment.

The most frequently talked about 'non-essential' expenses families tried to avoid or reduce were those for holidays and leisure activities, including those for children (for example, school camps). Public spaces and resources such as walks and games in nearby woodlands were used as a substitute for paid-for holidays in Spain, Ireland and Poland. Treats for children, gifts for birthdays and special occasions, and clothing were all strictly rationed in an attempt to reduce the cost of living as reflected by a participant in Lapland. 'Money is used for good quality of regular food with fresh vegetables, but the consumption of treats and refreshments is limited and controlled' (Finland/mother/agricultural education). Economising by cutting down on smoking, newspapers, internet, phone bills, going out to eat, drinking or other leisure activities also featured often in the conversations of the participants.

While housing costs may have declined after the crisis in some countries, in others such as the UK there has been a crisis of affordable housing. Lack of investment and decline in social housing stock constituted an important source of insecurity for low-income groups in some EU countries.

Reconfiguration of living space was used frequently. In Greece, Finland, Spain, Poland, Portugal, Ireland and Turkey, remaining with or returning to the family home was the most viable option for some participants. This meant different things for different people. In some instances, participants complained about lack of autonomy or reduced autonomy as a result of having to live with parents or other members of the family, not out of choice but out of necessity. In other instances, younger participants complained about not being able to 'move on' with their lives or to enter into relationships and build a family for themselves because of the duty towards older family members, especially towards parents, and continued to live with them in order to share their cost of living.

Bargain hunting occupied many low-income households within urban locations. Transport and distance prevented some families from engaging in similar activities in the rural locations. While some families chose to do their food shopping daily in order to catch the best offers, others explained how visiting shops often led them to spend more than they intended. Hence, they filled up the freezer to reduce the need for going to shops to buy bare essentials, such as bread and milk, as a way to deal with this problem (Ireland, UK). Buying lower quality products and out-of-date food were mentioned as a way to reduce outgoings. Use of second-hand markets, charity shops and flea markets for clothing, furniture and other household items was common.

Self-provision or producing goods and services for one's own consumption was also prominent in the narratives of participants as a way to reduce the monetary cost of living and better cope with hardship. For example, in Ireland some participants grew vegetables for their own consumption – potatoes, onions, cabbage, carrots and turnips – sometimes producing a surplus that could be given to friends and neighbours (Dagg and Gray 2015). Fishing, hunting and gathering wild fruits and mushrooms in Finland (Vuojala-Magga et al. 2015) and to some extent in Germany (Meier et al. 2015; Promberger 2017) and the collection of firewood from the forest in Spain (Arnal et al. 2015) as a substitute for costly fuel, were some of the examples reported. Fixing and maintaining own machinery, mending own cars and doing the carpentry for one's own furniture were also mentioned (see Chapter 7 of this volume).

Strict budgeting and stocking up for future consumption was a way of exerting some control over spending. In Spain, for example, rents constituted a large proportion of incomes, especially for those on welfare benefits, and were given priority. Then households had to decide what expense *not* to pay out: this may be part of the rent or the electricity or gas bill (Arnal et al. 2015). Some talked about strictly planning the cooked meals in order to serve them more than once. In Poland, a woman explained how she apportioned chicken into parts to cook and serve for several meals (Wódz et al. 2015). In Lapland, food for winter is stocked through net fishing and hunting in autumn and freezing the catch to preserve it. Some of these activities are carried out in groups and the caught, hunted and gathered goods are shared between the households (Vuojala-Magga et al. 2015).

A final theme that runs through the findings is the role played by informal exchange that may take the form of personal or social exchange, including gift-giving, some involving reciprocity, others solidarity or a personal or social duty towards others (see Chapters 2 and 7 of this volume). In Germany, there were examples of sharing cars, tools and magazine subscriptions, doing repairs for each other, giving or taking home-made jams, juice or liquor, home grown herbs, fruits and vegetables (Meier et al. 2015). In Lapland, reindeer herders exchanged the work of maintaining fences and watching animals to guard against predators in the wilderness. These services may be paid for in fuel or by a gift of reindeer, fish or meat (Vuojala-Magga et al. 2015).

Family support played a significant role in sustaining individuals and households through hardship across all countries but perhaps more so in some than others. In Greece, the older members in receipt of pensions shared their already reduced and limited earnings (Kambouri et al. 2015). In Turkey, farming households sent foodstuff such as fruits, vegetables, pulses, cracked wheat and so on to their children and relatives who had migrated and settled down in urban locations (Şengül and Aytekin 2015). In Spain, families helped by lending money for unforeseen expenses, preparing food for everyone, buying clothes or school supplies, or paying debts when other family members could not do this (Arnal et al. 2015).

IMPORTANCE OF ASSETS, USE OF DEBT, AND COMMON AND PUBLIC RESOURCES

Most participants in the nine countries covered in this study did not own many physical assets, except for houses, often with a mortgage. Participants in the UK were least likely to own their homes while those in Finland, Poland and Turkey were more likely. Most participants did not have savings. In some cases, participants, particularly from the UK and Portugal, reported selling personal possessions to raise funds, such as watches, wedding rings and furniture.

Perhaps the most important factor when looking at the use of assets and resources is participants' relationship with debt. This is to some extent linked to the centrality of debt, both sovereign and household, to the financial crisis. This was especially the case in the UK, Ireland, Spain, Portugal, Turkey and Greece but not so common in Germany, Poland and Finland. A participant in Greece found that, during the country's sovereign debt crisis, her employer could not pay her salary, which forced her to begin spending on credit cards in order to pay for essentials in her day-to-day life (Kambouri et al. 2015). This is especially notable in the UK where for many credit cards and overdraft facilities have become the norm in managing daily spending and other essential outgoings. In Poland, debt was used in an arguably more traditional way, to build assets and resources rather than to finance consumption (essential or otherwise). In Turkey, the striking difference is illustrated by one participant, who remarked:

> 'You cannot show me one single family who are not in debt. The only difference is that some of us have [a] big amount of debt to banks while some others' debt is not that big. We do not know how to pay it. Only we get further debt to pay the debt. The only relief is that we are all in debt [laughs].' (Turkey/M/40s)

Thus far, the analyses of household practices in this chapter have predominantly focused on private, traded and commodified resources. However, across the entire RESCuE sample use of public resources proved particularly important. In Portugal, vacant land in both urban and rural locations was used to grow vegetables and raise small livestock such as chickens and rabbits, which could then be used for food, and shared amongst multiple households (Capucha et al. 2015). In Lapland, public resources such as free healthcare, library services, affordable and accessible sports facilities and evening courses were seen as crucial for wellbeing. After attending a community college course, one participant even built his own boat, while another was able to start making their own clothes (Vuojala-Magga 2015: 18; see Chapter 2 of this volume). There are many similarities in the UK case, where local authorities provide libraries, children's centres, leisure centres, playgrounds and in some locations city farms – although austerity measures in the country have put some of this at risk.

Support by third sector organisations such as charities, churches and solidarity groups played a stronger role in some countries than others. In the UK, over one million individuals have been receiving food parcels every year from foodbanks since 2008 (Trussell Trust 2016),[3] which in our view reflected temporary spells of destitution for a significant proportion of the population. In Greece, assistance by the solidarity movements that have emerged since the economic crisis began is more prominent (Kambouri et al. 2015). In Finland, food delivery by the church or the organisations for the unemployed is found to be popular among nearly all the informants (Vuojala-Magga 2015, p. 18). In Turkey, clientelist networks play a functional role for all involved, including charity in return for loyalty and voluntary work; they also create animosity (Şengül and Aytekin 2015). There is evidence of using foodbanks in all of the nine countries covered in this study.

IMPLICATIONS FOR RESILIENCE

A major attraction of resilience in much of the literature is the emphasis on the potential individual agency of those facing hardship, contradicting the 'deficit approach' associated with established poverty studies that tend to view people in poverty as passive victims of circumstance (for example Royce 2009, p. 64; Lister 2002; Mullin and Arce 2008; Buckner et al. 2003). This emphasises the importance of individuals' and households' socio-economic decision making. Central to resilience is a focus on how individuals and groups, in times of adversity, are able to turn crises into opportunities while surviving many different pressures. However, these positive accounts, based upon individual agency, do not take into account social conditions, including class, gender, ethnicity, power relations, cultural norms, (post-)colonial influences, and so on (Dagdeviren et al. 2016, p. 6; Chandler 2013; Duffield 2012). It is these social conditions that define the boundaries of the possible in terms of the choices that can be made. For example, getting a second job to complement existing income is only possible if the labour market is buoyant enough to sustain it. Where this may have been possible, it may have come at the risk of inferior employment conditions with lower wages and precarious work.

Across the countries covered in this study, there were many examples of practices that encapsulate the ethos of resilience – beating the odds (Seccombe 2002). Families supported each other, made effective use of budgeting, employed bargain hunting, and made use of open or free access public resources in their quest to deal with austerity and hardship. In Germany, there was one participant who was able to maintain an old camper trailer allowing their family to go on holiday cheaply, or another who taught her children how to grow food. The result is not only an improved economic situation but also increased confidence and self-esteem that allows these people to strive for an improved quality of life (Meier et al. 2015, pp. 25–6). As the latter participant remarked:

'[My children can] look around if they are poor and on the margin and they can look back and remember what you can do from plants and from herbs. That they can shift for themselves ... What you can do from apples, that you can produce apple jelly. Then you have to buckle down to work.' (Germany/mother of more than three children/rural area)

Likewise, a number of Polish participants demonstrated a creativity that enabled them to take hobbies and talents and transform them into income-generating activities (see Chapter 7 of this volume). 'Some of the respondents improved their situation through painting pictures or playing on the accordion' (Poland/F/ rural area), 'making decorations made of tissue paper' (Poland/F/taking care of mother and two disabled sons), 'having their own music band' (Pl/husband/ urban area). Further education and/or retraining reflect vocational and spatial mobility and these could also be seen in a positive light.

The socio-economic practices of resilience employed by participants across all studied countries were dominated by cost-cutting practices. For example, efforts to contain the cost of living by significantly cutting down on food, energy and health costs were widespread across the countries covered in this study. The fact that these result in deprivations of basic but essential needs clearly shows that the resilience paradigm may gloss over the negative consequences of household action in times of hardship. Many participants found it difficult to plan any further ahead than the immediate future, posing problems for the development of resilience, which requires a long-term view that will guide the appropriate use and acquisition of resources.

Some of the findings suggest complex relationships between survival and coping with hardship and the socio-economic characteristics of households. Working-class or low-income participants, who had long-term experience of coping with poverty and hardship, fared better than 'the new poor' or formerly middle-class households in terms of coping and getting by. On the other hand, the middle-class households that were hit hard by the crisis seem to have access to a set of resources such as savings, a house and social connections that enables a speedier transition to a better economic state. Labour mobility is an important means for coping with hardship but achieving decent living conditions may be difficult, especially for international migrants, as a result of the multiple disadvantages they face in the host countries.

Moreover, the resilience approach has the potential to problematise structural issues in terms of individual pathologies. For example, willingness of participants to accept jobs for which they are overqualified or jobs that offer low and erratic pay and uncertainty may be viewed as resilience, but this hides the lack of choice and opportunities for better employment conditions and insecurity associated with non-standard employment conditions in the labour market. Lack of good opportunities is well reflected by the fact some people resort to practices that keep them afloat financially and socially but are not entirely legal, such as a UK participant who helped maintain roads 'off the books'.

Widening inequality in advanced capitalist societies since the 1980s is well known (Atkinson et al. 2011; Stockhammer 2015). The richest 1 per cent owned around half of global wealth in 2014 (Hardoon 2015). This is reflected in our study of low-income groups who lacked the assets and resources to fall back on when hit by a major personal or socio-economic crisis. Unemployment, low wages and insecure employment conditions implied that most participants had no savings to use against unexpected developments in their life. Difficulties of getting on the housing ladder, limited social housing and high rents in the private sector translated into a housing crisis for many people in countries such as the UK where housing costs contribute to a rise in poverty by one-third (DWP 2013). The implication of all this is that if we want families to cope with crises better then they must earn sufficiently well to build their homes and savings to counter the negative shocks in their life.

In addition to better employment conditions, social protection and welfare systems are the best barriers against hardship in times of crisis. Such an approach encapsulates the idea that resilience is primarily a product of individual agency, while acknowledging the conditioning factors of socio-economic structure, the supporting capacities of civil society and community organisations. Additionally, these factors require support through structural assistance – whether that is through direct transfers such as the welfare state, qualifications and skills provision through education, the development, maintenance and protection of good health, or providing adequate housing fit for purpose. Effective social security and welfare systems would enable households to weather suffering without needing to be preoccupied with the essential concerns of everyday survival.

Finally, the findings in this chapter show that open access or free public resources such as parks, libraries, child centres, leisure centres, health services, and social and training clubs enhance the quality of life for the most vulnerable population and directly or indirectly support resilience.

CONCLUSION

A striking convergence of socio-economic practices exists across Europe. In all cases, cutting down what are considered to be expendable elements of consumption, such as treats or spending on celebrations and holidays, surfaces as one of the primary means by which households try to exert some control over their budget. Those who face more severe hardship cut down on vital items, such as reducing the number of meals, or protein rich food like meat, which may be expensive, not putting on heating and forgoing medical treatment. These are clearly measures of deprivation and describing them as a strategy of resilience or coping with hardship would be to glamorise them.

The country-level studies contain a wealth of evidence about how people in hardship try to manage their limited resources. These include changes in how they shop, for example cycles of shopping or a search for bargains, and where they shop, for example discount stores, second-hand shops, across the borders, as well as greater recycling of used materials. Do-it-yourself and grow-it-yourself emerge as an important practice for own consumption to prevent further potential falls in the standard of living, although this is more common in some countries than others. Payment of bills is another area that requires careful consideration by households. Rent and utility bills frequently receive priority in the allocation of family budgets.

If degrees of resilience are classified into survival, coping, getting by and transcending hardship, a large proportion of the practices for dealing with hardship recorded in this research falls into coping and getting by and very few could be regarded as overcoming hardship. Not all socio-economic practices of coping with hardship produce positive results other than coping with hardship. Many lead to negative consequences, reflected by a range of deprivations and insecurity.

From a policy perspective, there are a number of facilitators that would enhance social resilience. First, improvements in labour market conditions, including the level of pay and security, are the most important means through which resilience against negative shocks and hardship can be built. It would enable people to save and invest against potential adversities. However, our findings show that informal, casual, short-term, irregular work is common in all countries, reflecting the precarious conditions of employment. This is likely to restrict the general resilience of working classes, which traditionally consisted of decent and sustainable jobs. Savings are important for meeting unexpected expenditures families have. However, the ability to save was limited amongst participants, particularly low-income earners, rendering them more susceptible to crises. Instead, there is greater use of debt and signs of over-indebtedness, more in some countries, such as the UK and Ireland, than in others.

Second, unemployment and ill health is sometimes inevitable and, when this happens, welfare and social security systems are still the most significant barrier against more severe forms of poverty and act as the most important vehicle for developing or maintaining socio-economic resilience. Third, open access or free public resources such as libraries, health centres, children's centres, advice and advocacy units and public spaces remarkably enhance aspects of people's lives, even if they are facing hardship in other areas.

At a more individual level, family in a broad sense emerges as one of the most important support units during difficult times, including providing help with housing, food, small loans and childcare. While duty and solidarity appear as the overriding motives in this, the findings also reflect the burden this creates for the family members who are at the giving end (Gray and Dagg 2019; see Chapter 9 of this volume). Participants also benefit from other forms of social and informal exchange involving reciprocity, solidarity and gift-giving, for example, amongst friends, neighbours, community organisations, faith-based or ethnicity-based institutions and political groups (see Chapter 7 of this volume).

NOTES

1. We acknowledge the problems associated with the term 'household' but use it to cover units involving co-habitation as well as families.
2. All names in this chapter are pseudonyms.
3. The actual numbers are likely to be much greater taking into account those who collect food parcels for their family rather than as an individual, those who use

foodbanks and charities not belonging to Trussell Trust and those who do not use foodbanks to avoid the stigma and shame despite needing food support.

REFERENCES

Anderson, W., White, V. and Finney, A. (2012), 'Coping with low incomes and cold homes', *Energy Policy* 49: 40–52.

Arnal, M; de Castro, C; Martín, P; Revilla, J. C and Serrano, A. (2015), *Socio-Economic practices of resilience: Spanish national report*, unpublished RESCuE project report.

Atkinson, A B.; Piketty, T. and Saez, E. (2011), 'Top incomes in the long run of history', *Journal of Economic Literature* 49(1): 3–71.

Baek, E. and DeVaney, S. A. (2010), How do families manage their economic hardship? *Family Relations* 59(4): 358–68.

Buckner, J. C., Mezzacappa, E. and Beardslee, W. R. (2003), 'Characteristics of resilient youths living in poverty: The role of self-regulatory processes', *Development and Psychopathology* 15(1): 139–62.

Caplan, L. J. and Schooler, C. (2007), 'Socioeconomic status and financial coping strategies: The mediating role of perceived control', *Social Psychology Quarterly* 70(1): 43–58.

Capucha, L., Calado, A. and Estêvão, P. (2015), *Socio-economic practices of resilience: Portuguese national report*, unpublished RESCuE project report.

Chandler, D. (2013), 'International statebuilding and the ideology of resilience', *Politics* 33(4): 276–86.

Dagdeviren, H. and Donoghue, M. (2015), *Socioeconomic practices of resilience: International report*, unpublished RESCuE project report.

Dagdeviren, H., Donoghue, M. and Promberger, M. (2016), 'Resilience, hardship and social conditions', *Journal of Social Policy* 45(1): 1–20.

Dagdeviren, H., Donoghue, M. and Meier, L. (2017), 'The narratives of hardship: The new and the old poor in the aftermath of the 2008 crisis in Europe', *The Sociological Review* 65(2): 369–85.

Dagdeviren, H. and Donoghue, M. (2019), 'Resilience, agency and coping with hardship: Evidence from Europe during the Great Recession', *Journal of Social Policy* 48(3): 547–67.

Dagg, J. and Gray, J. (2015), *Socio-economic practices of resilience: Ireland national report*, unpublished RESCuE project report.

Datta, K., McIlwaine, C., Evans, Y., Herbert, J., May, J. and Wills, J. (2007), 'From coping strategies to tactics: London's low-pay economy and migrant labour', *British Journal of Industrial Relations* 45(2): 404–32.

Duffield, M. (2012), 'Challenging environments: Danger, resilience and the aid industry', *Security Dialogue* 43(5): 475–92.

DWP (2013), *Statistics for households below average incomes*, London: Department of Work and Pensions.

Elder, G. H. (1974), *Children of the Great Depression: Social change of life experience*, Chicago: Chicago University Press.

Esping-Andersen, G. (1990), *The three worlds of welfare capitalism*, Cambridge: Polity Press.

Gray, J. and Dagg, J. (2019), 'Crisis, recession and social resilience: A biographical life course analysis', *Advances in Life Course Research* 42: 100293.

Hardoon, D. (2015), *Wealth: Having it all and wanting more*, Oxford: Oxfam, UK.

Heflin, C., London, A. S. and Scott, E. K. (2011), 'Mitigating material hardship: The strategies low-income families employ to reduce the consequences of poverty', *Sociological Inquiry* 81(2): 223–46.

Henly, J. R., Danziger, S. K. and Offer, S. (2005), 'The contribution of social support to the material well-being of low-income families', *Journal of Marriage and Family* 67(1): 122–40.

Hossain, N., Byrne, B., Campbell, A., Harrison, E., McKinley, B. and Shah, P. (2011), *The impact of the global economic downturn on communities and poverty in the UK*, York: Joseph Rowntree Foundation.

Jones, A. and Murphy, J. T. (2011), 'Theorizing practice in economic geography: Foundations, challenges and possibilities', *Progress in Human Geography* 35(3): 366–92.

Kambouri, N., Marinoudi and S., Petraki, G. (2015), *Socio-economic practices of resilience: The Greek case study*, unpublished RESCuE project report.

Lister, R. (2002), 'A politics of recognition and respect: Involving people with experience of poverty in decision making that affects their lives', *Social Policy and Society* 1(1): 37–46.

Lokshin, M. M. and Yemtsov, R. (2004), 'Household strategies of coping with shocks in post-crisis Russia', *Review of Development Economics* 8(1): 15–32.

Meier, L., Boost, M. and Promberger, M. (2015), *Socio-economic practices of resilience – the German case study*, unpublished RESCuE project report.

Mingione, E. (1987), 'Urban survival strategies', in M. P. Smith, and J. R. Foggin, (eds.), *The capitalist city*, Oxford: Basil Blackwell, pp. 297–322.

Mullin, W. J. and Arce, M. (2008), 'Resilience of families living in poverty', *Journal of Family and Social Work* 11(4): 424–40.

Piirainen, T. (1997), *Towards a new social order in Russia: Transforming structures and everyday life*, Aldershot: Dartmouth.

Promberger, M. (2017), *Resilience among vulnerable households in Europe. Questions, concept, findings and implications*, Nuremberg: IAB-Discussion Paper, 12/2017.

Rakodi, C. (1999), 'A capital assets framework for analysing household livelihood strategies: Implications for policy', *Development Policy Review* 17(3): 315–42.

Royce, E. (2009), *Poverty and power: The problem of structural inequality*, Lanham, MD: Rowman & Littlefield.

Seccombe, K. (2002), 'Beating the odds versus changing the odds', *Journal of Marriage and the Family* 62(4): 384–94.

Şengül, H. T. and Aytekin, E. A. (2015), *Socio-economic practices of resilience: Report on Turkey*, unpublished RESCuE project report.

Sherman, J. (2006), 'Coping with rural poverty: Economic survival and moral capital in rural America', *Social Forces* 85(2): 891–913.

Stockhammer, E. (2015), 'Rising inequality as a cause of the present crisis', *Cambridge Journal of Economics*, 39(3): 935–58.

Trussell Trust (2016), *Primary referral causes in 2015–2016 to Trussell Trust Foodbanks*. Available at: https://www.trusselltrust.org/what-we-do/ (accessed 3 October 2018).

Vuojala-Magga, T., Vola, J. and Tennberg, M. (2015), *Socio-economic practices of resilience: Finland national report*, unpublished RESCuE project report.

Wallace, C. (2002), 'Household strategies: Their conceptual relevance and analytical scope in social research', *Sociology* 36(2): 275–92.

Wódz, K., Nowalska-Kapuścik, D. and Mandrysz, W. (2015), *Socio-economic practices of resilience: Poland national report*, unpublished RESCuE project report.

7. Cultural aspects of resilience from the perspective of everyday practices of households affected by economic crisis

Monika Gnieciak and Kazimiera Wódz

INTRODUCTION

The focus of this chapter is on cultural practices undertaken by resilient households affected by economic crisis. In the following, we present the ways in which the resources of knowledge, values, and life skills were used as tools in coping with a crisis situation in the investigated households. The analysis closes with a discussion of conditions that make it possible to effectively use the types of capital available to the respondents – in particular, cultural capital – in the process of creating and implementing resilient practices.

THEORETICAL ASSUMPTIONS

Amongst numerous concepts of resilience, we have selected those which emphasise the social dimension of self-supportive measures, allowing for the analysis of social actions in response to difficult circumstances (see Gans 1962; Valentine 1968; Hall and Lamont 2013; Revilla et al. 2017). From this perspective, resilience is understood as a social process within which both individuals and social groups, such as families or communities, respond adequately to a sudden economic crisis in a manner enabling them to simulta-neously maintain and obtain resources needed to sustain their basic standard of living (see Chapter 5 in this volume). As Revilla et al. argue, "[without], doubt, this means that resilience is, above all, related to the consequences of action, which brings ... [one] to the distinction between resilience as absorption, adaptation or transformation" (Revilla et al. 2017, p. 7). Thus defined, resilient practices lead to a specific approach to cultural categories, with special empha-sis on their flexibility and natural disposition to transformation in the face of social change.

The perspective outlined above draws on that proposed by Raymond Williams (1961), a renowned British researcher in culture studies. According to him, culture is "a particular way of life, which expresses certain meanings and values not only in art and learning, but also in institutions and ordinary behaviour" (Williams 1961, p. 41). As a result, culture is a tool with the help of which both individuals and whole communities are able to adapt to changes that are taking place in social reality (Williams 1961, p. 45).[1] This understanding of culture as a repository of practices that enable adaptation to more or less dynamic changes within a social system complements the theory of cultural practices proposed by Michel de Certeau (1984). Cultural practices are connected with any kind of participation in culture, understood as a system of tacit and explicit values and norms which form the structure of everyday activities of both individuals and groups. De Certeau (1984) describes the culture generated within daily life practices as a process of continuous transgression, searching for solutions, and crossing boundaries imposed by social strategies and tactics in the process of adaptation[2] to individual needs. Individuals learn how to use the resources that are available to them so that they can be effective in a new and potentially difficult situation.

This approach to cultural practices is supported by the results of research into poverty. In *The urban villagers*, a classical study on the urban lower-class poor, Gans (1962) defines working-class culture – or, as he prefers to call it, subculture – as "a generally satisfactory way of adapting to the opportunities which society has made available" (Gans 1962, pp. 264–5; see also Valentine 1968, pp. 111–13). Further confirmation for this approach comes from research carried out in Poland in the poorest districts of Upper Silesia (see Wódz and Łęcki 1998; Wódz and Szpoczek-Sało 2014).

The theory of practices – where the categories of rules and resources constitute the structure for actions of individuals participating in the creation or recreation of operational strategy in their daily social lives – was proposed independently by two prominent sociologists: Anthony Giddens (2003) and Pierre Bourdieu (1996). Moreover, Bourdieu's theory of social capital makes it possible to define analytical units to describe adaptive actions undertaken by individuals and groups faced with social change. He categorises the resources accumulated by individuals in the process of acculturation into four domains: symbolic capital (symbolic resources, such as self-esteem and the sense of place in the social structure), economic capital (connected with the accessible financial and economic means), cultural capital (knowledge, norms and values of individuals) and social capital (related to networks and human relations), and demonstrates that, depending on the needs, individuals can draw on their creativity and flexibility to transform resources belonging to one domain into another type of capital, more useful in the process of adaptation to a crisis situation (Bourdieu 1996). This chapter presents this process of conversion on the basis of changes in cultural capital.

Cultural capital, which in certain conditions is convertible into economic capital or/and social capital, may be institutionalised in the form of educational qualifications (Bourdieu 1986, p. 84) and indicates a set of knowledge, skills, and "other cultural acquisitions, as exemplified by educational or technical qualifications" (Bourdieu 1993, p. 14) that a given participant in social life possesses. It is of cumulative character. It is worth noting that the approach proposed by the French sociologist has influenced resilience scholars, who, like Peter A. Hall and Michele Lamont (2013), suggest that capabilities that enable coping with life challenges "depend on access not only to economic resources but also to cultural and social resources embodied in networks, social hierarchies, and cultural repertoires" (Hall and Lamont 2013, p. 14). This is why, in this chapter, we apply Bourdieu's framework to demonstrate how subjects in the sample cases use the cultural, social, and symbolic resources available to them to create various preventive practices that help them face challenges generated by the economic crisis.

The theory of capitals facilitates a perception of the fundamental issue that conditions resilient activities: namely, the fact that resources are also of social origin and are based on ties between individuals, which allows for the transfer of knowledge, information, norms, values, aid and support. Thus, when conducting our analyses, we focused on resilient social practices which enable "subjects and groups to configure and respond to their structural position in the context of norms and resources that structure such practice" (Revilla et al. 2017, p. 8). We used categories of knowledge, norms and values in the sense defined by classical sociological authors. In the case of knowledge, one may talk about the system of opinions and views formed in social consciousness, like, among others, ideology, morality, art and science (Berger and Luckmann 2010[1966]). With reference to resilient activities, one may talk about categories of practical knowledge understood as both institutionalised and informal. Moreover, in this context, practical knowledge implies awareness of social realities and the ability to function in the universe of human relations thanks to accumulated experience (Hayek 1945). Knowledge of this type is difficult to verbalise; thus, it is so-called tacit knowledge (Polanyi 1974). Practical knowledge, according to its definition, is supposed to be applied to routine performance of actions, functions, etc., with the concurrent ability to use them creatively.

For the purpose of this study, values related to knowledge comprise any material or ideal objects to which individuals or communities manifest a respectful attitude, attributing to them an important role in their lives; additionally, the desire to achieve them is felt as some kind of compulsion (Ossowska 1947).[3]One can also define values as conceptions of the desirable that guide the way social actors select actions, evaluate people and events, and explain their actions and evaluations (cf. Kluckhohn 1951; Rokeach 1973; Parsons and Shils 1951; Schwartz 1999; see also Bauman 2012). The notion of value is related to that of social norm, defined as a rule, regulation or behaviour pattern. Norms are rules and regulations determining the morality, customs, and habits of a particular community (Szczepański 1963). "Knowledge, norms and values … manifest themselves in social roles, interpretive patterns, behaviour, communication and practices in their various patterns and ways, being stratified, gendered, but also diversified according to regions, subcultures, ethnicities, and group identities, individuals, and organised actors" (Promberger et al. 2014, p. 32).

KNOWLEDGE AND LIFE SKILLS

"I feel I am in a better position to deal with the crisis because I always lived in hardship. And those who have always lived in hardship, in my opinion, are more able to tackle the crisis than those that were suddenly caught by the crisis. … So, what did I do when the crisis hit? Well, one of the things I did was give up smoking. Because when we are in crisis, we must think where we are going to save … My experience was always running on very little money." (Portugal/F/Rural)

Practical knowledge related to resilience is based on a specific world view, the experiences and biographies of the respondents, the way they comprehend crisis and their place in the social structure (see Bourdieu 1996; Certeau 1984; and Chapters 1 and 2 in this volume). On this basis, we can divide our respondents into two categories (Wódz and Łęcki 2001, p. 239; Tarkowska 2004; see also Dagdeviren et al. 2017). The first category refers to households in which poverty is a long-term phenomenon; it has been part of the household experience for an extended period of time. People from these resilient households know some methods for dealing with problems in times of deprivation; the strategies and practices that they have developed allow them to live at a certain level. The second category refers to households in which a crisis situation is something new and sudden, and poverty is a big change in their life situation (see also Chapter 5 in this volume). In this case, they are going through a dramatic change, a trauma which divides their lives into two halves: "before" and "after" the crisis. Respondents belonging to this group learn resilience practices by gaining knowledge and skills, although this process is very stressful. For them, crisis is not only something new but also something personal. Many respondents from Germany, Ireland, the UK, and Portugal blame themselves for their current life situation. "Household respondents spoke of their 'stupidity' at not recognising the impact of the crisis on their household sooner, of the importance of immediately opening communication channels with creditors to renegotiate debt, and of the difficulty in accepting the transition of their subjective position from worker to welfare recipient" (Dagg and Gray 2016, p. 27). Individuals who belong to the so-called new poverty group painfully sensed the change in their social position following the crisis, which resulted in degradation, alienation and the social isolation of such individuals (Wódz and Łęcki 2001; Tarkowska 2004; see also Dagdeviren et al. 2017). This feeling is combined with a strong sense of loss of prestige and dignity. Sense of guilt combines here with the stigmatisation of poverty; it results from low prestige of occupations, unemployment, or relying on benefits. In contrast, representatives of "old poverty" take this kind of crisis, economic and otherwise, as a fact of life and try to position themselves as best they can to survive it when it happens. So, they concentrate on what they can change instead of worrying about things well beyond their control. As such crises hit almost everybody around them, they do not see their particular situation as something they experience because of their personal weaknesses or vulnerabilities. This might be good for their self-esteem (Şengül and Aytekin 2015).

Knowledge of how to manage crisis is based on so-called life skills, defined as abilities for adaptive and positive behaviour that enable individuals to deal effectively with the demands and challenges of everyday life (Mctavish 2000; WHO 1997, 1999) and, in the case of our research, that are related to everyday struggle with economic deficiency. They might be further described, following Danish et al. (2004, p. 40), as those skills that enable individuals to succeed in the different environments in which they live. Life skills may thus be "behavioural (enabling effective communication with peers and adults) or cognitive (enhancing efficient decision making); interpersonal (assertiveness) or intrapersonal (setting goals)".

Cultural production is related to particular resources: creativity and the ability to improvise. These resources are some of the basic skills that our respondents use in their daily lives. Without having too much money, any repair of domestic appliances, or at least small house renovation, requires resorting to their own efforts and manual skills. The respondents are often in a situation in which they have to act themselves, without using specialist help (plumbing, painting etc.). Thus, in a broader sense, creativity and improvisation refer to planning and management of expenses. In essence, coping with a crisis requires activating different skills which help people to survive. This refers to a set of practices related to thrift and "modest life", such as saving money, the habit of planning expenses, methods of "making ends meet" in an economic sense, and practices such as preparing preserves. People turn to traditional practices and ways of life. In fact, resilience practices often have less to do with inventing new practices and more to do with exploring accessible resources, networks and knowledge. However, this is not to say that such activities amount to the passive exploitation of the accessible resources, as resilient behaviours, also in this case, require from individuals skilful and

creative adaptation of resources when faced with ever appearing challenges
of daily life. The data analysis shows that these traits may be divided into
abilities (traits of individuals, i.e. developed or inborn personality traits that
enable coping with a crisis situation), skills (predispositions to undertake
specific actions based on experience and practice), and capabilities (resulting
from good management of both abilities and acquired skills of the individuals).
Moreover, resilient practices are based on specific transmission of knowledge,
skills, a network of favours and relationships developed within a household
exposed to economic crisis, and the social environment of the respondents.
These relations are based on many norms which help create "safe networks" of
support and knowledge.

Interviewer: How do you help each other in your circle of friends?

Respondent: One can repair printers. The other has some knowledge with computers. The next has a large farmhouse where he is collecting everything. He is good
at carpentry. He is frequently called for this. It works fine .... Everybody looks out
for somebody who can help. Because there is not much to receive from the state.
(Germany/F/Rural)

The principle of reciprocity is based on the assumption that aid must be given
back in the form appropriate for the needs of others and one's own capabilities
(Mauss 1973; Malinowski 2001; Lévi-Strauss 1969). This principle is based
mainly on the rule of exchange of knowledge, favours, and gifts within a social
environment (Gouldner 1992; Blau 1964; Homans 1967). This mode of action
is based on the sense of group solidarity of people affected by economic
crisis (not excluding relations of kinship and affinity). Activities based on the
principle of reciprocity and exchange enhance the sense of personal dignity of
the respondents, while simultaneously influencing the emotional dimension
of their well-being. They also shape an individual's sense of responsibility for
himself/herself and for others (family, friends, relatives, acquaintances).

   Thus, our research has demonstrated that cultural capital is related to particular resources – creativity and ability to improvise. The individuals studied
implement resilience practices not solely by gaining knowledge and skills,
but they also learn how to make use of them in unexpected situations generated by crisis. Activities of this type require skilful management of available
resources. The process of gaining cultural capital in the form of knowledge,
life skills, or information is based on specific social relations defined by the
norm of social exchange and the principle of reciprocity. They are based upon
group solidarity, which leads not only to obtaining resources that are difficult
to gain, but also to strengthening the sense of achievement, which stems from
the experience of being able to influence both one's own fate and that of others.

FAMILY AS A VALUE AND FAMILY VALUES: SUPPORT, WORK, AND EDUCATION

It should be emphasised that the most important support and exchange network is based on family relationships. Family is in the centre of life of our respondents, and it is an important precondition for many practices that help our respondents to survive. As demonstrated in literature and confirmed by our own fieldwork, family is one of the main conduits through which cultural resources are amassed and transferred. It can be understood as a collective unit in which burdens, but also resources and energies, are shared rather than loaned or traded from one member to another (Fennell 2004, p. 1456; see also Folbre 1994). Internal family assistance constitutes the basic source of support for respondents, which can be delivered in the form of emotional and practical support through the acquisition and transfer of skills and knowledge, and through providing a sense of belonging and purpose. Family plays a fundamental role in thinking about the future and planning ahead. The reports have revealed that respondents are careful in determining their plans for the future, which they perceive as uncertain and dependent on factors over which they have no control (Lewis 1966; Gladwin 1961; Sarbin 1970; Tarkowska 2000). They live under the constant pressure of unstable existence, without the worker's identity that provides a sense of security and a chance for development through job and lifestyle. However, all their efforts concerning children and their education seem to be strongly connected with thinking about the future. They take care of the future of their children, and they see it as a chance for change. Thus, assistance inside the family is not balanced, as parents frequently bear considerably larger expenses connected with supporting the family. The older generation is permanently looking after their adult children. As one Portuguese informant remarked:

> "The money just drains away. Some six months ago, [my younger son] wanted €1000 and appeared on my doorstep crying, with a debt to pay. And there I went again … Maybe it's my fault. If I just threw them on the street … But I can't. I am a father and a grandfather and I would never do such a thing [laughs]. … After all those years of hard work, one sees one's children and grandchildren in trouble … Some people just close the door. But I haven't got the courage to do it." (Portugal/M/Rural)

However, it is family that allows individuals to muster resources to face crisis.

> "When we fall upon hard times, we might know it is our friends and family who constitute the important 'safety net' they can rely on apart from social support from the state welfare. It can often be seen in our empirical material, as it is often told, that the family whether or not living in the same household seems to be the first instance

to turn to and the most important basis for emotional stability and confidence as well as for economic or care-related support." (Meier et al. 2015, p. 25)

Therefore, individuals without support, either financial or non-financial (emotional support, recognition, advice, etc.), are in a particularly unfavourable position. This is often the situation of immigrants who have left families in their country of origin. Family is still of overriding importance for them; however, they may not count on their direct support. New technologies, mobile phones, and internet allow immigrants to keep in contact with their families (Madianou and Miller 2011; Peng and Choi 2013); still, they cannot replace direct contact. Therefore, immigrants create networks based on ethnicity or religion, in which they create relationships based on mutually given help (Young and Willmott 1957; see also Wódz and Szpoczek-Sało 2014; see also Chapter 11 in this volume).

Another group of respondents are people who are not supported by their families. Their relationships deteriorate due to dispute, divorce, addiction of one of the household members (or the respondent), etc. Their situation is dramatic because they are cut off from the resources that constitute the foundations of resilience activities. The sense of loneliness and lack of support is particularly severe in such cases. Therefore, people who find themselves in such a position ask their friends or neighbours for help, and social welfare centres may become some kind of substitute for support and care structures.

After family, the second most important category in respondents' lives is work. It allows individuals to provide for the family, but it is also a value in itself. A job is understood not only in professional terms. It implies diligence, permanent occupation, and looking after possessions and family. In the case of the unemployed, any daily occupation, even in the form of voluntary service, gives meaning to everyday life. Thus, a job, both in the sense of a formal occupation and in the sense of the tasks that keep respondents busy, renders their daily struggle with crisis meaningful.

> "[B]ecause my job gives me strength. If I don't have a job, something strange happens to my brain … If you don't have a job, you feel different and stupid things come to your mind." (Poland/F/Rural)

When asked about their future expectations, the respondents said that they wanted to find a good job (sometimes they even talked about their dreams or wishes rather than about an actually planned future). It seems that it is due to this fact that, in the majority of communities, particular emphasis is put on the education of children, which it is hoped will help them find a good job in the future. Exceptions in this respect are Finland and Turkey. In Finland, difficult conditions in the North increase the importance of hard physical labour. In Turkey, among the poorest people:

> "education is not considered as a mechanism of getting out of the poverty trap anymore. ... [S]tudies conducted in the 1960s and 1970s about recent migrants to the city have identified education as the key mechanism of class mobility. This seems to have changed significantly. Granted, some families are still eager to send their children to school with expectations of upward mobility. But the difficulties of covering the expenses as well as lack of enthusiasm on the part of the children are shown as factors preventing them to do so. On the other hand, those few who have failed to find a proper job after receiving a university degree have become a deterrent against keeping children in school." (Şengül and Aytekin 2015, p. 16)

Households invest in education in various research areas, treating it as a necessary element of class mobility. In our respondents' awareness, "there is recognition that formal education is the main tool that will allow their children to climb socially and provide them with better living conditions and life aspirations" (Capucha et al. 2015, p. 7). As John says:

> "We never got to do anything so it would have been nice to give them the opportunities that we hadn't got. That's why I say, that's why I'm adamant to try and keep them in school for as long as I can because, you know, you just sit down and realise what you hadn't got and no matter what you do you have to have your Leaving [Certificate] and your education. It just goes on and on and on, you never have enough education." (Ireland/M/Rural)

The analysis of values of special importance for resilient individuals, the main findings of which are presented above, demonstrates that family is the most important resource for households affected by economic crisis. It constitutes the transferring and enacting framework for cultural patterns, life skills, and knowledge, enabling individuals to cope with hardships generated by conditions of crisis. The habitual skills transferred in the process of socialisation, the emotional and, quite frequently, financial support provide the basis for practices which facilitate coping with crisis. Being employed and able to manage one's time, so that one is able to get involved in activities promoting self-development, not only provides the sense of security in case of unexpected events but also fosters the hope for an opportunity to overcome current difficulties. In the long-term perspective, obtaining knowledge and experience, especially in the context of educating children, is understood as an activity enhancing the prospect of permanent escape from crisis through social advancement.

PARTICIPATION IN CULTURE

Apart from involvement in work and education, another important dimension
of resilient activities is participation in culture. On the basis of data regarding
participation in public cultural activities, the respondents may be divided into
consumers of culture, that is, informants who passively participate in culture,
and active participants in, or producers of cultural events. Both forms of participation in culture can be connected with resilience practices. "Producers" of
culture are creative and socially active people; their cultural resources can turn
into social resources and hence also into economic ones. Passive participants
can also actively learn about culture and look for information they need in the
everyday struggle with a crisis.

Participation in cultural life is based mainly on the principle of cooperation.
Making use of offers of cultural institutions often takes place within some
kind of social grouping and is the source of social relationships for people
with similar interests and hobbies, or who are in the same social situation.
Such relationships, in turn, become a space for building social solidarity and
mutual support. We can find examples of turning cultural resources into social
resources in our reports. For instance, a Spanish urban study draws attention
to:

> "a significant deployment of cultural activities within the public sphere, in cultural
> centres, libraries, theatres, day centres for older people and social services centres,
> as well as specific locations such as the sculpture museum, the music school, con-
> servatory, etc. ... In general terms, these activities come to function as spaces for
> building relationships, meeting with acquaintances and entertainment. Sometimes
> they are ways to get training and education that may help in finding work. The
> courses and workshops they organise provide the space for network expansion and
> consolidation of social resources, as well as being spaces that strengthen the social
> fabric." (Serrano and Revilla 2015, p. 25)

Individual initiatives connected with cultural production are often of economic
character, combining passions and hobbies of the respondents with attempts
to earn money by selling their products or using skills (dancing, acting etc.).
Cultural events in the neighbourhood (e.g. holidays, fairs, festivities) give
them a chance to do so. Such a lifestyle is exhausting; therefore, cultural
activity for most of our respondents is associated with passive leisure. Some
respondents choose cultural content as a source of inspiration for resilience
practices. These can be TV programmes or books on specific subjects, for

example, on agriculture, or non-fiction literature, such as biographies of people who have overcome crisis thanks to their own efforts.

"I started reading books, watching movies about successful people and reading inspiring quotes, and someone in these books said that a teacher will always find a disciple when he is ready." (Poland/M/Rural)

Making use of cultural offerings can take the form of activities verging on the illegal. Madeline, an informant from the UK, watches movies to relax, but as she admits, she cannot afford to go to the cinema, and that is why she downloads them illegally. On the basis of data collected in England, Dagdeviren and Donoghue have shown that, in cases such as Madeline's, even basic forms of participation in culture are limited by the social and economic situation of a household. According to these authors, this situation:

"relates directly to Bourdieu's argument that capitals are interrelated (Bourdieu 1986) – in this case financial resources condition the accumulation and use of cultural resources and the lack of cultural resources could (in some circumstances) restrict opportunities for building financial resources, and therefore restrict the acquisition of resources essential for developing and maintaining resilience. The cultural options for households facing hardship are limited; even if a household wanted to participate more frequently in high culture, for most this simply is not possible." (Dagdeviren and Donoghue 2015, p. 16)

Based on the analysis of cultural practices of the respondents, it is possible to show that there are mutual connections between cultural, social, and economic resources. Taking advantage of the offerings of cultural institutions often takes the form of some kind of social grouping, thus becoming a source of social relationships for people who share interests and hobbies or who are in the same social situation. In this way, social ties and local identities are strengthened. People exchange their experiences and knowledge, as a result of which new ties based on material and non-material exchange are created. Thanks to these links, they can pass on information about jobs or options of resilience activities. Emotional support and sense of belonging are also important. Using public spaces, such as libraries, reading rooms and clubs, may be connected with saving money (e.g. doing homework by the electric light available there) or with access to computers and the internet, as indicated in the Spanish report (Serrano and Revilla 2015). Organisation of cultural events, participation in amateur theatres, or conducting dance workshops may become an additional source of income, but also a source of personal satisfaction and the sense of authorship, as well as an effective method of collecting symbolic resources for individuals, namely, subjective self-esteem and assessment of social position. These mutually interconnected factors are presented in Table 7.1.

The majority of our respondents belonging to the so-called "new poverty" experience crisis in the form of more or less severe social isolation. This is caused by limited time and financial outlays, or the sense of shame related to the current economic situation of their household.

> "We used to go out at the weekends. We would go for a coffee and hang around. We either went by ourselves or with the children. We would go out for dinner and the like. Sometimes we would go to the cinema. This was back when I had a balanced life. Now, I don't even know what a cinema looks like anymore. I don't know what dining out is anymore [laughs]. I don't even know what going out for a coffee is like anymore." (Portugal/F/Urban)

Social isolation is the reason for "dissociation" from sources of knowledge and resilience, plunging individuals into an even more difficult crisis situation. In households with a developed network of social relations based on the principle of reciprocity and exchange, resilience practices and emotional stability were reinforced. Social relations constitute the foundations for the creativity of the respondents; relations based on the norm of reciprocity and exchange enable them to transform their hobby into a job (e.g. do-it-yourself (DIY) activities used to help in other resilient households), while the network of acquaintances enables access to information and exchange of experiences and knowledge. The ability to build social networks and social competences is one of the most important elements in programming resilient activities.

CONCLUSIONS

In this chapter, we focused mainly on the cultural capital constituting a helpful source of resilient activities and practices providing a response to the problems related to the economic crisis. All types of capital (economic, symbolic, social and cultural) are interconnected and of a systemic nature. Activities in one of the resources support the growth of the other ones. This observation coincides with Pierre Bourdieu's theory of capitals, according to which accumulation of resources in one of the capitals has impact on the others (Bourdieu 1996).

It is widely known (see Geremek 1989) and confirmed by our research that, in terms of symbolic resources, poverty is a state of social contempt. The respondents gave examples of unfair stereotypes or disrespect shown by people from their social environment. Poverty stigmatises and deprives people of a sense of self-esteem; it is almost a moral category (cf. Lewis 1966; Tarkowska 2011, 2012; Tarkowska et al. 2003). An individual in poverty, who is unable to meet social expectations concerning their assigned social roles – frequently for objective reasons – is faced with a negative evaluation by society (see Sarbin 1970, pp. 38–46). Efforts that our respondents make in order to independently "make ends meet" and get them out of poverty are

Table 7.1　　*Examples of transforming cultural resources into economic, social, and symbolic resources*

Cultural resources	Economic resources	• Selling products and services (at the fairs, workshops, private lessons etc.);
• Knowledge, hobby, talent, skill; • Organising cultural events (festivities, religious ceremonies, cultural events, for example, performances, workshops, for example dance, music); • Participation in workshops, courses (vocational, training), meetings, local social actions; • Making use of services of cultural institutions (libraries, reading rooms, clubs); • Making use of cultural offerings (cinema, theatre, opera, etc.).		• Additional/ seasonal source of income; • Mutual exchange of material and non-material goods (loans, taking care of children and the elderly, meals); • Saving money (electricity, Internet bills); • Information about jobs; vocational training.
	Social resources	• Overcoming social isolation; • Meeting with people having similar problems; • Exchange of information, services, help; • Positive social identities (e.g. an actor instead of unemployed person); • Strengthening local identity.
	Symbolic resources	• Building a sense of the world and place in it; • Finding the so-called good forms of help strengthening a sense of personal dignity; • Social solidarity; • Sense of authorship.

Source: Wódz et al. (2016).

activities that should provide them with the sense of self-esteem. The basic norms related to resilience are based on the following: the principle of reciprocity, exchange rule, group solidarity, sense of dignity and responsibility. To this one may add three basic values: family, work and education. These values and norms may provide the basis for resilient activities, but also for individuals' self-esteem. This fact is of crucial importance for the initiation of resilient practices. As Gladwin (1961, p. 83) observes, the poor are paralysed by a lack of faith in their own strength and in the meaningfulness of their activities. They do not plan their future, as they perceive it as uncertain, unclear and deprived of any significant point of reference. That is why, among other reasons, individuals from poverty-afflicted backgrounds fail to be successful in areas where the essential conditions for success are persistence and determination, such as education: "the poor are the worst educated social group and simultaneously the group with the smallest interest in becoming educated" (Matza 1966, p. 648). Respondents from resilient households tend to plan and organise the future for both themselves and their children, and they perceive education of their children as a chance for prospective social advancement. These individuals manage their time, that is, the resources they have, either in search of help for themselves, or in order to provide assistance to others.

Poverty not only stigmatises but also exposes individuals to social isolation, and there are numerous reasons behind this state of affairs. The first is connected with the problem of social stigmatisation and shame. It isolates individuals from their social environment and leads to breaking contacts with friends. Those particularly at risk of being stigmatised are immigrants, as this social status alone deepens their sense of isolation and alienation. Another reason is related to the organisation of respondents' lives, frequently revolving around obtaining employment in several places simultaneously. Obviously, the latter refers solely to employed respondents. Chapter 2 and others in this volume have confirmed that various social relations constitute the basis for resilient activities. Social isolation separates individuals from knowledge concerning activities which could potentially enable them to find a way out of the difficult situation and to manage in the times of deprivation. Hence, one of the elementary resilient activities is an attempt to terminate the state of social isolation, also through participation in local cultural life. Relations based on exchange of information and goods and on mutual help constitute the basic link for self-help activities.

Social environment has a decisive impact on the capabilities of the respondents. The conditions obtaining in the district/region of residence influence the scope of resilient activities. Their important element is participation in the cultural life of a community, for example, by making use of libraries and reading rooms (looking for knowledge and patterns of conduct, enhancing the chance of education for children). Workshops related to broadening interests inspire individuals to become involved in creative and preventive activities and, additionally, provide a positive impact on the psychological and emotional well-being of respondents. Co-organisation of celebrations and holidays related to the functioning of the community integrates its members and has an impact on the strengthening of self-help relations associated with exchange of information, knowledge and mutual services. All these aspects allow members of resilient households to function outside the poverty culture. When such individuals engage in various cultural activities requiring persistent and conscious participation, they break free from the daily routine. Apathy, a typical feature of poverty (Matza 1966, p. 469), decreases, driven away by activities leading to participation in the social life of broader communities, thus providing individuals with the sense of belonging and support. The sense of helplessness in reaching the assumed goals, also characteristic of poor environments (Sarbin 1970, p. 38), disappears, and individuals gain a sense of agency. Members of resilient households are willing to take responsibility for themselves as well as for others.

In the perspective adopted here, focused on the social dimension of self-help activities of both individuals and groups which react adequately to a sudden economic crisis (see Chapter 5 in this volume), resilient activities are associated with cultural resources of respondents and their habits related to the management of both time and material and economic goods. They are also associated with the knowledge of prosumption activities, DIY techniques, the use of household appliances, creation of self-help organisations, as well as the use of legal solutions that support resilient activities. Resilient behaviours stemming from cultural capital strengthen the creativity and flexibility of individuals in poverty to an even greater extent. On the one hand, such individuals are able to react ad hoc to the current situation on the basis of available resources. These behaviours are not permanent and tend to disappear as circumstances evolve, but their triggering stimulus activates a permanent predisposition for creative implementation of the possessed knowledge and experience. Additionally, we may also observe far more durable practices supported by values, subject to internalisation and consolidation. By functioning as behaviours rooted in habits, they are transformed into cultural elements and undergo intergenerational transmission, to be assimilated in the course of the socialisation process (Hannerz 1969).

The combination of behaviours based on the listed resources takes the form of a specific self-help *bricolage* (see Lévi-Strauss 1969, p. 30), which, from the resilience point of view, consists in a set of interconnected activities enabling individuals to cope with crisis through the creative use of the existing cultural capital. Norms, values and behaviour models available to individuals and groups through cultural transmission constitute the foundations of daily practices. Thus, we can observe a particular type of hierarchical structure, with the cultural environment providing the foundations for and the source of resources which shape resilient activities in the form of knowledge and skills.

NOTES

1. A comprehensive analysis of emergent elements which come into being in the process of acculturation – and which, in Williams' view, are a response to social change – can be found in a monograph *Restructuring Class and Gender. Six Case Studies* (Wódz and Gnieciak 2012), reporting on the results of the SPHERE research project investigating post-working-class communities.
2. Pulakos et al. (2000, p. 614) define adaptivity as involving the following capacities: creative problem solving, coping with uncertainty, learning new tasks and skills, and changing and developing new procedures in everyday life.
3. Maria Ossowska (ethicist and sociologist) is the author of theoretical concepts related to sociology of morality, a classical branch of Polish sociology, which is concerned with values, norms and behaviour patterns connected with the axiological system of European societies.

BIBLIOGRAPHY

Athanasiou, A., Kambouri, N. and Marinoudi, S. (2015), *Cultural practices in resilient households, Work package 5: National report on Greece*, unpublished RESCuE project report.
Bauman, Z. (2012), *Kultura jako praxis*, Warszawa: PWN [Eng. ed. (1999[1973]) *Culture as praxis*, London: Sage Publications].
Berger, P. and Luckmann, L. (2010[1966]), *Społeczne tworzenie rzeczywistości*, Warszawa: PWN.
Blau, P. M. (1964), *Exchange and power in social life*, New York: John Wiley.
Bourdieu, P. (1986), 'The forms of capital', in J. Richardson (ed.), *Handbook of theory and research for the sociology of education*, New York: Greenwood Press, pp. 241–58.
Bourdieu, P. (1993), *The field of cultural production: Essays on art and literature*, Cambridge: Polity Press.
Bourdieu, P. (1996), *Distinction: A social critique of the judgment of taste*, Cambridge, MA: Harvard University Press.
Capucha, L., Calado, A. and Estêvão, P. (2015), *Cultural practices in resilient households. Work package 5: National report on Portugal*, unpublished RESCuE project report.
Certeau, M. de (1984), *The Practice of Everyday Life*, Berkeley: University of California Press.
Dagdeviren, H. and Donoghue, M. (2015), *Cultural practices in resilient households, Work package 5: National report on the United Kingdom*, Unpublished RESCuE project report.
Dagdeviren, H., Donoghue, M. and Meier, L. (2017), 'The narratives of hardship: The new and the old poor in the aftermath of the 2008 crisis in Europe', *The Sociological Review* 18: 369–85.
Dagg, J. and Gray, J. (2016), *Cultural practices in resilient households in Ireland: NIRSA Working Paper No.84*, NIRSA - National Institute for Regional and Spatial Analysis, Maynooth University. Available at: http://mural.maynoothuniversity.ie/9016/ (accessed 7 October 2020).
Danish, S. J., Forneris, T., Hodge, K. and Heke, I. (2004), 'Enhancing youth development through sport', *World Leisure* 46(3): 38–49.

Fennell, L. A. (2004), 'Relative burdens: Family ties and the safety net', *45 Wm. & Mary L. Review* 1453: 1503–06.

Folbre, N. (1994), 'Children as public goods', *The American Economic Review* 84(2): 86–90.

Gans, H. (1962), *The urban villagers*, New York: Free Press.

Geremek, B. (1989), *Litość i szubienica: dzieje nędzy i miłosierdzia* [*The mercy and the gallows*], Warszawa: Czytelnik.

Giddens, A. (2003), *Stanowienie społeczeństwa: Zarys teorii strukturacji*, Poznań: Wydawnictwo Zysk i Spółka.

Gladwin, T. (1961), 'The anthropologist's view of poverty', *Social Welfare Forum* 88: 73–86.

Gouldner, A. W. (1992), 'Norma wzajemności. Preliminaria', in M. Kempny and J. Szmatka (eds.), *Współczesne teorie wymiany społecznej. Zbiór tekstów,* Warszawa: PWN, pp. 55–90.

Hall, P. A. and Lamont, M. (2013), *Social resilience in the neoliberal era*, Cambridge: Cambridge University Press.

Hannerz, U. (1969), *Inquiries into ghetto culture and community*, New York: Columbia University Press.

Hayek, F. A. (1945), 'The use of knowledge in society', *The American Economic Review* 35(4): 519–530.

Homans, G. (1967), *The nature of social science*, New York: Harcourt, Brace & World.

Kluckhohn, C. (1951), 'Value and value orientations in the theory of action', in T. Parsons and E. Shils (eds.), *Toward a general theory of action*, Cambridge, MA: Harvard University Press, pp. 388–433.

Lévi-Strauss, C. (1969), *Myśl nieoswojona*, Warszawa: Państwowe Wydawnictwo Naukowe.

Lewis, O. (1966), 'The culture of poverty', *Scientific American* 215(4): 3–10.

Madianou, M. and Miller, D. (2011), 'Mobile phone parenting: Reconfiguring relationships between Filipina migrant mothers and their left-behind children', *New Media & Society* 13(3): 457–70.

Malinowski, B. (2001), *Prawo, zwyczaj, zbrodnia w społeczności dzikich*, Warszawa: De Agostini.

Matza, D. (1966), 'Poverty and disrepute', in R. K. Merton and R. A. Nisbet (eds.), *Contemporary social problems*, New York: Harcourt Brace Jovanovich, pp. 289–302.

Mauss, M. (1973), *Socjologia i antropologia*, trans. M. Król, K. Pomian and J. Szacki, Warszawa: PWN.

McTavish, S. (2000), *Life skills: Activities for success and well being*, New York: Lippincott Williams & Wilkins.

Meier, L., Boost, M. and Promberger, M. (2015), *Cultural practices in resilient households. Work package 5: National report on Germany*. Unpublished RESCuE project report.

Nardelli, A. (2015), 'Unsustainable futures? The Greek pensions dilemma explained', *The Guardian*, 15 June.

Ossowska, M. (1947), *Podstawy nauki o moralności*, Warszawa: Czytelnik.

Parsons, T. and Shils, E. A. (1951), 'Values, motives, and systems of action', in T. Parsons and E. A. Shils (eds.), *Toward a general theory of action*, Cambridge, MA: Harvard University Press.

Peng, Y. and Choi, S. P. (2013), 'Mobile phone use among migrant factory workers in south China: Technologies of power and resistance', *China Quarterly* 215: 553–71.

Podsakoff, P. M., MacKenzie, S. B. and Paine, J. B. (2000), 'Organizational citizenship behaviors: Critical review of the theoretical and empirical literature and suggestions for future research', *Journal of Management* 26: 435–62.
Polanyi, M. (1974), *Personal knowledge: Towards a post-critical philosophy*, Chicago: University of Chicago Press.
Promberger, M., Huws, U., Dagdeviren, H., Meier, L., Sowa, F., Boost, M., Athanasiou, A., Aytekin, A., Arnal, M., Capucha, L., Castro de, C., Faliszek, K., Gray, J., Łęcki, K., Mandrysz, W., Petraki, G., Revilla, J. C., Şengül, T., Słania, B., Tennberg, M., Vuojala-Magga, T. and Wódz, K. (2014), *Patterns of resilience during socioeconomic crises among households in Europe (RESCuE). Concept, objectives and work packages of an EU FP 7 Project*, Nuremberg: IAB research report 05/2014.
Pulakos, E. D., Pilakos, E. D. and Donovan, M. A. (2000), 'Adaptability in the workplace: Development of a taxonomy of adaptive performance', *Applied Psychology*, 85: 612–24.
Revilla, J. C., Martín, P. and de Castro, C. (2017), 'The reconstruction of resilience as a social and collective phenomenon: Poverty and coping capacity during the economic crisis', *European Societies* 20(1): 89–110.
Rokeach, M. (1973), *The nature of human values*, New York: Free Press.
Sarbin, T. R. (1970), 'The culture of poverty, social identity, and cognitive outcomes', in V. Allen (ed.), *Psychological factors in poverty*, Chicago: Markham Publishing Company, pp. 29–46.
Schwartz, S. H. (1999), 'A theory of cultural values and some implications for work', *Applied Psychology: An International Review* 48(1): 23–47.
Şengül, H. T. and Aytekin, E. A. (2015), *Cultural practices in resilient households. Work package 5: National report on Turkey*, Unpublished RESCuE project report.
Serrano, A. and Revilla, J. C. (2015), *Cultural practices in resilient households. Work package 5: National report on Spain*, Unpublished RESCuE project report.
Szczepański, J. (1963), *Elementarne pojęcia socjologii*, Warszawa: PWN.
Tarkowska, E. (2000), 'Świat społeczny ludzi żyjących w ubóstwie', in E. Tarkowska (ed.), *Zrozumieć biednego. O dawnej i obecnej biedzie w Polsce*, Warszawa: Typografika, Warszawa, pp. 149–71.
Tarkowska, E., Warzywoda-Kruszyńska, W. and Wódz, K. (eds.) (2003), *Biedni o sobie i o swoim życiu*, Katowice – Warszawa: Wydawnictwo Naukowe 'Śląsk'.
Tarkowska, E. (2004), 'Dawna i nowa bieda: spojrzenie socjologa', *Zeszyty Towarzystwa Popierania i Krzewienia Nauk* 42: 34–45.
Tarkowska, E. (2011), 'Exluded and humiliated: On subjective and relational dimensions of poverty', *Academia* 2(26): 38–9.
Tarkowska, E. (2012), 'Bogactwo i ubóstwo jako problem etyczny', in W. Gasparski (ed.), *Biznes, etyka, odpowiedzialność: podręcznik akademicki*, Warszawa: PWN, pp. 44–52.
Valentine, C. (1968), *Culture and poverty*, Chicago: University of Chicago Press.
Vuojala-Magga, T., Vola, J. and Tennberg, M. (2015), *Cultural practices in resilient households. Work package 5: National report on Finland*, Unpublished RESCuE project report.
WHO (1997), *Program on mental health: Life skills education in schools*, Geneva: Division Of Mental Health And Prevention Of Substance Abuse.
WHO (1999), *Partners in life skills education: Conclusions from a United Nations inter-agency meeting*, Geneva: Department of Mental Health.
Williams, R. (1961), *The long revolution*, London: Chatto and Windus.

Wilson, W. J. (1987), *The truly disadvantaged: The inner city, the underclass and public policy*, Chicago, London: The University of Chicago Press.

Wódz, K. (ed.) (1992), *Przestrzeń – środowisko społeczne – środowisko kulturowe. Z badań nad starymi dzielnicami miast Górnego Śląska*, Katowice: Wydawnictwo Uniwersytetu Śląskiego.

Wódz, K. and Łęcki, K. (1998), 'Nowe i stare ubóstwo na Górnym Śląsku (Ubóstwo w rejonie pogranicza kulturowego)', *Kultura i Społeczeństwo* 1998(2): 73–90.

Wódz, K. and Łęcki, K. (2001), 'New and old poverty in Upper Silesia', in M. Buchowski, E. Conte and C. Nagengast (eds.), *Poland beyond Communism: 'Transition' in critical perspective*, Fribourg: University Press, pp. 239–55.

Wódz, K. and Gnieciak, M. (eds.) (2012), *Restructuring class and gender. Six case studies*, Kraków: Nomos.

Wódz, K. and Szpoczek-Sało, M. (2014), 'Miejscy wieśniacy w metropolii. Przypadek świętochłowickiej dzielnicy Lipiny', *Przestrzeń Społeczna (Social Space)* 4(1): 91–124.

Wódz, K., Łęcki, K., Gnieciak, M. and Dzienniak-Pulina, D. (2015), *Cultural practices in resilient households. Work package 5: National report on Poland*, Unpublished RESCuE project report.

Wódz, K., Gnieciak, M., Łęcki, K., Dzienniak-Pulina, D. and collaboration Ćwikła, P. (2016), *International comparative report on the cultural practices in resilient households*, Katowice: Instytut Socjologii University of Silesia.

Young, M. and Willmott, P. (1957), *Family and kinship in East London*, London: Routledge.

8. Turning points and critical moments in resilient European lives: a biographical longitudinal analysis

Jennifer Dagg and Jane Gray

INTRODUCTION

This chapter develops a comparative biographical analysis of resilience in the lives of Europeans experiencing hardship after the economic crisis, using concepts from the life course perspective in social science. Earlier in this volume, Boost et al. (Chapter 4) argued for an understanding of resilience as a social, historical and developmental process. Resilient practices take the form of patterns of action that mobilize specific resources that have accumulated over time. These resources are found within the wider socio-economic environment, but have also been 'personalized by the individuals in processes related to their history, their socialization and their experience, and have developed in part into knowledge, capacities and patterns of action' (p. 62). In this chapter we examine this 'personalization' of resilience from a qualitative life course perspective, focusing in particular on the processes through which people sought to 'turn their lives around' in the face of severe disruption to their biographical projects.

In the sections that follow, we begin with a brief discussion of the usefulness of the life course perspective for identifying and explaining resilience. We then show how many participants in the RESCuE study experienced the economic crisis as a 'perfect storm' of poorly timed events and transitions that threatened their ability to cope, placing them at risk of sustained 'downward' life trajectories. We then analyse narratives of 'turning points', through which some interviewees began to redirect their lives in response to this accumulation of hardship. We show how participants often described these processes as 'critical moments' when they struggled to adjust their identities in ways that restored a positive sense of anticipation. We argue that resilience often entails a significant transformation of social identity that requires time and space for individuals to accomplish, but which also has consequences that resonate across communities and societies. Finally, we insert a note of caution into scholarly debates about resilience through a discussion of how turning points and critical moments are always 'intermediate outcomes' (Abbott 2005, p. 2) and 'provisional identity claims' (Holland and Thomson 2009, p. 464) within lives as lived.

A LIFE COURSE PERSPECTIVE ON RESILIENCE

The life course perspective in social science provides an elaborated conceptual toolkit for capturing the complex interplay between social life pathways, changing historical and social contexts and the development of individual lives over time. Glen Elder Jr. first laid out five broad principles that subsequently guided an ever-increasing volume of multi-disciplinary research within the paradigm (Elder 1994,1998). More recently, a number of leading authors have sought to develop a more comprehensive and integrated theoretical foundation for life course research (Bernardi et al. 2019; see also Levy and Bühlmann 2016). For the purposes of this chapter, we will be focusing on three key concepts – *trajectories, turning points* and *anticipation.*

Trajectories can be understood as 'lines of development' (Sampson and Laub 1992, p. 66) that exhibit directionality over extended periods of time. Thinking about lives as trajectories has been especially valuable for demonstrating the dynamics of stress and resources that give rise to vulnerability within biographies, showing how disadvantages arising from past transitions and events may give rise to 'cumulative chains of adversities' that reduce people's capacity for resilience in the face of new challenges (Spini et al. 2017, p. 17). Trajectories take the form of interlocking sequences of *transitions* and *events* across multiple domains (such as work and family) across the life span. The pattern of transitions within a life trajectory comprise four interdependent dimensions: timing, ordering, reversibility and duration (Aeby et al. 2019, p. 52). Thus the degree of 'goodness of fit' between the timing of events and transitions, normative expectations about the sequencing and alignment of social statuses, and wider patterns of socio-historical change, all affect the 'specific resources and patterns of action' (Chapter 4 of this volume, p. 62) that build up over time within life trajectories. In addition, events and transitions may give rise to either positive or negative 'spillover effects' across life domains, with consequences for vulnerability or resilience (Spini et al. 2017, pp. 9–11). Later in this chapter, we show how such spillover effects combined with past life experiences and the effects of economic crisis to create an accumulation of critical life challenges for many participants in the RESCuE study.

In addition to understanding lives as developmental trajectories, the life course perspective also recognizes that biographical pathways can sometimes change direction. These bifurcations are analysed through the concept of 'turning point'. Bernardi et al. (2019, p. 4) define a turning point as: 'A radical deviation or disruption in the trajectory an individual has been on or from one that was personally or socially expected in the future.' This definition recognizes that turning points can only be identified in retrospect and that they entail 'a discontinuity in anticipation' (Bernardi et al. 2019, p. 4). The concept of *anticipation* reflects the emphasis on subjective agency within the life course perspective (Hitlin and Kwon 2016). Anticipation is critical to human agency or 'planfulness' (Elder 1994, p. 6), not only because people make choices in light of their future expectations, but also because it reflects their subjective perception of how much they can affect their own futures (Bernardi et al. 2019, p. 4; Hitlin and Kwon 2016).

Elsewhere we have argued that severe external shocks, such as the recent economic crisis, can overthrow people's biographical projects (Gray and Dagg 2019). In order to turn their lives around – to take actions towards resilience – they must recover a sense of positive anticipation, including belief in their own efficacy, or 'mastery' (Bidart 2019; Hitlin and Johnson 2015). This may require a reconfiguration of their biographical projects, including a change in how they narrate their 'biographical selves'. Within the literature on late modern theories of the self, these subjective turning points have been identified as 'critical moments' – events within life narratives that appear to have consequences both for the shape of individual lives and for their identities (Thomson et al. 2002, p. 339). Critical moments are considered to be 'fateful' in cases where individuals take action to shape their futures in ways that entail a reconfiguration of their identities (Holland and Thomson 2009, pp. 454–5). People's capacities for converting critical moments into fateful ones depends on the resources and resourcefulness to which they have access (Holland and Thomson 2009, p. 458). Below, we describe how our interviewees' narratives of resilient turning points included three shared and overlapping themes: recovery of a sense of agency; unexpected intervention by others; and a reconfiguration of identity often involving the adoption of new ethical frameworks.

In summary, this chapter examines the resilience practices of poor households from a biographical life course perspective. We focus first on how the economic crisis created severe challenges for participants leading to the disruption (Bury 1982) of their biographical projects. We show how the severity of these challenges must be understood in the context of their past life trajectories. The cumulative impact of past transitions, negative spillovers across life domains and the immediate effects of the crisis, combined to create a 'perfect storm' of adversity for many participants. We then turn to an examination of the critical processes through which some people began to reconfigure their biographical projects, recovering a sense of positive agency and anticipation, as they attempted to turn their lives around. While our approach centres on individual biographical projects, it is important to emphasize that, consistent with the life course perspective, we do not attribute resilience to 'random' events or the unique characteristics of individuals. As Abbott (2005, pp. 10–12) has elaborated, individuals are the bearers of an 'encoded historical experience' that at any given moment 'constitutes a set of possibilities and constraints within which various actors must work in the present'. Our goal is to develop a comparative biographical analysis both of the 'assets, liabilities and constraints' that shape people's capabilities for resilience in different contexts and of the 'moment to moment relation in which everything can change'. This analytic endeavour, in our view, is key to an adequate sociological understanding of resilience (Keck and Sakdapolrak 2013). In the next section, we begin with a brief discussion of the methodology underpinning our analysis.

METHODOLOGY

As described earlier in this book, the methodology of this study proceeded through the collection of in-depth interviews with representatives of urban and rural households in nine European and European Area countries. Follow-up, photo-elicitation interviews were conducted with a subset of participants in each country. The criteria for study area and case selection are described in detail in Chapter 1 of this volume. The household interviews included two substantive phases: a biographical interview and a topic interview. The biographical interview began with a non-directive opening question such as 'Could you elaborate your personal history, from childhood to present times?', followed by flexible probing to elicit as rich a narrative as possible. Some country teams incorporated the use of a 'life grid' or 'lifeline' tool to assist participants to recall events and experiences, improve chronological accuracy and as an aid to comparison across cases (Nico 2016; Parry et al. 1999; Wilson et al. 2007).

Following transcription and analysis of the interviews, each country team submitted a national report on *Biographical and longitudinal aspects of resilience* to the research team at Maynooth University in Ireland, which was responsible for this work package. The national reports were written and presented using guidelines provided by the Irish team. Those guidelines centred on the four 'pillars' of life course research identified by Elder (1994) in a classic article, namely: (1) lives and historical times (how, depending on year of birth, individual life paths intersect in different ways with long-term patterns of macro-social change); (2) the timing of lives (how well the timing and sequencing of transitions from one socially defined life stage to another fits with normative, institutional and historical contexts) and the impact of spillover from one life domain to another at key transitions; (3) linked lives (how people experience social change across their lives within the 'small worlds' of family, friends and others with whom they interact on a regular basis); (4) human agency (people's capacity and belief in the possibility of making plans and taking action to shape their futures). This chapter focuses principally on a comparative analysis of the findings submitted under the second pillar – the timing of lives – with its focus on transitions and turning points. However, since each of the four pillars is analytically separable but they are substantively interwoven across individual lives, we also draw on evidence and analyses provided by the country teams under the other three headings.

ILL-TIMED EVENTS AND TRANSITIONS

Life course transitions can be 'ill-timed,' either because they occur at ages or in an order that is not well supported by social norms or institutions within particular historical periods, or because they are poorly synchronized with the dynamics of social change (Elder 1994). People's capacity for resilience may be negatively affected, either because an accumulation of untimely transitions has increased their vulnerability, or because the timing of an external shock coincides with stressful life transitions, often leading to 'negative spillover' from one life domain to another (see Spini et al. 2017). Both patterns of ill-timing occurred within the biographical narratives of the study participants.

Because of their importance for life trajectories, early and out of sequence transitions in young adulthood, such as leaving school, entering the work force and starting a family, may be especially consequential. Recently, however, scholars have begun to identify a pattern whereby the timing and sequencing of early life transitions have become protracted and complex, leading to a growing diversity of 'packages' of transitions (Billari and Liefbroer 2010; Furstenberg 2013; Schoon 2015). In this context, their identification as 'ill-timed' becomes more problematic, to the extent that institutions and societal norms adapt to changing practices. Nevertheless, it is clear that some 'packages' of transitions continue to pose challenges for future life paths in ways that vary by welfare-state regime (Buchmann and Kriesi 2011) and by social class (McLanahan and Percheski 2008). However, research has also demonstrated that, within individual lives, different configurations of transitions do not lead in any determinist way to given outcomes. As Schoon (2015) emphasized, many young people are able to 'turn around' an initially problematic transition. Moreover:

> 'The timetable for when to achieve certain transition markers appears to be variable and depends on the resources available to the individual. Family background, gender, individual capabilities, and preferences play an important role in shaping transition behaviours, and depending on their circumstances, young people have to develop different strategies for successfully balancing demands and resources.' (Schoon 2015, p. 128)

Clearly, from a resilience perspective, it is important to understand the institutional contexts that facilitate diverse pathways and support people's capacity to overcome poor timing in early life transitions within their life trajectories. We must also pay attention to the social timing of later life transitions – notably the transition to retirement. Working-class people and women are more likely to retire early and to retire *involuntarily*, due to circumstances such as ill-health and unemployment, with implications for well-being in older age (Radl 2013).

The themed national reports of the project partners included a range of examples of poorly timed transitions that contributed to people's experience of and adaptation to the crisis. These included challenges to life trajectories associated with early school-leaving, early retirement and, most commonly, early family formation. Amongst Portuguese participants, early family life transitions, together with early school-leaving, often represented the beginning of life trajectories characterized by a pattern of reactive decision-making, that is by urgent responses to circumstances in the context of scarce resources, where the possibilities of alternative routes were already severely restricted (Capucha et al. 2016, p. 39). Early pregnancy is also mentioned as a personal crisis within individual lives in the Polish national report: 'Let's say that I am the cause of my crisis. Of course, I am happy that I have a son, but everything could be different. I gave birth to Kuba when I was 17. I wasn't prepared for this at all' (F, born 1980s, quoted in Wódz et al. 2015, p. 10).

Other cases in the national reports illustrated how the impact of early childbearing and solo parenthood on future well-being varies according to welfare regime and the socio-cultural environment, as well as to the historical period in which the transition took place. The authors of the Finnish national report observed that an orderly pattern of early family life transitions continues to be the norm in Finnish Lapland (Vuojala-Magga et al. 2015, p. 17). Young women have children at an early age, supported by their extended families. Many are single mothers, having freely chosen to leave their husband and boyfriend with the support of their families. In Ireland, the lifetime consequences of early family formation varied considerably by year of birth. Amongst those born in the 1950s, the social consequences of an unplanned pregnancy could be managed if the couple married quickly in the context of the favourable economic climate of the 1970s. Larry (Ireland, M, born 1950s) reflected that, ironically, 'you were able to survive in those days on an apprenticeship and married and with a kid, isn't it mad?' (quoted in Dagg and Gray 2017, p. 27). By contrast, in an example of negative spillover between work and family life domains, those participants born in the 1960s and 1970s faced fewer moral sanctions around non-marital pregnancy, but found themselves negotiating continuing institutional constraints that had consequences for their well-being, especially in the context of growing female labour force participation. For working-class women, in particular, this led to 'early and disorderly' sequences of transitions as they grew up and established their families during the Celtic Tiger era of economic growth (from the mid-1990s to mid-2000s) that in turn affected their capacity to cope with the succeeding economic crisis (Dagg and Gray 2017, pp. 26–8). However, the Spanish national report included an unusual example of how early parenthood enhanced one participant's ability to cope with the crisis by leading to the development of skills she would later draw on when her husband became unemployed:

> '[I]t was a change, a bit ..., because to go from being at home with Mum and doing nothing [little housework] to having my own house, a family, to have to ..., to administering the house, money, being responsible for a husband and a baby.' (Spain/F/born 1980s, quoted in Martín et al. 2015, p. 10)

While early family life transitions had repercussions that accumulated across individual lives, poorly timed transitions to retirement also had significant consequences for some study participants. The economic crisis after 2008 prompted many states to push forward plans for increasing the age at which people became entitled to public pensions (Casey 2012). However, the national report from Portugal provided examples of unplanned early retirement precipitated by redundancy due to age-related physical inability to work, followed by an extended period of unemployment. These (male) participants did not see themselves as unable to work but rather found themselves drifting towards retirement as opportunities for employment became ever-fewer (Capucha et al. 2016, p. 39). The Irish report included an example of planned retirement that, in retrospect, turned out to be poorly timed. Larry (M/born 1950s) saw retirement as an opportunity to address a number of challenges in his life, including reducing the costs of commuting to his newly built home in the countryside. However, he found that his earnings were much more reduced than he had expected and this contributed to a downward spiral in his household finances, making it increasingly difficult for him and his family to make ends meet (Dagg and Gray 2017, p. 32).

As we have seen, ill-timed life transitions do not necessarily lead to sustained downward trajectories. Especially when economic circumstances are auspicious, people can avoid negative long-term consequences, although there are gendered differences in the impact over time of changing patterns of spillover between work and family life. However, the narratives collected for the study revealed how the convergence of 'ill-timed' transitions and other unexpected life events within challenging macro-socioeconomic contexts, including the Great Recession, often generated multiple complications, initiating steep downward trajectories that proved extremely difficult to overcome. There were many such combinations of unexpected transitions and events described within the national reports, but those that occurred most frequently centred on family life, health and employment status.

Changes in Partnership Status

As well as 'out of time' childbearing (discussed above), separation and divorce were commonly reported unexpected family transitions that impacted on people's vulnerability to economic adversity. These transitions are examples of 'reversibility' to previously held statuses within the life course, a pattern thought to be increasingly common in late modernity (Aeby et al. 2019, p. 52). In many cases the framing and consequences of these transitions were highly gendered, insofar as women tended to be in an economically weaker position following separation. (This was a strong theme in the reports from the UK, Poland, Portugal and Spain.) How well participants were able to manage the shock of a partnership breakdown not only depended on the extent of support they received from family and friends – and from their ex-partner – but also on the timing of the separation and on whether or not it coincided with other life challenges. For example, in the UK, one participant's experience of divorce coincided with a period of economic instability in the 1980s, giving rise to an overwhelming fear that she would not be able to cope with single parenthood, leading ultimately to her becoming suicidal (F, born 1950s, in Dagdeviren et al. 2016, p. 13). When separations took place in the context of violent or abusive relationships, often associated with women and children being forced suddenly to leave their homes, the impact of limited capacity for earning was exacerbated. The Polish national report revealed how death of a partner can create similarly gendered challenges for resilience when bereavement is accompanied by financial difficulties:

> 'My husband died one and a half years ago, we took out a loan to buy an apartment, which I have to pay off now. Therefore, by moving to my mom, I could rent my apartment to a young couple. Loneliness was also a reason to come back to live with my mother. I don't have children, I was very emotionally involved with my husband and he died so unexpectedly.' (Poland/F/born 1990s, quoted in Wódz et al. 2015, p. 10)

Health and Illness

The absence of institutional support for individuals and families facing illness was a significant factor inhibiting resilient responses to economic adversity and, as we discuss further below, when the onset of illness or disability co-occurred with other unexpected events during the recession, it created almost insurmountable problems. This problem was especially noted in the reports from those countries most affected by the financial crisis – Greece,

Ireland, Portugal and Spain. A few examples will suffice to illustrate this pattern.

'In Greece, V. lost her job in the recession, but this was aggravated when she was diagnosed with a very serious health problem as a result of which she had to undergo surgery and stay hospitalized for a long period of time. Without the support of her mother, who was in receipt of a pension, V. would have been unable to meet the extra expenses not covered by social security.' (Petraki et al. 2015, pp. 16–17)

'In Portugal, a participant (F, born 1970s) discovered, after a workplace accident, that her employer had failed to make the correct social security payments that would have entitled her to benefits. She sought help from her sister-in-law, who is a lawyer, without any initial success. As a result, she experienced a significant loss of income and is forced to depend on her mother and mother-in-law for financial support' (Capucha et al. 2016, p. 41)

The authors of the national report from Spain noted that:

'Many of the transitions experienced by the interviewees are related to health problems, most notable amongst the males over fifty years of age. It is linked to work history and acts as a precursor to periods of unemployment and early retirement. In this sense there is a severe lack of institutional protection for situations of vulnerability arising from health problems, which further translates into severe inequality from case to case as the capacity to be resilient in the face of such problems depends largely on the personal (and family) resources of the individual.' (Martín et al. 2015, p. 15)

Employment and Unemployment

Next to family transitions, unemployment and other changes in employment status were the most frequently discussed 'ill-timed' events in the national reports. Strikingly, in every country, losing work became a major challenge to resilience when it was accompanied by other problems, most notably illness or disability. In many of the narratives described in the reports, unemployment was experienced at the centre of a 'perfect storm' of income loss, illness and caring responsibilities. One quotation from the Portuguese report depicts vividly the psychological and emotional consequences of the stress that such a combination of challenges can cause:

'At that time, I started crumbling. I started crumbling because my husband was crumbling. I talked to our family doctor about it. My husband couldn't get a job, his unemployment benefit was at an end. He woke at 4 or 5 in the morning. "Oh, go to sleep", "I can't sleep", "But you have to sleep, otherwise you will be banging your head to the walls soon." "I can't sleep. What am I going to do with my life?" It all coincided: my husband breaking, my mother getting ill, I myself failing to get any money – everything was striking me at the same time.' (Portugal/F/born 1970s, quoted in Capucha et al. 2016, p. 27)

In many instances, participants found themselves at the centre of such a storm because of discriminatory or opportunistic behaviour by employers and because state institutions failed to protect them from the fallout of problems arising from ill-health or disability. From the Polish report we learn about the experience of one woman who explained:

> 'Half [a] year ago, [an] aunt of my husband had a stroke and she has become paralysed. Me and my husband took leave to take care [of] her. In the meantime, we wanted to find someone that can take care of her. When I came back to work, after 14 days, my boss told me I am fired … he said that due to [the] disease of my aunt, I will be absent at work more frequently.' (Poland/F/born 1980s, quoted in Wódz et al. 2015, p. 9)

In low-wage sectors and in the context of weak labour regulation, employers can take advantage of employees faced with illness or caring responsibilities, to make them redundant in difficult economic times, or to avoid meeting other obligations.

There were a number of narratives relating the difficulty that formerly self-employed people encountered in obtaining government assistance when they lost their income. In both Ireland and Portugal this emerged as a serious set of challenges to resilience. John felt strongly that the Irish government should have stepped in to help small businesses at the onset of the crisis, and that people going into business should be better informed about the risks:

> 'Take the start of the recession what was the first thing the government should have done? What do you think? Now all the businesses are going downhill, all the self-employed are going downhill, they should have stepped in there with money and maybe a contract, whatever the case may be to try and get it stabilised so it wasn't going as far as it was. There are people, I have mates who come in and committed suicide, friends of mine committed suicide over it which there was no need for whatsoever. If the government only stood in because more or less they were like myself. Their businesses went down, they were hard workers, they had families, they had nowhere to turn, absolutely no place to turn.' (Ireland/M/born 1970s, quoted in Dagg and Gray 2017, p. 32)

In the Portuguese case, some of those who had previously owned their own businesses faced significant loss of income following retirement (Capucha et al. 2016, p. 26).

In summary, the collected interviews show how the impact of the Great Recession was felt through accumulations of unforeseen transitions and events that altered peoples' lives in unanticipated ways, affecting their ability to respond to other life challenges. These experiences not only impacted individual life trajectories, but also their wider family networks and the households in which they live. In particular, people's lives were affected by structural reforms associated with the financial crisis, such as the deregulation of labour markets and austerity policies. Moreira et al. (2015) described how the deregulation of labour markets across Europe, particularly in southern European countries, was associated with changes to employment protection legislation, wage costs, internal flexibility, unemployment protection, collective bargaining and the introduction of active labour market policies. These reforms exacerbated adversity for people who were already experiencing hardship in countries with underdeveloped welfare systems, especially in relation to health care, resulting in severe everyday life challenges and threats to the future well-being of families and households.

Our research revealed how persistent negative trajectories often emerged when people's attempts to negotiate life transitions were met with a complex of individual challenges, such as relationship difficulties (at home, in the workplace or the wider community) or ill-health, together with the financial challenges arising from unemployment or business failure. This convergence of a multiplicity of 'ill-timed' events in individual biographies was particularly prevalent in those case-study countries most affected by the recession – Greece, Spain, Portugal and Ireland. In the next section we describe how some participants strove to convert this storm of crisis events into a turning point that re-directed their lives.

CRITICAL MOMENTS AND TURNS TOWARDS RESILIENCE

As we saw above, 'turning points' are identified as key events or processes through which individual lives take a different direction, either positively towards a more adaptive trajectory, or negatively, towards entrenching a downward spiral. In the discussion of 'ill-timed' transitions above, we have provided examples of how such events led to negative trajectories for many participants in the RESCuE study, especially when they occurred in the context of a 'storm' of problems that contributed to overwhelming economic and emotional stress. In this section we discuss participant narratives of critical moments through which their lives turned in more positive directions. These narratives have a number of overlapping features: recovery of a sense of positive anticipation; unexpected intervention by others; and a reconfiguration of identity often involving the adoption of new ethical frameworks.

Agency: Recovering a Sense of Positive Anticipation

As we described above, life course research prioritizes the concept of agency and 'planfulness' within biographical projects (Elder 1994; Hitlin and Elder 2006; Hitlin and Kwon 2016). However, severe external shocks, such as the global financial crisis, can give rise to 'biographical disruption' (Bury 1982), requiring people to quickly reconfigure interpretations of their past lives and generate new orientations to the future (Bidart 2019). Across the national reports, recovering a sense of agency lies at the heart of narratives relating to critical moments in individual lives. Participants whose narratives displayed a sense of self-efficacy and positive anticipation of the future often expressed belief in their capacity to reinvent themselves through education and training. For example, one Portuguese immigrant participant, who had lost his job but secured qualifications through continuing education, displayed a qualified level of optimism about his future:

'[My project for the] future … is to have a job. And be able to face this 12th grade to open doors to get [into] an institute or something like that where I could do a more [advanced] training. And in the future, even yesterday I was thinking: I intend to translate my diploma in English. If things don't go right, well. And if I have the nationality on my hand, look. Let's see if we follow the Prime-minister's advice! [Referring to the former-PM advice to young unemployed adults to migrate to other countries and find jobs there].' (Portugal/M/born 1970s, quoted in Capucha et al. 2016, p. 45)

For some participants, recovering a sense of agency entailed an initial deterioration in their economic circumstances. For example, women who made the decision to leave abusive relationships often encountered greater economic hardship at first, as well as the emotional turmoil involved:

'I already had put in my head that, however difficult it may be … but I never thought it was so difficult, that this journey would be so painful … I'm living out of my comfort zone. It was to [leave] behind a good car, a good house, a good life and I will leave all that and I'll have to start alone … [S]omething changed in me, I didn't want [it] anymore and I went there battling against material goods, you know? Against everything I believed.' (Portugal/F/born 1970s, quoted in Capucha et al. 2016, p. 43)

Other participants expressed optimism about the future through their hopes and aspirations for their children.

'We're pushing everything to keep the kids right and that's the main thing. If you keep the family right everything else should fall into place.' (Ireland/John/M/born 1970s, quoted in Dagg and Gray 2017, p. 42)

Linked Lives: The Importance of Unexpected Help

A considerable body of research, including evidence presented in this book, has shown how people look for support from the 'strong ties' of family and community at times of adversity. However, recent scholarly research has high-lighted the previously underestimated importance of 'disposable' (Desmond 2012) and 'opportunistic' (Small 2013) ties at times of crisis. Narratives of turning points in our study often included accounts of unanticipated inter-vention by others. Spontaneous help from 'unpredictable' sources – that is, from people with whom participants did not feel strongly bound within ties of mutual obligation – sometimes played a decisive part. Unexpected support came from more distant kin, spontaneously from friends or neighbours, or from public officials and charity workers who took a personal interest in one's case. The Irish national report documented a number of cases in which unexpected help from relatives outside the immediate family circle played a decisive part at moments of crisis. For instance, Seamus described how an aunt of his, who lived overseas, made a critical intervention:

> 'During this period [she] came to visit, she came every second year. When I was really down, she could see there was something wrong, we were trying to hide it so I told her and she said holy Jesus I'll help you. So she gave us the money to pay off [the bank].' (Ireland/M/born 1950s, quoted in Dagg and Gray 2017, p. 37)

The Turkish national report includes an account by a participant whose life was turned around unexpectedly by the woman who became his wife:

> 'In 1996, I opened a textile atelier in Okmeydanı ... My business was doing great for a while ... Then all of a sudden, the crisis swept off us all. It was the crisis of 1998 ... I had to close the atelier. For two years I tried different things such as selling simit [Turkish bread] off the road. Then I got tired and depressed. ... Because I was tired and failed to handle the situation, I ended up in prison for a whole year. In the middle of this big crisis I met my wife. We knew each other before, but we were not in touch. Having learnt that I was in prison, she contacted me and supported me there by sending letters and paying visits. After coming out of prison, we both started working in textiles as the sector was doing well again and both earned quite well for a while and then we got married. I should say she took me from the edge of the cliff.' (Turkey/M/born 1960s, quoted in Aytekin and Şengül 2016, p. 14)

The Spanish team documented spontaneous acts of gift giving by neighbours. For example, one interviewee found bags of food and clothes on her daughter's hanger at school, while another found bags of clothes in her living room that had been passed through the window by her neighbours after a flood (Martín et al. 2015, p. 16). Other Irish participants described unexpected interventions on the part of people with whom they had formal institutional ties. Rachel

(Ireland/F/born 1980s) described how, when she desperately wanted to change her social housing accommodation because of how badly her son was being bullied in the local community, the county council 'were not listening to me at all'. However, her doctor wrote a letter on her behalf and provided 'a big file ... saying we had to get out of there as it wasn't fair on [my son]'. This facilitated her family's move to a more rural setting and represented a turning point in her life (Dagg and Gray 2017, pp. 38–9).

Reconstructing Biographical Projects: Ethical Frameworks

The experience of unemployment often triggered a process of re-configuring the self. Having no networks of support to keep him in London, a UK participant (M, born 1970s) sought a 'quieter kind of life' in a rural area, even though this involved an initial period of sleeping rough. In the Finnish, Spanish and Portuguese reports there are additional examples of people moving (or moving back) to rural locations in an effort to address the challenges in their lives. While this frequently took the form of finding support from families of origin, it also often involved either the adoption of a new ethical framework or the rediscovery of older values.

Ethical framing within positive turning points also occurred in urban contexts, for example where participants prioritized autonomy, dignity or other professional values in their working lives (Ireland, Portugal). In a number of instances across the national reports, the (re)discovery of religion, including new forms of spirituality, was central to the positive reconfiguration of self. In Ireland, Sam (M, born 1970s) described how an accumulation of negative events, including ill-health, relationship difficulties and unemployment, triggered a phase in his life that he called his 'awakening', portrayed in his interview as an upward trajectory: 'Because there were a few things that just made me look at everything differently. I take everything apart now, even my religion, I questioned it, I picked through it and I made more sense of it than I did before' (quoted in Dagg and Gray 2017, p. 35). For one UK participant, the more traditional structures of formal religion provided the means to redirect his life:

> 'Well the big [turning point], the one that's changed the trajectory of my life would be joining the Church, they push you to do stuff which you wouldn't ... I mean volunteering, I mean I volunteered before I joined the Church but volunteering was a biggie if you like because as I always stayed so far in my comfort zone we could be on Mars to do something like that, mixing with the type of people who get in there. And then after joining the Church somebody said "Are you prepared to do any help around the Church? Do you want to serve us?" So the next thing I found myself carrying a cross and serving a long time.' (UK/M/born 1950s, quoted in Dagdeviren et al. 2016, p. 19)

For some younger participants, becoming a parent acted as a fateful moment. In Ireland, becoming a father at age 17 was a positive turning point in James' (M, born 1990s) young life, which had hitherto been on a downward trajectory characterized by problems with school and the recent decease of one of his own parents: 'When my child was born, it was the happiest thing I'd ever felt like, it was the happiest moment in my life. Just seeing the child being born, life changed there and then.' Now James has returned to education, is hoping to find work and is putting a little bit by for his child's future (Dagg and Gray 2017, p. 35).

DISCUSSION

This chapter has explored the different ways in which the trajectories of lives impact on people's resilience through turning points towards the recovery of positive anticipation in the reconfiguration of biographical projects. In our discussion of the timing of lives, we have seen how patterns of transition from one socially defined life stage to another intersect with the dynamics of social change in complex ways. At the level of individual biographies, 'poor timing' and the impact of spillovers from one life domain to another can give rise to varying vulnerability and resilience to shocks such as major economic crises, depending on historical and social context. Our analysis revealed how the historical timing of transitions that are 'earlier' or 'later' than the norm, or that occur in sequences that are less well supported by societal institutions, impacts on people's capacity to overcome the initial disadvantage associated with them. Patterns of vulnerability and resilience are shaped by how the 'dynamics of resources and stress' (Spini et al. 2017) evolve over time within varying social, institutional and historical contexts.

When they occur in the context of growing economic opportunity or when they receive strong institutional support, people are often able to negotiate the challenges associated with 'ill-timed' or 'complex' patterns. However, the 'Great Recession' had a profound effect on many people's lives in the form of multiple severe, unanticipated, adverse events. Our principal finding here is that people are least well able to cope with such shocks when they occur at the centre of a 'storm' of challenges that overwhelm them. Many of the participants in the RESCuE study were not simply coping with economic threats to their standard of living; they were also coping simultaneously with abusive or fragile family relationships, discrimination by employers or welfare officials and, most notably, with ill-health or disability. Working-class and poor people are more exposed to health problems to begin with, due to the nature of their work or their living conditions. The impact of negative 'spillovers' between work and family life domains varied by gender. Several chapters in this book demonstrate how austerity measures that have rowed back on support for health care and on labour market protections have piled challenges on already struggling people in ways that undermine their resilience. Even in countries with relatively well-developed welfare states the systems of support in place do not appear flexible enough to accommodate the needs of people experiencing multiple life challenges, a point that we return to below.

Finally, we examined some of the conditions associated with events and processes that participants identified as positive turning points in their lives. We showed how narratives of such 'critical moments' often included accounts of unanticipated help from unexpected sources and were associated with a reconfiguration of participants' identities in ways that promoted a sense of agency and the rediscovery of self. Accounts of the re-shaping of lives were commonly framed through an ethical lens. They involved taking a stance on doing what is 'right' – for themselves and their families, for the community or the environment.

CONCLUSION

We began this chapter with a discussion of the usefulness of a biographical life course approach to understanding resilience. We have focused on three key concepts from within this approach, namely: trajectories, turning points and anticipation. Through an analysis of the timing of transitions and events in participant life trajectories, we showed how many people experienced the Great Recession as a 'perfect storm' of ill-timed, adverse events that created negative spillovers across their life domains, and a severe risk that their lives would turn in the direction of sustained downward trajectories. People experienced this disruption to their biographical projects as a loss of agency or 'self-efficacy' (Hitlin and Kirkpatrick 2015). We then showed how some participants provided narratives of positive turning points in the face of such critical moments in their lives, often in response to assistance from unexpected sources – that is, from 'disposable' or 'opportunistic' social ties. Consistent with the literature on 'fateful moments', we showed how these accounts of positive turning points incorporated narratives of the recovery of agency and a positive sense of anticipation through the reconfiguration of identities, often in ways that involved the adoption of new ethical frameworks.

Although these narratives are very striking, we think it is important to note that, while such 'fateful moments' may play a decisive part in enabling a turnaround in people's lives, in the sense that they are associated with the restoration of an agentic sense of self, they are often also associated with at least a temporary acceptance of reduced economic circumstances and in many cases depend on critical interventions by others. Furthermore, turning points must always be considered 'provisional claims;' the narratives constructed by researchers and participants always sit within the space between 'life-as-told' and 'life-as-lived' (Holland and Thomson 2009). In most cases people will require either an increase in economic prosperity or a transformation in the institutional environment in order to convert critical moments into turning points towards sustained positive trajectories. From a policy perspective, our analysis provided strong evidence that the de-regulation of labour markets and the scaling back of investment in social protection added to the risk that adverse experiences would lead to sustained downward trajectories by contributing to the accumulation of multiple challenges at the critical moments through which people encountered the crisis. Converting turning points into resilience will require a renewed commitment to social protection, in order to provide people with time to reconfigure their identities, in addition to social investment approaches that can provide the basis for critical interventions.

BIBLIOGRAPHY

Abbott, A. (2005), 'The historicality of individuals', *Social Science History* 29(1): 1–13.
Aeby, G., Jacques-Antoine Gauthier, J. and Widmer, E. D., (2019), 'Beyond the nuclear family: Personal networks in light of work-family trajectories', *Advances in Life Course Research* 39: 51–60.
Aytekin, E. A. and Şengül, H. T. (2016), *Longitudinal and biographical aspects of resilience: Work package 6, national report (Turkey)*, unpublished RESCuE Project Report.
Bernardi, L., Huinink, J. and Settersten, R. A. (2019), 'The life course cube: A tool for studying lives', *Advances in Life Course Research* 41: 100258.
Bidart, C. (2019), 'How plans change: Anticipation, interferences and unpredictabilities', *Advances in Life Course Research* 41: 100254.
Billari, F. C., and Liefbroer, A. C. (2010), 'Towards a new pattern of transition to adulthood?', *Advances in Life Course Research* 15(2–3): 59–75.
Buchmann, M. C., and Kriesi, I. (2011), 'Transition to adulthood in Europe', *Annual Review of Sociology* 37: 481–503.
Bury, M. (1982), 'Chronic illness as biographical disruption', *Sociology of Health and Illness* 4(2): 167–82.
Capucha, L., Calado, A. and Estêvão, P. (2016), *Longitudinal and biographical aspects of resilience: Work package 6, national report (Portugal)*, unpublished RESCuE Project Report.
Casey, B. H. (2012), 'The implications of the economic crisis for pensions and pension policy, Europe', *Global Social Policy* 12(3): 246–65.
Dagdeviren, H., Donoghue, M. and Luz, S. (2015), *Longitudinal and biographical aspects of resilience: Work package 6, national report (United Kingdom)*, unpublished RESCuE Project Report.
Dagdeviren, H., Donoghue, M. and Promberger, M. (2016), 'Resilience, hardship and social conditions', *Journal of Social Policy* 45(1): 1–20.
Dagg, J. and Gray, J. (2017), *Longitudinal and biographical aspects of resilience in Ireland*, Maynooth, Ireland: NIRSA Working Paper No.85. Available at: http://mural.maynoothuniversity.ie/9015/ (accessed 2 September 2020).

Desmond, M. (2012), 'Disposable ties and the urban poor', *American Journal of Sociology* 117(5): 1295–35.

Elder, G. H., Jr. (1994), 'Time, human agency, and social change: Perspectives on the life course', *Social Psychology Quarterly* 57(1): 4–15.

Elder, G. H., Jr. (1998), 'The life course as developmental theory', *Child Development* 69(1): 1–12.

Furstenberg, F. F. (2013), 'Transitions to adulthood: What we can learn from the West', *The ANNALS of the American Academy of Political and Social Science*, 646(1): 28–41.

Gray, J. and Dagg, J. 2019. 'Crisis, recession and social resilience: A biographical life course analysis', *Advances in Life Course Research* 42(100293): 1–12.

Hitlin, S. and Elder, G. (2006), 'Agency: An empirical model of an abstract concept', *Advances in Life Course Research* 11: 33–67.

Hitlin, S. and Johnson, M. K. (2015), 'Reconceptualizing agency within the life course: The power of looking ahead', *American Journal of Sociology* 120, 1429–1472.

Hitlin, S., and Kirkpatrick J. M. (2015), 'Reconceptualizing agency within the life course: The power of looking ahead', *American Journal of Sociology* 120(5): 1429–72.

Hitlin, S. and Kwon, H. W. (2016), 'Agency across the lifecourse', in M. J. Shanahan, J. T. Mortimer and M. Kirkpatrick Johnson (eds.), *Handbook of the Lifecourse*, Cham: Springer, pp. 431–49.

Holland, J. and Thomson, R. (2009), 'Gaining perspective on choice and fate: Revisiting critical moments', *European Societies* 11(3): 451–69.

Keck, M. and Sakdapolrak, P. (2013), 'What is social resilience? Lessons learned and ways forward', *Erdkunde* 67(1): 5–19.

Levy, R. and Bühlmann, F. (2016), 'Towards a socio-structural framework for life course analysis', *Advances in Life Course Research* 30: 30–42.

Martín, P., Arnal, M., Revilla, J. C., Serrano, A. and de Castro, C. (2015), *Longitudinal and biographical aspects of resilience: Work package 6, national report (Spain)*, unpublished RESCuE Project Report.

McLanahan, S., and Percheski, C. (2008), 'Family structure and the reproduction of inequalities', *Annual Review of Sociology* 34(1): 257–76.

Moreira, A., Alonso Dominguez, Á., Antunes, C., Karamessini, M., Raitano, M. and Glatzer, M. (2015), 'Austerity-driven labour market reforms in southern Europe: Eroding the security of labour market insiders', *European Journal of Social Security* 17: 202–25.

Nico, M. L. (2016), 'Bringing life "back into life course research": Using the life grid as a research instrument for qualitative data collection and analysis', *Quality & Quantity* 50(5): 2107–20.

Parry, O., Thomson, C. and Fowkes, G. (1999), 'Life course data collection: Qualitative interviewing using the life grid', *Sociological Research Online* 4(2). Available at: http://www.socresonline.org.uk/4/2/parry.html (accessed 2 September 2020).

Petraki, G., Kambouri, N., and Marinoudi, T. (2015), *Longitudinal and biographical aspects of resilience: Work package 6, national report (Greece)*, unpublished RESCuE Project Report.

Radl, J. (2013), 'Labour market exit and social stratification in Western Europe: The effects of social class and gender on the timing of retirement', *European Sociological Review* 29(3): 654–68.

Sampson, R. J. and Laub, J. H. (1992), 'Crime and deviance in the life course', *Annual Review of Sociology* 18: 63–84.

Schoon, I. (2015), 'Diverse pathways: Rethinking the transition to adulthood', in P. R. Amato, A. Booth, S. M. McHale and J. V. Hook (eds.), *Families in an era of increasing inequality*, Cham/Heidelberg/London/Dordrecht/New York: Springer International Publishing, pp. 115–36.

Small, M. L. (2013), 'Weak ties and the core discussion network: Why people regularly discuss important matters with unimportant alters', *Social Networks* 35(3): 470–83.

Spini, D., Bernardi, L. and Oris, M. (2017), 'Toward a life course framework for studying vulnerability', *Research in Human Development* 14(1): 5–25.

Thomson, R., Bell, R., Holland, J., Henderson, S., McGrellis, S. and Sharpe, S. (2002), 'Critical moments: Choice, chance and opportunity in young people's narratives of transition', *Sociology* 36(2): 335–54.

Vuojala-Magga, T. Vola, J. and Tennberg, M. (2015), *Longitudinal and biographical aspects of resilience: Work package 6, national report (Finland)*, unpublished RESCuE Project Report.

Wilson, S., Cunningham-Burley, S., Bancroft, A., Backett-Milburn, K. and Masters, H. (2007), 'Young people, biographical narratives and the life grid: Young people's accounts of parental substance use', *Qualitative Research* 7(1): 135–51.

Wódz, K., Faliszek, K. and Nowalska-Kapuścik, (2015), *Longitudinal and biographical aspects of resilience: Work package 6, national report (Poland)*, unpublished RESCuE Project Report.

9. Gender regimes in vulnerable households during the recession – what has changed and what not?

Concepción Castrillo, Mª Paz Martín, María Arnal and Araceli Serrano

INTRODUCTION

This chapter focuses on the relationship between gender and resilience in households strongly affected by the economic crisis and subsequent recession of the last decade. More specifically, in the first section the aim is to analyse the ways in which different *gender regimes* in the households studied helped or hampered their capacity to overcome hardship during this period, while the second section explores the ways in which different coping styles and the strategies set in motion to overcome difficulties in turn influenced gender relations at the household level, shaking up existing gender orders.

The basic concept that forms the starting point for our analysis is that of *gender regime*, as conceptualised by Connell (1987, 2009). According to this author, there is a historically constructed *gender order* which hierarchically structures gender relations in different domains, in both the public and private spheres. In addition to this general order, there are also *gender regimes*, which constitute this structure of hierarchical relations in smaller, more specific domains, such as individual households, for example. At this micro-social level, gender regimes sometimes reproduce and sometimes differ from the more general dynamics of existing gender orders (Connell 2009, p. 73).

This chapter focuses on household *gender regimes* and the ways in which they may affect and be affected by the household strategies put in place to overcome hardship. A number of different elements were used to frame the gender relationships in the households studied: how the household is organised (in relation to the diversity of different family structures), the distribution of the workload, the time employed and activities carried out by individuals within the employment–reproductive work binomial, and caregiving provided to other members of the household and/or community.

It is important to remember that household *gender regimes* are affected not only by internal household dynamics, but also to a large extent by the welfare state in which the household exists, namely its corresponding *care regime* (Bettio and Plantenga 2004), both of which have a strong impact on these internal dynamics. The countries compared in this chapter[1] are characterised by the diversity of their gender arrangements (Pfau-Effinger 1998), which gender orders and cultural elements. In the ex-socialist countries studied (East Germany and Poland), while much progress has been achieved in terms of women's entry into the labour market (even though they still tend to occupy junior positions in their corresponding companies), inequalities continue to exist in relation to household and care work (Kaminsky 2016; Boost et al. 2016). Northern (Finland) and central European (Germany) countries, along with the United Kingdom, have achieved higher rates of male involvement in the home (care tasks). Countries with a Catholic tradition (Ireland), Mediterranean countries (Spain, Portugal and Greece, in this order) and Turkey, all of which have a more family-based care regime, continue to report high levels of gender inequality in both the labour and domestic spheres (Ollo and Goñi 2019).

We shall now briefly analyse how the recession has affected gender relations in the European countries studied, before exploring the two-way relationship which exists between gender regimes and households' capacity to overcome hardship.

GENDER, CARE AND EMPLOYMENT DURING THE RECESSION

Most of the literature on the effects of the recession on gender relations analyses these trends from a macro-social and quantitative perspective, focusing mainly on public policies and employment. Studies carried out at a household level from a qualitative perspective are scarcer. We found few studies that analysed the relationship between household capacity, practices and strategies for overcoming hardship and *gender regimes*, or which examined how these practices and strategies may 'shake up' pre-existing *gender orders*.

Recessions and periods of change may constitute an opportunity for transformation and a move towards greater equality; however, they may also trigger regressions (Enloe 2013). From the perspective of employment, and in relation to the last economic crisis, the gender segregation of the labour market in general protected women during the subsequent recession, since large-scale job losses mainly occurred in masculinised industries and sectors. Nevertheless, during the austerity period, this segregation affected women more intensely than men, since the sectors that suffered most were those involved in the public provision of services and care, which are more feminised (Karamessini and

Rubery 2014, p. 324). Moreover, it is important to remember that austerity policies affected women not only in their capacity as employees, but also as users of and substitutes for social services (Gálvez 2013).

In addition to the above, gender equality policies have gone from being an integral part of employment strategies prior to the recession, to being relegated so far to the sidelines as to have become almost invisible (Karamessini and Rubery 2014, p. 333), both in the European Union (EU) as a whole and in its constituent member states (Villa and Smith 2014; Kantola and Lombardo 2017).

The impact of the recession and its consequences for women differ substantially between the different regions of Europe, being less severe in countries with a stronger tradition of equality policies, such as the Nordic states, and harsher in southern European countries, whose welfare states follow the Mediterranean model, characterised by heavy reliance on the family (Salido 2016). In countries in which the gender order is not firmly rooted in the dual earner model, policies and services which seek to promote gender equality are more likely to have come under greater threat during the recession (Rubery 2014; Távora and Rodríguez-Madroño 2018).

Some studies argue that the recession has resulted in an intensification of women's workload since it has increased their participation in the labour market (particularly among working-class and older women),[2] while at the same time intensifying their care work, due to the fact that, as mentioned earlier, cutbacks in public spending on social services affect women much more than men (Gálvez 2013, pp. 93–4; Walby 2015). Indeed, some survival strategies set in motion by families consist precisely of intensifying the work carried out by their female members, resulting in a 're-privatisation' of care and 'responsibility for life' (Gálvez 2013: 95). The privatisation of care and domestic work is particularly clear in households in which one or all of the adults are unemployed, since they have less resources to pay for these services, coinciding (temporarily at least) with cutbacks in the public provision of services (Briales 2015).

Prior to the recession, the configuration of gender relations in the home environment had a major influence on the distribution of productive and reproductive work since, in clearly unequal households, structural hierarchies were further compounded by intra-household inequalities (González de la Rocha and Grinspun 2001). In households characterised by more rigid gender arrangements, when women are unemployed, the norms of common-sense dictate that it is only logical for them to spend more time on care-related tasks, since they are not working outside the home. However, this situation is accompanied by an individualised sense of unease, along with a certain degree of ambivalence and feelings of guilt. In the same context, unemployed men resist taking on a more active role in the domestic sphere, and the conflict generated by their new situation is often shifted to their relationship with their spouse (Briales 2015). In households which had a more flexible gender arrangement prior to the recession, the fact of the male partner losing his job may trigger a questioning of assigned roles, as well as the assumption of a more engaged type of fatherhood in relation to care (Roy 2004).[3]

In those contexts in which the recession prompted previously 'inactive' women to enter the labour market, this change is often accompanied by a somewhat positive evaluation of their new situation and a shift in their con-ception of family gender roles; while for those women already in paid employ-ment, the recession may serve to reinforce their perception of their job as vital to the household economy and to strengthen their conviction of the importance of their financial independence (Távora and Rodríguez-Madroño 2018).

GENDER REGIMES IN HOUSEHOLDS IN HARDSHIP

Gender and Households' Capacity to Overcome Hardship

Prior to the recession, in almost all cases, the men in the households examined for this chapter were the breadwinners and based their identity to a large extent on the fact of having a job. In the case of women there is more diversity, although, in general, they tended to combine their role as the principal carers in the domestic sphere with different types of relationship with paid employ-ment (equal breadwinner with their male partner, part-time employment taken voluntarily or involuntarily in order to ensure compatibility with their care responsibilities, sporadic or informal employment and, in some cases, volun-tary withdrawal from the labour market in order to raise a family). In a small number of participating households, prior to the recession the female partner was the main breadwinner while the male partner was unemployed.

The different ways in which households are organised in terms of gender are strongly influenced by 'gendered moral rationalities' (Duncan and Edwards 1999) and the opportunities offered by different institutional contexts for both employment and the organisation of care. They are also impacted by other elements pertaining to the life histories of their members. Households' prior gender organisation was found to affect their capacity to overcome hardship during the recession. We shall now examine some examples of particularly significant types of households in the study, in terms of resilience.

One highly significant case is that of *single-parent households*. In all countries participating in the project, these types of household (mainly formed by women with at least one minor in their care) are the most vulnerable and experience the greatest difficulties overcoming hardship.[4] In addition to being more financially vulnerable, the adults in these households also find it harder to reconcile the demands of work and family responsibilities, which means that their ability to overcome hardship depends more on institutional support or other informal networks of friends and family.

Another example of a less resilient type of household is those with *traditional and inflexible gender regimes*. These regimes not only have a negative impact on women's autonomy and power, they also hamper the household's ability to overcome hardship. Inflexible female roles mean that women are less available for employment, in a context in which women's employment, even if precarious, is often indispensable in order to counteract falling salaries or male unemployment, particularly in working-class families.[5] For their part, inflexible male roles are accompanied by greater reticence to assume responsibility for the additional care burden imposed by reduced income, thereby preventing effective reconciliation of work and family demands and making conflict within the household more likely (Briales 2015). Among the vulnerable households participating, the second trend was found more frequently than the first, as we found more cases of men who were reticent to take over domestic and care tasks in the home than women reticent to engage in paid employment. Furthermore, the reluctance observed in some households in relation to women going out to work had more to do with the problems involved in paying someone else to do the domestic and care tasks they had previously performed free of charge than with strictly traditional ideologies or habitus.

A third example was found in Finland. This country, whose report reflected a more diverse kind of household composition, offers some interesting examples of *household organisation beyond the nuclear family*, which offer a greater range of possibilities and strengths for coping with difficulties. For example, one informant (Finland/F/mid 30s) reported living in two households, one together with her partner and his extended family within a reindeer herding community, and her own single-person household. This enabled her to occupy different positions and gender roles. Whereas in the first household she occupied a more traditional role within a rural, subsistence economy, having her own individual household and a job outside the herding community enabled her to maintain other networks outside the family and community ones and to maintain her autonomy and financial independence (Vola and Tennberg 2016, p. 9).

Shaking Up the Gender Order: The Consequences of Resilience Strategies for Gender Relations at Home

There were three types of consequences of resilience strategies for gender relations at home. The first is related to female habitus and care practices. The second has to do with gender roles at home as a consequence of unemployment. Finally, the third relates to the reorganisation of households and support networks.

Taking the lead: female habitus as a tool for resilience
In the first place, female habitus was a tool for resilience. As outlined in the
different national reports, the strategies employed by households in hardship
to overcome their problems are frequently based on women's overburdening
and self-sacrifice (this is the case particularly in Spain, Greece, Portugal and
Germany). In periods in which social vulnerability affects broader swathes
of society more deeply, as it has done over the last decade as the result of the
recession, the activation of women's disposition to care may help families
survive, but it often comes at the cost of their health and wellbeing. Households
are not harmonious units of totally homogeneous interests, and neither are they
without hierarchies and power dynamics (sometimes less and sometimes more
explicit, and sometimes simply the result of inertia).

The discourses of women in vulnerable households with dependent minors
are largely articulated around their own actions to ensure their children's
wellbeing and the distress that is generated as a result of this. They are also
frequently linked to the frustration felt as a result of not being able to give them
everything they think they should.

This type of discourse is fundamental for constructing the figure of the 'courageous mother', a mother willing to sacrifice everything and employ any kind
of strategy necessary to ensure that her children's needs are met.

> 'It is like you've already sold everything, but for my child I'd sell anything I had to.
> Even if I had to go out and start stealing, I wouldn't hesitate, I'd do it in a flash. My
> children will have no unfilled needs.' (Spain/mother of four children/unemployed)

The prominence of the protective woman-mother figure in times of crisis takes
different forms and is organised around different dimensions of care. These
include direct material care (identified in Portugal), the orchestration of care
through the activation of networks and relationships with other stakeholders
within the household's immediate environment (Spain, Germany) and emotional care (Spain, Ireland).

The first of these dimensions implies everyday actions *prioritising the
wellbeing of the family, and particularly that of children* (at least in terms
of nutritional sufficiency). In cases of more severe financial hardship, direct
material care manifests as *privation* strategies, or, in other words, in mothers
renouncing their own needs in order to satisfy those of their children. Self-care
is relegated to second place, and the emphasis is firmly on protecting the most
vulnerable members of the household, particularly children:

> 'If I and my [older] daughters don't have butter, we'll eat a simple piece of toast,
> dipped in coffee, and that's it. But I can't tell my son: "Look, I made some toast with
> coffee – eat it!". … I must always think about having food for him. Because he is the
> youngest and the most fragile and we all have to protect him. I can't let him become

aware [of our difficulties]. We can't afford a nice steak with chips and an egg on top for us – but, for him, we cannot let him down. It is important that he has an adequate diet. The food bank helped me with cereals and cookies for him. They sent milk and instant cereal. I managed to balance it out. If I don't have milk, I'll drink coffee. But for him, there must be plenty.' (Portugal/mother/late 30s/urban area)

The second dimension of female prominence in the field of family care is the *activation of assistance networks and resources in the local environment.* As observed in the households participating, women are the principal liaisons with different stakeholders who can fulfil the role of support network and provide occasional help in the event of a pressing need. These tasks correspond to the management of and mediation with other institutions and social stakeholder dimensions and form part of reproductive work (Carrasquer et al. 1998).

The stakeholders contacted vary widely, ranging from extended family, friends and acquaintances (such as neighbours and people living nearby, teachers and other parents at the children's school) to religious aid organisations, lay and/or self-managed associations and public social services. Although the relative weight of each of these different types of stakeholder/resource varies between the diverse institutional and cultural contexts of the participating countries, one common element is that households tend to use different combinations of them, rather than just one. Help provided by religious charity organisations is present in the discourses of many interviewees, particularly as a result of the deficiencies of the public social services, which were further affected by the cutbacks made as part of the austerity drive.

Physically turning up at the places where help is provided implies having previously gathered information about them and identified the resources available to meet the needs of different members of the household. It also implies remaining alert to any changes in those needs. All this constitutes an area of household care that is usually the responsibility of women and which is linked to planning and the global perspective (Hochschild and Machung 2012), tasks which are particularly invisible and add to the mental burden of care.

Furthermore, in vulnerable contexts which require external aid, this activation of resources frequently involves a certain amount of shame linked to the household's inability to comply with the social norm of financial independence. As explained in the German case (Boost et al. 2016), women are better able to overcome and cope with these feelings of shame because, as one interviewee explained, shame is a 'luxury' that those in need simply cannot afford. This trend was also identified in Spain. Martín and Arnal (2016) highlighted the fact that this role of 'super mum' or 'courageous mother' also implies a great deal of emotional work, in the sense in which Hochschild uses the term (1979). In other words, it obliges women to manage and regulate their own emotions in order to adapt them to social norms. In this case, they must work to overcome feelings such as sadness or shame, which do nothing to help the family struggle through.

The third dimension in which the prominence of female care is evident in families in hardship is linked to *emotional care*. Regulating one's own emotions (mentioned above) tends to be a component of (or at least is closely connected to) another type of emotional work carried out by women, which manifests in dealing with other people's feelings (James 1989, p. 15) and taking emotional care of others (Duncombe and Marsden 1993). This type of care is particularly important in those households in which the male partner is unemployed. The association between employment and masculinity (Morgan 1992) and the pre-eminence of the role of breadwinner for the masculine identity often generates disruptions to the expectations and social positions of men during times of recession, resulting in severe emotional distress that only serves to compound the already pressing financial difficulties experienced by these households. Women frequently act as emotional buffers for men in these situations, as illustrated in the case of the informant quoted below, who explains how he only managed to carry on thanks to the help and support provided by his wife:

> 'So, at Christmas time … we had no money, we had nothing and the building society was banging on the door and I went down to the Social Welfare Office in [name of town] and told her my story. At this stage now I was going through clinical depression because the doctor was treating me and I was on these [medication], and only for my wife I probably would have committed suicide.' (Ireland/father of two/ part-time worker)

As mentioned earlier, emotional care of others tends to be combined with work on one's own emotions. In this sense, a trend can be identified in relation to the female disposition to hide one's own distress as a means of protecting others or preserving harmony in households in extremely precarious situations. In such cases, women become buffers for the distress felt by other members of the household, a role which renders their own distress invisible:

> 'I think as well, sometimes especially in a family situation, the wife might be car-rying most of the burden and doesn't want to worry the husband, the kids. And you will go on your visitation and there would be this off load of distress ….' (Ireland/ expert)

All these dimensions of care in which women take on a leading role in contexts of vulnerability turn them into *tools* for resilience, and imply the use of strategies for coping with difficulties that may result in overburdening and have a negative impact on their emotional and physical wellbeing.

Gender (dis)arrangements as a response to unemployment

Among one subgroup of participating households an unintended change occurred in gender positions within the employment/care relationship. This change mainly occurred in households in which women became the principal breadwinners, while men (who were unemployed) were forced to take on more responsibility in the domestic sphere. This in turn implied the transformation of certain practices, although it did not necessarily involve a change in the symbolic gender order, and nor did it automatically give rise to greater equality.

Across the countries investigated, different situations and positions were observed in those households in which such a change had taken place. For many women, being in paid employment had already become vital to their identity and wellbeing prior to the recession. However, among those who found themselves 'pushed' onto the labour market by the recession or as a result of their male partner being made redundant, some claimed that the new situation proved an 'awakening'.[6] Nevertheless, the extreme precariousness of the conditions in which these women join or re-join the labour market often severely limits both their autonomy and their subjective wellbeing in this new situation. On many occasions, women are forced to accept informal jobs in extremely precarious feminised sectors – working, for example, as domestic employees or carers of elderly or dependent people, a circumstance that merely exacerbates their perception of injustice and exploitation.

As men are concerned, they were generally found to develop one of two stances or attitudes in response to this potential change in roles. The first is what could be termed an attitude of 'silent counterrevolution'. This is the stance adopted by men for whom being unemployed has a strong emotional impact, and who (as mentioned above) become new subjects in need of care. This type of situation prevents a more stable transformation in gender roles which would result in their greater involvement in domestic and care tasks. It is also a position supported by a high degree of social consensus regarding the fact that men suffer more than women during a recession, as well as the aforementioned 'invisible' nature of women's distress, both of which are reflected in discourses such as the one below:

> 'Yes, it has been harder on him than on me. Because a man, you know, has to take care of his family, so it's harder. You have to recognise that.' (Spain/mother of two/ rural area)

The second stance observed among men in this type of situation is characterised by a greater involvement in care tasks. Different examples of this were found in various participating countries. One paradigmatic case is that of a household in Finland in which the unemployed male partner became the main caregiver, not only of the nuclear family itself, but also of certain members of the extended family and other members of the community. In addition to mitigating certain aspects of gender inequality, this also prevented the man himself from feeling isolated and socially excluded.

Nevertheless, certain inequalities were also found in predominantly male and female care models. When men become more actively engaged in care, they often tend to perform one-off activities, rather than take over routine daily tasks. Moreover, many see their involvement in this sphere as something that will cease as soon as they find a job. Therefore, even in these situations, one cannot really talk about stable transformations:

> 'He's not affected now I don't think, he just hates sitting at home. He's a lad that likes to be on the go the whole time. He loves the kids, he loves staying at home with the kids but if there's any work to be had he'd be out there doing it.' (Ireland/ mother of 3/rural area)

This auxiliary nature of men's involvement in caregiving is evident also in women's discourses, even in those cases such as the one quoted below. At the moment of the interview, the man's long-term situation of unemployment had still not served to consolidate equality in the domestic sphere, and his role was still viewed as that of 'helping' the main caregiver (i.e. the woman):

> 'When he worked, you know? Well, he'd come home at night and couldn't help me. I had to do everything. And then, when he lost his job, well he has helped since then, at least with the girls. He takes them to school, and if I have to go out, well he's there for them. I don't have to worry. He'll pick them up for me if I can't make it. And I do the same for him.' (Spain/mother of three/migrant)

Simultaneously with this potential (although, as we have seen, limited) change in roles triggered by male unemployment during the recession, a counter movement also developed which sought to reinforce the existing status quo. This counter movement, which consists of a trend towards intensifying male work and 're-domesticating' women, is linked to both unemployment and the fact that the jobs women find are often temporary, intermittent and/or poorly paid, and are therefore 'not really worth it' for the households in question. Indeed, when both members of the couple making up the nuclear family are unemployed, priority is generally given to the man finding a job. The preference for male over female work is partially explained by practical reasons linked to the habitual salary gap in favour of men (Távora and Rodríguez-Madroño 2018), and should also be understood within the general framework of social tolerance for female unemployment (Torns 2000) and the consideration of female work as an 'auxiliary' measure in moments of crisis (Gálvez 2013), which is often located on a continuum somewhere between formal and informal employment (Williams 2009; Torns and Recio Cáceres 2012). Many households do not consider it 'worthwhile' for women to work, since, due to the poor conditions they are often forced to accept (temporary, informal and part-time employment), the money coming in does not compensate for that which must be spent paying someone else to do the care tasks they themselves would otherwise do free of charge. Although this situation is perhaps more common in southern European countries, it exists also in some of the stronger welfare states (Williams 2009), as shown in the cases from Finland, Germany and the UK. Poorer employment conditions and the intensification of work in the domestic sphere are two factors that together constitute a negative feedback loop in female biographies (Gálvez 2013). In some cases, it is only the fact that women can delegate care tasks to other members of the extended family (mainly grandmothers) that makes it 'worthwhile' or even possible for them to go out to work.

The hyper-availability of male workers during recessions (as if they were subjects with no responsibilities other than those linked to the labour market) results in them accepting long working hours, or 'flexible' or intermittent time-tables which take up the entire day or require them to travel long distances on a daily basis. This in turn increases the workload in the domestic sphere, which usually falls to the female partner. Moreover, this situation is legitimised by the narrative of the 'male working hero', which extols men's sacrifice and virtues as tireless workers and is frequently combined with the fact that women conceal their own efforts, thus rendering them invisible. The praise showered on men's super-presence in the workplace tends to ignore the implications of their absence in the domestic sphere:

> 'My husband works 25 hours a day, and there are only 24. And I often think, "How does he do it?" He's lucky if he gets 3 hours' sleep. We'll have to do something about it soon, because sometimes I think to myself: "Any day now something terrible is going to happen to him". Because he's been like this for a year now, and there's bound to be consequences. It frightens me. Sometimes he only gets four or even three hours' sleep a day.' (Spain/F/self-employed)

The narrative of the 'male working hero' is complemented by that of the 'male carer hero' identified in the Irish case (Dagg and Gray 2016). Such a discourse emphasises and celebrates unemployed men who take over certain care tasks, a narrative reinforcing the view of masculinity as something far removed from this type of responsibility, portraying those men who care for members of their family as heroes in merit of special praise.

Reorganising households and support networks
Financial difficulties lead to the activation of different networks as a strategy for overcoming hardship. Networks can be institutional, informal or

family-based, depending on the different welfare state contexts. Sometimes, and specifically in contexts in which there are fewer public services, this activation of networks may involve changes in the way households are organised. These changes take on various forms and may have different consequences in terms of gender.

Athanasiou et al. (2016) outline significant examples of these different ways of reorganising households and their relationship with resilience in Greece. The case of one Greek informant offers an example of a new kind of household organisation characterised by solidarity and the renegotiation of care outside the nuclear family, which becomes possible and is developed in activist contexts which enable the politisation of care and mutual support practices. These new kinds of organisation are based on horizontal decision-making, shared consumption and expenses and collective solidarity in times of hardship. This can help to compensate for the difficulties generated by the high level of job precariousness in southern European countries, characterised by neoliberal policies and the deregulation of the labour market. These practices constitute resilient strategies which enable people to cope with difficulties in better material and relational conditions. Moreover, they also reflect a non-patriarchal gender organisation, based on horizontality and co-responsibility.

Nevertheless, this reorganisation of households as a strategy for overcoming hardship may take on less egalitarian forms, at least in terms of gender. This is the case reported by another Greek informant who, after having left the family home for a while to live by herself, moved back in with her parents and other relatives. While this move provided her with a certain degree of financial security, in exchange she was forced back into the role of a female domestic carer. Although her narrative attaches value to care work, it also highlights the fact that being unemployed restricts her autonomy, and the need to move back to the small town in which her family lives limits her ability to pursue her professional career, resulting in a certain ambivalence when reflecting her own position in the household.

On other occasions, reorganising life in response to the recession and financial difficulties involves activating extremely precarious female support networks, which occasionally structure themselves to form new households. In moments of hardship, women tend to support other, more vulnerable people in their immediate and (particularly) family environment (often other women), and act as buffers for their difficulties, while at the same time leaning for support on other female figures, thereby creating chains of mutual aid aimed at mitigating vulnerability. This is the case of one informant in Spain – a single mother who lives not only with her son but also with her separated sister and her two dependent children. All these people live on the informant's unemployment benefit and the (minimal) child support payments received from her son's father. The two single-parent nuclear families support each other, with occasional help from the sisters' mother, who contributes by buying them meat once a month, despite also being unemployed. Another similar case is that of a Greek informant, who, like her sister, also leans on her mother for support. Here again we see the female disposition and self-sacrificing motherhood acting as the principal buffers of situations of hardship:

> 'My mother is a pensioner. She receives a 460 Euro pension and supports three households: mine, her own, and our country house. My sister has recently moved in with her in order to avoid the extra expenses … My mother, my mother only my mother can do this.' (Greece/F/casual worker)

Thus, as Athanasiou et al. (2016) point out with respect to Greece, the inter-generational circle of care (which in any case is patriarchal and based on the sexual division of labour) is broken, since rather than the informant taking care of her own family and her retired mother, the situation is the other way round. However, this circle is not broken in such a way as to enable a move towards greater social co-responsibility for care tasks, which is extremely complicated in periods of austerity. Rather, it exacerbates the existing vulnerability of women from different generations.

CONCLUSIONS

In this chapter we have explored the gendered ways in which vulnerable families have coped with the hardships imposed by the economic crisis and recession of the last decade and the austerity policies applied in response.

In general terms, women, as the main caregivers in the domestic sphere as well as in the sphere of marketised care work, have found their workload increased as a result of greater vulnerability, particularly in contexts in which social welfare policies are weaker and have suffered the negative impacts of austerity. The recession, austerity and increasing vulnerability have triggered discourses which extol family values and norms linked to ideas of protection and solidarity. This emphasis on the family as the core which protects and must be protected does not necessarily always legitimate inequality, but it does tend to in those frequent situations in which women assume responsibility for caring for those affected by this greater vulnerability, without being the objects of an equivalent degree of reciprocal care.

This trend is evident in many of the strategies employed by families to over-come hardship, which are mainly based on the activation of the female roles, role expectations and experiences, often perceived as a disposition to care for others. These dispositions are further fed by the 're-domestication' of women, which in certain contexts is the consequence of a lack of employment opportu-nities or the possibility of only accessing jobs that are so precarious, unstable or poorly paid that they fail to compensate for the need to hire a third person to do the reproductive work that they would otherwise do for free. As explained above, the overburdening of women (particularly women-mothers) in these situations is manifested in the form of direct care (particularly privation strategies, in which women sacrifice their own needs to satisfy those of the rest of the family), the organisation and orchestration of care though the activation of available networks that may provide some help and support to households, and emotional care for their male partners, who are suffering from unemployment and the destabilisation of their identity that this entails.

Alongside these elements, we have also outlined a number of other strategies for coping with hardship which introduce a greater degree of ambiguity into the reorganisation of gender regimes at a household level as the result of the economic recession. In addition to the aforementioned re-domestication of women (who are overburdened as the agents 'responsible' for the family's resilience), there is also a reverse trend which 'pushes' women onto the labour market. However, the precarious conditions in which they find themselves on that market severely limit their chances of emancipation in this new situation. Male unemployment offers an opportunity for men to play a more active role in domestic and care tasks. This was the case in various households from different countries participating. Different degrees of involvement were observed in different households, in both quantitative and qualitative terms, thereby indicating that men having more time available does not automatically prompt them to assume a leading role in reproductive work. In addition to some transformational dynamics in male care, both inside and outside the nuclear family, other cases identified included that of 'temporary male carers' and men whose activities in this field continue to be considered auxiliary, a praiseworthy 'aid' provided to their female partners.

Gender organisation in terms of how households are configured and the diversity of family structures is also relevant when analysing resilience. Single-parent households were found to have higher social vulnerability indicators in all participating countries and strict, traditionalist families were also found to be in a poorer position for coping with hardship. The reorganisation of household and family structures as a strategy for coping with recession may challenge gender hierarchies when it is based on politicisation, equal distribution of care and solidarity, although it can also serve to reinforce the existing ones when a return to the family home provides security in exchange for care at the cost of the professional development and autonomy of young women.

The ways in which households are organised and the strategies they set in motion to overcome or cope with the hardship generated by the recession and austerity measures have ambivalent effects on their *gender regimes*. Some of the trends outlined here reflect clear 'doing gender' dynamics (West and Zimmerman 1987) in everyday interactions within households. These dynamics not only maintain, but also strengthen the hierarchical relationship between men and women in the family environment, reinforcing both female practices and female subjectivities in relation to their leading role in care. Others, however, such as the distribution of care tasks and their delegation to unemployed men and other agents outside the nuclear family have a potentially transformational effect. In other words, they could potentially 'undo gender' (Deutsch 2007; Risman 2009), since they question previous practices and assumptions, or at least 'redo' it (Connell 2010), reconfiguring gender relations with some elements persisting and others being modified.

These changes and continuities are more feasible in some welfare states, care regimes, traditions and norms than in others. In all, however, by re-privatising care and protection against vulnerability and pushing the responsibility for them firmly back into the family environment, austerity policies have a regressive effect on social co-responsibility and gender equality, the consequences of which are particularly felt by those more vulnerable households, which are more exposed to unemployment and precarious employment, and which are less able to pay for the outsourcing of reproductive work.

NOTES

1. For more information about the RESCuE project please see Chapter 1 of this volume and http://rescueproject.net/ (accessed 25 August 2020).
2. Indeed, in the EU, the gender gap in employment rates diminished by over 2% between 2007 and 2012 (Gálvez 2013, p. 93).
3. In this sense, it is important to bear in mind that, in quantitative terms, and according to data published by Eurostat, in all the countries participating in the RESCuE project for which data are available (Poland, Finland, the United Kingdom, Spain, Portugal and Greece), employed women spend more time engaged in domestic and care work than unemployed men, with Greece being the country with the largest differences and Poland the one with the smallest (Eurostat 2010). These trends suggest that, in those families in which the male partner is unemployed and the female one in work, gender arrangements and trajectories in the gender division of labour may have as much or more weight than time availability in the distribution of domestic responsibilities, thereby hampering a possible change of roles between financial and care providers. Furthermore, according to the same source, the difference between the average amount of time spent on domestic and care work among unemployed and employed men is, in all countries, less than the difference between unemployed and employed women, which suggests that, when they lose their job, women increase the time spent on these tasks to a greater extent than men in the same situation.
4. EU households classified as 'single person with dependent children' had an AROPE (at risk of poverty or social exclusion) score of 47% in 2017 and 48.4% in 2014 (when the RESCuE fieldwork was carried out), as opposed to 22.4% and 24% (respectively) for the entire population of households.
Source: Eurostat https://ec.europa.eu/eurostat/statistics-explained/index.php/Children_at_risk_of_poverty_or_social_exclusion (accessed 25 August 2020).

5.   This is especially the case for Spain and Portugal, as has also been reported by Távora and Rodríguez-Madroño 2018, p. 629.
6.   The term 'awakening' is a metaphor used by a Moroccan woman living in an urban environment in Spain, who had been 'pushed' into training and to search for employment when her husband lost his job (Spain/mother of three children/ migrant).

BIBLIOGRAPHY

Athanasiou, A., Kambouri, N., Marinoudi, T., and Petraki, G. (2016), *RESCuE Project National report (Greece), WP 11, Gender, ethnic and migration aspects of household resilience*, unpublished RESCuE project report.
Bettio, F., and Plantenga, J. (2004), 'Comparing care regimes in Europe', *Feminist Economics* 10(1): 85–113.
Boost, M., Kerschbaumer, L., Schneider, A., Hacker, A., Promberger, M. (2016), *RESCuE Project National Report (Germany), WP 11, Gender, ethnic and migration aspects of household resilience*, unpublished RESCuE project report.
Briales, A. (2015), 'El paro como desorden del ordenamiento de la vida cotidiana', in C. Prieto and I. Aler (eds.), *Trabajo, cuidados, tiempo libre y relaciones de género en la sociedad española*, Madrid: Ediciones Cinca, pp: 191–214.
Capucha, L., Calado, A., and Estêvão, P. (2016), *RESCuE Project National Report (Portugal), WP 11, Gender, ethnic and migration aspects of household resilience*, unpublished RESCuE project report.
Carrasquer, P., Torns, T., Tejero, E. and Romero, A. (1998), 'El trabajo reproductivo', *Papers* 55: 95–114.
Connell, R. (1987), *Gender and power: Society, the person and sexual politics*, Stanford, CA: Stanford University Press.
Connell, R. (2009), *Gender: Short introductions*, Cambridge: Polity Press.
Connell, R. (2010), 'Doing, undoing or redoing gender? Learning from the workplace experiences of transpeople', *Gender and Society* 24(1): 31–55.
Dagg, J. and Gray, J. (2016), *RESCuE Project National Report (Ireland), WP 11, Gender, ethnic and migration aspects of household resilience*, unpublished RESCuE project report.
Deutsch, F. (2007), 'Undoing gender', *Gender and Society* 21(1): 106–27.
Donoghue, M. (2016), *RESCuE Project National Report (United Kingdom), WP 11, Gender, ethnic and migration aspects of household resilience*, unpublished RESCuE project report.
Duncan, S. and Edwards, R. (1999), *Lone mothers, paid work and gendered moral rationalities*, London: Palgrave Macmillan.
Duncombe, J. and Marsden, D. (1993), 'Love and intimacy: The gender division of emotion and emotion work: A neglected aspect of sociological discussion of heterosexual relationships', *Sociology* 27(2): 221–41.
Enloe, C. (2013), *Seriously! Investigating crashes and crises as if women mattered*, University of California Press.
Eurostat (2010), *Time use survey*.
Gálvez, L. (2013), 'Una lectura feminista del austericidio', *Revista de Economía Crítica* 15: 80–110.

González de la Rocha, M., and Grinspun, A (2001), 'Households, crisis and work', in A. Grinspun (ed.), *Choices for the poor: Lessons from national poverty strategies*, New York: UNPD, pp. 55–87.

Hochschild, A. (1979), 'Emotion work, feeling rules, and social structure', *American Journal of Sociology* 85(3): 551–75.

Hochschild, A. and Machung, A. (2012), *The second shift: Working families and the revolution at home*, New York: Penguin.

James, N. (1989), 'Emotional labour: Skill and work in the social regulation of feelings', *The Sociological Review* 37(1): 15–42.

Kaminsky, A (2016), *Frauen in der DDR*, Berlin: Links Verlag.

Kantola, J. and Lombardo, E. (eds.) (2017), *Gender and the economic crisis in Europe: Politics, institutions and intersectionality*, London: Palgrave Macmillan.

Karamessini, M., and Rubery, J. (2014), 'Economic crisis and austerity: Challenges to gender equality', in M. Karamessini and J. Rubery (eds.), *Women and austerity: The economic crisis and the future for gender equality*, London: Routledge, pp. 314–51.

Martín, P., and Arnal, M. (2016), *National report (Spain), WP 11, Gender, ethnic and migration aspects of household resilience*, unpublished RESCuE project report.

Morgan, D. H. J. (1992), *Discovering men: Critical studies on men and masculinities*, London: Routledge.

Ollo, A. and Goñi, S. (2019), *¿Qué medidas pueden ayudar a conciliar la familia y el trabajo?*, Observatorio Social la Caixa. Available at: https://observatoriosociallacaixa .org/-/medidas-familia-trabajo (accessed 25 August 2020).

Pfau-Effinger, B. (1998), 'Gender cultures and the gender arrangement – a theoretical framework for cross-national gender research', *Innovation: The European Journal of Social Science Research* 11(2): 147–66.

Risman, B. (2009), 'From doing to undoing: Gender as we know it', *Gender and Society* 23(1): 81–84.

Roy, K. (2004), 'You can't eat love. Constructing provider role expectations for low-income and working-class fathers', *Fathering* 2(3): 253–76.

Rubery, J. (2014), 'From women and recession to women and austerity: A framework for analysis', in M. Karamessini and J. Rubery (eds.), *Women and austerity: The economic crisis and the future for gender equality*, London: Routledge, pp. 17–36.

Salido, O. (2016), 'El impacto de género de la crisis en los países del Sur de Europa', *Revista Española de Sociología* 25(2): 277–9.

Távora, I. and Rodríguez-Madroño, P. (2018), 'The impact of the crisis and austerity on low educated working women: The cases of Spain and Portugal', *Gender, Work and Organization* (25): 621–3.

Torns, T. (2000), 'Paro y tolerancia social de la exclusión: el caso de España', in M. Maruani, C. Rogerat and T. Torns (eds.), *Las nuevas fronteras de la desigualdad. Hombres y mujeres en el mercado de trabajo*, Barcelona: Icaria, pp. 311–26.

Torns, T. and Recio Cáceres, C. (2012), 'Las desigualdades de género en el mercado de trabajo: entre la continuidad y la transformación', *Revista de Economía Crítica* 14(2): 178–202.

Villa, P. and Smith, M. (2014), 'Policy in the time of crisis: employment policy and gender equality in Europe', in M. Karamessini and J. Rubery (eds.), *Women and austerity: The economic crisis and the future for gender equality*, London: Routledge, pp: 273–94.

Vola, J. and Tennberg, M. (2016), *RESCuE project national report (Finland), WP 11, Gender, ethnic and migration aspects of household resilience*, unpublished RESCuE project report.

Walby, S. (2015), *Crisis*, Cambridge: Polity Press.
West, C. and Zimmerman, D. (1987), 'Doing gender', *Gender and Society* 1(2): 125–51.
Williams, C. C. (2009), 'Beyond the market/non-market divide: A total social organisation of labour perspective', *International Journal of Social Economics* 37(6): 402–14.

10. Space and resilience – a scalar analysis of household resilience in Europe

E. Attila Aytekin and H. Tarık Şengül

INTRODUCTION

> 'To be in a happy mood I always purchase a nice spring bouquet. Here [is] a bunch of daffodils. I have this always on my table [...] Because it improves the mood. First, I had a nice bunch of tulips and now I have these daffodils. I need this. Because then I have a glimpse of hope from the start of the day just when I enter the living room. For me it is really important to do this [...], especially at the moment because I hit rock bottom.' (Germany/F/unemployed)

It is striking to see that a person, such as the woman in the epigraph, who is struggling to make ends meet, regularly spares money to buy flowers for her living room. This is a good illustration of the complexity of the symbolic as well as material practices households engage in order to be resilient during times of crisis. It also, through the significance of 'home', attests to the unmistakable and irreducible spatiality of these practices.

This chapter investigates the spatial dimension of resilience of urban and rural households which are under economic duress in nine European countries (Aytekin and Şengül 2016). Given this geographical extent, there is a great deal of diversity among the cases in terms of socio-economic, demographic and spatial characteristics. The economic structures and labour market characteristics of the urban and rural cases also diverge. We have nevertheless employed a common methodology and theoretical framework to analyse the findings from these diverse cases with the general goal of comprehending the relevance of space to resilience.

The spatiality of poverty and survival strategies of the poor is by now a well-established avenue of research (Mingione 1996; Wacquant 2008; see Fainstein and Fainstein 2018 for a review of the literature). Recently, a new literature that builds on the earlier research but also critically incorporates concepts such as resilience and materiality has developed. One of the main points of contention in the growing literature is whether it is better to understand resilience within an agent-centric conception. One line of critique against this conception draws attention to its affinity with neoliberalism (Joseph 2013). Another critical position departs from a Deleuzian perspective, and calls for shifting the focus from the subject to 'assemblages', underlying the contextually-bound and constantly changing character of resilience (Higgins and Larner 2017; Grove and Pugh 2015). A third position also strives to move away from the active-vs-passive agent or powerful-vs-powerless subject dichotomies and stresses the importance of the web of social relations and structures in conditioning, that is, enabling or hindering, resilience (Dagdeviren et al. 2016). Individual creativity, resourcefulness of families, personal traits, etc., play a role in practices that affect resilience positively or negatively; yet, these do not occur in a vacuum. Resilient households, in times of distress, successfully use a set of freedoms while acting in a set of given constraints (Promberger 2017, 8). While we draw insights from the first and second modes of criticism, our position in this chapter is closer to the third one; we concentrate on space in that it produces opportunities as well as constraints for resilience practices.

On a more general theoretical level, the approach we adopt stipulates that space is not a simple container, but a medium; not abstract and universal, but concrete and specific; not substantial but relational; not neutral but meaning- and power-laden, not timeless but temporal. Space, then, is a social product, and this has two important implications. First, once constituted, 'the spatial' is not reducible to 'the social'. If space has a specificity beyond the social, then it would have some impact upon social relations. The second implication is that a multiplicity of spaces, which are cross-cutting, intersecting, aligning with one another, or antagonistic to each other, exist simultaneously in the spatial practices of human beings in their day-to-day practical activities (Massey 1994; Lefebvre 1991; Tilley 1994).

The quotidian activities of people cover an enormous range from the most symbolic through the social to the most immediately material. The developing literature that underlines the importance of 'materiality', therefore, is a welcome contribution to the relational notion of space (Bennett 2010; Löw 2016). Materiality of space refers, of course, to the physical things themselves such as bodies, housing buildings, gardens, cafés, various kinds of objects, artefacts and infrastructure such as roads and transportation facilities. But it also draws attention to the significance of the specific arrangements of objects and people (Löw 2016), the capacity to make and unmake objects, and the control or lack thereof over material resources (McCormack 2009, pp. 62–4). In the context of spatiality and resilience, then, the concept of materiality draws attention to context-specific, shifting yet effective arrangements between objects and people that either enable or hinder resilience.

To unfold the great complexity of those arrangements and the practices of resilience that are involved, we employ the TPSN – territory (T), place (P), scale (S) and networks (N) – framework (Jessop et al. 2008). This framework allows one to focus on the territorial dimension by placing emphasis on bordering, bounding, parcelization and enclosure, which involves construction of inside/outside divides. As we discuss below, many residents of the localities that we deal with live around such conceptions at different scales and these presuppositions are quite central to their resilience. Likewise, place refers to proximity, spatial embeddedness and a real differentiation, which are quite important for individuals and households in reaching various resources and mobilizing their own resources within households and community networks. Scale is crucial in understanding household resilience as horizontal and vertical differentiations are constituted at various scales. Finally, networks are important to understand the level of interconnectivity and interdependency of households and other dynamics affecting household practices.

While we take the implications of all of the four dimensions into account, we attribute a special role to scale and organize the chapter around four scales: supra-local, local, home and body, in this order, from the highest to the lowest scale. Our goal in doing so is to present a more holistic account of the spatiality of household resilience in European countries as well as to stress the importance of networks. Practices that bring about the resilience of households are diverse and multifaceted, and scale provides an indispensable tool in analysing the wide range of such practices without losing sight of their interconnections.

CONNECTIONS WITH THE SUPRA-LOCAL

When analysing the level of connections of the localities with the supra-local, we deal with their connections to the global, national and regional scales. We have summarized the complex forms and levels of connection of the cases we have studied to these higher scales in Tables 10.1 and 10.2. It should therefore suffice to stress the remarkable points that come out of this complicated picture.

First of all, in general, access to higher scales of space creates more opportunities for households to be resilient, and confinement to lower scales hinders it because practices confined to the lower scales tend to create problems for households in the longer run. The analysis of connections to the global scale, which is the highest scale in our analysis, however, reveals that connections to the global do not automatically increase the capacity for resilience. Immigration as a connection to the global, for one, could have both positive and negative effects on the households in a locality. We see this quite well in the case of Greece, which has been the gateway to Europe for many immigrants and refugees. Immigration could mean the arrival of a robust population group to a locality and could also create the opportunities for the development of more effective solidarity networks involving both the recent immigrants and the more established residents of a neighbourhood. Immigration, however, also creates tensions among residents of certain areas, leading some to perceive the neighbourhood as alien or hostile. The stigmatization that could accompany heavy immigration to neighbourhoods could also act as a barrier to resilience.

Moreover, not only the level, but the form in which the households are connected to the global scales also counts. The Turkish urban neighbourhood in the study is linked to global networks through textile manufacturing, and houses tens of confectionery workshops. Many of them are part of export networks that start in other Istanbul neighbourhoods and end in Russia, Eastern Europe or central Asia. The exporter manufacturers collect orders from abroad and outsource part of the production to workshops. If no orders come from the exporters, the workshops have no work and have to close temporarily. Given the fragility of such assemblages, it is a business that depends on short-term consumer demand and is very vulnerable to fluctuations in the economy, linking the neighbourhood to the global economy from a disadvantageous position.

An important dimension of the isolation or connectedness of an area to higher scales is the situation concerning the labour market and the stigma attached to poor neighbourhoods, which could be a serious obstacle in this sense. The Greek urban case investigated, a metropolitan city quarter, is viewed by outsiders as a poverty ghetto, while increasing international immigration to the neighbourhood strengthens the negative perception of this locality. In Poland, too, there is a stigma attached to one of the neighbourhoods as a poverty ghetto and an essentially undesirable place to live in. In the Turkish case, the Istanbul neighbourhood in question is associated not only with poverty, but even more emphatically with 'terrorism' since it is a politically active neighbourhood. One of the consequences of stigmatization is exclusion from larger labour markets and being constrained to the local scale for employment. In addition, it brings out a situation where households cannot have access to supportive networks that operate at the supra-local scales. The combined effect of these two forms of exclusion is a further strengthening of the 'trap' the lower scales constitute for households in distress. Thus, the stigmatization of poor neighbourhoods on class, ethnic or political terms, or on the basis of various combinations of the three factors, constitutes a very effective limit on the households' capacity for resilience.

THE LOCAL SCALE

In developing resilience, poor households often rely on extra-household resources. The networks that exist in the community and the neighbours and

Table 10.1 Level and forms of connectedness of the urban cases to higher scales

Urban case	Regional (to a major city; to other cities; to other neighbourhoods; to the region in general)	National	Global
Germany	well-connected within the region	well-connected with road and rail networks	weak but somewhat connected through consumption
Poland	well-connected	state policies have largely failed, but the Church provides some connections	weak
Spain	located within the metropolitan area of Madrid and very well-connected with it	area is not easily accessible from cities other than Madrid; Church plays an important role in connecting to the national	well-connected through immigration networks
Britain	well-connected but somewhat stigmatized	some national-level services are provided; emigration to urban areas	well-connected through immigration networks
Greece	part of the metropolitan area of Athens	weak	well-connected through immigration networks
Turkey	economically and socially isolated from the rest of Istanbul, although physically accessible	various religious networks provide links	well-connected through export networks in textiles
Finland	well-connected through road and railway networks	the state has actively striven to strengthen the connection; tourism also links the region to the rest of the country	ties with the global have been severed due to the economic downturn
Ireland	located within the metropolitan area of Dublin	good connections with the rest of the country through Dublin	well-connected through immigration networks
Portugal	well-connected to Lisbon through public transport; part of the labour market of the metropolitan area	housing market depends upon private financial networks; state's role is limited	connected through immigration networks

Table 10.2   Level and forms of connectedness of the rural cases to higher scales

Rural case	Regional (to a major city; to the region; to nearby villages)	National	Global
Germany	villages have links with towns in the region; but public transport is not very effective	there is a high number of welfare recipients	weak ties through consumption
Poland	public transport is not reliable but the villages are well-integrated with the regional labour market	due to the high number of welfare recipients and pensioners, economy is dependent on the national scale	weak
Spain	good road connections but no reliable public transport; integrated with the labour market of Madrid	the Church plays an important role in linking the area to the national	wine export links the area with European Union (EU) commercial networks
Britain	no large city; inhabitants are dependent on public transport, which is not very reliable, for services	the high cost and limited availability of transport weakens connections	weak
Greece	connected to Athens through road network and suburban railway system	the Church plays an important role in linking the area to the national	both older and more recent waves of immigration have created connections with the global

Rural case	Regional (to a major city; to the region; to nearby villages)	National	Global
Turkey	close to Ankara but public transport is almost non-existent; constant immigration to the city	physically close to the national highway network, but very little actual social connection	weak
Finland	larger towns are physically far away	being a border region, connections with Norway and Russia seem relatively strong	tourism, energy and mining sectors and its geopolitical position strongly links it to global networks
Ireland	part of the hinterland of an urban area	the area has attracted urban-to-rural immigration from the rest of the country	limited; mostly through immigration
Portugal	the town is very well-connected but the villages are not; public transport is not reliable	the town is connected but in villages private cars seem necessary	weak

community members who live in the surrounding built environment constitute an important element of such resources. This point, however, should be qualified on the basis of three additional factors.

First, one needs to distinguish between different types of networks. The distinction between weak and strong ties in social networks (Granovetter 1983) is relevant to our discussion of household resilience since the networks formed by outward-looking weak ties could be quite effective in finding jobs, a flat, reaching an unknown resource, etc. This is because networks with strong ties, which are formed around friends, family or kin members, and which provide valuable emotional and social support, nevertheless tend to circulate a limited amount of information in contrast to the differential networks that provide wider information about a range of social resources.

Second, the impact of the locality and the community, however, is not always friendly or helpful to the household. Even if outward-looking supportive networks based on weak ties exist in a locality, some households could have serious difficulty in having access to them. We have actually come across several cases where poor households do not have a chance to make use of the beneficial networks that operate on the local scale. In the Istanbul neighbourhood under study, Alevi households are systematically excluded from the networks that are Sunni Islam-based and/or supported by the district or metropolitan municipality which are controlled by political Islamists. Even if Alevis have formed their own formal or informal networks, they are often resource-poor and face obstacles in their dealings with the authorities.

Third, a worse situation occurs when the immediate environment becomes a threat or is considered to be so by individuals and households who are forced to live in isolation from the wider community. This could stem from the absence of funds or time to participate in community life as well as a pressing perception that the community has changed rapidly and is almost unrecognizable to its residents. In addition to this feeling that could engulf long-term residents in an area, immigrants could also perceive the community as unwelcoming or even threatening. Thus, while the existence of relevant local networks is very important for household resilience, community could also become irrelevant or even a threat in the eyes of the residents.

There is also differentiation between urban and rural areas in the formation of supportive networks. In urban areas, workplaces could be physically far away from living places or otherwise isolated from the latter. Accordingly, the local networks in urban areas are often tied to living places rather than workplaces, as we see in the German or the Turkish cases. In rural areas working and living places often overlap, and so do the supportive networks. In fact, in rural areas, such networks go beyond the everyday life and are often built into workplaces as well. The Finnish rural case is quite illustrative in this sense, where the reindeer herders have networks that have become institutional in the form of cooperatives. But those networks are not only professional ones; as they include family, kin and mutual support systems they serve as one of the key contributions to the resilience of households. In urban areas, local networks often do not extend into work but they nevertheless are important components of communities that contribute in different ways to household resilience. The support provided by neighbours could be material as well as emotional, as Chapter 11 of the present volume illustrates.

The assistance offered by the neighbours, however, could be irregular and, therefore, not reliable. This is not surprising, as in poor neighbourhoods most households face similar hardships, which we see clearly in the issue of borrowing money. Given the fact that most people in poor neighbourhoods live under financial strain, having money to lend to neighbours would be rare. Therefore, lending mostly takes place between the family and kin members rather than with the members of the larger community. Although money is at times exchanged between neighbours and friends, the amounts involved are often limited – in the case of an Angolan interviewed in Portugal, for example, as low as 2 euros. On the other hand, in the case of Turkish villagers, we see them overcoming this difficulty by acting as mutual guarantors for agricultural bank loans.

Finally, since resilience is not only material but also psychological, the local scale is important for providing emotional support to individuals and house-holds in duress. Several respondents in different countries point to the feeling of the neighbourhood as a safety net not only due to the material exchanges but also by knowing that there is a supportive environment if needed. But there is no guarantee that the community would be supportive in actual circumstances. In many cases poor people who live under adverse conditions are compelled to withdraw from active social life due to the shrinking of the financial resources to be devoted to communal activities. Moreover, as other people in the same community often face the same problems of limited resources or mental distress, community would have no such positive affect. A Portuguese respondent has put it neatly: 'To go out ... to go drink a coffee with someone means spending money [laughs], which we don't have. To go to someone's home is equivalent to spending money, even if it's only gas and we don't have it [laughs]' (Portugal/F/unemployed cook).

In the worst case, the social relations at the local scale could create a hostile environment which would undermine resilience. Whatever the reason for an absence of feeling of belonging to a community, such absence often leads to a widespread reactionary sense of place, as communities adopt a generalized tendency to draw hard boundaries and stigmatize those who fall outside its limits (Massey 1994, p. 146ff). In many cases, such a sense is associated with the changing demographics and the spatial transformation of the area. An Irish mother of two has expressed this feeling: 'I can't work in [urban location] anymore, I don't know anybody in there. I would be afraid to walk up Patrick St on my own anymore because I feel like I'm in a foreign country' (Ireland/F/living in a large provincial town). Not feeling 'at home' and perceiving the locality as a threat is not always limited to the 'native' population. In some cases, immigrants could also have quite a negative perception of the neighbourhood. In almost any case, the 'other' that plays the major role in stigmatization of the area is the one who is weak and poor, whether he/she is immigrant, unemployed, criminal, addictive or deviant. However, on the other side of the coin, there are two cases where the well-off person is seen as a threat to the community life by the residents. Both the neighbourhoods studied in Istanbul and London have for some time been threatened by gentrification and there the residents feel that they are under the threat of displacement by the rich and the powerful coming in from outside.

THE SCALE OF HOME

Since our main unit of analysis is the household, we pay special attention to the scale of home in the exposition of the conclusions of our research. In this section we discuss the relation of the scale of home with resilience around four points: the impact of ownership, growing food at home, its immaterial benefits and its changing boundaries.

It is well known that poor households could find themselves in a position to allocate a large portion of household income to rent (Tinson et al. 2016). Thus, it could be presumed that whether the households own the place they live in has a big impact upon their resilience. Nevertheless, there is no direct correlation between home ownership and resilience, even in general terms. In so far as our nine European cases are concerned, only in Finland is home ownership the dominant form of housing tenure. In certain cases, namely Portugal, Turkey and the UK, households that rent their dwelling places clearly form the majority. In Germany, Greece, Ireland and Poland, homeowners and tenants could be more or less equally found among the respondents and one should note that home ownership is found more in rural areas than urban ones. We see the positive impact of home ownership on resilience in some of the countries, most notably in Germany. Although home ownership in Germany is quite rare among the households that are in the lowest income quintile, the households that are more resilient tend to own their homes.

Yet, the aspirations of many deprived households to own a home notwithstanding, homeownership could be a burden, not an asset, for households because of heavy taxation, or mortgage payments. In Greece, the new property tax which was imposed in 2011 at exorbitant rates, has reversed the perception of property as a guarantee and made it a burden for poor people. The law particularly affected the 'new poor', i.e. the middle and upper classes that have been experiencing downward social mobility. In Spain, since mortgage payments were related to the high incomes households had before the crisis, the inability to make the mortgage payments became an important factor that decreased household resilience after the crisis.

Whether owned or not, home can have different functions in addition to the basic one of shelter. A studio apartment, a small flat, a larger flat, house with or without a garden, a yard, cellar or additional buildings such as a shack, stable, etc. enable or disable a range of practices. While smaller dwelling places tend to limit the inhabitants' use of home to functions like shelter, consumption, reproduction, relaxation, etc., larger ones may create the opportunity for home to be a unit of production, too.

. A large number of households in rural areas consume home-grown food. In Finland, many households have backyards which they use to produce various kinds of vegetables. In Germany, we see among rural households the use of home to grow legumes and vegetables. In the Irish and Polish rural localities, in addition to growing herbs, legumes and vegetables, keeping hens and chickens in the back garden is common. In Spain, relationship to land is crucial for rural households and often a garden is used to produce food. In urban areas, the practice of growing food at home is less common, which has various reasons. The first is the unavailability of space required to produce food, as smaller dwelling units almost prohibit it. This is the case, for example, in the Turkish urban neighbourhood, where the great majority of apartments are small and there are very few detached houses remaining in the neighbourhood. The same applies to Greece where the houses even in the rural areas are too small to devote some space to agricultural activities. Another impediment to self-production of food is pollution, which has become a major problem, especially in some rural areas. The rural case of Turkey where the scarcity of water and labour discourage households from producing self-grown food is another example attesting to the importance of factors other than the availability of land.

A factor that also accounts for the relative rarity of growing food at home is the choice some households make about the use of home space. Even if there is some extra space at home, these households might opt to use it not for growing food but for leisure and relaxation purposes. While these two functions, namely food-growing and relaxation, may not be necessarily mutually exclusive in a spatial sense, in some dwelling units, they are. Households could care for larger houses as a means to cope with stress and thereby prefer to use backyards or gardens for recreation. In general, households could prefer larger dwelling places not for strictly economic reasons, but simply as a means to provide psychological relief.

This brings us to another major function of home: the immaterial benefits it provides. As several examples from different countries make clear, a well-kept and nicely decorated place promotes self-esteem and increases the ability to cope with stress. The quote at the beginning is a marvellous example of the immaterial contribution of home to resilience. Conversely, as some residents from Finland, Poland, Spain and the UK have pointed out, low-quality housing could be a major source of stress.

The crisis also compelled the households to go beyond the physical limits of home and, in a sense, redefine the boundaries of home. Some of those practices implemented during crises also depend on the previous (pre-crisis) structures and practices. For example, in Greece, it has been common for family members to live close by and the spatial relations among the extended family members have been mobilized following the crisis. We have seen a similar tendency in urban Turkey where households tend to live very close to the related households. Apparently, spatial proximity of kin or family networks outside the home proved to be a substantial advantage in times of crisis. Nevertheless, there are examples from Finland and Germany where economically and psychologically functional networks of kin stretch through wider space.

Perhaps the most visible impact of the last recession on the household structure and borders of home is the tendency on the part especially of the young people to go back to live with their parents. In Greece, the impact of recession and austerity was more devastating for younger generations, since older generations, despite reductions, continue to enjoy greater financial security because of savings and pensions. As a result, the notion of the household was transformed as previous intergenerational patterns were reversed. Instead of elderly relatives moving in with their progeny to be taken care of by younger women in the family, today it is more common for adults to return back to the family home to live with their parents. We have discerned a similar tendency in Spain, Portugal and Turkey. This, needless to say, provides a great financial advantage to families and individuals under duress by allowing them to cut several costs (rent, electricity, heating, food, etc.) and also provides them a sense of security and care. Living with parents, however, has also its disadvantages. Moving in with parents after having an independent home for a while could be seen as a sign of failure in life. In this sense, then, what we see is a practice that is good for the economic well-being of households, but has social and psychic costs.

THE SCALE OF BODY

Inspired by Bourdieu's definition of body (see Shilling 2003, p. 110), we focus in this section on two ways in which body is relevant to resilience. In one sense, resilience could be defined as a condition of protecting one's own body as a form of physical capital. This relates mostly to the use of the body to produce economic capital. Moreover, the conceptualization of the body as a form of physical capital simultaneously allows us to recognize an intimate relationship between the development of the body and people's social location, and management of the body as central to the acquisition of status with reference to such social location. In the second sense, then, the body is relevant to resilience because of its role in the production of cultural and social capital, which are necessary for access to networks or certain practices of getting by.

Many practices of resilience during times of crisis are organized in and around the body. Those practices that convert the body as physical capital to economic capital are frequently used by households and are quite effective in the short run. There are many examples in which the most direct consequences of economic crisis are warded off by households with body-based practices, such as working longer hours, consuming less and not seeking medical assistance even when it is necessary. While these provide effective relief in the short run, they are not reliable in a longer term as they take a high physical and mental toll on individual bodies and thus undermine resilience in the middle and long run, contrary to the practices that provide cultural and social capital to the owners of the body.

Faced with the economic crisis, one of the first responses of distressed households is to cut the expenses at the household level. The attempts to reduce the expenses are necessarily highly selective, starting from non-essential items and services like going out to coffee shops, restaurants and cultural activities. The situation, on the other hand, is more complicated for some households in relation to reducing the expenses as they often make sacrifices on the quality and quantity of the food they consume in a dramatic way, as this quote reveals:

> 'There was actually days there, there was one week there I didn't eat for four days. I gave it to the kids instead and I gave it to him because he is at work and the kids need it for school. I didn't eat, and I just told the kids I wasn't hungry but I was, but I just gave it to them instead. I would rather give to them, I would rather for them to eat, they need it for school and he works, I do without it. I'm used to that. It doesn't bother me now. [...] I won't eat anything now until [my husband] gets paid on Friday so it doesn't bother me, I'm just used to it at this stage.' (Ireland/female/four children)

Some practices of resilience depend on people physically forcing themselves, and such practices obviously take a toll on the body. One of the most common of such practices is to work longer hours. Several respondents have mentioned having to work more hours, or even in an extra job, to cope with financial problems. The outcome is an exhaustion that does not seem to go away. When working long hours, fatigue and poor-quality housing is coupled with low-quality food intake, falling sick is almost inevitable. Sickness creates additional problems for poor households. If they do not have healthcare cover, such households are often forced to give up regular healthcare, as it may be quite expensive. A quite common practice is not to see a doctor unless absolutely necessary, as this quote from a person who was on the verge of homelessness illustrates:

> 'When I'm sick I eat a couple of hot paprikas. When I have flu, excuse me, I drink a couple of glasses of raki. I drink hot tea and wear warm clothes. It slowly gets better. When you go to the doctor, excuse me, a shot is 30 liras. Serum costs money. Hospital bed costs money. If you have documents, they will take care of you, right? I don't have a document or insurance. So, I cure myself.' (Interviewer: When was your last time when you went to see a doctor?') '2004 or 2005' (Turkey/male/early 30s)

Indeed, one of the worst possible consequences of coping practices that centre on the body is permanent damage to the body. This is especially true for individuals who 'overuse' their bodies as seen in the following quotes.

> 'When I was young, I raised my brothers and sisters. I helped my mother. When I got married, I raised a family ... I had to take care of my husband, his sister, his mother. [...] I was only looking after other people and, in the end, realized that I suffered from osteoporosis. When I went to the doctor, he asked me: "Where were you all these years, what have you been doing to yourself?"' (Greece/female/mid-80s)

> 'I came here at the age of 17 from the village [...] It's been 40–45 years. I've worked as a porter, collected scrap metal in the streets. There was no wheelbarrow at the time. [...] My left shoulder stands 3 cm shorter than the right one, because of lifting heavy things.' (Turkey/male/retired worker)

Against the tendency to consider even the practices that cause permanent body damage as practices of resilience, one could argue that the practices that lead to chronic disease or disability cannot be deemed practices of resilience. There are households that cope with similar problems without permanent bodily damage or death, so they would be the ones that should be considered resilient. Although this is consistent with the concepts of resilience and of the household/family applied throughout the project (see Chapter 1 of this volume), two caveats could be raised against this point. First, we have defined the household, rather than the individual, as our unit of resilience. Therefore, we should not reject the possibility that sacrifice of the body by one household member leads to the resilience of the household. Second, we need to reconsider our time frame when thinking about resilience. Sacrificing physical well-being might lead to resilience of one household compared to others on the short timescale, even if in a longer time frame it might contribute to a deterioration of the quality of life due to health problems.

In addition to the physical problems, poverty, distress, resilience practices that 'force' the body, and concerns about the future affect people's mental health badly. The final stage in the pressure on the body with regards to coping is what we may call the dissolution of the body. Some individuals who cannot use their body for cultural and social capital are forced to depend too much on their body as physical capital. This, coupled with the immense physiological pressure deprivation creates, could lead to suicide. The research has provided rare but striking examples of this tendency towards the dissolution of the body.

CONCLUSION

This chapter has been an attempt to understand the impact of space on resilience of households. Although the sheer number and diversity of the cases studied is striking, we have nevertheless strived to focus on and emphasise commonalties. Departing from a relational notion of space, and considering resilience as a social and spatial phenomenon, we have analysed the impact of space on resilience at different scales as either restraining or enabling material, social and symbolic practices of resilience.

Most households have a limited degree of territorial control in their relation to supra-local scales such as the global and the national. While the state is the most important actor that links the local to the national, there are other institutions such as religious networks that perform the same function. The net impact of state and non-state actors that connect the households to upper scales on resilience is not pre-given and depends on the strength, persistence and inclusiveness of the assemblages which the households become a part of.

Households frequently rely on networks that exist at the local scale for extra-household resources in developing resilience. While both weak and strong networks could increase the household capacities for resilience, given that many households share the same limited resources in the face of economic adversity, outward-looking weak networks are more important in this sense. However, certain households might have difficulty in reaching these networks, chiefly for political reasons. In addition, the local scale could become irrelevant or even an obstacle to resilience when households and individuals face social isolation or feel no meaningful sense of belonging to their respective communities.

Home is the scale of the household as a social entity. Given the proportion of income which deprived households expend on rent, it is understandable that many of them strongly aspire to home ownership. Ownership, however, could also become a major drawback to practices of resilience under certain circumstances. In addition to its main function of providing shelter, a probable use of home space to increase resilience could be to grow food in a garden or backyard. Even if such practices exist in many rural and a few urban households, some households prefer to use the extra space in their homes for leisure and recreational purposes. Home plays a key role in the mental resilience of the households as a well-kept and nicely decorated place promotes self-esteem and helps to cope with stress, which shows that certain symbolic practices at the scale of home provide valuable emotional support for those who struggle with hardship and thus contribute to resilience in a considerable way.

All the problems that stem from the economic crisis affect the body at some point. We have focused in the present work on two issues that are relevant to the relation between body and resilience, namely body as a form of physical capital and its role in the production of cultural and social capital, which are necessary for access to networks. The practices that centre on the body as physical capital are frequently used and quite effective in the short run but are not reliable in the longer term due to their high physical and mental costs. Using the body in the production of cultural and social capital, on the other hand, paves the way for resilience as these forms of capital facilitate access to networks that link the household to higher scales.

After this summary of analysis of the relation of space and resilience in nine European countries that we have organized around four scales, we would like to finish with three conclusions.

First, defined in spatial terms, resilience refers to the ability of households to have access to higher scales and not to be 'trapped' in the scales of body and home. When practices of resilience take place mostly at the body scale, they have a dramatic impact, bringing about several physical and mental problems. On the other hand, solidarity networks that operate at the neighbourhood/ village scale are important in determining the level of isolation, and hence, the obstacles to resilience of poor households. As a result, while practices that revolve around home vary widely from country to country, most poor households strive to engage in resilience practices that go beyond the physical limits of home.

Second, while access to higher scales is important for resilience, it does not make a household automatically resilient. This has emerged most clearly with respect to the connections of households with the global scale. Under globalization, social relations have become more spatially stretched-out than before. This leads to closer connection between people living in different places, and residents of a locality are increasingly affected by processes that operate at scales higher than the local. The net impact of close connections with the global is, however, often negative on their chances of maintaining resilience. Connections to the national do not fare better, either. The intensive austerity programmes several governments across Europe engaged in following the global recession caused a decrease in the state's role as a meaningful actor in people's lives and households' resilience. Moreover, other networks, such as the religious ones, that form a connection to the national scale could be inadequate, or not inclusive enough.

Lastly, given these serious problems the scales of body, home and the supra-local present for resilience, the local scale seems to be the most important in bolstering the opportunities of household resilience. As we have seen, however, the local could also seriously hinder household capacity for resilience. To understand the positive and negative role of the local on resilience, we shall distinguish between progressive and reactionary senses of place, which brings us to the fourth concept in the TPSN model we have espoused.

Rather than seeing places as homogeneous entities, it is better to conceive them as sets of social relations linked into networks that cross space and scale. Doreen Massey has discussed the reactionary responses people give to social change and difficulties associated with it in a different context, yet one which is applicable to the post-crisis situation in Europe:

> 'An (idealized) notion of an era when places were (supposedly) inhabited by coherent and homogeneous communities is set against the current fragmentation and disruption [...] But the occasional longing for such coherence is none the less a sign of the geographical fragmentation, the spatial disruption, of our times. And occasionally, too, it has been part of what has given rise to defensive and reactionary responses – certain forms of nationalism, sentimentalized recovering of sanitized "heritages" and outright antagonism to newcomers and "outsiders".' (Massey 1994, pp. 146–7)

In our scale-based analysis, a progressive sense of place is related to, on the one hand, access to networks that link a particular place to other places as well as to higher scales and, on the other hand, the degree of inclusiveness of those networks. When a progressive sense of place dominates social relations in a village or an urban neighbourhood, this is a major enabling factor for household resilience. Resilience in this sense refers to the collective making of a progressive sense of place as opposed to a reactionary one.

Economic crisis has forced European households to engage in a number of symbolic and material practices to fight off the immediate detrimental outcomes of the downturn and, then, to secure household resilience in the longer run. Some of these practices are fully concentrated on the body and the household or rely upon hierarchical and/or clientelist networks and produce a reactionary sense of place. Others connect lower scales to higher ones, make use of horizontal networks, and simultaneously produce a progressive sense of space. The second group of practices are more effective and reliable in the long run for the resilience of households in that they significantly enlarge the set of freedoms the household can use and weaken the constraints that limit the household capacity to act.

BIBLIOGRAPHY

Athanasiou, A., Kambouri, N., Marinoudi, S., Petraki, G. (2016), *Workpackage 7: The spatial dimension of households' resilience: Greek case study*, Athens: RESCuE Research Project.
Aytekin, E. A. and Şengül, H. T. (2016), *Workpackage 7 international report: Spatial aspects of household resilience*, Ankara: RESCuE Research Project.
Bennett, J. (2010), *Vibrant matter: A political ecology of things*, Durham, NC: Duke University Press.
Capucha, L., Calado, A. and Estêvão, P. (2016), *WP7 – the spatial dimension of households' resilience: Portuguese national report*, Lisbon: RESCuE Research Project
Dagdeviren, H., Donoghue, M., Promberger, M. (2016), 'Resilience, hardship and social conditions', *Journal of Social Policy* 45(1): 1–20.
Fainstein, N. and Fainstein, S. (2018), 'Spatial dimension of poverty', in A. Andreotti, D. Benassi and Y. Kaepov (eds.), *Western capitalism in transition*, Manchester: Manchester University Press.
Granovetter, M. (1983), 'The strength of weak ties: A network theory revisited', *Sociological Theory* 1: 201–33.
Grove, K. and Pugh, J. (2015), 'Assemblage thinking and participatory development: Potentiality, ethics, biopolitics', *Geography Compass* 9(1): 1–13.
Higgins, V.and Larner, W. (2017), 'The resilient subjects', in V. Higgins and W. Larner, *Assembling neoliberalism*, London: Macmillan, pp. 1–17.
Huws, U. (2016), *The spatial dimension of households' resilience: UK workpackage 7 report*, Hatfield: RESCuE Research Project.
Jessop, B., Brenner, N. and Jones, M. R. (2008), 'Theorizing sociospatiality', *Environment and Planning D* 26(3): 389–401.
Joonas, V., Vuojala-Magga, T. and Tennberg, M. (2016), *Report – workpackage 7 Finland: The spatial dimension of households' resilience*, Rovaniemi: RESCuE Research Project.
Joseph, J. (2013), 'Resilience as embedded neoliberalism: A governmentality approach', *Resilience* 1(1): 38–52.
Lefebvre, H. (1991), *Production of space*, Oxford: Blackwell.
Löw, M. (2016), *The sociology of space: Materiality, social structure and actions*, London: Palgrave Macmillan.
Massey, D. B. (1994), *Space, place, and gender*, Minneapolis: University of Minnesota Press.
McCormack, D. (2009), 'Materiality', in A. Latham, D. McCormack, K. McNamara and D. McNeill (eds.) *Key concepts in urban geography*, London: Sage, pp. 62–9.
Meier, L. and Promberger, M. (2016), *Work package 7: The spatial dimension of households' resilience – the German case study*, Nuremberg: RESCuE Research Project.
Mingione, E. (1996), *Urban poverty and underclass*, Oxford: Blackwell.
Promberger, M. (2017), *Resilience among vulnerable households in Europe: Questions, concept, findings and implications*, Nuremberg: IAB Discussion Paper.
Revilla, J. C. and Calderón, D. (2016), *Wp7 the spatial dimension of households' resilience: Spanish RESCuE Team*, Madrid: RESCuE Research Project CuE.
Shilling, C. (2003), *Body and social theory*, Sage: London.
Tilley, C. Y. (1994), *A phenomenology of landscape: Places, paths, and monuments*, Oxford: Berg.

Tinson, A., Ayrton, C., Barker, K., Born, T. B., Aldridge, H., and Kenway, P. (2016), *Monitoring poverty and social exclusion*, London: New Policy Institute.

Wacquant, L. (2008), *Urban outcasts*, Cambridge: Polity.

Wódz, K., Klimczak, J. and Nowalska-Kapuścik, D. (2016), *Polish national report workpackage 7: The spatial dimensions of households' resilience*, Katowice: RESCuE Research Project.

11. The paradoxes of resilience and social, political and community participation in Europe

Araceli Serrano, Juan Carlos Revilla, Mª Paz Martín and Carlos de Castro

INTRODUCTION

The concept of resilience is increasingly being used in academic studies to refer to mechanisms by which people overcome adversity through certain capacities or actions that, while individual in origin, are clearly conditioned by the social context and subjects' social position as well as being embodied in their personal histories (Dagdeviren et al. 2016; Estêvão et al. 2017). This new body of research understands resilience as having a complex, processual and multidimensional character. Similarly, we understand resilience as a social phenomenon whereby people's capacity to be resilient is highly dependent on the resources they can draw on when faced with difficult life situations. As such, resilience depends on a wide variety of social, cultural and structural factors that condition courses of action and social practices and differentiate them between social groups and subjects (Promberger et al. 2014, 2016; Revilla et al. 2018).

The aim of this chapter is to connect the aforementioned conceptualization of resilience with community and political participation in a context of increasing individualization and social fragmentation. We start by analysing the dynamics of individuation, social fragmentation and community decline that, in different ways, have intensified during the economic crisis in the populations where we carried out our case studies and identify some of the primary drivers of these processes. Subsequently, we consider the opposing dynamics of increasing community relations and re-politization that are represented by social movements and social innovation initiatives, together with other practices that have no explicit political content but can be understood as being oriented toward social and community integration. In the final section, we analyse how participation practices (or the lack of them) are related to modalities and degrees of resilience and show how these practices and dynamics favour both household and collective community resilience.

Following the irruption of the 2008 economic recession, western democracies experienced a deep political/democratic upheaval and a crisis of social cohesion and solidarity which triggered a twofold effect: (a) an increase in social inequality, instability and fragmentation in societies that were already weakly articulated; (b) a reconfiguration of the frameworks of understanding of political participation and social bonding, and consequently people's engagement with the community, the collective, the political, and the social (Serrano et al. 2013), as well as their notions of what it means to be a citizen. In fact, these two processes can be thought of as related to each other, since people's de-politization can often be a consequence of the crisis of legitimacy of modern states and modulated by the socio-political and institutional tradition in each country. Hence, more equal societies reduce the barriers that tend to restrict the participation of deprived groups, which also reduces social and political disengagement. For instance, several authors (Bourdieu 1999; Castel 1999; Putnam 2000; Kaztman 2001; Merklen 2005; Morales 2006) consider that vulnerability and precarity tend to foster social disintegration and fragmentation, individualization and isolation. Among collectives living in hardship, these factors impede the articulation of organized political and community-related action due to their lack of resources (social, cultural, symbolic, and so on). However, other authors argue that the deterioration of living conditions creates the conditions of possibility for more active social participation and the emergence of social movements and local groups and solidarity initiatives (Herrera and Cívico 2015). Thus, the crisis could mean the development of collective consciousness and political participation in some vulnerable communities.

Hence, in our societies, new social movements and social initiatives are proposing and enacting community-related alternatives to dominant individualistic social processes. Some of these alternatives are of a profound political nature and affirm that 'a different world is possible', while others are more oriented toward solidarity and the fostering of social inclusion without directly challenging the system. Finally, the fragmentation of social bonds is also leading to the construction of exclusionary communities amongst some social groups along national or local and/or religious or ethnic lines. The analysis identifies and discusses several paradoxes of social and political participation as they relate to household resilience.

These processes of radical individualization, similarly to the opposing processes of strengthening communities and re-politization, are evident in the analysis of in-depth interviews undertaken in households in situations of vulnerability (in each country, 24 interviews were undertaken, evenly split between the urban and rural case study), together with key informant

interviews (at least eight per country), and ethnographic work in both settings – rural and urban – across nine European countries: Finland, Germany,
Greece, Ireland, Poland, Portugal, Spain, Turkey and the UK. Each country's
institutional traditions, political culture, and social and economic structure
influence these individualization processes, the possible disappearance of
traditional community relations, as well as the emergence and strengthening
of communities and re-politicization, all of which contribute differently to
household resilience.

The analysis takes Tönnies' (1979[1887]) classical distinction between
Gemeinschaft (community) and Gesellschaft (association) and adapts it to the
needs of this study. To illustrate, if one thinks of communities as close-knit
groups, with clear boundaries and limited exchange with outside people, then
the usefulness of the concept is quite limited in our complex mass societies.
In this sense, the notion of social network (closer to association) is perhaps
more appropriate for an analysis of the kind of loosely integrated groupings
that are found in our individualized societies (Bauman 2002; Beck and
Beck-Gernsheim 2002). People connect with others with different degrees of
intensity and in an open way. However, the concept of network lacks the affective component that community entails and the reality that few social networks
actually develop identity and emotional attachment, in the sense of belonging.
It is in this context that emotionally laden networks could be understood as
communities, even if they are not the close-knit, geographically proximate
groups that we once thought of.

DECLINE OF COMMUNITIES AND SOCIAL ISOLATION

In general terms, many of our case studies are experiencing radical processes
of individualization in their community lives. Although this trend is evident
in all or most societies, it has quite distinct manifestations and dimensions
in the areas we studied. The composition of many communities that were
relatively homogeneous has diversified and become weakened, which makes
community life more challenging (Revilla et al. 2013). In some case study
areas, such as in Ireland, Spain, Greece, Germany and the UK, key informants and some household members believe that this has come about with the
arrival of migrants, either national or international. In other case areas, such
as the mining communities in the Polish national report, the decomposition
of working-class communities is seen to lie at the heart of the problem. In the
UK, Greek and German urban cases, gentrification is viewed as the main issue,
while the deterioration of urban and rural areas was highlighted in the Turkish
and Greek reports. Both of these processes – gentrification and deterioration –
can act to drive out parts of the former population and change neighbourhoods'

social composition (reported in the Greek, UK, German and Turkish studies). The stigmatization of certain areas and a polarization between old and new areas was also evident in the urban cases. Through different mechanisms, these processes give rise to social fragmentation, and feelings of abandonment and distrust amongst impoverished communities, most of which are located in urban areas that experience more rapid transformations.

Furthermore, worsening socio-economic parameters should create the conditions, such as having extra time, for more active participation in associations and community and political life. Yet, insecure and poor employment conditions often foster competitive practices which, together with the effort invested in alternative sources of making ends meet, results in a lack of time (or even energy) to participate in community life. Some of the people in our fieldwork revealed that they were too consumed by work and household needs to engage in leisure or other participatory social activities. These dynamics can be understood as some disciplining effects of crisis and precarity (Sennett 1998; Alonso et al. 2011).

In some countries, in particular those with more fragile social, political and labour market institutions, the advent of the crisis has been particularly conditioned by the effect of a pre-crisis bubble (especially in Spain, Portugal, Greece, Poland and Ireland) in a way that has encouraged and intensified the trend towards individualization and the decline of community life. This effect produces isolation dynamics because, first, it entails a rupture at the very basis of social life in a capitalist system where consumption and labour are at the core. Thus, the crisis disrupts the central social dynamics of consumption and work as the dominant form of sociability. Second, it is a powerful mechanism for the production of emotions like social shame, distrust and envy that reduce social interaction. On the one hand, these dynamics promote competitiveness for limited resources. On the other, feelings of shame, associated with hardship and scarcity, produce a retreat into the private sphere, rendering cultural, political or social participation difficult, even in the local context of a neighbourhood. An example from the German case study helps to illustrate:

> 'People are different today. Some are more envious. Because one has money and the other doesn't. And this is how it starts. In the old days, everybody had the same amount of money, nearly. Nearly the same. In the past during the weekends, when there was a get-together, you just had to bring some beer … This doesn't happen today. Today this might happen with some unemployed people. […] People helping each other out in the neighbourhood, that's gone.' (Germany/single mother/mid-40s)

Moreover, a socio-spatial infrastructure can also be a barrier to participation, as the structuring of urban neighbourhoods may favour anonymity and lead to reduced social interaction amongst residents, which in turn fosters isolation.

Furthermore, participation in associations and organizations is also impeded by spatial distance, which can only be overcome if people have the necessary functional mobility resources (see also Chapter 10 on spatial dimensions of resilience).

In general, in the fieldwork, references to nearby community spaces, and to related collective activities, were scarce and the analysis suggests that interaction amongst the different populations was diluted and exceptional rather than the norm. For some, simple, physical proximity makes them feel part of a community, even if their link with other community members is rather superficial and only characterized by crossing paths in common social spaces with little intimate contact. Hence, these isolating tendencies, devoid of associative or participative activities beyond immediate friends and family, are reinforced by social processes that place consumerism as the main mechanism of social integration. We can observe this tendency in an extract from the UK case report:

> 'My street is lovely. My street is really, really nice, I know all my neighbours really well ... know my downstairs neighbours ... I know all of them and I know all of the people in my local shops and stuff ... I, I guess it depends to what extent, like I wouldn't really ask them to do anything for me other than maybe take a parcel in.' (UK/F/short-term unemployed)

Individualism is on the rise to the extent that, in some contexts, like in the UK and Germany, we found examples of how being independent is considered a sign of social integration and of middle-class status. For example, a discourse of voluntary self-isolation was evident in an interview with a German respondent who considered herself to be socially integrated in socio-economic terms 'without having a pressing need for integration into the nearby neighbourhood' (Meier et al. 2016, p. 10). 'Here, everybody does their own thing. And right now I am at a point where I am just glad when I can close the door and have silence. That's how it has developed for me' (Germany/F/unemployed).

However, a wish to recover past community life was often expressed, in idealistic terms, as a way to reactivate mutual help between neighbours. Coinciding with other research (Meier 2013), these narratives reveal a romanticism and nostalgia for the past. Some embodied experiences or memories have also acquired a mythical status in some communities, like the mining area in Poland where memories of solidarity during the rule of the former Communist German Democratic Republic were important to local identity. Other examples include the traditional rural communities in Spain, Greece, Portugal or Ireland, where people spoke about how everyone used to know their neighbours and help each other out. In Southern European countries, the metaphor of the family was often used to represent this idea of living together, while strengthened social bonds in the rural UK case study were related to a predominance of the personal dimensions of social relations. The following interview extracts are examples from the Portuguese and Spanish rural areas:

'Yes, yes. There are people from [rural area] that I have a good relationship with. And I have friends who live in [nearby town] and I have friends in [nearby town]. People who live with me, too, we are family. Life has difficulties. When we are here, Africans, we need to know where our family is. If not, you may have problems at home, being alone. You have to visit family and friends, and let them visit you.' (Portugal/M/mid-60s/urban area)

'My grandmother told me about that type of thing [how it used to be when her grandmother was younger], that if she didn't have something her neighbour would give it to her and if they didn't have something she'd give it to them.' (Spain/mother of two children/rural area)

Derived from these processes, in the vast majority of our cases, one can find a lack of participation in groups, associations or social networks, along with a tendency toward de-politization, apathy and lack of mobilization. For instance, in the Polish case studies, respondents talked of the 'democracy deficit', and felt they had no influence on this situation and even expressed an aversion to having any knowledge about the political and social situation.

In the Portuguese cases, crisis and austerity seems to have fostered an even greater degree of political apathy, with extremely low levels of conventional and non-conventional participation, and significant declines in the trust of associations, organizations and political institutions. In Ireland, participants' responses point to a conformist attitude as a national characteristic. This is related to an important 'crisis of legitimacy' (Kountouri 2015) that has been intensified by the economic crisis and austerity and has impacts on the traditional political parties and the institutionalized forms of political and social participation, especially in Spain and Greece.

SOCIAL AND POLITICAL PARTICIPATION AND REVITALIZATION OF COMMUNITY

Although of a reduced level, in the case studies analysed there was quite a rich diversity of spaces for social participation and collective activities. However, the impact and community-building capacity of the different practices observed was quite varied. Here, Tönnies' (1979[1887]) dichotomy between community and association (Gemeinschaft and Gesellschaft) is a useful analytical axis that can help us describe these processes. Table 11.1 gives an overview of the identified participation patterns along this axis.

Closer to the associative side of the dichotomy, some households establish passive contact with groups and associations simply to acquire basic necessities (help receivers), while others become more actively involved, as members

Table 11.1   Forms of social participation

Type of bond	Status	Types of grouping	Contribution
Association	Beneficiary	Help & care institutions	Mainly material
Social network	Vertical links	Product or service exchange associations	
		Local political participation	
		Voluntary civic associations	
Community	Participant	Religious groups	Symbolic
	Bottom-up	Neighbourhood associations	Material
	Horizontal links	Cultural groups	
		Political movements	

Source: Serrano/Revilla/Martín/de Castro, own elaboration

of an exchange agreement, for example. This is often the way families and individuals approach organizations that provide support and care. Likewise, this is also characteristic of product or service exchange associations (school-books, clothes, toys, time banks, and so on). In both cases, there is little sense of community, although in some cases these practices produce feelings of gratitude or indebtedness. As such, some forms of collaboration within neighbourhoods and communities have also increased, establishing support and collaborative initiatives, especially in the rural context and in smaller communities. In the German, Greek and Irish cases, close social circles of informal mutual assistance were also found in the urban areas. However, they seemed to have an exclusively economic rather than political nature (indeed they could be categorized as an economic resource of the community – Meier et al. 2016).

> 'I got involved in the community group and we hold meetings here every couple of weeks and then I go to the [name of a NGO] meetings and feedback and all the needs of the community, if it's only the antisocial behaviour or people dumping rubbish, there's a lot of violence going on around the place, drug dealing and things like that, robbed cars coming into the area speeding around the place so you need somebody just to be feeding back all that. So we are doing that, we go around and try to collect money from the houses to fund the grass cutting because the council is not cutting the grass.' (Ireland/mother of one child/social housing)

These are spontaneous networks set up to exchange and share wood, food, garden products, clothes or even help with house maintenance. Therefore, in these countries a sort of baseline communitarian economy of informal exchange takes place. From the perspective of households, these are resilient tactics, but they have little impact at a wider communitarian or political level.

Alternative forms of association were also evident in the participation of people in organizations that promote citizen welfare or provide support and aid in the context of scarcity. These organizations act primarily as a counterbalance to individualism and the reduced role played by the State, while participation is mainly associated with voluntary work. Especially present in countries with a liberal tradition, such as the UK and Ireland, both *beneficiary* and *volunteer* participate as individuals, the first as a victim of life decisions or circumstances, the latter as a citizen helping fellow citizens on an individual and personal basis. Hence, they generate biographic solutions to systemic problems (Beck 2001) and more committed modalities in the individuation process (Beck 2000).

> 'I did an awful lot of work in the schools, I was a parent helper, that was voluntary, I put my name down for so many activities, like I'd go out on all the school trips, and then at our local library one of the librarians said, "We're looking for a volunteer to run an afterschool homework club in the library with the computers and the internet", so I volunteered. I loved doing that.' (UK/F/long-term unemployed)

During the economic crisis, austerity measures and a reduction in private donations threaten the existence of organizations that provide support and care services to households in situations of hardship. This, consequently, causes a decline in forms of association, which relates as much to subjects' experience of time and resource restrictions as the decrease in public investment in these organizations.

Participation in formal politics (political parties and trade unions), which could also be understood as being closer to the associative pole, was notable for its general absence in the households that participated in the study. As a matter of fact, a clear delegitimization and distrust of traditional political parties and trade unions was a common thread that ran across generations and nations. These institutions were viewed as self-serving and were represented in a very negative light.

> 'In any case, all unions in such jobs, they always have money. Because they take money from the employers, who are ... you know. In theory, they mediate supposedly for the workers too, but in reality, they make deals and take the money and sign contracts for the salaries to be reduced.' (Greece/M/20 years old)

On the other hand, the examples of formal political participation that we found consisted of local political involvement born out of a commitment to and participation in local groups and associations, which contributes to a more inclusive idea of citizenship.

Looking to the community side of Tönnies' dichotomy, some participants, mainly urban, referred to social relations and social networks articulated through active participation in associations or organizations of a different kind: religious associations (mainly in the Spanish and Turkish case studies), neighbours' associations (in the Spanish and Finnish study areas), leisure associations (Irish case study), and so on. In these cases, solidarity (and a sense of community) is built or stimulated by different social and political organizations rather than informally or from the bottom up. This is evident in the urban areas in Turkey, Spain, Greece and Ireland where associations have an important role in the articulation of coexistence and the production of social cohesion that goes beyond the material and economic domain.

Hence, there is an emergence and multiplication of new forms of participation that constructs social bonds around common projects focused on helping and improving collective wellbeing, as well as the horizontal organization and co-participation in hybrid (in terms of nationality, religion or ethnic origin) value-oriented groups.

Many of these social organizations and associations of mutual solidarity concentrate their efforts on specific groups or needs, such as: food and clothes banks, legal assistance for households at risk of eviction, self-help groups for disabled or sick people, urban vegetable gardens, and so on. These organizations are also willing to encourage participation in their activities, be they users, beneficiaries or non-affected people. However, this 'activation' of help recipients is not an easy task. Households in situations of hardship rarely have the time or the material and symbolic resources required to provide help to someone else or even to feel at ease in such a role. Sometimes they do not feel part of the solidarity group's project for cultural reasons, as it is alien to their political socialization. Nevertheless, participating or getting involved in one of these organizations or associations represents a step toward the transformation of subjects and/or their situation.

Additionally, cultural or subcultural organizations bring together people who are connected by common interests or affinities, like music, playing sport, theatre, dance or other leisure activities (much like aesthetic communities; Maffesoli 1990). Due to the main purposes of these organizations, they are more likely to be horizontal, in the sense that all members participate and are part of a common project. In this sense, there is no divide between participant and beneficiary, such as in other organizations. Participation in activities organized by these organizations potentially produces the basis for some form of common identity. For instance, in the Irish case study, the local band seemed to also function as a local cultural organization, whose importance made it representative of the whole town, a token of local identity. In the rural Spanish case study, the brotherhood groups (bearers) that carry the palanquins during the Easter religious processions have a similar role in the community. In these activities, such as concerts, processions or sporting events, local non-participants become the beneficiaries.

On the other hand, the research also identified a strengthening of some communities where solidarity was articulated on the basis of the similarity or homogeneity of participants (ethnic, national, religious or local) to the exclusion of non-members. This often took the form of a 'defensive retreat' against a supposedly threatening Other (Colectivo IOE and Ortí 2007), which could be related to increasing uncertainty and fears for personal security in these times of crisis.

In this sense, in all the urban case studies in the participating countries, a worse present is identified by many inhabitants. This is related to an increase in criminality, violence and danger in public areas, and was often associated with drug gangs and migrants and usually in ghettoized communities. Indeed, in the Turkish urban case, the decline of the neighbourhood was attributed, frequently, to the economic crisis and the influx of refugees (Aytekin and Şengül 2016). Hence, migrants become the scapegoats for a deteriorating socio-economic situation in which they are viewed as competitors for scarce resources (jobs or social benefits). An extract from an interview in Ireland provides a good example of these exclusionary tendencies:

'Well I've lived here all my life, ya know what I mean, [...] so to be fair I know nearly everyone but since the last five/six years I know it sounds shocking but the amount of foreigners they're putting in, they're putting in loads of them and I notice it as well there's a load of them on the road up here and they do not put a bin tag on their bins and their bins get collected, I just can't understand that at all.' (Ireland/ mother of three children/rural area)

This was often the case in the rural areas too, which on the surface seemed much more cohesive and united, but this was usually a result of having more homogeneous communities in geographically isolated areas (in the sense of having very little or no integration with other municipalities and cities in the region). Therefore, differences, whenever and however they occur, usually imply a great cleavage in the population and sometimes boost attitudes of 'restrictive communitarism' (Serrano et al. 2019). The rural case in Turkey was a paradigmatic example of local community cohesion, based on the homogeneity and isolation of the village. On the other hand, the Spanish rural case area was, to a degree, representative of a restrictive communitarism as the community was not very open to strangers and foreigners.

'All the clothes I have are from Caritas [church-run charity], I haven't bought myself clothes in more than ten years, I haven't bought anything. But my circumstances don't matter a jot, the Moros [pejorative term for North Africans] are first in line, then the Gypsies, and then last of all the Spanish. That's why. The Moros have everything laid on, then the Gypsies, and then us afterwards, when there's nothing left. I just don't see the logic.' (Spain/mother of four children/unemployed/ urban area) 'if you tell me you've no work, well you're out, because you're not going to take advantage of my assistance [social welfare], when there are people from my country that need it. What's happened to us? We've had a lot of immigration, Romanians, Ecuadorians, from everywhere.' (Spain/mother of two children/rural area)

In various contexts, new forms of community processes, linked to political participation and civic engagement, have also emerged as a result of the crisis, albeit the widespread narrative is one of weakening community ties in most of the case study areas. As was observed in the Greek report, there is an unprecedented growth of political mobilization and participation that has affected every sphere of daily life. An important part of participation in this context is related to the re-emergence of 'street politics' through demonstrations, campaigns, occupations, protests, and so on. This was especially the case in Spain and Greece, but also in Germany, where it is linked to the emergence of the Pegida (nationalist, right-wing political) movement and its opponents. In other countries, such as Ireland, the conflict related to water charges, an austerity tax, gave birth to the Right2Water movement.

Along with this growing street mobilization, we find the consolidation of movements, groups, platforms, associations and new political parties, all of which build spaces and structures that serve for protesting and making claims to legal rights and so on. During the last number of years in the Spanish and the Greek urban cases, many spaces and structures have come into existence, such as self-support groups, anti-racist groups, pro-minority rights movements (ethnic, sexual, migrants, and so on), anti-eviction platforms, collaborative initiatives, and so on. Most of these are based on the collaboration and participation of citizens, acting to promote a diverse range of social initiatives that serve to develop political activism and the construction of collaborative spaces amongst the most deprived people.

In the context of these new forms of participation, we also found several formal structures with radical right and neo-Nazi ideology (i.e. Golden Dawn in Greece, Alternative for Germany in Germany or the True Finns Party in Finland) that develop political mobilization activities and some social initiatives, such as food banks, clothing exchange, exclusively for national, white and heteronormative populations. In these cases, community bonds are fostered at the expense of fragmenting and creating conflict within the population. Hence, these groups create a kind of community resilience that is fostered at the expense of excluding, sometimes with aggression, a significant part of their wider societies.

RESILIENCE IN THE CONTEXT OF COMMUNITY AND POLITICAL PARTICIPATION

In relation to resilience, the key idea being emphasized in this chapter is the community-related and political participation of the individuals and households in the study. The influence of such participation on their resilience can be expressed in positive and negative terms, which we recount in this section.

In negative terms, and across all nations under study, the situation of the more isolated households in our sample clearly shows the different ways in which an absence of relevant social participation can trigger individualization processes that have severe consequences on their potential for resilience. In a practical sense, this means that these households lack the social networks that are necessary to hear about useful information, such as potential job opportunities, associations that can be of help or support, public allowances for people in need, and so on. Nowadays, much of this information can be obtained through the internet, but the direct experience or knowledge of people known to the subject make it easier to make a call or to go straight to where help can be obtained. For instance, if it were not for a close relative, one of the rural Spanish households would most likely have never attended the anti-eviction platform (PAH) meetings and hence never have obtained the advice and support that helped them to keep their house. The Polish fieldwork also shows how much easier it is to find employment for those who have a broad network of connections, especially if the available jobs are in the informal market (Wódz et al. 2016, p. 28).

In a deeper sense, our analyses highlight the important contribution that social relationships and participation make to psychosocial wellbeing and how this is often lacking for more isolated households.

On the more positive side of things, involvement into community and politics presents two types of contributions to households' resilience: firstly, in terms of material needs (food, housing, energy/fuel, clothing, educational spaces, work and health) and, secondly, with social, spiritual and symbolic needs (identity, dignity, participation, affective support, leisure, sociability, conflict mediation, cultural integration, spiritual support and so on). Most of the practices include, simultaneously, both types of contribution.

It is interesting to observe how the source (community-related or political) of these contributions changes from one country to another, according to the different ways of constructing communities and political involvement, which in turn relates to the socio-economic situation and the traditional ways that citizenship is built in each context.

In the Turkish urban area, belonging to kinship and politically sectarian networks provides considerable material benefits to households in the form of direct material assistance, various forms of financial assistance, jobs or even shelter. In the rural area, homogeneity dilutes this restrictive component, so 'there is nobody to exclude' and community-related resilience depends exclusively on informal social networks.

In the Greek urban and rural areas, these two features (restrictive socio-communitarian attitudes and membership of informal social networks) converge. Here, the Church, the municipal government and attachment to local associations, trade unions and kinship networks provide households with material and symbolic resources of resilience, but also block any possibilities of experiencing alternative concepts of belonging and networking. Furthermore, this restrictive socio-communitarian frame of resilience was particularly present in the Greek urban area, where being a Greek national was a condition of becoming a beneficiary of the Church (Athanasiou et al. 2016, p. 15).

However, in contrast to this, an experimental collective model of producing both community-related and political resilience was also developing in the Greek urban case area. It includes the establishment of politically engaged solidarity and mutual aid groups based on development through self-organization. This model varies from pure material assistance to people in situations of hardship to active and cohesive political mobilization and even to the construction of new forms of cohabitation that transcend the traditional family model. Hence, it produces emotional alliances based on alternative networks of mutual support. Its most interesting asset is its potential to build an alternative source of resilience, where a renewed version of political and symbolic contribution leads to a material contribution. The Spanish case is quite similar to the Greek one, but it is important to note that we found hardly any narratives on these alternative socio-political practices, which was only evident through ethnographic fieldwork rather than the Spanish participants' interviews.

In the Irish and German case studies the crisis appeared to have provoked the emergence or strengthening of the role of cooperative and inclusive community and social practices. In principle, these initiatives make a mostly economic-material contribution (exchange/sharing: essentials, home repair, hairdressing, transport), but their activities can also form the basis for the development of personal and emotional bonds. However, or in opposition to the Spanish and Greek cases, these dynamics seem to be almost completely free of political interests or a collective engagement with the space (village or neighbourhood) where they take place. In Ireland and Germany, these inclusive practices have become as relevant as socio-familiar practices in Mediterranean countries. Furthermore, at least in the Irish case study, Community Development Centres were identified as very important for economic resilience. Hence, although people are not politically active, they rely in many cases on government agencies and local government offices to support resilience practices, even if such support has been drastically reduced through austerity (Gallagher et al. 2016). In the UK, Polish and Portuguese case studies, the strength of hegemonic ideological and cultural pattern of individualism seems especially strong and makes the symbolic and material contribution to resilience by community-related and political practices quite weak. In these countries, with the exception of some specific examples of socio-political reactive activism in UK (that is, Focus E15 – mothers against council evictions), the main sources of economic help are benefits from social institutions and, above all, individual strategies. In the UK these individual strategies and efforts often come hand in hand with de-consumption/inverse consumption practices, like pawning and gambling. One of the UK respondents, for example, commented that the opening of a pawn shop and a betting shop next to each other was an example of this (national) system of individual(ist) resilience. The UK rural area was reported to produce a much more communitarian form of resilience because interaction is more personalized (one on one), allowing for greater empathy.

In the Portuguese case studies, this tendency to individual resilience gravitates more to family practices, but, apart from that, isolation predominates. Beyond public institutions and external interventions there were very few examples of self-organization and a sense of community or subcultural organizations and activities that produce social cohesion and a sense of belonging. So, while the economic contributions of these socio-familiar networks may be diverse (according to the needs and capability of offering assistance in each household), the symbolic contribution is mainly emotional and represents restrictive belonging.

> 'I depend a lot on my parents' help. I have to work for many hours … Me and my daughter eat in my parents' house every day. We don't want for anything. She practises swimming and they pay for it. If she needs a pair of shoes, clothes, they buy them. It is an enormous help I have. But my parents are 72. It is very stressful for them to see me in this situation. At that age they begin to think that they won't last much longer. And they begin to worry about what will happen to me and to their grand-daughter.' (Portugal/mother/mid-40s/rural area)

In the Polish case studies, the restructuration of post-industrial areas in the post-communist era is having a diverse impact on the Upper Silesia industrial region. Nevertheless, in conditions of hardship, the general tendency is towards individualism and isolation.

The Finnish case studies are distinctive. In the rural case area, economic contributions to the community-related forms of resilience are based on work, which is organized in reindeer cooperatives, takes the form of informal mutual help and is based on social exchange. These networks also make important symbolic contributions: a sense of belonging, solidarity, identity and sociability. In the urban case, attempts to keep services close to home create a strong community spirit and endow its inhabitants with a degree of community-related socio-political awareness, in addition to the production of material improvements to the village.

> 'Also, the working community, you have to feel that you belong to it, it is not just something where you walk in the morning and walk out in the evening. This is especially important when you work with challenging issues.' (Finland/father of more than five children/rural area)

CONCLUSIONS

In general terms, the analysis shows that the different forms of community-related social and political participation contribute positively to the implementation of practices of resilience in order to cope with adversity. Participation and inclusion in groups, initiatives, associations and organizations governed by community principles and with political aims generate synergic forms of resilience that ease the confluence of diverse practices and strategies of coping with the crisis. This occurs as much at an individual as at a household and community level, but also aids psychosocial wellbeing and group empowerment. They are synergic because they feed individual forms of resilience, especially participation in politically oriented endeavours focused on the transformation of socio-economics and power relations.

However, the present state of society increasingly produces processes of individualization that frays community bonds within vulnerable populations that inhabit fragmented and tensioned spaces, leading to disorientation, isolation and the fostering of participation-inhibiting feelings like shame or powerlessness. Furthermore, in many social contexts the crisis has indeed eroded the possibilities of social participation in terms of the availability of material, temporal and symbolic resources.

On the other hand, and simultaneously, under certain circumstances and with diverse manifestations and intensities, some bonds of solidarity and mutual help emerged, sometimes intensely, when they were, in reality, supposed to dilute and disappear. Old forms of community, more frequent in the rural case areas and in certain groups (ethnic, religious), as well as new mutual help support initiatives (especially in urban contexts) were found to have multiplied in all social contexts, while coexisting with tendencies towards isolation and individuation. In some contexts, participation was limited to local networks that targeted material aid and reinforced neighbourhood collaborative bonds. On other occasions voluntary organizations substituted for the shrinking role of public institutions as sources of support for people in situations of hardship. In some other cases we found many new forms of social participation developed by bottom-up organizations that reinforce solidarity (community-like) bonds and mutual help, while strengthening social cohesion and a sense of collective identity.

In some contexts, like in Spain and Greece, these initiatives often take the form of social mobilizations that have experienced a certain consolidation or institutionalization and have a clear political and protest role. Thus, new political parties and new forms of participation and empowerment emerge locally in response to social problems triggered by the economic crisis and therefore foster new forms of communication and participation in the public sphere while contributing to the survival and participation of the most crisis-affected families. However, the participation of these families directly in political mobilization, as our fieldwork shows, is scant even though they benefit from their actions.

At the same time one can witness the emergence of groups and organizations articulated around a defensive and excluding communitarianism that promotes the individual and household resilience in restricted communities, but at the expense of fostering conflict and endangering social cohesion and harmonious cohabitation. These practices relate as much to community resilience strategies understood as a whole as their diversity and complexity.

On the whole, the results identify several paradoxes of social and political participation as it relates to household resilience. First of all, social participation continues to be an important asset for resilience and coping with adversity while it is simultaneously rendered more difficult in these individualizing times. This weakens the social fabric and thus also weakens deprived households. Second, when the opposite strengthening or emergence of communities takes place, social organizations and networks seem to become a substitute for a retreating welfare state and thus a justification for neoliberal policies. Finally, even though they may be positive for resilience, community dynamics also have a darker side, since they can open the way for the exclusion of some collectives, especially in groups that restrict solidarity along cultural, ethnic or religious lines.

As a consequence, even if social participation has proved valuable for resilience, civil society and social participation cannot in themselves substitute for welfare states since they lack their redistributive capacities and their universal attention to social needs, as seen in the history of the development of welfare states in western societies. However, some policy trends appear to promote the replacement of welfare states by civil society. Our analyses show that even civil society initiatives are highly dependent on welfare provision and have suffered from public budget cuts. And even if we contemplated a positive answer to the suggestion, the question of the approach to such activity would remain: could civil society ever take on a rights-based and universalist approach in a decentralized provision strategy in the same manner as the State and avoid the exclusion of certain social groups? It is not easy to see how it could.

BIBLIOGRAPHY

Alonso, L. E., Fernández, C. and Ibáñez, R. (2011), 'Del consumismo a la culpabilidad: en torno a los efectos disciplinarios de la crisis económica', *Política y Sociedad* 48(2): 353–79.
Athanasiou, A., Kambouri, N., Marinoudi, S. and Petraki, G. (2016), *Communities, participation & politics. Work package 8. Greek report*, unpublished RESCuE project report.
Aytekin, E. A. and Şengül, H. T. (2016), *Communities, participation & politics. Work package 8. Turkish report*, unpublished RESCuE project report.
Bauman, Z. (2002), *Modernidad líquida*, Buenos Aires: Fondo de Cultura económica.
Beck, U. (2000), *Un nuevo mundo feliz: la precariedad del trabajo en la era de la globalización*, Barcelona: Paidós.
Beck, U. (2001), *La sociedad del riesgo: hacia una nueva Modernidad*, Barcelona: Paidós.
Beck, U. and Beck-Gernsheim, E. (2002), *Individualization: Institutionalized individualism and its social and political consequences*, London: Sage Publications.
Bourdieu, P. (1999), *La miseria del mundo*, Akal: Madrid.
Capucha, L., Calado, A. and Estêvão, P. (2016), *Communities, participation & politics. Work package 8. Portuguese report*, Unpublished RESCuE project report.
Castel, R. (1999), *La metamorfosis de la cuestión social: una crónica del salariado*, Barcelona: Paidós.
Colectivo IOE and Ortí, A. (2007), *La convivencia en Madrid. Discursos ante el modelo de desarrollo de la ciudad y la instalación de población inmigrante*, Madrid: Estudio encargado por el Observatorio de las Migraciones y de la Convivencia Intercultural de la ciudad de Madrid. Available at: http://www.colectivoioe.org/uploads/cd378eccdc4f7742c20992da3b66cfa4a452bf99.pdf (accessed 28 August 2020).
Dagdeviren, H., Donoghue, M. and Promberger, M. (2016), 'Resilience, hardship and social conditions', *Journal of Social Policy* 45: 1–20.
Donoghue, M. (2016), *Communities, participation & politics. Work package 8. British report*, unpublished RESCuE project report.
Estêvão, P., Calado, A. and Capucha, L. (2017), 'Resilience. Moving from a "heroic" notion to a sociological concept', *Sociologia, problemas e practicas* 85: 9–25.
Gallagher, K. Gilmartin, N. and Gray, J. (2016), *Communities, participation & politics. Work package 8. Irish report*, unpublished RESCuE project report.
Herrera, M. R. and Cívico, I. (2015), 'En los Tiempos del Malestar: Movimientos Sociales, Acción Colectiva y Participación Política', paper presented at the REPS Conference, Barcelona, Spain, 5–6 February.
Kaztman, R. (2001), 'Seducidos y abandonados: el aislamiento social de los pobres urbanos', *Revista de la CEPAL*, 75: 171–89.
Kountouri, F. (2015), 'Participatory types in Greece during the 2000's and the debt crisis: The significance of socio-demographic variables and media uses', *Επιθεώρηση Κοινωνικών Ερευνών* (*The Greek Review of Social Research*) 144(144): 45–67.
Maffesoli, M. (1990), *El tiempo de las tribus*, Barcelona: Icaria Editorial.

Meier, L. (2013), 'Encounters with haunted industrial workplaces and emotions of loss: Class-related senses of place within the memories of metalworkers', *Cultural Geographies* 20(4): 467–83.

Meier, L., Promberger, M., Boost, M. and Müller, J. (2016), *Communities, participation & politics. Work package 8. German report*, unpublished RESCuE project report.

Merklen, D. (2005), *Pobres ciudadanos: Las clases populares en la era democrática (Argentina, 1983–2003)*, Buenos Aires: Editorial Gorla.

Morales, L. (2006), *Instituciones, movilización y participación política: el asociacionismo político en las democracias occidentales*, Madrid: Centro de Estudios Políticos y Constitucionales.

Promberger, M., Huws, U., Dagdeviren, H., Meier, L., Sowa, F., Boost, M., Athanasiou, A., Aytekin, A., Arnal, M., Capucha, L., Castro de, C., Faliszek, K., Gray, J., Łęcki, K., Mandrysz, W., Petraki, G., Revilla, J. C., Şengül, T., Słania, B., Tennberg, M., Vuojala-Magga, T. and Wódz, K. (2014), *Patterns of resilience during socioeconomic crises among households in Europe (RESCuE). Concept, Objectives and Work Packages of an EU FP 7 Project*, Nuremberg: IAB research report 05/2014.

Promberger, M., Marinoudi, T. and Martín, P. (2016), 'Unter der erschütterten Oberfläche: Sozioökonomische Praktiken, Zivilgesellschaft und Resilienz in der europäischen Krise', *Forschungsjournal Soziale Bewegungen, special issue: Kapitalismus und Zivilgesellschaft* (3): 86–97.

Putnam, R. (2000), *Bowling alone*, New York: Simon and Schuster.

Revilla, J. C., Jefferys, S. and Tovar, F. J. (2013), 'Collective identities in the age of restructuring: Old and new class, space and community-based identities in six European regions', *International Sociology* 135: 13–36.

Revilla, J. C., Martín, M. P. and Castro, C. (2018), 'The reconstruction of resilience as a social and collective phenomenon: poverty and coping capacity during the economic crisis', *European Societies* 20(1): 89–110.

Sennett, R. (1998), *The corrosion of character: The personal consequences of work in the new capitalism*, New York: Norton.

Serrano, A., Martín, P. and de Castro C. (2016), *Communities, participation & politics. Work package 8. Spanish report*, unpublished RESCuE project report.

Serrano, A., Martín, P. and de Castro, C. (2019), 'Sociologizando la resiliencia. El papel de la participación socio-comunitaria y política en las estrategias de afrontamiento de la crisis', *Revista Española de Sociología* 28(2): 227–47.

Serrano, A., Parajuá, D. and Zurdo, A. (2013), 'Marcos interpretativos de lo social en la vivencia de la "nueva pobreza"', *Cuadernos de Relaciones Laborales* 31(2): 337–82.

Tönnies, F. (1979[1887]), *Comunidad y asociación*, Barcelona: Ediciones Península.

Vola, J., Tennberg, M. and Vuojala-Magga, T. (2016), *Communities, participation & politics. Work package 8. Finnish report*, unpublished RESCuE project report.

Wódz, K., Mandrysz, W. and Klimek, M. (2016), *Communities, participation & politics. Work package 8. Polish report*, unpublished RESCuE project report.

12. Social economy and household resilience[1]

Witold Mandrysz and Kazimiera Wódz

INTRODUCTION

Social economy entities, to be widely understood as organized actors, non-government and not solely private for profit, acting primarily for social concerns, are crucially involved in providing social services to poor and other vulnerable populations, and they are well known and well established throughout Europe. They run food banks and counselling offices in almost all European countries, but almost everything else varies considerably, making it hard to develop clearer demarcations, to identify consistent structures, or even to develop a definition which is not fraying at the seams. Nevertheless, this chapter makes an attempt to do exactly this, in order to investigate the impact of social economy entities to the development and maintenance of poor households' resilience.

The first part of the chapter presents a short description of the conceptual framework of social economy and social entrepreneurship and its development as part of the cohesion policy of the European Union (EU), as a normative, political and conceptual background. The second section presents differences and similarities in defining and understanding the concept of social economy and its background in the nine countries investigated (see Promberger et al. 2014), in order to identify and understand the actual condition of social entrepreneurship and social economy activities in different European countries. It is the basis for a typological attempt to conceptualize different kinds of social economy. The third part of the chapter is based mainly on fieldwork findings. It is based on statements of participants on their interactions with social economy entities, the everyday practices of social economy entities, and how they contribute to the resilience of the households and communities observed.

CONCEPTS OF SOCIAL ECONOMY

Helen Haugh (2005, p. 2) defines social economy as a 'collective term for the part of the economy that is neither privately nor publicly controlled'. Amin et al. define social economy as 'not-for-profit activity geared towards meeting social needs' (Amin et al. 2002, p. 1), and there are further definitions in the literature. Almost all definitions share a common denominator ex negativo by stating the social economy to be non-state and non-solely for profit but differ widely in the following dimensions:

• Limited to the field of social services versus operating in different sectors but having social objectives (among others).
• Non-profit versus not only for profit/with social goals.
• Is active participation of members, volunteers, clients in production and decisions a necessary condition or not?
• Private enterprises with social goals or side goals included or not?

Thus, details depend on the specific definition but, widely understood, the conceptual space of the term social economy includes non-profit organizations as well as associations, cooperatives, mutual organizations, foundations, profit-oriented private enterprises in the social sector as well as those with more than just marginal social goals. Some synonyms and related terms are also used, such as community economy and community capitalism. Social economy thus oscillates between the idea of a socially engaged capitalist economy, on one hand, and an alternative to a capitalist form of community or organization, non- or low-marketized economic activity, on the other. In the first, the crucial variable could be the extent or degree to which social issues are relevant; in the second, a crucial variable could be the degree of de-commodification (see Esping-Andersen 1990) in terms of a relative distance to market procedures and prices.

Before proceeding to discuss how social economy is understood in Germany, the UK, Poland, Portugal, Spain, Greece, Ireland, Finland and Turkey it is necessary to consider in more detail some ambiguities in the understanding of social economy.

The social economy and its supporters assume that their sector plays an important role in the creation of new jobs and other forms of support for people threatened by social exclusion. They emphasize social economy to be a significant factor in local development and providing more services that allow human needs to be satisfied in a better way (European Commission: Euricse 2013). It may also create a complex system of management (community economy), involve non-governmental organizations in the activities of local authorities, and affect the establishment of local and neighbourhood forms of economic cooperation and mutual support. One developmental goal of a thus-defined social economy is to create an inclusive local labour market (Zybała 2007).

It is estimated that the social economy in Europe, understood as cooperatives, mutuals, associations, foundations and social enterprises, engages over 14.5 million paid employees, equivalent to about 6.5% of the working population of the EU-27 and about 7.4% of the EU-15 countries. These figures also include the vast majority of social enterprises using legal forms strongly associated with social economy, such as social cooperatives and entrepreneurial associations (European Commission: Euricse 2013, p. 45).

Some current attempts to define social economy are associated with the Social Economy Charter CEP-CMAF of 2002.[2] It states that social economy organizations are social and economic entities operating in all sectors. They are distinguished from other economic activities mainly by their objectives and their characteristic form of entrepreneurship, which include social aspects. These companies are particularly active in certain areas, such as social protection, social services, healthcare, banking, insurance, agricultural production, consumer issues, associative work, crafts, housing, neighbourhood services, education and training, and the area of sports, culture and recreation. Still there is some confusion at the fringes, as certain cooperatives may be purely in pursuit of profit or entrepreneurial functions by socializing risk costs among members – such as a maintenance cooperative of flat proprietors, a mutual loans cooperative for spirit and wine wholesalers, which hardly can be seen as a contributor to the solution of social problems or a benefactor for society as a whole. On the other hand, working-class cooperatives for housing, gardening, building, health insurance and consumption have been very early and crucial parts of what today is called social economy – and some of them still are.

Since the 1990s, the European Commission has contributed significantly to the development of the idea of social economy and social entrepreneurship. For example, its 'Communication on Promoting the Role of Voluntary Organisations and Foundations in Europe' (European Commission 1997) highlighted the importance of the non-governmental organization (NGO) sector in both counteracting social exclusion and developing social policy. Another important step was the implementation of the EQUAL Community Initiative, which was part of the EU strategy for creating a greater number of better workplaces and for ensuring broad access to them. To create a favourable environment for the development of social business in Europe, the European Commission developed the Entrepreneurship 2020 Action Plan 2012.

'The concept of social enterprise overlaps with the traditional social economy organizations and cuts across legal forms, as an entity that operates as a social enterprise might choose to be registered as an association, cooperative, charity etc., as a private enterprise, or as one of the specific forms set up in recent years under national legislation.' (European Commission: Euricse 2013, p. 31)

There is a debate about the position and the responsibility of social economy entities in providing social services. Sometimes it is argued that, although the entities of social economy may not fully replace the support of public aid institutions, or may not enable people affected by social exclusion to find a proper job, broadly defined entities of social economy may nevertheless be more successful and productive in providing social services than public institutions.

> 'In this sense, it is always worth considering whether what is offered by social welfare could simply be provided more effectively by a social economy entity, particularly when it is also capable of earning its own funds.' (Giza-Poleszczuk and Hausner 2008, p. 16)

But such arguments can also prove controversial in two respects. First, social economy may reduce the expenditure burdens on the state not only by better organization or by introducing profits for co-founding, but also by reducing the scope, quality and coverage of services, and last but not least, 'through the exploitation of social economy workers, generally [being] paid less than their peers who are in the public sector doing equal or equivalent work' (Capucha et al. 2016, p. 6). Second, more generally, it is controversial to shift social policy tasks and responsibilities which are based on civil rights from state authorities under political control to businesses or NGOs which are controlled far less. Third, there is little empirical evidence so far, that private or NGO suppliers are actually more efficient or effective than public suppliers. Where respective literature exists, there are no clear results in favour of the social economy or private suppliers, and some hints speak of a better or more comprehensive performance of public suppliers against private ones in the long run (Winterhager 2006; Davies 2008; Bennmarker et al. 2009; Krug and Stephan 2013). At least in some of these studies the investigated private suppliers would fall under the definitions of social economy. It also has to be mentioned that, at least in some European countries, the social economy uses and redistributes public money to a huge extent, which may look like gaining income from a market from a microeconomic perspective, but is just a shift in who does the last mile of redistributing public money; and the dependency on public money seems to open the gate for implementing public governance in private and Third Sector suppliers of social services, making them a 'just in time' supplier (Aiken and Bode 2009).

In the UK in 2014, large charities received 'at least £3.1 billion' in public money, accounting for around '24% of their incoming resources' (Norton 2014, p. 1). Some have suspected that in recent times it has been 'public services "on the cheap", rather than local innovation, [that] constitute the real motivation for the government's interest in the social economy' (Di Domenico et al. 2009, p. 982; Donoghue et al. 2016, p. 3).

Opposite those critical remarks, affirmative positions perceive the social economy as a force that strengthens social inclusion and civic participation in favour of individuals and communities, which may enhance the processes of social and political inclusion. Some authors argue that social economy organizations have the potential to strengthen social capital through participative processes, collective activities and social innovations, with the goal of resolving common problems (Olsson 2003). Moreover, as other authors say, social economy may encourage citizenship participation, allowing the most socially excluded collectivities to participate not only in collective goods, but also at least potentially in community decision-making processes (Sanz 2013; cited in Serrano et al. 2016, p. 3).

For socio-economic development, not only are community relations – such as close ties and desire to cooperate – very important, but so too are external connections which link the community to institutions, organizations or other communities and which accrue benefits in the form of resources, financial or non-financial support and new markets (Putnam 2001; Woolcock and Narayan 2007). 'Social enterprises in particular and the Third Sector in general, as sites of both social reintegration and provision for social need, are increasingly seen as sources of social capital of a particular sort' (Amin et al. 2002, p. 7). Moreover, in countries like Turkey, where the social economy is underdeveloped, the concept of social capital emerges more prominently in order to permit understanding of different mechanisms (Poyraz et al. 2016, p. 12).

As said, there is not sufficient evidence on how (which kind of) social economies perform practically, in terms of what they offer, with whom they compete, and which comparative outcomes are generated. Certain kinds of social economy are far from new but just appear under a new observation label, from huge charities to class-based cooperatives. Other entities enter parts of the field where the welfare state never reached out directly, or has been withdrawing before, thus acting in a complementary or substitutive way, while – as far as we see – just very few social economy entities in the field of poverty and labour market integration actually compete with welfare state authorities[3] – and just those few would fulfil one precondition for a methodologically rigid evaluation, which is offering roughly the same social service but based on a different organizational form and different inputs. Apart from very few studies, there is little such evaluation done, known or published, a gap which cannot be closed or narrowed by this chapter. Consequently, the next sections will be a description of organizational patterns in their association to country-level social policy, some first evidence of the functionality and usefulness of services offered to poor and resilient households, leading into a few hypotheses for further research.

PATTERNS OF SOCIAL ECONOMY

Based on the empirical information collected, it is possible to identify certain 'patterns' of understanding and defining social economy, which constitute the legal, institutional and cultural circumstances underpinning how social economy entities function at the level of individual countries. The following classification is an attempt to identify certain patterns of action of social economy entities. Such patterns may, to some extent, help to explore the relationship between the different ways of understanding and implementing the idea of social economy and social entrepreneurship, and the levels of resilience of individuals and households.

The main criteria for the following categorization are:

- The dominant or highly relevant way in which social economy and social entrepreneurship entities are defined in particular countries (NGO sector, social cooperatives and social enterprises, community economy entities).
- The scope, type and degree of connections between these entities and public institutions.
- The dominant financing method and level of 'marketization' of activities falling within the scope of social economy (financing under public subsidies, obtaining grants, running a business to achieve social goals).

Four basic patterns were identified:

1. The charity economy.
2. Mixed non-state social service and support providers.
3. Labour market (re-)integration entities.
4. The collective/community-based economy.

These four types are described in detail below, and illustrated by different country cases, although they are not consistently associated to certain countries (see Table 12.1).

The Charity Economy

In this pattern, a large amount of social services are offered by huge charities, often based on religious, philanthropic or class-based early-modern social movements, organizations or foundations – Caritas, the Diaconia, Santa Casa da Misericórdia, the Red Cross, the Rowntree Foundation, Oxfam, the Arbeiterwohlfahrt, just to name a few. These nationwide or even international organizations are to a great extent funded by welfare state money through refunds, reimbursements, tax privileges or direct payments, and through donations or church money, but very little through profit activities. Offering their services to public authorities through market-like procedures like applications for funding calls may occur but is not the usual case. Such huge charity providers, NGOs, operating in the broad sphere of social services are the most visible social economy entities in countries where authorities delegate social services (at different levels – central/federal, regional/state, local/municipal) to charities, which results in a strong market and political position. They are well respected and professionally prepared, and their operations are based on well-educated and experienced staff and large numbers of volunteers. Such organizations have dominant positions and a respective political and legal status, for example, in Germany and Portugal, but are very visible also in other countries like Spain, the UK, and others. Quite often, these organizations are structured as a roof or federation – or holding – of numerous minor organizations with some limited autonomy as separate legal entities in terms of business legislation (Gruber 2014). Those huge charities can offer a wide and differing country-wide range of services, be it directly or through subdivisions: they run orphanages, hospitals, childcare units, foodbanks, counselling offices, self-help groups, homeless persons' support centres, charity shops, bank accounts for donations, community libraries, women's shelters and numerous other services.

'Talking about Social Economy in Germany means also talking about the welfare state. It is a special feature in Germany that the Third Sector is (still) often and mostly financed by the welfare state. This shapes the picture of the German Social Economy system as a place where mere charity and independence from state funding is a rare phenomenon. Social services are mostly offered by non-profit charitable organizations, while the most important are the six major independent charities in Germany, [...]. These charities are mostly funded by state resources and social security contributions.' (Boost et al. 2016: 4)

We should add that this is not only limited to Germany, and we have also to add that donations play an important role, especially in the charity economy, but usually second to public money. And, to be precise: welfare state money does not mean that this money necessarily comes directly from state budgets. At least in Germany, which we hold to be the constitutive example for this type, main sources of funding for those charities are budgets owned by publicly controlled but non-governmental entities, such as the public pension insurance, the public unemployment insurance, the public health insurances, which pay the charities for running hospitals, treating patients, counselling unemployed and other tasks. Obligatory contributions to social security institutions are also known at least from Turkey, Greece, Spain, Finland, Portugal and the UK, of which some goes through huge NGOs, charities, for supplying respective services. Those top charities providing social services are not only able to use welfare state financial support. Being publicly recognized and respected, they are very effective at attracting support from private donors and are well prepared to apply for EU supported projects, and hold tax or organizational privileges – or even own state-warranted monopolies on certain resources like the lottery business (Spain and Portugal). All these factors make the financial and organizational situation of such entities better than that of other actors in the Third Sector. They have a respected say in social policy, as their members and activists are well represented in political parties, policy advisory boards and expert circles, even holding up representation offices in capital cities. Apart from the undoubted advantages of this model, in which strong non-government charities supply a broad range of social services commissioned by public institutions, there are also certain risks, due to their level of dependence on the welfare state on one hand, and an 'oligopolization' of the Third Sector by the strongest charities on the other. Such structures may limit the developmental potential and creativity of organizations operating on a minor scale. Some of their subdivisions may have the legal form of registered enterprises, but their ownership is far from being entrepreneurial in terms of norms and values.

Mixed Non-state Social Service and Support Providers

This includes civil society organizations as well as social enterprises. Usually they are smaller than the organizations of the first type, a bit more independent from public money, and they usually are not seen as a charity and do not regularly collect and receive donations. When they get public money, they do so through market-like relations to a great extent – such as applying to provide certain services in a state programme. Social economy entities of this type include non-government and non-profit organizations as well as profit-oriented social entrepreneurs. The type occurs more strongly in countries or fields of activity where both a strong position of the Third Sector and quite a high level of decentralization can be observed. NGOs and the authorities in certain countries were open to strong trends in the development of social entrepreneurship in the 1990s and early 2000s (Finland, Ireland, UK). Finnish and UK national definitions of social enterprise refer to a partial non-profit distribution constraint. In Ireland and Finland, publicly funded schemes targeting social enterprises are very limited or non-existent. In the Finnish case, it has been a deliberate policy choice not to develop such schemes for social enterprises.

In Finland, according to the EU assessment, about 7.65% of employed people work in the field of social economy. The research shows also a significant growth (6.73%) of this kind of employment between 2002/2003 and 2009/2010. The percentage of unpaid voluntary workers in associations is

estimated to be 39% (Monzón Campos and Chaves Ávi 2012, pp. 34–8). From
1990 to 2009, private operational units in the social economy grew in number
from 741 to 4,272, of which 36% were maintained primarily by various associations (Kostilainen and Pättiniemi 2013). A survey conducted in 2009 argued
that about 15,000 enterprises in Finland regarded themselves as social enterprises due to having social goals (Karjalainen and Syrjänen 2009), depending
on the applied criteria (Tennberg et al. 2016, p. 2).

There is also substantial growth of the Third Sector in the UK:

> 'The UK's social economy expanded rapidly between 2000 and 2008, with income
> rising 39% and expenditure 35% (NVCO, 2012: 17). Paid employment in the
> sector increased from 546,000 to 642,000 from 2001 to 2007, an increase of 18%.
> Income from individuals increased by 32%, or 4% per annum, while income from
> government increased by 55%, or 7% per annum (NVCO, 2015: 42)'. (Donoghue
> et al. 2016, p. 3)

The emergence of the concept of social economy in Ireland is closely related
to a number of international and national reports that focused on the potential
for job growth. In Ireland 'the social economy was broadly understood as that
part of the economy between the private and public sectors which engages in
economic activity in order to meet social objectives' (Dagg and Gray 2016,
p. 3). According to an official report published in 2012, social enterprises
employed between 25,000 and 33,000 people in over 1,400 enterprises, with
a total income of €1.4 billion. In general, social enterprises were not seeking
additional state funding (Dagg and Gray 2016, p. 7).

Labour Market (Re-)integration Entities

The main focus in this type is on differently organized actors – social cooperatives, social enterprises and others – with the common denominator of (re-)
integrating people into the labour market, which is to be achieved by training,
further education, subsidized labour, internships and other support measure-
ments. In Poland (as well as in other Eastern European countries) this situation
was also associated with the rather weak position of the non-governmental
sector, which in the 1990s and early 2000s in general was fragmented, acting
mostly on the basis of the voluntary engagement of its members, with a lack
of professional staff and financial stability. In recent years, the position of
the NGO sector in the social economy market has become much stronger,
but during the implementation of the idea of social economy, the so-called
Work Integration Social Enterprise (WISE) was the dominant form in
Poland. The model is based on the idea of building entrepreneurship through
implementation of social economy, defined mainly as social cooperatives
and social enterprises in the form of social inclusion of excluded people, or

through the occupational activation of such people in institutions of vocational reintegration.

In Poland as well, social economy means rather variable institutional and legal forms, such as social enterprises, social cooperatives and social integration centres, whose primary purpose is to prevent social exclusion and professional activation of marginalized people in socio-economic terms. However, it also means business activities within the organization of the Third Sector (Rymsza 2007, pp. 175–6).

Labour market oriented social services provided by social economy units also occur in other countries, often funded by the government through own or EU funds but fielded through local social economy entities of different organizational forms – small NGOs, charity spinoff companies, private companies.

The Collective/Community-based Economy

Within this type, social economy is understood as economic activities, but including social purposes apart from, or beyond, mere labour market integration, and together with another productive purpose of the unit. This type includes local grassroots activities as well as more formal ones. The first kind, often bottom-up, informal, and not initiated or supported by public institutions, is based on local relationships, norms and social ties. It can be found mostly in Mediterranean countries like Greece, Spain, and to some extent Portugal and Turkey – where a more formal, legally demarcated or profit-based social economy is underdeveloped or reduced in times of crisis.

In Greece, the so-called no-middlemen movement is such an example of a community-based social economy. Small and medium-sized enterprises and small family businesses (the prevailing Greek model of economic life), which were on the verge of closing down, struggling to remain afloat and facing unpaid invoices, started to sell their products directly to consumers for cash at fixed prices. They operated through non-profit collectives, instead of through intermediaries – i.e. shop managers, middlemen, wholesalers and traders – thus returning to economic habits from the past (Athanasiou and Marinoudi 2017).

This model is exemplified by the actions taken, not only by small neighbourhood communities but also by large production projects, combining the commitment and resources of many people and institutions. However, their characteristic feature is the fact that their implementation is possible thanks to mutual trust, a willingness to cooperate and a sense of bonding. They contribute, not only to the development of the people directly involved in them, but also to that of the entire community and, thus, to a high level of social identification and acceptance.

The second kind of community-/collective-based social economy shares those characteristics of closeness, shared interest and social bonds, but is more traditional and more formal – the class- or group-based cooperative would be an approximative concept for this. One example is a Spanish wine cooperative, which belongs to 2,000 small wine farmers and olive oil producers who sell their products to the cooperative and receive an agreed price. The cooperative creates workplaces and job opportunities for community members and offers other services, including information, training and counselling. The wine-production cooperative is a source of identity and pride not only for producers, workers and other staff, but also for the town as a whole (Serrano et al. 2016). Other than the grassroots initiatives already mentioned, class-based cooperatives seem to exist all over Europe, in sectors of agriculture, forestry, hunting, housing and building, consumption, and even as a tiny minority in banking and finance, and can be considered one of the most traditional forms of social economy – Elinor Ostrom refers to Spanish irrigation cooperatives which have operated well for six centuries (see Ostrom 1990), and are far from anything that could be called a tragedy of the commons. The social element often is an unseparable by-product of a different main purpose, such as organizing or administering a crucial resource or business function needed by every member of the collective. But, in analysis, the social ties, benefits, participation and controls are a crucial factor for both the wellbeing of the members and the long-term survival of the cooperative (Ostrom 1990).

Very often, the benefits of this type of social economy are restricted to members, and membership itself is restricted to a certain social group or community and/or associated with entry fees. Cooperation and mutual support are an element reserved exclusively for those who are recognized as members of the local community, religious group, political party or economic group (vine growers), thus they are to different degrees more collective or even 'club' goods than public goods. In such cases, bonding social capital is of great importance, together with a tendency to close off the community/group from outsiders, or from everything that is foreign and unknown.[4] As far as the village or little town community is concerned, being different is often frowned upon and it may even be dangerous for those who show such unconventionality. 'Even when rural masses migrate to the big cities, the cultural traits of the former community and the attitudes and values of the individual, change rather slowly' (Kalaycıoğlu 2002, p. 72; Poyraz et al. 2016, p. 16).

THE ROLE OF SOCIAL ECONOMY IN THE DEVELOPMENT OF HOUSEHOLD RESILIENCE: PRACTICAL EXAMPLES

Social economy entities may generally function as producers, distributors and providers of public or collective goods and services, which otherwise would not be on offer at all, or would only be offered at market prices which could

Table 12.1   *Patterns of social economy (in the field of anti-poverty policies)*

Pattern of social economy	Socio-legal understanding of social economy	Important social economy pattern in practice	Country examples in …
1. The charity economy	Huge non-profit NGOs (charities), to a large extent founded by public resources. No explicit legal definition of social enterprise – *de facto* corporations and cooperatives with a 'public benefit' status.	Dominant position of the biggest Third Sector organizations which are respected and professionally prepared. Huge entwinement between public sector and charities.	Germany, Portugal
2. Mixed non-state social service providers	Both the NGO sector and social entrepreneurship. Strong position of the Third Sector; high level of decentralization.	NGO sector – diverse and competing for public funds. Social enterprises operating on the open market selling goods and services mostly to public authorities.	Finland, Ireland, partly UK
3. Entrepreneur/ labour market inclusion type	Broad definition centring entities of socio-professional reintegration.	Significant importance of public EU funds in promoting the idea of and understanding social economy in terms of labour market integration. Mostly top-down initiatives supported and financed in their initial phases by public institutions.	Poland, Germany, others
4. Community economy (communitarian) type	Understood as an activity closely related to economic activities but for social purposes.	A bottom-up subtype, informal, not initiated or supported by public institutions. Great importance of local relationships, norms and ties, and a more formal type of class- or group-based cooperatives.	Spain, Greece, Turkey, partly Portugal, Germany, UK

create severe access barriers to low income households. But low income households' access to the goods and services provided by social economy may be very selective, depending not only on the information, knowledge and relationships of the potential clients, but also on the supply side – precedence, coverage, quality, resources and accessibility of social economy units. Thus, where available and functioning, social economy entities can produce affordances/resources which may help people to get by in socio-economically restricted situations. They thus support resilience, but only for those who manage to access the goods and services, which not all families do.

Many of the examples of social economy that are presented in the following can indeed more or less be described as charities in the sense of type 1 above.

Moreover, to a far extent, most examples show organizations/institutions that are established by, in cooperation with, or supported by public institutions or local government. Nevertheless, there are also some examples of social entrepreneurship as well as of 'community economy', such as the no-middlemen movement in Greece and agricultural cooperatives in Spain.

The most frequent observation on the interaction of vulnerable households with the social economy are charities supporting individuals and households facing hardship by 'crisis intervention', counselling, and distributing food and clothes.

'The [name of the association] offers one super-market bag for every household once in two weeks. The families who take part in the activities mostly suffer from poverty and unemployment. The people who are in need of these offers are primarily immigrants […].' (Greece, Expert interview, quoted from Athanasiou and Marinoudi, 2017)

'I was receiving [food] through [local organization], which is up here … It was very important, particularly regarding my son, who was always my main concern. The fruit was rather poor – it's leftovers from supermarkets. They gave me instant cereal, biscuits and milk and also food for the rest of the family: olive oil, dry pasta, canned sausages, rice, tuna. Sometimes, they would send yogurts for my son. They gave according to what they got. I used to go there once a month and they would give me a decent amount. Sometimes they gave us frozen food. Of course this was very helpful!' (Portugal/mother/late 30s/urban area)

'The RSI [minimum guaranteed income scheme] team here [at the SCM[5]] was the only one that helped us, because we didn't qualify for unemployment benefit. [My husband] never qualified for the benefit because he was the managing partner. And I was also managing partner of the theme park firm, so I didn't qualify either. I contributed to the Social Security for two years – and in the end I wasn't entitled to anything. And all the jobs I had afterwards were never stable – I worked by the month. It was basically covering for someone's holidays or ramping up a few hours. It was not enough for getting the benefit. The only one [we qualified for] was the RSI.' (Portugal/mother/late 40s)

This kind of support is necessary for meeting the basic needs of vulnerable individuals and households, for supporting survival strategies and for creating circumstances for building resilience in the context of dealing with hardship or extreme poverty. Such institutions, like foodbanks, are redistributing donations, employing mostly unpaid voluntary workers, using premises owned or made available by a charity, NGO or municipality, and administered by charity or NGO staff and some voluntary workers.

Some respondents state that improper labour market inclusion makes people dependent on support from aid institutions or the NGO sector, and that this also becomes a pattern perpetuated by the processes of socialization in subsequent generations. Thus, social economy interventions are no general recipe to prevent welfare dependency, if they do not improve inclusion into sufficient labour.

'They don't have prospects, they need someone who gives them a job, not the money. [...] They get money and social pathology is the same. I sometimes see small children in such communities, and I think they will be just like their parents.' (Poland/husband/urban area)

In the national reports there are some examples of entities that create work-places for their clients/supported individuals. In most cases these workplaces result from publicly financed projects with short-term employment. This means social economy entities in such cases work with public money and an elaborate division of labour with governmental welfare state institutions.

'In the recent years, the Centre for Social Integration has been executing projects for long-term unemployed people benefiting from social welfare and disabled people taking part in 6-month programmes of social employment (Poland).' (Wódz and Mandrysz 2016)

'Some of the associations, such as Skolt Sámi Foundation, are able to use the state and municipal support to employ people, at least for short-term with so called "work market support" and "salary support" system (Finland).' (Tennberg et al. 2016)

The respondents speak in a very positive way about the projects that allow them to get some stability – not only those based on financial support, but also those associated with engagement in a fixed profitable activity. Aside from financial resources this kind of position also offers access to social relation-ships (bonds and sense of belonging), and to daily activities associated with the need for responsible behaviour and cooperation.

'[I] started working here under the CE [Community Employment Programme in Ireland] scheme and I loved it. [...] I worked here for, I think it was 3 years, on the scheme and then being a Traveller I got another 2 years and then when my time was up it was terrible. It was more or less that I missed it as well but I used to come down voluntary and I used to come down and do the clubs ... but then [project coor-dinator] called me down for an interview for the caretaking job came up and I said that would suit me fine so I came down and I did the interview in here and I got the job and I was here for another 4 years ... it's really like a second home to me at this stage and then it was funded by the [county] communities together and it was great.' (Ireland/lone mother/mid 40s/urban area)

Nevertheless, there is criticism on the side of the clients, targeted at social economy units which are commissioned to field governmental social protec-tion policies: bureaucracy, failing to meet the needs of clients/residents, and spending the resources ineffectively are among the respective arguments.

'[T]hese forms of support allow only short-term employment [...]. Therefore, the current state approach to employment is criticized – as the local employment offices have been closed, services digitalized and the support for individuals to become employed are just "short-term tricks" (Fin. Expert)' (Tennberg et al. 2016, p. 11f.).

Moreover, such poorly paid and short-term subsidized employment was criticized for failing to help people into decent employment with sufficient wages or being misused as cheap labour by employers instead of supporting transitions into decent jobs.

> '[She] really likes her one-euro-job and it helps her to stay resilient. Nevertheless, she also criticizes the Jobcentre and the one-euro-job as she sees no real perspective to get a normal job, earn more money and leave Hartz IV.' (Germany/single mother/ mid 40s)

In some cases, the programmes related to social employment are criticized for the lack of long-term effects associated with some forms of employment and the absence of any opportunity to secure a stable income when the project is over.

> 'The employees of the Club of Social Integration emphasize that the problem is the situation in which employers willingly employ trainees or make use of other forms of subsidized employment, because they can have an employee working for free due to the fact that their remuneration is refunded. However, many employers do not employ trainees when their period of employment is over and they look for other "employees working for free" (Poland).' (Wódz and Mandrysz 2016, p. 24)

The strongest examples of criticism against social economy organizations suspected that the respective social economy actors serve the interest of their staff first, by focusing on acquisition of new projects instead of providing help to their clients.

> '[S]ome of the beneficiaries themselves question the role of the NGO's actions. [...] As he argued with emphasis, "all the money for immigrants that are coming from the European Union were spent on other purposes. They take money for immigrants, but they ask me to translate for them voluntarily" (Greece/husband/mid 40s/migrant). It is obvious that they reproduce their existence by exploiting the precarious workers who lack citizen and labour rights in the social context of Greece under the existing political circumstances.' (Athanasiou and Marinoudi 2017, p. 15)

To sum up, most resilient and non-resilient households who encountered help from social economy organizations did so from the charity type, some from the collective economy (grassroots initiatives and cooperatives), from labour market integration organizations, and a few from social enterprises. The help received ranged from direct support through money or foodstuffs to counselling and labour market reintegration schemes, the latter to a huge extent based on programmes and funds from governments and administrations, but in that case being fielded by social economy units. Criticism from the clients arose in four major issues: lack of sufficient budget, short programme durations, few transitions into decent, non-subsidized labour, and self-interest of the organizations countering the effectiveness of help (Table 12.2).

CONCLUSIONS

Social economy and social entrepreneurship have become important elements in certain programmatic statements of the modernization of social policy in the EU (European Commission 2011b), claiming that traditional models of the welfare state turned out to be inefficient in different economic and demographic situations, and the problem of unemployment did not find satisfying solutions in traditional forms of social policy. The standard activities of employment and social welfare services are held to be insufficient and the costs of public social services to be much higher. Currently, the relative popularity of the social economy concept seems to be a part of a wider attempt to turn from the model of the welfare state to the so-called welfare society (European Commission 2011a), or, in other words, release the state burden in social policy by shifting the responsibility and costs back to society.

Given such heroic programme statements as well as the lack of systematic evaluation (see Bouchard 2010) the yield seems to be small so far, even if we apply a very inclusive definition of social economy. There are the same huge charities doing what they've always done, often in close cooperation with the welfare state (Type 1), and often internally diversified. There is a considerable, somewhat growing amount of smaller and specialized non-state units, with a high variation in purposes, functions and organizational forms (Type 2). There is a selection of entities running labour market reintegration programmes, usually a business that is neither a charity nor a civil society organization but a kind of company in public or private control (Type 3) – and there are traditional cooperatives and community organizations (Type 4). In the sector of anti-poverty policies and anti-unemployment policies, excluding the health sector, there is hardly any competitive relation between social economy entities and the social policy activities of the governments, which would allow for a comparative evaluation. It also must be said that the money within the social economy system directly or indirectly consists of state funds, other public money and donations to a huge extent. Thus, there is a huge interdependency between state and social economy actors. If we do not want to talk about a dependency of the second on the first, we certainly can talk about entwinement or possibly entanglement – or of a beneficial

Table 12.2   *The role of social economy practices in individual households and community resilience and its limitations*

Pattern of social economy	Contribution of social economy practices in individual households and community resilience	Limitations
Type 1: Charity economy	Wide range of help and social services – 'crisis intervention', charity, distributing food and clothes, providing services, education and training.	Decent jobs mostly for professional charity staff, hardly any further labour market effects. Can alleviate poverty and buffer extreme hardship, but not much support provided in leaving poverty. Sometimes offering unpaid voluntary work or temporary subsidized jobs to beneficiaries and clients.
Type 2: Mixed non-state social service and support providers	Providing various forms of social service, as in the first case, by various types of NGOs; also creating work positions (or social employment) in social entrepreneur entities.	Competition between NGO entities; short-term projects unable to create long-term strategies for clients; existing support helps to cover necessary expenses but limits job seeking. Social entrepreneur or managerial activities are sometimes accessible only for skilled and productive workers, which may increase exclusion of members of vulnerable groups.
Type 3: Labour market (re-) integration entities	Social enterprises with the main purpose of labour market (re-) integration constitute the dominant form of social enterprises in this type, achieved through the provision of a very wide range of goods and, e.g., social services of general interest.	The vocational integration activities (training and courses) are often criticized for lack of the possibility for employment after the training. Entities implemented with financial support of public institutions often exist only as long as they are under the respective support scheme.
Type 4: The collective/ community economy	Their characteristic feature is the fact that their implementation is possible thanks to mutual trust, willingness to cooperate and a sense of bonding. Their effect may exceed the development of the people directly involved but benefit the whole community, thus a high level of social identification and acceptance may occur.	In some cases, cooperation and mutual support is reserved exclusively for members of the local community, religious group or political party. Also, there may be some adversity or inertia to changes.

partnership (Capucha et al. 2016). There is not much evaluation research at all, and even less when it comes to random assignments and control group comparisons, which we well know from clinical trials but little from the field of social policy. The goods and services they produce are nevertheless useful from the perspective of the households asked, helping to stabilize, supplement the means of living, and create and maintain social integration. If we look ahead to Chapter 14 of this volume, we will meet some examples at closer quarters. But there will be no great surprise or innovation in the intervention methodology or practice – except in those countries with low welfare state activities. And it has to be stated that integration into sufficient income jobs through social economy support of whatever kind is a rare event, possibly even rarer than practical support in getting by in everyday life. The main reason why households experience economic hardship (as the findings in this volume show) is strongly associated with unemployment or low incomes of household members, due to unsuccessful job search efforts, lack of local labour force demand, or other insufficient conditions on the demand or supply side. Even though the 'traditional' activities of the social economy, based on charity and social services, are very important – sometimes essential – for dealing with everyday problems, this kind of support rarely leads to exits from the situation.

While there is some remarkable support in alleviating poverty through charity work, subsidized labour, counselling and redistributing goods, and increasing job opportunities through further education and training, the work of profit-based or private social economy units, social capitalism or other 'innovative' actors in social policy mostly does not give additional contributions to the field. Such additions may only occur where certain functional roles have been unfilled before, which especially seems to apply for providers of education, training or work practice for poor or jobless people and in post-transformation countries in Eastern Europe. Furthermore, it seems that rootedness is a key for the resilience of social economy units themselves: charities are rooted through their ethical or religious backgrounds, donations and voluntary work, and the collective economy is rooted in class origins, shared interest, microculture and local backgrounds. Both have been around for decades or centuries, while newly funded and often strongly programme-dependent enterprises are mostly prone to shorter life cycles. Nevertheless, there is not much systematic and empirical research into this issue, which certainly deserves more attention in the future.

NOTES

1. The authors are grateful to Markus Promberger and Marie Boost for substantive comments, and to Sarah Price for language refinements.
2. Cooperatives, mutual societies, associations and foundations (CMAF) deemed it essential to establish a permanent dialogue on European policies that are of common interest. In November 2000, they set up the European Standing Conference of Cooperatives, Mutual Societies, Associations and Foundations (CEP-CMAF). In January 2008, the CEP-CMAF changed its name to Social

Economy Europe (see http://www.socialeconomy.eu.org (accessed 28 August 2020)).
3. This may be different for the healthcare sector, especially in the field of hospitals and care homes for the elderly.
4. It should not be forgotten that solidarity is not only a matter of ethics and altruism, but also a regulation of competition, where an exclusion of outsiders can increase the benefit of insiders (Offe/Wiesenthal 1980, Parkin 1974).
5. The Santa Casa de Misericordia (SCM) is a Catholic organization for supporting people in need, established in the late fifteenth century, thus one of the oldest NGOs in existence.

BIBLIOGRAPHY

Aiken, M. and Bode, I. (2009), 'Killing the golden goose? Third sector organizations and back-to-work programmes in Germany and the UK', *Social Policy & Administration*, 43(3): 209–25.
Amin, A. (2003), 'The economic base of contemporary cities', in G. Bridge and S. Watson (eds.), *A Companion to The City*, Malden, USA, Oxford, UK, Carlton, Australia: Blackwell Publishing, pp: 115–29.
Amin, A., Cameron, A. and Hudson, R. (1999), 'Welfare as work? The potential of the UK social economy', *Environment and Planning A* 31(11): 2033–51.
Amin, A., Cameron, A. and Hudson, R. (2002), *Placing the social economy*, London: Routledge.
Athanasiou, A. and Marinoudi, S. (2017), *National case study reports on the social economy & household resilience – Greece*, unpublished RESCuE project report.
Bennmarker, H., Grönqvist, E., and Öckert, B. (2009), *Effects of outsourcing employment services: Evidence from a randomized experiment*, IFAU-Institute for Labour Market Policy Evaluation, Working paper No. 2009-23, Uppsala: Institute for Labour Market Policy Evaluation.
Böckenhoff, A. (2016), 'Die europäische Debatte um soziale Innovation: Chancen und Risiken für die Sozialwirtschaft', *Sozialer Fortschritt* 1–2: 24–31.
Boost, M., Müller, J. and Kerschbaumer, L. (2016), *National case study reports on the social economy & household resilience – Germany*, unpublished RESCuE project report.
Bouchard, M. J. (2010), *The worth of the social economy: An international perspective* (No. 2), Bern: Peter Lang.
Capucha, L., Calado, A. and Estêvão, P. (2016), *National case study reports on the social economy & household resilience – Portugal*, unpublished RESCuE project report.
Carpi, J. A. T. (2008), 'The prospects for the social economy in a changing world', *CIRIEC–España, Revista de Economía Pública, Social y Cooperativa*, Special Issue 62: 7–33.
Dagg, J. and Gray, J. (2016), *National case study reports on the social economy & household resilience – Ireland*, unpublished RESCuE project report.
Dail Éireann (1999), 'Social economy. Written Answers', Dail Éireann debate, 16 November, 510(6). Available at: http://oireachtasdebates.oireachtas.ie/debates%20authoring/debateswebpack.nsf/takes/dail1999111600072?opendocument (accessed 26 August 2020).

Davies, S. (2008), 'Contracting out employment services to the third and private sectors: A critique', *Critical Social Policy* 28(2): 136–64.

Di Domenico, M. L., Tracey, P. and Haugh, H. (2009), 'Collaboration the dialectic of social exchange: Theorizing corporate social enterprise', *Organization Studies* 30(08): 887–907.

DG Employment, Social Affairs and Inclusion, Unit C2 (2015), *A map of social enterprises and their eco-systems in Europe*, Synthesis Report, Luxembourg: Directorate-General for Employment, Social Affairs and Inclusion, European Commission.

Donoghue, M., Wearmouth, A. and Dagdeviren, H. (2016), *National case study reports on the social economy & household resilience – United Kingdom*, unpublished RESCuE project report.

Esping-Andersen, G. (1990), *The three worlds of welfare capitalism*, Princeton: University Press.

European Commission (1997), *Communication on promoting the role of voluntary organisations and foundations in Europe*. Available at: https://ec.europa.eu/growth/content/communication-commission-promoting-role-voluntary-organisations-and-foundations-europe-0_en (accessed 26 August 2020).

European Commission (2011a), 'A renewed EU strategy 2011–14 for Corporate Social Responsibility', COM (2011) 681. Available at: http://ec.europa.eu/enterprise/newsroom/cf/_getdocument.cfm?doc_id=7010 (accessed 26 August 2020).

European Commission (2011b), 'Commission Communication: Initiative for social entrepreneurship'. Available at: http://eur-lex.europa.eu/LexUriServ/LexUriServ.do?uri=COM:2011:0682:FIN:PL:PDF (accessed 26 August 2020).

European Commission: Euricse (European Research Institute on Cooperative and Social Enterprises) and Commission Staff (2013), *Social economy and social entrepreneurship*. Social Europe guide. Available at: https://sofisam.se/download/18.3453fc5214836a9a472a0430/1472023483855/EU+kommissionen,+Social+Economy+and+Social+Entreprenreurship.pdf (accessed 26 August 2020).

Geddes, M. and Benington J. (2001), *Local partnership and social exclusion in the European Union. New forms of local social governance?*, London and New York: Routledge.

Giza-Poleszczuk, A. and Hausner, J. (2008), *The social economy in Poland: Achievements, barriers to growth, and potential in light of research results*, Warsaw: Foundation for Social and Economic Initiatives.

Gruber, C. (2014), 'Zum Konzept der Sozialwirtschaft', *Soziales_kapital* (11): 1–12.

Haugh, H. (2005), 'A research agenda for social entrepreneurship', *Social Enterprise Journal* 1(1): 1–12.

Immonen, N. (2006), *Yhteisötalous Suomessa, Sisäpiirin slangia vai uutta yhteistyön taloutta*. Tampere: Tampereen Seudun Osuustoiminnan Kehittämisyhdistys ry.

Kalaycıoğlu, E. (2002), 'Civil society in Turkey: Continuity or change?', in B. Beeley (ed.), *Turkish Transformation: New Century-New Challenges*, Eothen: Huntingdon, pp. 59–78.

Karjalainen, A. and E. Syrjänen (2009), *Onko Suomessa yhteiskunnallisia yrityksiä?*, Helsinki: Suomen Lontoon instituutti.

Kostilainen, H. and Pättiniemi, P. (2013), 'Evolution of the social enterprise concept in Finland'. Available at: https://www.researchgate.net/profile/Riitta_Maija_Haemaelaeinen/publication/318902235_Palveluinnovaatiot_ja_sosiaaliset_nakokulmat_julkisissa_hankinnoissa/links/59845182458515946723cca8/

Palveluinnovaatiot-ja-sosiaaliset-naekoekulmat-julkisissa-hankinnoissa.pdf#page=
40 (accessed 26 August 2020).

Krug, G. and Stephan, G. (2013), *Is the contracting-out of intensive placement services
more effective than provision by the PES? Evidence from a randomized field experiment*, Bonn: IZA Discussion Paper 7403.

Lah, U. G. K. P. M. (2009), 'Social economy and social responsibility: Alternatives
to global anarchy of neoliberalism?', *International Journal of Social Economics*,
36(5):626–40.

Laurinkari, J. (ed.) (2007), *Yhteisötalous – johdatus perusteisiin*, Palmenia: Helsinki.

Melinz, G., Pennerstorfer, A. and Zierer, B. (2016), 'Social economy and social work
in Austria', in G. Fábián and A. Toldi (ed.) *The Changing faces of social economy
across Europe: A perspective from 7 countries*, Debrecen: University Press,
pp. 41–73.

Molloy, A., McFeely, C. and Connolly, E. (1999), *Building a social economy for the
new millennium*, Derry: Guildhall Press.

Monzón Campos, J. L. and Chaves Ávi, R. (2012), *The Social Economy in the
European Union*, report drawn up for the European Economic and Social Committee
by the International Centre of Research and Information on the Public, Social
and Cooperative Economy (CIRIEC). Available at: http://www.ciriec.uliege.be/wp
-content/uploads/2015/12/EESC_CIRIECReport2012_EN.pdf (accessed 26 August
2020).

Norton, W. (2014), *Transparency begins at home: Why charities must state who funds
them*, London: Centre for Policy Studies Pointmaker. Available at: https://www.cps
.org.uk/files/reports/original/170605124309-TransparencyBeginsatHomeFINAL
.pdf (accessed 26 August 2020).

Offe, C. and Wiesenthal, H. (1980), 'Two logics of collective action: Theoretical notes
on social class and organizational form', in M. Zeitlin (ed.), *Political power and
social theory*, Cambridge, MA: Cambridge University Press, pp. 67–115.

Olsson, J. (2003), *Una vision de la economía social europea. La economía social y el
tercer sector: España y el entorno europeo*, Rioja: Escuela Libre.

Ostrom, E. (1990), *Governing the commons: The evolution of institutions for collective
action*, Cambridge: Cambridge University Press.

Parkin, F. (1974), 'Strategies of social closure in class formation', in F. Parkin (ed.),
The social analysis of class structure, London: Routledge Library Editions, pp:
1–18.

Poyraz, U., Aytekin, E. A. and Şengül, H. T. (2016), *National case study reports on
the social economy & household resilience – Turkey*, unpublished RESCuE project
report.

Promberger, M., Huws, U., Dagdeviren, H., Meier, L., Sowa, F., Boost, M., Athanasiou,
A., Aytekin, A., Arnal, M., Capucha, L., de Castro, C., Faliszek, K., Gray, J., Łęcki,
K., Mandrysz, W., Petraki, G., Revilla, J. C., Şengül, T., Słania, B., Tennberg, M.,
Vuojala-Magga, T., Wódz, K. (2014), *Patterns of resilience during socioeconomic
crises among households in Europe (RESCuE). Concept, objectives and work pack-
ages of an EU FP 7 project*, Nuremberg, IAB-research report 05/2014.

Putnam, R. D. (2001), *Bowling alone: The collapse and revival of American community*, New York: Simon & Schuster.

Rymsza, M. (2007), '*Druga fala ekonomii społecznej w Polsce a koncepcja aktywnej
polityki społecznej*', in T. Kaźmierczak and M. Rymsza (eds.), *Kapitał społeczny. Ekonomia społeczna, Instytut Spraw Publicznych*, Warsaw: Instytut Spraw
Publicznych, pp. 175–93.

Seanad Éireann (2000), *Social Economy Programmes. Adjournment Matters.* Wed. April 5, 162(22). Available at: http://oireachtasdebates.oireachtas.ie/debates %20authoring/debateswebpack.nsf/takes/seanad2000040500009?opendocument (accessed 26 August 2020).

Serrano, A., Revilla, J. C. and Garcia, M. (2016), *National case study reports on the social economy & household resilience – Spain*, unpublished RESCuE project report.

Tennberg, M., Vola, J. and Vuojala-Magga, T. (2016), *National case study reports on the social economy & household resilience – Finland,* unpublished RESCuE project report.

Winterhager, H. (2006), *Private job placement services –a microeconometric evaluation for Germany*, Mannheim: ZEW Discussion Paper No. 06–026.

Wódz, K. and Mandrysz, W. (2016), *National case study reports on the social economy & household resilience – Poland*, unpublished RESCuE project report.

Woolcock, M. and Narayan, D. (2000), 'Social capital: Implications for development theory, research, and policy', *The World Bank Research Observer* 15(2):225–49.

Zybała, A. (2007), *Rynek pracy społecznie integrujący, zadania dla lokalnych partnerów*, Dialog. Pismo dialogu społecznego 2, Warsaw: Ministerstwo Pracy i Polityki Społecznej.

13. Aesthetics, self-reliance and resilience

Aida Bosch and Markus Promberger

INTRODUCTION

The following chapter deals with the role of aesthetics and self-reliance for developing resilience under difficult, fragile circumstances of hardship. The following analysis is based on the photographs taken by the interviewees in the qualitative nine country study (Promberger et al. 2014), the results of which are presented in this volume. At first, aesthetics and aesthetical practice were not an analytical priority in the investigations, but soon proved to be an important issue. Visual fieldwork had originally been included in order to detect inexpressible but relevant aspects of everyday life and self-perceptions of the participants' lives as well as cultural and community related activities, and for having the option for methodological triangulation.

During data collection and analysis, the symbolic significance and beauty of the participants' visual footage emerged in some of the case studies, necessitating inclusion in the analysis in its own right. A methodological setting deliberately open for non-anticipated or non-hypothesized surprises from the field was chosen. These emerging findings connected well to theory and research relevant for our topic. Developmental psychology emphasizes the role of aesthetics in education for identity formation; social workers and psychological practitioners around the world encourage people to practise aesthetic self-expressions in fine arts, literature and music in order to cope with disadvantages, difficult life situations and even traumas. Class or youth (sub-)cultures have been studied extensively as (self-)expression of social positions and conflicts, and according to structures of feelings (Williams 2014). Visual anthropologists have enriched and broadened, if not challenged, text-based cultural analysis by investigating images and other non-text artefacts. Moreover, being an *animal symbolicum* is a crucial feature of human identity (Cassirer 1992[1944]), which has to be seen as an anthropological foundation of culture, and aesthetic self-expression is the means of producing, modifying and reproducing culture (see Williams 2014). Even more so, aesthetic self-expression is of vital concern, both as a foundation and a result of the process of life (see Scheler 2009[1928]; Plessner 2017[1928]; Fischer

2012), not necessarily for humans alone. When we focus on human phenomena and human cultural surroundings this counts even more so. Georg Simmel (1995[1901]) conceives aesthetics as a means to overcome or at least to alleviate the physical or emotional heaviness ("Schwere") of life, which is clearly of relevance for households in or close to poverty. The following chapter will investigate if and how this applies.

The visual footage surprisingly showed that, in addition to factors like available common goods, social embeddedness, and economic and cultural resources like values and education, there was a surprising richness of aesthetic practices. These practices may constitute a relevant part of redefining one's self and becoming and staying self-reliant, in order to be able to cope with or even to transform critical situations and circumstances into a resilient way of life.

EMPIRICAL APPROACH AND GENERAL FINDINGS

As part of the study, families were asked to take pictures of their lives using a simple digital camera provided by the researchers, and to explain their pictures to the research team in a photo elicitation interview. Previously, an inspirational guideline was developed for taking the photographs, offering associative themes to process photographically which could be freely interpreted, such as "Where I live", "A mealtime", "Family and friends" and "What gives me strength". This guideline was intended to provide a facultative rather than an obligatory framework for a photo series in order to stimulate dialogue and self-dialogue in a field of action and observation that not only consisted of what could be said or accessed easily but included implicit knowledge and could also touch on feelings of shame and stigmatization or experiences of discrimination. It turned out to be significant here for the success of the empirical fieldwork that these thematic frameworks provided the participants with an open, colloquially formulated invitation to describe themselves and express themselves creatively in their photographic work. In this way, the more than 500 interviews of several hours' duration which took place with about 100 experts and 240 families or households were accompanied by several thousand photographs taken by participants themselves.

Before we come to the visual analysis, a brief summary is going to introduce the main findings of the study in general. It turned out that only a small number of vulnerable households are resilient (see the discussion in Chapter 17 of this volume). However, the resilient households reveal an astounding range of socioeconomic practices and frequently show highly developed cultural connections outside the formal labour market (see Chapters 6 and 7 of this volume). These are accompanied by highly developed relationships within multifaceted social networks outside welfare state institutions: family networks, groups of friends and colleagues, neighbours, exchange networks and customer networks. Here, a strong tendency becomes apparent towards mixed economic forms, different sources of livelihood and several interlinking polyvalent practices in the sense of mixed functions and purposes which – also in the sense of a diversity that supports resilience – complement each other and can replace each other. This structure is particularly pronounced in households which fall into the self-reliant oíkos[1] type. Several households of this type show activities like fishing, picking berries and gathering mushrooms. Both from the observers' and their own point of view, this not only improves the diet but replaces monetary expenditures for food and leisure activities, and, at the same time, it is family time. It opens the possibility for recreational contact with nature and conveys knowledge from generation to generation. Swapping vegetables over the garden fence, neighbours helping each other or joining in with local clubs not only delivers useful material results or renders public goods accessible but improves social standing and social integration at the same time – and also provides information on job opportunities or contracts.

Resilience implies vulnerability and can be accompanied by risks to society, communities or even people themselves and their families. Health problems and family difficulties in connection with overwork and low income deserve a mention here – although these also affect non-resilient, low income families. Nevertheless, the overall situation of resilient households is better than that of equivalent non-resilient households, although this can change rapidly if relevant practices no longer work or attempts to compensate fail. It should be noted that resilience does not lift the families concerned very much above their non-resilient counterparts with respect to income and risks. However, there is nonetheless a significant difference in the material, cultural and social resources available, and in their dependence on welfare benefits, activity, motivation, self-esteem, life satisfaction and quality. In the case of vulnerable households, three things are generally important for developing and main-taining resilience. First is a welfare state that not only provides direct support when households' resilience strategies fail, but offers low-threshold, accessible public goods which are used precisely by those families that do not draw direct benefits, whether this be free access to nature or to public or civil society infrastructures, from the energy and water supply to food or clothes banks to information and education opportunities. Second is a varied and comprehensive concrete social network where it is not only about exchanging trivia but where goods, opportunities and a social sense of belonging are co-produced and shared. Third are cultural norms, values, knowledge and skills which make low-commodified life contexts outside the consumer-orientated market conceivable and viable and enable self-sufficient economy and individualism. Despite all the fluidity of resilience, several different, relatively stable life patterns were identified as types in the confines of the project. One of these was the self-reliant oíkos, which is particularly fruitful regarding the question of aesthetic practices in developing resilience. Before moving to study such a case more thoroughly, we will outline our methodology of visual analysis.

METHODOLOGY: THE AESTHESIOLOGICAL HERMENEUTICS OF IMAGES

Photographs are a product of a technical representation process, and, as such, they store patterns of perception and action, thus simultaneously reinforcing them. The photograph comprises a mimetic action: a scene is duplicated and recorded in the image. The photographic action changes how the time that goes by is dealt with. A scene, object or person is chosen in a certain setting at a certain point in time and is cut out of the stream of time. This singular cut-out of a fleeting event is recorded and can be looked at again and again. Here, the photograph is not just storing symbols of meagre importance but is an imprint of the "Real", as Roland Barthes (1981) called it. At the same time, the photographic act moulds the situation represented by showing it from certain selected angles. What is worth wresting out of transience and holding onto? Why are some scenes chosen over others? From what angle is the scene shown? What is permitted to be shown in the picture and what is not? What cut-out is permitted and how are the individual elements composed? Is a specific normative or aesthetic idea introduced into the picture?

Due to its capacity to record and duplicate events, photography generally embraces a tendency to affirm and reinforce its contents. Taking family photography as an example, Pierre Bourdieu showed that, in the private use of photography, it is not every subject occurring in the family that is recorded but only the special moments of family life which one likes to remember and which strengthen family cohesion (Bourdieu 1981[1965]). Quite in accordance with the idea stemming from Émile Durkheim (1981[1912]), in private photography the collective is ritually venerated, which is why the situations that are recorded visually are predominantly those that consolidate the community. As a rule, there is a characteristic inherent to private photography that mirrors and reinforces the collective and individual identity – thus already augmenting resilience per se. It is therefore to be assumed that photography tends to be practised in families and households that are more stable (despite all dislocations). Taking photographs generally is associated with doing better, thus it means adopting a social and aesthetic practice of resilience. When analysing the pictures, therefore the selectivity of the material must be taken into account, but this selectivity is definitely useful when researching resilience and sampling relevant cases.

The pictures were analysed using the methodology of aesthesiological image hermeneutics (see Bosch 2017; Bosch and Mautz 2012 for more detail). The focus of the analysis lies on the synergy of aesthetics applied, the objectified attitude and picture content. This methodology is based on iconographical and iconological analysis which has been developed by historians of fine arts and then transferred and refined for the social sciences. One crucial issue in that transfer was to include the study of the punctum (Barthes 1981), which means the direct, non-analytical impact of the image on the researcher/observer, and therefore bringing in the direct sensual and aesthetic qualities inherent in the picture itself – this is why this methodology is an aesthesiological one.

The photographic image shows the photographer's attitude to the depicted object. The image communicates this attitude and suggests it to the observer. The photograph acts as an intermediary, an objectified element of a physically and spatially positioned attitude to the subject of the picture. Is the object presented made smaller or larger? Is it worshipped or idolized? Is the access to the image motif intended to document the object and show it in the cold light of day? Does it let the object speak for itself or does it wish to impose its own idea on the object?

The process presented here requires to be practised in a research group that is as heterogeneous as possible in order to bring in different sections of social contextual knowledge. This enables the forming of competitive hypotheses to validate the result of the analysis, in other words, to extend interpretation beyond the level of individual perception. In the first step, each member of the analysis team notes down spontaneous feelings, perceptions and associations that arise when they see the picture for the first time – which is a kind of experimental practice. After this notation of the punctum, the studium begins – as suggested by Roland Barthes in his *Camera Lucida* (1981). The individual contents, elements and aesthetic features of the picture as well as interdependencies and interactions in the picture are analysed step by step until all the results are consolidated at the end of the analysis. In the following, we show this method in a very condensed form by taking one picture as an example; see Bosch (2017) for a summarized recommendation concerning the steps of the aesthesiological image hermeneutics analysis. The picture in this chapter was selected with respect to its relevance in terms of aesthetic practices for resilience in households living in poverty.

STUDYING AN EXEMPLARY IMAGE

The analysis of pictures and images is an extensive procedure; its crucial steps will be briefly introduced in this section, leaving the elaboration of the details to the co-producing reader. We start with the punctum (step 1). In the picture presented in Figure 13.1, the punctum is multi-layered and confusing. One can see a room which contains many objects and elements. The first impression of this room is being light, comfortable and filled with different things, some of them strange and idiosyncratic, which give the effect of a polyphonic choir with both high and deep voices. The rough, very weathered surface of the wood in the foreground also exudes a sense of individualism. What could be the connection between these things? In the next step, we take inventory of the exact study of the picture with the pre-iconographic description (step 2). This step takes a great deal of time, as there are plenty of separate elements and things to be seen, standing in a specific arrangement. Tools, decorative objects, furniture and parts of the house, food and technical devices can all be seen in detail. At this level of analysis, all elements of the image must be patiently described from a naive perspective in order to rigorously reconstruct the details of the image, based on everyday knowledge. In the next step, the iconographic description (step 3), all the formal design elements are analysed. These include dominant lines and draw the viewer's eye toward colours, light conditions and composition. Almost in the centre of the picture we can identify a dark, apparently rusty, roughly cylindric and pleated sheet metal object of indeterminate origin and function, a battered pleated tube. It is standing on a horizontal wooden beam, which represents the dominant axis in the picture.

Figure 13.1   Picture of the Miller family's kitchen–diner, German case study

Its original form has obviously been greatly altered by weathering and the influence of the elements.

Other beams with large cracks and an expressive wood surface with a strong grain form vertical and diagonal axes in the picture. These axes are supplemented by a plethora of objects in all sorts of different shapes. The dominant colours in the picture are the yellowish and brownish shades of the wood and wall, complemented by the white wall in the background. The blue light from the laptop in the bottom right section of the picture stands out in contrast to the warm shades in the photograph and corresponds to the two blue pictures found in the top left segment of the photograph. Small splashes of red and a little green created by individual objects in the picture also catch the eye. The perspective and composition selected are an obvious attempt to get as much of the setting in the eat-in kitchen into the picture as possible, with all individual objects included. The iconographic interpretation (step 4) which now follows asks about the photographer's intention in terms of content and aesthetic ideas, as reflected in the formal composition of the picture. The choice of diagonal beams in the foreground as a perspective is unusual, as are some of the objects that can be seen in the picture. The object at the centre of the picture is particularly puzzling. The setting of the other items around this object reflects a consciously arranged, albeit slightly chaotic order that was to be captured in the picture. The picture has obviously been taken by an amateur, although it also does speak of a certain photographic ability, as the multitude of things that can be seen do not just disintegrate into a mess but seem to reflect the sense of aesthetics they have been bestowed with, despite the partial disorder. In the iconological description (step 5), all the elements and things to be seen in the photograph are analysed in relation to their possible symbolic content.

Most of the objects in the picture seem to be things that have been found, old objects from flea markets, homemade objects or arts and crafts. Only a few of the technical devices visible in the lower section of the picture – the computer, the loudspeaker and the lamp – and likewise a small amount of food packaging in the background appear to be ordinary objects that have been bought. Everything else seems to elude the laws of the marketplace. The dark, rusty object in the centre in particular (which could perhaps be a piece of stovepipe, a very deformed tin can or part of a vehicle, for example) not only runs counter to the usual aspirations to form but also defies common market logic. Adjacent to it on the beam are two large jars containing pebbles, and there are large, rounded stones lying next to the jars. Articles that have been collected or made by hand and things with a history predominate in this room. In the upper, central section of the picture, one can see a wreath braided out of dry twigs which has been hung on the ceiling and decorated with Easter eggs in dark patterns. In addition, there are red and green hearts made of felt hanging from the wreath and from a hanging wire basket. On the right, one can see a particularly lovely fossil snail at the back; there are also snail or mussel shells on top of the object in the centre. At the top left there are all sorts of old pots, cans and jugs to be seen made of clay, enamel or aluminium. The formal idiom of the things shown reveals characteristics of weathered, individual objects full of history which have been looked after, restored or newly made with love and attention, things made of wood or other natural materials with striking, weathered or eroded surfaces formed by age or other natural forces – a language of symbols that seems to stand in contrast to a commodified culture of rapidly changing fashions and the constant influx of new consumer products. It is solely the computer and the technical equipment associated with it which look like a nod to modern, consumer-orientated lifestyles geared towards speed. However, these technical objects have often been positioned very low down in the room underneath the dominant centre beam. They are ready for use but are put in a subordinate place until they are required.

In the iconological interpretation (step 6) which now follows, the results of the previous steps are combined and supplemented by additional context information on the pictures from the context of the project. From the interviews, we know that this photograph is one of many taken by a woman living with her partner and more than three children in the east of Germany. The family was able to buy an old house for very little money in an area at risk of flooding and renovate it themselves with a great deal of effort. Every couple of years the house is flooded almost to the top of the first floor – the house that is their place to live, a base that enables them to lead a good, resilient life despite their low income – and then the house is under water up to almost the top of the first floor. The family has prepared itself to live with this situation and react to it. After the flood, they join forces with neighbours from the village to mutually help in the clean-up, and the family is well integrated into local clubs and associations. Both adults in the family are skilled woodworkers, and offer their skills to friends and neighbours, often in exchange for other goods and services. The woman has several small project-like jobs such as tourism, social measures and busking. Her contribution helps to keep the family afloat financially, albeit in precarious arrangements and, due to the manifold stress, sometimes in a precarious state of health. Her husband works as a craftsman, not only on informal construction sites but also in alternative cultural conversion and development projects. If we take this information and return to the results of our analysis so far, we see how remarkable and individual the arrangement of the things in the picture is – things they have found or made themselves, looked after and appreciated. We see a system of corresponding objects in which the highly valued things are not only the useful ones, but primarily those used and worn out, historical and symbolic. There are many objects in the room which have been formed or deformed by water; the pebbles in the glass particularly refer to the water that eroded them, as do the rusty object in the centre and the fossils. When one knows that the place is at risk of flooding, this symbolism seems particularly remarkable as a kind of aesthetic resilience that counterbalances the risks with the traces of beauty caused by the water. The old vessels for pouring and ladling to be seen in the upper section of the picture and the contrasting soft shades of blue in the picture seem to lend even more visual support to this interpretation. The interviewed mother does photography as a hobby, is quite good at it and submitted a large number of photographs to the project. For her, as she says, photography is an aesthetic anchor in a highly demanding everyday life: the family literally keeps its head above water with a great deal of self-supply work, unusual means and strategies, ties to networks and aesthetic practices. Even though this arrangement is always precarious, it certainly shows the significance of aesthetic individualism in vulnerable life contexts.

The intention of such an analysis is not to evaluate the aesthetics chosen in each case; even commonplace, tasteless or seemingly anti-aesthetic arrangements can play an important role in life practices at the brink of poverty. There are several more examples whose beauty and hermeneutic meaning only unfold at the second or third patient glance, while the image chosen here makes it easier to demonstrate the relevance of aesthetics in resilient practices.

AESTHETIC SELF-RELIANCE AND RESILIENCE

The case reconstructed above is representative of a specific type of resilient family that has been labelled the self-reliant oíkos (Promberger 2017, p. 43 and Chapter 7 of this volume). It occurs in most of the nine countries investigated, and is characterized by values, patterns of interpretation and action which strongly differ from the usual standards of consumer and labour society and the corresponding identity formations. In this type of resilience, autonomy, creativity and alternative structures of meaning are at priority, not only in terms of thought, reflection or life aspirations but also in everyday practice. In some cases, the aesthetic aspect of actions is a consistent core factor of *every* practice, whether embedded in an occupation, in the family or in other networks. Nevertheless, this type of aestheticization is not observed in all families, and aesthetic practice as a component of resilience can also be found in other types, although most clearly so in the self-reliant oíkos type. The aesthetic practices which we observed fed on different sources: biographical, professional or family connections on the borderline between craftsmanship and art, between nature and civilization, and at the border between a traditional or alternative, artisanal, community-orientated life and a modern, acquisitive life. It is on these boundaries, in the conflict between contradictory life concepts, where aesthetic self-reliance is born. Here, we do not conceive of aesthetics as being primarily an element of commodification, market and distinction (see

Reckwitz 2012), an element of consumption and seduction (see Baudrillard 2012), or an element of domination and fluid social power (see Foucault 2012), but as a self-reliant, resistive practice that at least partly evades easy consumerism and creates aesthetic patterns which are not emerging smoothly, seamlessly and flawlessly, but reveal and communicate the self-reliance and resistance of their creation and background right in their expression. We must learn to read, understand and appreciate these aesthetic patterns. Some of them correspond to an educational background, with elements of cultural capital. Fragmentary academic backgrounds or craft skilled craftsmanship can be found to shape resilient people's values, abilities and affordances and how they see life, and allow for respective aesthetic self-expression.

Other patterns of aesthetic self-reliance feed on a traditional connection to nature, which is pronounced to varying degrees in the different countries due to the varying natural conditions and plays a part in different life practices in the European case studies. When confronted with the modern age, this self-reliant practice baulks at a commodified and industrialized lifestyle and reverts to residual cultural elements, reviving and cultivating them in an aesthetically self-reliant fashion. Here, tradition is no longer just tradition but is emphatically interpreted in a new way, precisely because of the confrontation with the commodified lifestyle of the dominant modern age. Cultural and aesthetic based self-reliance allows a distancing from the dominant patterns of life choices but is only possible when the embeddedness in social structures like village communities, neighbourhoods, extended family, subcultures and communal structures exists. Further aesthetic patterns we observed fed on a strong need for order in a life which tends to be chaotic and uncertain. These can include aesthetic preferences that may not initially reveal themselves to the scientists shaped by their middle-class backgrounds, and which some would be inclined to describe as kitsch. However, this misses the point of this aesthetic practice. We found an excessive habit of doing jigsaw puzzles of over a thousand pieces, for example, or to organize porcelain figurines such as animals, flowers and other things in unusual arrangements. At first sight, these are not sophisticated aesthetic objects in terms of accepted aesthetics. However, this aesthetic practice also stabilizes identities though the person's own work towards achieving a meaningful and symbolically structured order, creates connections for community formation and helps to brave external threats and crises. The intention here is not to romanticize or glorify resilience and self-reliant aesthetics. Resilience itself is too vulnerable; too rarely does it lead to a way out of life circumstances teetering on the brink of poverty – and too great is the price that life on the poverty line can exact. However, it is often precisely the aesthetic and individualistic aspects of this life practice which, despite all the strokes of fate, adversities, challenges and their own feelings of being overwhelmed, lead to the people affected remaining stable and socially integrated, perceiving themselves as having the power to act, and, saturated with experience, reporting plausibly that they lead a good life.

NOTE

1. For the self-reliant Oíkos and on self-reliance see Chapter 14 of this volume.

BIBLIOGRAPHY

Barthes, R. (1981), *Camera Lucida: Reflections on Photography*, London: Farrar Straus & Giroux.

Baudrillard, J. (2012), *Von der Verführung*, Berlin: Matthes & Seitz.

Bosch, A. and Mautz, C. (2012), 'Für eine ästhesiologische Bildhermeneutik, oder: Die Eigenart des Visuellen. Zum Verhältnis von Text und Bild', in H.-G. Soeffner (ed.), *Transnationale Vergesellschaftungen. Verhandlungen zum 35.DGS-Kongress in Frankfurt am Main, Bd. 2,* CD-ROM, Wiesbaden: VS Verlag für Sozialwissenschaften.

Bosch, A. (2017), 'Das Bild als Aktant. Theoretische und methodologische Implikationen des Visuellen', in M. R. Müller and H.-G. Soeffner (eds.), *Das Bild als soziologisches Problem. Herausforderungen einer Theorie visueller Sozialkommunikation*, Weinheim: Beltz/Juventa, pp. 91–107.

Bourdieu, P. (1981[1965]), *Un art moyen: Essais sur les usages sociaux de la photographie*, Paris: Les Editions de Minuit.

Cassirer, E. (1992[1944]), *An essay on man*, New Haven, CT: Yale University Press.

Durkheim, É. (1981[1912]), *Les formes élémentaires de la vie religieuse.* Paris: Alcan.

Fischer, J. (2012), 'Interphänomenalität. Zur Anthropo-Soziologie des Designs', in S. Moebius and S. Prinz (eds.), *Das Design der Gesellschaft*, Bielefeld: transcript verlag, pp. 00–00.

Foucault, M. (2012), *Discipline and punish: The birth of the prison*, New York: Vintage.

Glaser, B. and Strauss A. (1967), *The discovery of grounded theory: Strategies for qualitative research*, New Brunswick, London: Aldine Transaction.

Harper, D. (2002), 'Talking about pictures: A case for photo elicitation', *Visual Studies* 17(1): 13–26.

Kluge, A. and Negt, O. (1981), *Geschichte und Eigensinn*, Frankfurt am Main: Suhrkamp.

Plessner, H. (2017[1928]), *Die Stufen des Organischen und der Mensch*, Berlin, Boston: De Gruyter.

Promberger, M., Huws, U., Dagdeviren, H., Meier, L., Sowa, F., Boost, M., Athanasiou, A., Aytekin, A., Arnal, M., Capucha, L., Castro, C., Faliszek, K., Gray, J., Łęcki, K., Mandrysz, W., Petraki, G., Revilla, J. C., Şengül, T., Słania, B., Tennberg, M., Vuojala-Magga, T. and Wódz, K. (2014), *Patterns of resilience during socioeconomic crises among households in Europe (RESCuE). Concept, objectives and work packages of an EU FP 7 project.* Nuremberg: IAB research report 05/2014.

Promberger, M. (2017), *Resilience among vulnerable households in Europe. Questions, concepts, findings and implications*, Nuremberg IAB, Discussion paper 12/2017.

Reckwitz, A. (2012), *Die Erfindung der Kreativität. Zum Prozess gesellschaftlicher Ästhetisierung*, Frankfurt am Main: Suhrkamp.

Scheler, M. (2009[1928]), *The human place in the Cosmos*, Chicago: Northwestern University Press.

Schütze, F. (1983), 'Biographieforschung und narratives Interview', *neue praxis* 13(3): 283–93.

Simmel, Georg (1995[1901]), 'Ästhetik der Schwere', in R. O. Kramme and A. Rammstedt (eds.), *Georg Simmel Gesamtausgabe, Bd. 7, Aufsätze und Abhandlungen 1901–1908*, Frankfurt a.M.: Surhkamp Verlag, pp. 36–42.

Soeffner, H.-G. (2014), 'Zen und der "kategorische Konjunktiv"', in M. R. Müller, R., J. Raab and H.-G., Soeffner (eds.), *Grenzen der Bildinterpretation. Wissen, Kommunikation und Gesellschaft*, Wiesbaden: VS Springer, pp. 55–75.

Spittler, G. (2001), 'Teilnehmende Beobachtung als Dichte Teilnahme', *Zeitschrift für Ethnologie* 126(1): 1–25.

Trinczek, R. (1995), 'Experteninterviews mit Managern: Methodische und methodologische Hintergründe', in: C. Brinkmann, A. Deeke and B. Völkel (eds.), *Experteninterviews in der Arbeitsmarktforschung. Diskussionsbeiträge zu methodischen Fragen und praktischen Erfahrungen*, Nuremberg: Beiträge zur Arbeitsmarkt- und Berufsforschung 191, pp. 59–68.

Williams, R. (2014), *Keywords: A vocabulary of culture and society*, Oxford: Oxford University Press.

PART IV

Conclusions and implications

14. A typology of resilient households

Markus Promberger, Marie Boost and Janina Müller

CONCEPTUAL CONSIDERATIONS

The study on the incidence of resilience and living practices of resilient low-income households underlying this book started with the idea that socio-economic resilience is based on resources which were hidden, out of sight or obsolete from the perspective of mainstream poverty research (see Promberger 2017). Such resources can be differentiated and classified. In his famous studies on social inequality and class, Pierre Bourdieu (2011[1986]) had proposed a distinction between economic, social and cultural capital as concepts, which are practically overlapping, mutually complementary and substitutive to a certain degree. He pursued these concepts in order to obtain a clearer picture of class structures within a society than was possible by just analysing economic income or wealth, as the prevailing liberal stratification and Marxist class theories of his time did. But, it is theoretically unsatisfactory to talk about sorts of capital when analysing social groups where the respective resources are far from being capitalized or even marketized. Poor households are poor because they are not sufficiently equipped with capitalizable resources. But despite having no capitals available, they might or might not have resources, and have developed practices which can make life easier, which is the topic of this chapter. Therefore, we propose to use alternative or more fundamental concepts like resources or affordances (see Chapter 2 of this volume) instead of talking about sorts of capital.

But it still seems fruitful to follow Bourdieu in his distinction between the economic, social and cultural, for the following reasons. The human condition mainly consists of the fact that humans must do something purposeful with their environment in order to survive. Moreover, being non-specifically equipped in physical terms (Gehlen 1988) but highly capable in thinking, and grouping (Plessner 2019[1928]), planning and acting (Elder 1994; Clausen 1998), and, as Aristotle said, being a social animal, these human specifics raise the chances of survival dramatically and – together with labour – enable the formation of a cultural, economic and social life, which then again becomes a framework for future action (Giddens 1984). Classical studies like Durkheim's (2014[1893]) social division of labour, Polanyi's idea of economy–culture relations (2001[1944]), and Mauss' (1954[1925]) analysis of the deep interrelatedness of economic, cultural and social aspects of life and practice bring us closer to the necessity of including economic, cultural and social resources in our studies of low-income households' practices.

But such attempts to identify and classify the available resources of poor households have not found their way into poverty research: there is wide and recent qualitative research on welfare benefits, their coverage and capacity to ensure a livelihood (such as Engel and Hirseland 2016; Kreher 2012), not to mention classical sociological and anthropological studies on living in poverty and unemployment (Jahoda et al. 1988[1932]; Lewis 1959; Rowntree 2000), and also on households at the brink of poverty (Meier et al. 2003; Daly 2016; Hooper et al. 2007). All of them provide deeper insights into the experience of poverty than statistical surveys of who is over or below a poverty line. But, astonishingly, little is known from a perspective of resource use, resource classification, and the daily practices of resource combination. And – even more surprising – the methodologies and approaches developed in social history, economic anthropology and economics of private households in development research have hardly ever been transferred to the analysis of poverty in contemporary welfare states, just to name the mixed economy approach of social historians (Malcolmson 1988), economic anthropology and their cultural economy concept (Hann 2000), the livelihood or sustainable livelihood approach in development research (Glavovic et al. 2002; Holt and Littlewood 2017) as well as the importance of local knowledge (Garibay-Orijel et al. 2012), skills (Vuojala-Magga 2009), and household strategies (Warde 1990; Wallace 2002).

Closing this gap in a conceptual and empirical way was one of the aims of this volume and the underlying empirical work. The previous chapters have revealed some of the diversities of household strategies and practices to improve livelihoods and well-being of the persons concerned. This has given hints that there are indeed various associations identifiable between different varieties of economic, cultural and social practices. This chapter shows that these variations and associations of practices are not random, but cluster into a typology of resilient low-income households. But before we proceed to develop the different types of resilience in or close to poverty, we should again emphasize that these are special and rare forms of socieconomic resilience, under conditions where other, more common patterns of socioeconomic resilience fail, and we should briefly describe these other forms of resilience for comparison.

First, any families or households exposed to crisis or other challenging factors, might face threats to their standard of living, when their main source of livelihood begins to fail. For households headed by propertied citizens, in other words the bourgeoisie, who are able to live on returns from capitalized business, properties, land or real estate revenues, a failure of their sources of rent or profit means that these sources change their function from capital into a stock for consumption, such as when using up a fortune or converting assets into money for consumables. Resilience among propertied citizens then would consist either of having enough of such means of existence to cover a longer period or to recover the sources of revenue from any types of wealth or assets available, or, if not, starting to sell their labour power (see Offe and Wiesenthal 1980). The point of comparison of resilient and non-resilient cases, then, according to Simmel's definition of poverty (1906), would be the situation and development of their peers. Without elaborating this further here, these considerations reflect an ideal type of the usual resilience of propertied citizens.

Second, for non-propertied citizens who have to live mainly from non-capitalized small entrepreneurial income or from wages, being self-employed, small entrepreneurs and, the largest numerical group, dependent labourers whether white or blue collar, the main source of livelihood is their own labour power. As Offe and Wiesenthal (1980) have shown, this source has to be sold (or precisely, hired out) in order to function, as it can hardly be stored for bad times or used for direct consumption. Given this lack of elasticity and the absence of relevant assets or means, the regular resilience for this social group would mean to become re-employed, with a sufficient income, as soon as possible, after consuming savings and social insurance benefits in an interim period. This ideal type could be described as 'standard working-class resilience', recognizing that in certain historical periods this may not apply to the majority of workers in a practical sense, but always, and for most of them, does so as a desire or pattern of orientation. But where assets and wealth are absent, sustainable labour market or small business success fails or is not an option, and households are declining into poverty with no quick return into substantial employment and earned income, we speak of vulnerability 'as a weakening process and as a lack of resources' (Spini et al. 2013, p. 19), and we search for patterns of resilience different from the non-functioning standard ones – which is the issue discussed in this chapter.

Almost all households interviewed had to employ different and more than one strategy to survive, cope, get by or even transcend hardship (see Chapter 6 of this volume). These strategies emerge from complicated living circumstances, poor labour market options (often in areas remote or subject to economic decline) and family commitments. These strategies arise from various affordances aside from standard labour contracts, and are driven by certain value orientations (Holmes 2018). Despite the difficulties they encounter, the households observed are trying to provide a living, applying alternative practices characterized by special knowledge, by high levels of creativity as well as commitment and involvement in social networks, often accompanied by social and cultural values of mutual support, cooperation and cohesion, and an ability to adopt to changing circumstances of life despite adverse conditions. Based on the performed strategies and practices (see also Chapter 6 of this volume), five different types of resilience could be identified. They are performing a multitude of different practices, which are mostly plurifunctional, providing not only a material, but also an emotional/ psychological or social surplus mostly through subsistence labour and mutual help (*self-reliant oîkos* type). Some others are becoming small entrepreneurs, accepting a high workload to avoid dependency on the welfare state (*small entrepreneur/bricoleur* type), while a third group specializes in enforcing their social security entitlements *(resilience through actively enforcing citizens' rights)*. Relying on a supportive community (*community* type) as well as the influence of personal transformations and turning points (*biographical development and healing* type) can additionally contribute to foster resilience through developing a sense of belonging and self-confidence. The latter is a type of resilient household where the socioeconomic and resource-based concept of resilience shows substantial overlap with the psychological understanding of resilience (Werner 1992).

There is a line of collective resilience in most European countries which has been institutionalized through time and social conflict, stepwise forming what we know today as the welfare state. It did not come into existence by grace, mercy or insight, but mainly by the struggles of the working classes and their political, trade-union and self-help organizations, supported by Christian and philanthropic anti-poverty movements in the late nineteenth and early twentieth centuries, as well as by the pressure for compromises forced on the ruling elites by war and fear of revolution. This line of collective or social resilience nowadays includes catch-all poverty legislation with basic income support in most European countries, and in certain countries it is usually topped up by temporary wage substitute benefits for unemployment, sick and parental leave. Nevertheless, these supports vary in coverage, duration and value from country to country. For example, it is quite hard to live on those supports in some provinces of Spain, where many of the benefits are temporary, related to special situations in families (single parents, childbirth), or limited to a few hundred euros per year – as in the case study of the García family discussed below. In Greece, most social benefits have been abolished or dramatically reduced since the European financial and economic crisis after 2007. They are no longer of much relevance in the lives of poor Greek citizens, whereas civil society and people's self-organized redistributions (food banks, soup kitchens) grew considerably, but can hardly replace the functions of a developed welfare state. On the other hand, in Germany and most of Scandinavia, basic income support plus civil society organization services allow for a life where basic needs are covered to a relevant extent, although there have been major cuts, reorganizations for the worse for a substantial proportion of the households concerned, and problems at the fringes since 2005 (Promberger 2015; Kohl 2000; Butterwegge 2014; Lessenich 2013; Kananen 2014; Valkonen and Vihriälä 2014).

This means, although the typology is derived from case examples from all countries investigated, and therefore applies to all of them in general, the incidence of the respective households may vary, and the respective internal patterns of each type, as well as the degree of relevance of different dimensions, may still show some variation by country. Nevertheless, the internal variation is less than the external variation (see Hempel and Oppenheim 1936) – or in other words, the similarity within a type is high, while the similarity between types is low, which are standard constituents of classifications including typologies (see Kuckartz 2010, p. 555).[1]

TYPE 1: RESILIENCE THROUGH ONE'S OWN MEANS AND VALUES – THE *SELF-RELIANT OÍKOS*

'We do everything by ourselves, as far as we can and we have an iron law, going like I help you and you help me. [...] We do not take any money. We exchange work for work. [...] Money is not everything. You cannot eat money and it doesn't make you happy or healthy.' (Ms Miller[2]/Germany/mother of more than three children/ rural area)

The first type of vulnerable household showing resilience is what we propose calling the *self-reliant oíkos*. Self-reliance is a not very satisfying translation for what Negt and Kluge (1981) called 'Eigensinn'. This German term has a history of its own, having emphasized negative characteristics like waywardness or self-will in the nineteenth and early twentieth centuries, but since Negt and Kluge (1981) has increasingly been used to describe independence, creativity, self-determination and resistance in difficult situations, which were seen as a precondition of working-class self-organization. The Greek term 'oíkos' then, refers to the household not only as a unit of shared consumption, kinship and intimacy, but also as the most important unit of production (Finley 2002[1965]).

Let's take a closer look into a significant case study: the Millers, a family with many children, live in a small village in a German rural area. Both parents are skilled woodworkers. Ms Miller has also some uncertified academic skills in education and social work. Due to the poor labour market situation of the area, the couple has developed considerable creativity to ensure a livelihood. While she holds a mix of different jobs, working as a tourist guide, street

Figure 14.1   Spinning wheel

artist and education supervisor for unemployed youth, her husband and father
of the children is part of a craftsmen's network, doing house and flat refur-
bishment and renovation, often without formal payment, but on the basis of
mutual favours, gifts or wages in kind. Besides that, he works on renovating

and improving the family home, making furniture and repairing the two old family cars, and supports the local youth culture centre with his work. A few years ago, they bought a cheap small house in a flood endangered area for some thousand euros, learning to live with the regular flood every few years and sharing the risk and mutual support with their neighbours. Besides her various jobs, the wife knits clothes, spins wool (Figure 14.1) and does gardening with considerable yields of fruits and vegetables. The family enjoys spending time not only in the local youth and culture centre or in other civil society events, but even more so in nature-related activities, such as hiking, and gathering herbs, berries or mushrooms. They emphasize that nature is for free and offers plenty of opportunities. Although they are new residents, the family is fully integrated in the local life of the community. All their practices, such as repairing, constructing, collecting, gardening, reciprocal help and gift exchanges, merge into a mixed economy, providing a simple but satisfying and socially integrated life, without having to apply for social benefits – although, due to unstable and variable incomes, they live close to and sometimes below the poverty line. Although not claiming benefits, they are eligible for certain labour market reintegration schemes, which they sometimes make use of. Their self-conception is backed up by values that put community, family and solidarity at the core, as well as co-producing and participating in local cultural activities, civil society organizations, like neighbourhood associations, as well as informal professional networks, do-it-yourself-culture, mutual and gift exchange and handcraft- and nature-related knowledge, while explicitly rejecting concepts of career and economic success. Their material standard of living is higher than usual around the poverty line, owning a house and two (old) cars, an old camping trailer for a family holiday several weeks once a year, not to mention the above-average quality of food supply due to their intensive gardening activities. Nevertheless, the family's resilience shows aspects of fragility, due to high workload, permanent uncertainty and the need to work without a break, whether at home or elsewhere. At the time of the interview Ms Miller has just overcome a delayed respiratory disease, which points not only towards the fragility of resilience but also to one interface where the family has to relate to welfare state services.

The multitude of the household practices among the *self-reliant oíkos* families allows for mutual substitution and keeping up the livelihood model in general, even when one particular practice fails. 'Don't put all your eggs in one basket' or the equivalent German, Finnish or Polish expressions were a characteristic saying of these families. The mix of different practices further improves their quality of life, compared to non-resilient households, as gathering, repairing and do-it-yourself activities are far more than just practices for saving, or ways to meet extraordinary expenses, like new clothes or a special menu. It also gives meaning to their everyday life and allows social integration through mutual support, barter and gift exchange. It is further part of their self-image and a way to express themselves in a creative way. A wide social network also increases the potential to find out new job possibilities on a formal and informal basis. But there is not just a *multitude* and *diversity* of practices. Characteristically, most practices pursued are each *plurifunctional* in themselves: similar to the practices of the Miller family, a single mother from Finland goes into the nearby forest to collect blueberries in the late summer. This not only replaces purchases, saves money and increases food quality, but is also a family event that strengthens cohesion and the transfer of knowledge from parents to kids. As the interviewees emphasize, such practice is not only recreational and relaxing, but also a part of the family's self-definition, consisting of an alternative value system and aesthetic self-expression, in which – and there are many cases of this type amongst the families we observed – *nature and solidarity replace market success*. One could even say that such cases show an entwinement of social, cultural and economic aspects or functions in a way which has been significant for pre-modern life in general, not only in the ancient Greek concept of *oíkos* or exchange practices of so-called 'primitive societies' (Mauss 1954[1925]), but also in lower social classes at the dawn of the industrial age (Malcolmson 1988), in industrial workers' biographies until the mid-twentieth century (Deppe 1982), or in present day rural households of developing countries (Banerjee and Duflo 2011), where livelihood diversification is sometimes argued for as a development strategy (Ellis 1998). Economic practices are usually affiliated to a certain cultural framework. Residual patterns of culture, such as plot gardening, secondary harvests on other people's soil or informal craftwork, having been made obsolete or redundant by social differentiation and progressive divisions of labour, as described by classical social theory from Durkheim via Parsons to Luhmann (1984), are re-emerging or have always been there in resilient households and families at the fringes of poverty.

Given the still high uncertainty of living conditions and the risks associated with overwork, we might ask where the above-average quality of life of the self-reliant oíkos households in comparison to other poor households comes from. First, subjectively and most important, they themselves describe their lives as better than a normal life on welfare, with different positive above-average outcomes. Main points reported in their narratives and observed by the fieldwork are a self-owned and maintained home, giving them independence and lowering housing costs, a richer diet, being able to travel, good family coherence and time, a strong sense of belonging and embeddedness in several communities which they relate to their economic practices, and their well-maintained craftspersons' or other professional identities. Second, the health risks in the observed cases fairly equal typical health risks that come along with precarious employment (see Lewchuk et al. 2008) and are lower than those associated with long-term unemployment. It also has to be noted that many of the families of this type, like most other resilient families observed, have access to standard healthcare.

This type of resilience occurs amongst households in most countries of investigation. It is strongly visible in northern and central Europe, occurs here and there in rural and even urban sites of southern Europe, but appears much less frequently in Ireland and the UK.[3] The *self-reliant oíkos* is strongly but not completely associated with rural or small-town settings and formal or informal property orders which allow for use of natural resources on public land, no man's land or unfenced private or self-owned land. Resources of the *self-reliant oíkos* typically include cheap housing facilities, often inherited or self-bought at very low prices, a lack of options for formal labour market integration, but sufficient possibilities for network and community based economic activities. Significant risks of the *self-reliant oíkos* households are overwork and related health problems, quite similar to what is known from households involved in precarious labour or precarious self-employment (e.g. Benach et al. 2014; Lewin-Epstein and Yuchtman-Yaar 1991), but also family tensions or ruptures, or under certain circumstances a lack of sufficient entitlements to welfare state services if their diversified but still small livelihood fails. The *self-reliant oíkos* uses multiple resources, among them many active and economically functional local and translocal networks, common goods and nature. The welfare state comes into play less as a provider of transfer incomes but more as a guarantor of public goods, in some countries including free education and healthcare, a supporter of the social economy, and lender of last resort where own strategies and practices fail.

TYPE 2: SELF-EMPLOYED RESILIENCE – *THE SMALL BRICOLEUR–ENTREPRENEUR*

'And here, I fixed some chairs. You apply some oil or so, makes them look more chic and new, easier to sell then. [...] And this, is a kitchen cupboard, I built some drawers for it, because the original ones got lost. Now, we can sell that one too'. (Mr Schmidt, Germany/grandfather/mid-50s/self-employed)

Fixing broken furniture can be a practice to save money as it compensates for buying new items, or it can be a practice to gain some money by reselling it and, naturally, it shows a certain value orientation towards the importance of re- and upcycling as well as saving resources. The photograph in Figure 14.2 shows a kitchen cupboard under repair. Mr Schmidt obtained it through his flat clearance business, which is based on some tools, an old lorry and a backyard workshop in a small-town neighbourhood. Mr. Schmidt provides services like flat clearances, building maintenance and all kinds of estate-based repair.

According to the customs of his trade, he disposes of waste, charging his customers for that, but keeps any goods worth repairing, converting and reselling. He is working externally for his customers, but also in his private workshop and garage. Items repaired or converted are then sold by him and his wife in their self-run second-hand shop. Both are working very hard to gain a small, unstable income depending on the varying demand. Most months of a year, their income isn't any higher than the basic welfare benefits. Nevertheless, they prefer earning their own money as they want to be active and avoid the strong legal restrictions for combining own earnings with welfare state benefits. Low-income self-employed in Germany are not only subject to dense monthly reporting to tax authorities, but also to welfare administration, potentially having to partly repay social benefits already received. The family became self-employed after the husband had for years tried to get a stable position in various nearby companies. He used his wide set of knowledge and practical skills to fit himself into many different jobs and duties. But due to the small-town environment and the decline of industries, every company he started working for had closed within a short time. So, he suffered years of repeatedly going in and out of employment, unemployment and welfare, but then decided to change his work life, in order to become independent from wages or welfare by working hard constantly on his own to get by. Mr Schmidt even extended his activities by extending the range of building maintenance and caretaker services at offer, like cutting trees, mowing the lawn, sweeping paths or clearing snow in winter, on top of doing just flat clearances. Presently, this strategy seems to pay off, but the disadvantages are also visible. Putting work first under any circumstances, no matter how demanding in terms of time and strain, creates some vulnerability with respect to income stability and at the same time increases risks of burnout and physical decline. More so, as Mr Schmidt has already suffered from cancer and a stroke. Furthermore, both are frequently absent from home, which restricts them from seeing and supporting their children and grandchildren living next door.

This case is an example of resilient households living from small business profits, and they represent the most at-risk part of what is called precarious entrepreneurs in the literature (Bührmann and Pongratz 2010).[4] They make their business from other households' leftovers, delivering micro services, taking high risks on very low margins and recognizing affordances where others see just waste. Other entrepreneurs would quite soon turn their back or never enter such business at all. These persons and households can be characterized as *bricoleur–entrepreneur*, combining special skills and practical knowledge with available resources, like a garage, car, tools, networks and a high personal motivation. This *bricoleur–entrepreneur* constitutes a second type of resilient household. In some way he or she is a Schumpeterian entrepreneur (Schumpeter 1942), engaged in a process of creative destruction. But he/

Figure 14.2   Making new kitchen cupboard drawers

she does not do the destructive part him-/herself, but instead works creatively on destroyed or abandoned goods – like Mr Schmidt – or with neglected people, like another case doing self-employed pedagogical work with disadvantaged people. In such environments, the *bricoleur–entrepreneur* comes into play, discovering what's lost by others and at hand for him/her, then doing creative repair, conversion and transformation work. As a bricoleur in the sense of Lévi-Strauss (1962), the *bricoleur–entrepreneur* stands for creativity with things and persons having been subject to loss, degradation or deprivation to form something unusual but useful, or making sense in an unexpected way. Parsimony and alternative values play a certain role here. And, again, skills – from skilled craftsmanship to university education (often unfinished or obsolete) plus lots of practical experiences in former regular jobs – seem to be as crucial as personal networks for setting up projects, discovering useful items and services or finding customers. Nevertheless, the surprisingly high level of planning, skill and aesthetics that could be observed suggests rejecting the negative connotations implied by the initial concept of Lévi-Strauss (1962). Often, not only the products of the *bricoleur–entrepreneur*, but also his/her biography is a bricolage. Furthermore, there is not much distinction between leisure and working time, as the *bricoleur–entrepreneur* is combining his/her personal interest in craftwork with the aim of gaining an income. This mix allows a multitude of possibilities to make a living. Nevertheless, unlike the *self-reliant oikos*, subsistence production, gift exchange and sharing outside the nuclear family play a relatively small role in the livelihood composition.

The *small bricoleur–entrepreneur* actually self-produces mainly for money and markets, which are co-structured by networks. These households, often as a couple or family, do not work to stock their home with self-made products, for wages in kind or for just a favour in turn, but seek to gain a monetary income from their activities, not refraining from setting up formal cooperation with fellows of the trade, customers or funders when necessary. Nevertheless, the business often has some strong ethical background, be it explicit or implicit – like making waste stuff useful again, working for fair prices, or working not only for profit but also for the good of underprivileged persons or society in terms of education or social projects. Case examples in this study include not only the Schmidt family or the mentioned educational entrepreneur working with disadvantaged children, but also an electronics street vendor in Greece, and a Syrian refugee family running a small basement textile factory in Turkey, just to name a few. They all live around the poverty line, but are managing to get by well without any transfer incomes[5] and are proud of it, feeling distinctively more free or independent compared to living from the precarious dependent labour available in the area – or welfare.

TYPE 3: RESILIENCE THROUGH ACTIVELY ENFORCING CITIZENS' RIGHTS

'These are the authorities […] this is what I have to do […] writing everything, objections, review requests, I have to turn that wheel every day. Now, I have to fill-in a request for co-payment exemption of my health insurance …' (Germany/ father/mid-40s/early retirement)

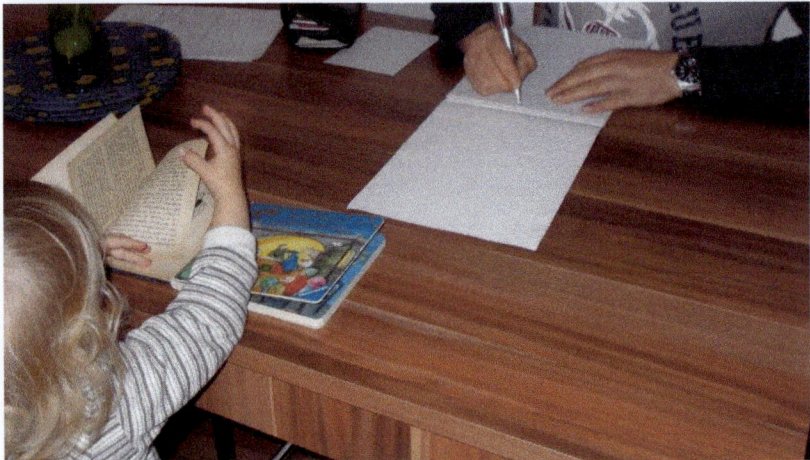

Figure 14.3   Turning the wheel: writing claimant letters

Conflicts, even legal disputes with welfare authorities are a part of the daily lives of many persons and families receiving welfare benefits, but some fight more intensively to claim their rights. Family Bauer suffered many misfortunes. After the reunification of Germany Mr Bauer, a trained agricultural worker, struggled to receive stable employment, but he never obtained a permanent position. He participated in several education and job creation programmes without much success. Then, in the early 2000s, he was attacked by a stranger and suffered a basal skull fracture. Due to the severe consequences of his injury he went into early retirement. Now he is fighting to fully receive the additional transfer incomes and support grants that members of his family are entitled to – such as free school meals for his daughter, or defending against sanctions which were imposed on him when he started legal actions against an authority decision. Nevertheless, he continues his legal actions, demanding his family's legitimate rights, as he explains in the interviews (Figure 14.3). The hub of their activities is their family life with two children; giving them a good bridge into life is the declared goal of Mr and Ms Bauer. Outside family, they have a few distant relatives, but their main network consists of experts and counsellors supporting them in their claims against the authorities.

Focusing on the characteristics of this and similar cases, this third type can be called *resilience through actively enforcing citizens' rights*. This type is quite familiar to many social workers, policy practitioners and researchers studying vulnerability in developed welfare states. It is centred on cases who, although living from transfer incomes alone, are not passive welfare recipients, but strive to actively enforce their citizens' rights, either to maximize their outcome to the extent possible, or to realize parts of their entitlement they had been denied access to by discretion of the welfare authorities. They are, in a sense, professionals of their own welfare case, as their level of activity and knowledge is comparatively high in terms of effort, time and scope in their interaction with authorities – which makes a constituent of this type of resilience. But as the amount of achievable welfare benefits varies in the different welfare states, so does the shape and incidence of this type: in comparatively weak welfare states, e.g. Spain or Portugal after the 2007 crisis, formal transfer incomes, even if optimized, need severely to be complemented with other resources, such as extended family support, small informal jobs, neighbourhood networks or charity support, as welfare alone does not allow for sufficient livelihood. This may be the reason why the incidence of this type of resilience is reported mostly from countries like Finland or Germany, where welfare benefits are comparatively high. This type of resilience is different from the types mentioned before: although it requires knowledge and agency, and clearly improves the living of the households concerned, it does not reduce their dependency on support money.

TYPE 4: RESILIENCE BASED ON COMMUNITY AFFILIATION – *THE COMMUNITY PLUS TYPE*

The fourth type of resilient households[6] around the poverty line is distinctively characterized first by a strong relation to a specific community beyond their own family and second by an additional high importance of values like religion, solidarity, charity and mutual help. Communities in general may play an important role in the formation of resilience, which is discussed more extensively in Chapter 11 of this volume. The community relation discussed here usually is a special one: it is not what we usually discuss in terms of social capital, social networks or active citizenship. It is affective, direct and strongly value based. And these values are not completely situated in a rational framework only, but have roots in spirituality, transcendency and a very emphatic sense of community. It has also to be noted that each of these cases relates to just one community, and this affiliation is one of the strongest motifs they refer to in their self-taken pictures and interview narratives. Nevertheless, in addition, cases of this type usually show remarkable overlaps with either the aforementioned *self-reliant oíkos*, the *bricoleur–entrepreneur*, or the *biographical development and healing* type described later, adding a strong emphasis on being affiliated to one particular community, which is the reason for the 'plus' label. The following case example of the García family, a Peruvian immigrant family in Spain, gives an impression.

The Garcías, husband and wife in their 30s, mid-level education, three children aged between 2 and 15 years, are living in an urban area in Spain. Mr García immigrated to Spain in the early 2000s. He is a skilled information technology (IT) worker, had also worked in a call centre, as a waiter, delivery driver, IT technician, cleaner and DJ for little hours and little money, sometimes undocumented. His wife and daughter followed him to Spain a few years later. Ms García also works on temporary contracts and for small money. Due to their low labour income and children before and at school age, they receive some small public benefits of less than 1,000 euros per year in total. As this isn't enough for a living, they finally decided to seek out help in the local parish. Besides their bad financial situation, the family also suffered poor social integration and felt the urge to become members of a community. As their local parish is very active in terms of fostering neighbourhood and social integration in a problematic urban area, it became a place of social connections and inclusion for this family. Little by little, this contact, initially having been instrumentally motivated, changed into an emotional supportive and mutually helpful relation by joining multicultural discussion groups and other events. As time went by, closer and stronger relationships emerged through this group and the parish. New friendships were built and the feeling of being able to rely on them grew. After years of being socially isolated, the family now feels that they are starting to have a social life in Spain. Now, according to their account, they are actively involved in the parish and feel a sense of belonging and responsibility. The whole family have become active members of the church community and engage wherever possible. The social exchange and the feeling of being a respected member of a community increases their self-esteem and well-being. Mr García expresses this as follows:

> 'As we couldn't make ends meet, we got to know the parish, which is where Caritas is […] because otherwise we would not reach [the end of the month]. […] There we met the Father and more people, […] who treated us like a family, it's true. That's where my girl is doing catechesis for communion. And so, my wife […] will also be baptized there. We are in a small group, in the parish, […]. It's a pretty good group, we get along pretty well and it's very nice […]. That allowed us to get closer to the parish and to God, in some way. We did not know anyone here before, but now we do. We have something to do, we go out […]. And we have socialized a lot with the parish, even now, my wife does not want to move away […]. Because now, we feel a little more at ease, […] we feel more integrated than before. In that sense, that is to say, the parish has been the starting point and very important to socialize.' (Mr García/Spain/father/mid-30s)

A key period of their immersion into the community was the preparation of their daughter's first communion. The first communion means to formally include a child as an active member of the community of Catholic Christianity and Christ in general, and into the local parish. Developing social or community activities around this *sacramentum* (sacred procedure) is a core activity of any Catholic parish around the world; in our Spanish case the first communion involves the whole families of the concerned children for at least about one year. As the photograph in Figure 14.4 shows, activities like a shared meal after the service are common practice with practical and spiritual meanings in this parish.

In the long run these informal contacts, which had improved dramatically through this period, are the reason why the García family developed a sense of belonging and decided to stay in Spain. Their first integration into the framework of benevolence and charity was surpassed quickly and extended towards a general form of social integration in the community. The community is the main narrative of the Garcías as well as other cases of this type, beside which all other narratives play only a small role. Evolving into relations of social exchange, taking and giving back, and developing social relations and a sense of belonging out of this mutual relation (see Mauss 1954[1925]) increased their well-being in the long run. Additionally, their socioeconomic situation improved when community integration and networks increased, offering them a wide range of individual and collective resources, as the parish unifies different people with different knowledge and skills.

Figure 14.4   Sharing a meal at the church community

Community, as it is used here, refers to a group of people sharing a special belonging, usually involving close relations, direct communication, mutual non-commodified help and solidarity among their members, and a common basis of values. These are generated by co-presence of their members or by an image of the community in their minds and a feeling of comradeship to each other (Tönnies 1957[1887]; Anderson 1983). Within modern societies, community participation is increasingly based on a (more or less) free choice, shared living conditions, developments and interests (Stinchcombe 1965), norms and values, while in postmodern societies, temporary and virtual communities add to the morphology of community, with older forms still existing, although often endangered or reshaping themselves. Active community involvement depends also on the person's feelings of fitting in and corresponding with their aim and course of action. Emotional bonds, social recognition and a sense of belonging referring to the feeling of being an essential part of a community allows their members to feel useful, valued and accepted (Hagerty et al. 1992).

The example of the García family, and others collected through this study, clearly shows that, in times of crisis and precariousness, community integration (provided by a parish, volunteer association, friends or neighbours) can play an important stabilizing role. They provide low threshold help (practical as well as emotional) without further ado. Beyond the safety net of family and community, the welfare state provides a certain degree of social security for its citizens. But due to a mix of neoliberally motivated cutbacks, aggravated by the impact of economic crisis, a stronger reliance on communality can be observed in countries (see Revilla et al. 2018, and chapters 9 and 15 of this book), where the lack or decline of state welfare is partly and limitedly compensated by community relations.

Resilient low-income families of this type are integrated in different kinds of communities that satisfy various basic human needs, like sociality, a sense of belonging, socioeconomic support and daily routines. As mentioned above, formal organizations, where participation is a possibility without obligation, may provide a positive impact on their members through becoming active or by receiving aid (or both at the same time). In certain cases, formal organizations, such as churches, charities or civil society associations are anchor points where passive participation turns into active involvement. The initial contact is initially established with the formal side of the organization, based on needing help, but as time goes by, informal relationships are growing: first under the umbrella of the organization, later detached from it. A *sense of belonging* and *recognition* emerges and contributes to positive identity formation and a positive self-perception. Based on this *friendship, supportive social networks* arise from this community work, leading to knowledge exchange and mutual help. Further, especially when participating actively or contributing financially, members are co-creating the institution and promoting the *social life* of the local community and, consequently, the *cultural life* of the neighbourhood. Hence, they build *cultural resources* and benefit from them. A high community affiliation furtherly generates *socioeconomic benefits* supporting solidarity networks as a source for *mutual help* and *knowledge exchange*, e.g. about possible job opportunities or new ways of handling long existing problems, either by inspiration or by direct suggestions how to act. Furthermore, regular participation within community organizations *gives structure to the day*, generates meaningful time and modifies the perception of time from something superfluous to a valuable good and brings back a certain positive daily routine – things which easily get lost in poverty and unemployment (Jahoda et al. 1988[1932]). This shows that the community affiliation is *plurifunctional*, as it fulfils different purposes at the same time. The higher the impact that communities have on the interviewees' lives, the more resilient practices appear. However, community affiliation can also cause negative effects, for example when the affiliation to a certain neighbourhood causes stigmatization or when the community referred to is linked to crime, nationalism, racism or other inhuman world views (see also chapter 10 in this volume). Community affiliations have sometimes been accused of supporting 'poverty traps' (Williams and Windeback 2000) – but this could not be confirmed

(Cattell 2001). On the contrary, community affiliation in the observed cases clearly supported agency, psychosocial stability and contributed to increasing economic activities.

TYPE 5: BIOGRAPHICAL DEVELOPMENT AND HEALING

Some of the interviewees' narratives revealed significant turning points.[7] These were often associated with important biographical key incidents and transitions – standard passages (Glaser and Strauss 1971; Van Gennep 2013[1909]) such as graduation or marriage, but also 'irregular' status passages associated with severe biographical crises such as illness, divorce, job loss or trauma, a passage into social states of sickness, unemployment, poverty or other statuses. In that sense, some resilient cases presented a distinctive narrative pattern incorporating major negative life events, and the contingency, trauma and pain they caused, as well as – often metaphorically strong – a subsequent process of transformation and healing. This type of resilience occurred when people reconfigured their biographical projects in ways that facilitated a renewed sense of efficacy and hopeful anticipation of the future (see Gray and Dagg 2019 and Chapter 8 of this volume). We propose to call this type *biographical development and healing*.

Mr Donovan, a married father of two young children in his mid-40s, represents this type well. When the Irish research team met him for an interview in 2014, he described himself as in a phase of 'awakening' from a low point that he had reached in 2008. But, for Mr Donovan, this low point was also the culmination of an extended period of difficulty in his life that pre-dated the economic crisis. Having returned to Ireland from working overseas in the 1990s, he and his girlfriend purchased a house in her hometown, where they continue to live. Once married, they decided to sell their first home and buy another one that needed renovating. Mr Donovan found the renovation work therapeutic as it coincided with frustration and anger stemming from the grief of his father passing away and the demands of parenting young children. During this time, his marriage also ran into difficulty and his wife moved out of the family home with the children for two months. Mr Donovan identified these events – of his father passing, of becoming a father, anger and marital difficulties – as the beginning of his 'spiral years', a period that continued until the onset of the recession when he was made redundant from construction work, and his wife became unwell. Simultaneously, relationships with extended family became fraught, the household budget had reduced significantly, and Mr Donovan himself also became unwell.

However, Mr Donovan described how this low point in his life represented a turning point that marked the beginning of his 'awakening years'. During this time, he made a conscious decision to take some time out before seeking new work, and to really think about what he would like to do. This process of awakening took the form of a thorough re-examination of his understanding of the world:

'Because there were a few things that just made me look at everything differently. I take everything apart now, even my religion, I questioned it, I picked through it and I made more sense of it than I did before [...] I went into a lot of detail and research on a lot of things all around the world, things that happened, conspiracies, you name it and I had to back off. It just gets too much. Knowing about it, understanding it and being aware of it is one thing but when it gets to the stage where it's controlling your life then it's counter-productive. I see it as knowledge is power. The more you know, the more you can understand, the better you can deal with it. Doesn't necessarily mean that it has to bring you down and has to encroach on your regular life. So I sort of refocused, got to more of 'around me' sort of issues. Deal with what I can within reasonable boundaries I suppose.' (Mr Donovan/Ireland/father/mid-40s)

A few years after being made redundant all his family's savings and redundancy payments had depleted. To enact change, Mr Donovan began working at a local resource centre as a youth worker. His wife took on part-time work that did not adversely affect her health or welfare benefits. Her part-time hours together with Mr Donovan's income from working at the resource centre enabled the family to get by. Around the same time, a chance encounter introduced Mr Donovan to Reiki:

'Again that sort of fell into my path, I'd had an awful lot of problems with my back for years ... I went to a GP once and he gave me some tablets and he stood on my back, I wasn't very impressed so I thought right maybe the GP isn't the right way to go for this sort of problem so [...] I was given this number by my mother-in-law and I was told "this bloke's a healer, he might be able to help you out", so I gave him a ring and I made an appointment and went to see him and I got three treatments in the space of about two weeks – brilliant [...] It was at that stage that I found out he was a Reiki practitioner, he was a Reiki master [...] So then when he mentioned he was taking on students and teaching, absolutely. So I did the first level, practised just at home on family members for the guts of a year then did the practitioner's level.' (Mr Donovan/Ireland/father/mid-40s)

Mr Donovan is now focused on completing a course to become a qualified Reiki practitioner, as well as thinking about adding qualifications for other holistic therapies over the next few years. With these qualifications he envisions that he might be able to support himself and his family if he returns to college to do a course in counselling or psychotherapy. In the long term, he hopes that he will be able to merge his qualifications to provide a holistic set of therapies for people.

Figure 14.5   Alternative belief systems – attending the Festival of Fires

Mr Donovan's case illustrates well how the recovery of agency and a positive sense of anticipation often entailed reconfiguring biographies through the adoption of new value systems and revised ethical frameworks (see Dagg and Gray, this volume), symbolically well expressed in the picture Mr Donovan took at an alternative culture festival (Figure 14.5). Following Rutter (2013, p. 478 ff.), a turning point in the life course marks an event where there is a 'discontinuity with the past that removes disadvantageous past options and provides new options for constructive change'. A turning point changes the way an individual thinks or acts. Life is different from before, as there is a detectable change in the development trajectory. When negatively connoted, major life events or turning points can affect health temporarily or for longer periods of time (Folkman 1984). Crisis and negative events can provoke the experience of being a victim, helpless against circumstances. But the concept of turning point is more commonly associated with positive changes in life direction than with negative ones, and more with regaining agency than with being stuck in an evil fate (Riemann 1987; Promberger et al. 2021) – very much as in the life narrative of Mr Donovan. According to Rutter, for individuals in need of healing 'recovery may derive from turning point – experiences in adult life' (Rutter 2006), as turning points can provide additional psychosocial resources, such as, for example a positive change in their peer group when an individual gets married (Sampson and Laub 2003). Heuristically, case study evidence shows that turning points often involve positive interventions from a third party (Promberger et al. 2021; Dagg and Gray, this volume). Resilient turning points may be associated with a change in a person's time-orientation (Dilthey 1992[1910]; Promberger et al. 2021, p. 5). Past-oriented thinking can lead to feelings of subjection and passivity as past events cannot be changed (fate), whereas future-oriented thinking probably causes feelings of activity because there might be possibilities to take influence (agency) (see Hitlin and Johnson 2015). Mr Donovan began to look towards the future when he began a new career as a youth worker and adopted a revised set of values centred on alternative medicine. Healing, as we find in this type of resilience, seems to correlate with overcoming fate and achieving agency. This concept is also known in psychological theories as the concept of self-efficacy (Bandura 1993), which is the mental foundation for individuals to successfully modify their life situation.

This process of biographical development and healing, increasing future orientation, turning to agency and therefore changing life conditions, characterizes the development of resilience in vulnerable households of our fifth type. As a solid basis for this, authentic third-party interventions, interactions with materialities such as plants, animals, crafts and arts work, and new personal relationships, often in this sequence, help interviewees like Mr Donovan to regain agency and stability (Promberger et al. 2021). The biographical healing type of resilience was often but not exclusively found in single person or single parent households (Promberger 2017, p. 19), and the common goods of having access to supportive infrastructures – like hospitals, psychological or medical counselling, facilities for victims of domestic violence, or community resources, such as garden plots or opportunities for part-time employment, as in the case of Mr Donovan. Nevertheless, in Mr Donovan's case, the chain of steps out of vulnerability is not yet at its end. He may require more support for further education and opportunities for participation in the labour force. This indicates that many cases of biographical development and healing might need different anchors or further support to stay in the active role, leave social benefits and support, and develop furtherly.

OVERVIEW AND COMPARISON

Just a small proportion of households living around the poverty line are resilient at all – although quantitative evidence is still missing. But those who are resilient show a broad scope of different socioeconomic practices embedded in certain cultural patterns, and being organized within social networks or, more precisely, family, neighbours or different kinds of communities, many of these issues related to common goods of varying kinds. Moreover, these households can be described by keeping or regaining a positive self-perception, attitude and agency. Thus, they take their lives in their hands and strive for change themselves, sometimes triggered by external help. There is also a strong tendency to what social historians call a mixed economy (Malcolmson 1988), involving households' own small assets as well as common goods, knowledge, skills and culture, together with social and community relations – but with different combinations leading to the described typology – of which an overview is shown in Figure 14.6.

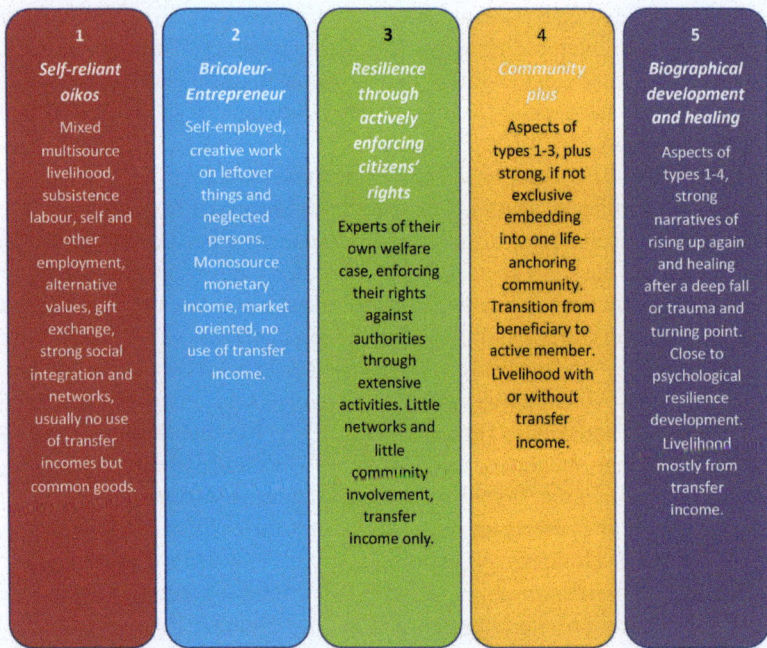

1 Self-reliant oíkos	2 Bricoleur-Entrepreneur	3 Resilience through actively enforcing citizens' rights	4 Community plus	5 Biographical development and healing
Mixed multisource livelihood, subsistence labour, self and other employment, alternative values, gift exchange, strong social integration and networks, usually no use of transfer incomes but common goods.	Self-employed, creative work on leftover things and neglected persons. Monosource monetary income, market oriented, no use of transfer income.	Experts of their own welfare case, enforcing their rights against authorities through extensive activities. Little networks and little community involvement, transfer income only.	Aspects of types 1-3, plus strong, if not exclusive embedding into one life-anchoring community. Transition from beneficiary to active member. Livelihood with or without transfer income.	Aspects of types 1-4, strong narratives of rising up again and healing after a deep fall or trauma and turning point. Close to psychological resilience development. Livelihood mostly from transfer income.

Figure 14.6   Types of resilient households around the poverty line

Three remarks and three findings conclude this chapter. First, this typology is tentative. There are hints in literature for an 'ascetic individual' type as well, living from transfer income but very parsimonious and ascetic by values, with little network and family relations, mostly living alone (see Bosch 2015). Second, bearing in mind what was said at the beginning of this chapter, it has to be stated that this typology for reasons of clarity does not display three points of comparison which of course were a background in the comparative work as explicit or implicit points of reference: first, the non-resilient poor households; second, the standard case of working-class resilience in developed capitalism – which is to be able to stay in the labour market and find more or less sufficient labour after loss or crisis, be it with or without institutional support; third, the resilience of households which are not actually poor or working class.[8]

And, third, it is very important to emphasize that belonging to such a type is not necessarily a permanent condition: households under observation were slowly proceeding or quickly moving after a critical event, such as declining after losing a job and not being able to find a new one, but then slowly stabilizing by subsistence labour, or starting from the position of being a marginalized immigrant with insufficient labour and without any social support towards becoming a well-respected and integrated community member – or leaving a refugee camp to start running a basement textile business, employing many of the wider family. Chapter 8 of this volume shed further light on the biographical processes behind these movements.

What are the major findings, beyond the typology itself? One finding is the multifunctionality of practices, and the multiple and diversified livelihoods. It arises from the observation that living in a poor but resilient household means making use of purposeful mixtures in many aspects of life. The effectiveness and efficiency which is ascribed to or demanded from modern work lives – like living from the one job one is best at, investing most power into the most promising source, maximizing the income from selling one's labour force, targeting the most improvement possible in a career, putting all one's eggs in one basket – has been dropped in order to give way to a different pattern of life: when living around the poverty line, vulnerability can obviously be reduced and socioeconomic stability improved where livelihood comes from mixed sources, obtained by diversified practices, which are multifunctional themselves in terms of their economic, social and cultural functions and meanings. Their interconnectedness reduces the investments required besides one's own labour ('we are already here in the forest, why don't we collect some firewood') – and the sources and practices are often able to substitute for each other at short notice, most strongly, if not paradigmatically so in type 1, the *self-reliant oikos*, and to a certain degree in type 2, the *entrepreneur–bricoleur*, less so but still visible in the other types. It has to be noted that in these two first types, the dependency on welfare payments is lowest and self-sufficiency highest. Resilient households are functioning more like internally diversified ecosystems and less like what we expect from modern households in (post)-industrial market societies, optimizing their most proficient source of income. We have to admit, if we go back in history, human survival and development seemed strongly based on such multiple sourced livelihoods through a long period of human existence – just think about the hunter and gatherer, farmer–craftsmen, farmer–labourers, labourer–entrepreneurs, merchant–travellers, fishermen–seamen, weavers–housewives among our own ancestors just one or two centuries ago.

Second, we had to learn that resilience of vulnerable households is vulnerable itself and it can involve risks. These may be risks for society, risks for community, or risks for the person or household itself. Health problems, in relation to overwork or substandard access to health provision and healthcare threatens resilient and other persons living at the poverty line. Within families, this often concerns adults, who try to minimize the risk for their kids and take on a higher burden themselves. Family rupture is another risk that resilient families share with non-resilient families, but, as some of our cases show, when resilience includes families that reacquire a role as a unit of production, ruptures are even more menacing. Self-endangerment through risky practices can also take place. While there was no electricity or gas tapping observable, insecure heating and cooking devices or fuels could be observed here and there. Community risks may arise from practices which overstretch the family's share in public goods (i.e. by water or electricity tapping, over-extraction of natural resources, free riding public transport, or by participating in social or gift exchange only on the 'taking' side) or generate public safety risks (living in illegal or insecure buildings or gas tapping), but there were no such observations during the project duration. Illegal or grey practices (small theft, fraud, squatting, undocumented labour or entrepreneurship) might pose risks to society in general but were either rarely observed among the resilient households of the project, or yielded very little impact. Generally speaking, the instability of income generation and the general situation of living in scarcity seems to be the major risk for households, followed by the connection between overwork, money scarcity, below average access to healthcare and bad health, in some cases accompanied by substandard housing. Situations can change quite quickly where the practices carried out before are no longer helpful. Of course, the observed families try to balance or compensate for them by substituting one practice for another, but during a severe economic crisis or natural disaster this can reach its limits quite quickly. Moreover, risks may distribute asymmetrically in households with respect to gender or generations (see Chapter 9 of this volume). In some cases, women, especially mothers, have a higher risk of overwork due to extensively combining family obligations with work and income generation. We must keep in mind that all income generation activities these households undertake are not very well paid, so they have to make extensive use of their labour force. This may bring them in conflict with their health interests and family relations. Resilience also requires certain institutionalized social conditions. Among these we can find a highly relevant role of common goods, and the developed welfare state in a wider sense, as we will see now.

Third and finally, there is little resilience which does not require the welfare state or some basic public order in one or another role. These roles may range from a minimum level as a guarantor of public safety and fundamental provisions for survival, such as police, justice, disaster protection, via a slightly advanced level by supporting a property order and culture which tolerates or allows for free use of public space, or for small secondary use of public and other persons' private land. But present developments, as well as comparisons of everyday life of poor households, shows some remarkable issues going beyond these basic levels: living on little money is obviously easier where either the welfare state or other collective actors exempt and protect some important means and conditions of living from full marketization, meaning a certain level of de-commodification: energy and water supply, waste treatment, housing and public transport, public safety, health and old age provisions, up to education and information are usually less available for low-income households if supplied for market prices only, and many of the common or public goods used by resilient families and other low-income groups fall into those categories. And where the welfare state does not provide them sufficiently, they are less available for those with little money. This function of the welfare state, of which the public was well aware in the first decades of the twentieth century, has moved out of sight a bit in recent decades, but is nevertheless crucial – the rising social and political conflicts on housing prices of the post 2010 years are just one indicator. The medium or maximum level of welfare state intervention of course are provisions of basic income support and other monetary entitlements, which come into play in the lives of resilient low-income households as a fallback option, temporary support, partial or full support where resilient households' strategies fail or cannot develop, and the findings indicate that resilience can develop to higher levels the better the framework of the respective welfare state allows for this.

NOTES

1. It has to be mentioned that there are quite different approaches to what a typology or typological research actually is or should be. Aside from what could be called "social types" (le Grand 2019) like the "stranger" (Schütz 1972), the "organization man" (Whyte 2013), "the poor" (Simmel 1908), or Bauman's "flaneur" (Bauman 1995), and aside from the introspective theoretization of Weber's ideal types (1914), however justified for other questions, the typology concept in this chapter follows the epistemological propositions of Lazarsfeld (1937) and Hempel and Oppenheim (1936) and the inductive comparative programme of Glaser and Strauss' *The Discovery of Grounded Theory* (1967): A set of n variables or observables identified as relevant by casewise comparison, guided by start heuristics and further developed by emerging structures of relevance constitute a property space within which clusters of values can be identified, where the internal variation is smaller than the external variation. Such a cluster can also be called group, class – or type. Taking Hempel/Oppenheim seriously, it may matter in precision and sharpness, but not epistemologically, whether these values are perfectly measured

on a precise scale, yes/no estimations by experts or observers, or relatively vague more/less impressions of the kind we find in ethnography or other qualitative research. This definition has clear advantages neither having to rely on Weber's genial introspection, nor risking to produce strong research artefacts with labelling effects, but being operable and applicable to quantitative and qualitative data (see Promberger 2011).

2. All interviewee names in this chapter are fictitious.
3. This could in principle result from a sampling bias, but more likely from the availability of common goods, which is important for low-income households' resilience, but comparably low in the UK and Ireland.
4. It has to be noted that precarious entrepreneurship is a standing topic in research on developing countries (e.g. Stensrud 2017), but so far has found little attention in post-industrial societies.
5. Of course, such strategies can fail – see case examples in Promberger et al. 2019, or the wide literature on precarious self-employment (Bührmann and Pongratz 2010).
6. We are grateful for the support of the Spanish RESCuE team María Arnal, Carlos De Castro, Paz Martín, Juan Carlos Revilla, Araceli Serrano who generously supported us with visual and textual footage for this type.
7. Gratitude goes to our co-editors Jenny Dagg and Jane Gray, who wove this Irish sample case into the typology presented here.
8. See the introduction to this chapter.

REFERENCES

Anderson, B. (1983), *Imagined communities: Reflections on the origin and spread of nationalism*, London, New York: Verso.
Bandura, A. (1993), 'Perceived self-efficacy in cognitive development and functioning', *Educational Psychologist* 28(2): 117–48.
Banerjee, A. V., and Duflo, E. (2011), *Poor Economics. A Radical Rethinking of the Way to Fight Global Poverty*, New York: Public Affairs.
Bauman, Z. (1995), *Life in fragments: Essays in postmodern morality*, Cambridge, MA: Basil Blackwell.
Benach, J., Vives, A., Amable, M., Vanroelen, C., Tarafa, G. and Muntaner, C. (2014), 'Precarious employment: Understanding an emerging social determinant of health', *Annual Review of Public Health* 35: 229–53.
Bosch, A. (2015), *Konsum und Exklusion: eine Kultursoziologie der Dinge*, Bielefeld: Transcript Verlag.
Bourdieu, P. (2011[1986]), 'The forms of capital', in I. Szeman and T. Kaposy (eds.), *Cultural theory: An anthology*, Chichester, Malden: Wiley-Blackwell, pp. 81–93.
Bührmann, A. D. and Pongratz, H. J. (eds.) (2010), *Prekäres Unternehmertum: Unsicherheiten von selbstständiger Erwerbstätigkeit und Unternehmensgründung*, Wiesbaden: Springer-Verlag.
Butterwegge, C. (2014), *Krise und Zukunft des Sozialstaates*, Wiesbaden: VS Verlag.
Cattell, V. (2001), 'Poor people, poor places, and poor health: The mediating role of social networks and social capital', *Social Science & Medicine* 52(10): 1501–16.
Clausen, J. (1998), 'Life reviews and life stories', in J. Z. Giele and G. H. Elder (eds.), *Methods of life course research: Qualitative and quantitative approaches,* Thousand Oaks, CA: Sage, pp. 189–212.

Daly, M. (2016), 'Money-related meanings and practices in low-income and poor families', *Sociology* 51(2): 450–65.

Deppe, W. (1982), *Drei Generationen Arbeiterleben: eine sozio-biographische Darstellung*, Frankfurt am Main: Campus.

Dilthey, W. (1992[1910]), *Der Aufbau der geschichtlichen Welt in den Geisteswissenschaften*, Berlin: Suhrkamp.

Durkheim, E. (2014[1893]), *The division of labor in society*, Simon and Schuster.

Elder, G. H. (1994), 'Time, human agency, and social change: Perspectives on the life course', *Social Psychology Quarterly* 57(1): 4–15.

Ellis, F. (1998), 'Household strategies and rural livelihood diversification', *The Journal of Development Studies* 35(1): 1–38.

Engel, F. and Hirseland, A. (2016), 'Ich meine, das reicht hinten und vorne nicht. Ansätze nachhaltigen Wirtschaftens bei Hartz IV-Beziehenden', *Vierteljahrshefte zur Wirtschaftsforschung* 85(3): 69–79.

Finley, M. I. (2002[1965]), *The world of Odysseus*, New York: NYRB Classics.

Folkman, S. (1984), 'Personal control and stress and coping processes: A theoretical analysis', *Journal of Personality and Social Psychology* 46: 839–52.

Garibay-Orijel, R., Ramírez-Terrazo, A. and Ordaz-Velázquez, M. (2012), 'Women care about local knowledge, experiences from ethnomycology', *Journal of Ethnobiology and Ethnomedicine* 8(25): 1–12.

Gehlen, A. (1988), *Man, his nature and place in the world*, New York: Columbia University Press.

Giddens, A. (1984), *The constitution of society: Outline of the theory of structuration*, University of California Press.

Glaser, B. G. and Strauss, A. L. (1967), *The discovery of grounded theory: Strategies for qualitative research*, New York: Adline de Gruyter.

Glaser, B. G. and Strauss, A. (1971), *Status passage*, London: Routledge & Kegan Paul.

Glavovic, B., Scheyvens, R. and Overton, J. (2002), 'Waves of adversity, layers of resilience: Exploring the sustainable livelihoods approach', in D. Storey, J. Overton and B. Nowak (eds.), *Contesting development: Pathways to better practice, proceedings of the Third Biennial Conference of the Aotearoa New Zealand International Development Studies Network* (DevNet), New Zealand: Massey University, Institute of Development Studies, pp. 289–93.

Gray, J. and Dagg, J. (2019), 'Crisis, recession and social resilience: A biographical life course analysis', *Advances in Life Course Research* 42: 100293.

Hagerty, B. M., Lynch-Sauer, J., Patusky, K. L., Bouwsema, M. and Collier, P. (1992), 'Sense of belonging: A vital mental health concept', *Archives of Psychiatric Nursing* 6: 172–7.

Hann, C. (2000), 'Echte Bauern, Stachanowiten und die Lilien auf dem Felde', in J. Kocka and K. Offe (eds.), *Geschichte und Zukunft der Arbeit*, Frankfurt: Campus, pp. 23–53.

Hempel, C. G. and Oppenheim, P. (1936), *Der Typusbegriff im Lichte der neuen Logik*, Leiden: A. W. Sijthoff.

Hitlin, S. and Kirkpatrick Johnson, M. (2015), 'Reconceptualizing agency within the life course: The power of looking ahead', *American Journal of Sociology* 120(5): 1429–72.

Holmes, H. (2018), 'Unpicking contemporary thrift: Getting on and getting by in everyday life', *The Sociological Review* 1(8): 1–17.

Holt, D. and Littlewood, D. (2017), 'Waste livelihoods amongst the poor – Through the lens of bricolage', *Business Strategy and the Environment* 26: 253–64.

Hooper, C.-A., Gorin, S., Cabral, C. and Dyson, C. (2007), *Living with hardship 24/7: The diverse experiences of families in poverty in England*, London: Frank Buttle Trust.

Jahoda, M., Lazarsfeld, P. F. and Zeisel, H. (1988[1932]), *Die Arbeitslosen von Marienthal. Ein soziographischer Versuch über die Wirkungen langandauernder Arbeitslosigkeit*, Frankfurt am Main: Suhrkamp.

Kananen, J. (2014), *The Nordic welfare state in three eras: From emancipation to discipline*, Farnham: Ashgate.

Kohl, J. (2000), 'Der Sozialstaat: Die deutsche Version des Wohlfahrtsstaates – Überlegungen zu seiner typologischen Verortung', in S. Leibfried and U. Wagschal (eds.), *Der deutsche Sozialstaat. Bilanzen – Reformen – Perspektiven*, Frankfurt, New York: Campus Verlag, pp. 115–52.

Kreher, S. (2012), *Von der 'Leutenot' und der 'Not der Leute': Armut in Nordostdeutschland*, Wien: Böhlau.

Kuckartz, U. (2010), 'Typenbildung', in G. Mey and K. Mruck (eds.), *Handbuch qualitative Forschung in der Psychologie*, Wiesbaden: VS Verlag für Sozialwissenschaften, pp. 553–68.

Lazarsfeld, P. F. (1937), 'Some remarks on the typological procedures in social research', *Zeitschrift für Sozialforschung* 6(1): 119–39.

le Grand, E. (2019), 'Conceptualising social types and figures: From social forms to classificatory struggles', *Cultural Sociology* 13(4): 411–27.

Lessenich, S. (2013), *Die Neuerfindung des Sozialen. Der Sozialstaat im flexiblen Kapitalismus*, Bielefeld: Transcript.

Lévi-Strauss, C. (1962), *The savage mind*, Chicago: University of Chicago Press.

Lewchuk, W., Clarke, M. and De Wolff, A. (2008), 'Working without commitments: Precarious employment and health', *Work, Employment and Society* 22(3): 387–406.

Lewin-Epstein, N. and Yuchtman-Yaar, E. (1991), 'Health risks of self-employment', *Work and Occupations* 18(3): 291–312.

Lewis, O. (1959), *Five families: Mexican case studies in the culture of poverty*, New York: Random House.

Luhmann, N. (1984), *Soziale Systeme. Grundriss einer allgemeinen Theorie*, Frankfurt am Main: Suhrkamp.

Malcolmson, R. W. (1988), 'Ways of getting a living in eighteenth-century England', in R. Pahl (ed.), *On work: Historical, comparative and theoretical approaches*, Oxford: Blackwell, pp. 48–60.

Mauss, M. (1954[1925]), *The gift*, London: Cohen & West.

Meier, U., Preuße, H. and Sunnus, E. M. (2003), *Steckbriefe von Armut. Haushalte in prekären Lebenslagen*, Wiesbaden: VS Verlag.

Negt, O. and Kluge, A. (1981), *Geschichte und Eigensinn*, Frankfurt am Main: Zweitausendeins Verlag.

Offe, C. and Wiesenthal, H. (1980), 'Two logics of collective action: Theoretical notes on social class and organizational form', *Political Power and Social Theory* (1): 67–115.

Plessner, H. (2019[1928]), *Levels of organic life and the human: An introduction to philosophical anthropology*, New York: Fordham University Press.

Polanyi, K. (2001[1944]), *The great transformation: The political and economic origins of our time*, Boston: Beacon Press.

Promberger, M. (2011), *Typenbildung mit quantitativen und qualitativen Daten: Methodologische Überlegungen*, Nuremberg: Institute for Employment Research, IAB Discussion Paper No. 12/2011.

Promberger, M. (2015), 'Nueve años de Hartz IV: evaluación de una reforma del bienestar', *Cuadernos de Relaciones Laborales* (1): 35–64.

Promberger, M. (2017), *Resilience among vulnerable households in Europe: Questions, concept, findings and implications*, Nuremberg: Institute for Employment Research, IAB Discussion Paper No 12/2017.

Promberger, M., Meier, L., Sowa, F. and Boost, M. (2019), 'Chances of 'resilience' as a concept for sociological poverty research', in B. Rampp, M. Endreß and M. Naumann (eds.), *Resilience in social, cultural and political spheres*, Wiesbaden: Springer VS, pp. 249–79.

Promberger, M., Hieber, S. and Hirseland, A. (2021), *Wendepunkte in Armutsbiografien*, Nuremberg: Institute for Employment Research, IAB Discussion Paper, forthcoming.

Revilla, J. C., Martín, P. and de Castro, C. (2018), 'The reconstruction of resilience as a social and collective phenomenon: Poverty and coping capacity during the economic crisis', *European Societies* 20(1): 89–110.

Riemann, G. (1987), *Das Fremdwerden der eigenen Biographie: narrative Interviews mit psychiatrischen Patienten*, München: Fink.

Rosenthal, G. (1995), *Erlebte und erzählte Lebensgeschichte: Gestalt und Struktur biographischer Selbstbeschreibungen*, Frankfurt am Main: Campus.

Rowntree, B. S. (2000), *Poverty: A study of town life*, London: Policy Press.

Rutter, M. (2006), 'Implications of resilience concepts for scientific understanding', *Annals of the New York Academy of Sciences* 1094(1): 1–12.

Rutter, M. (2013), 'Annual research review: Resilience – clinical implications', *The Journal of Child Psychology and Psychiatry* 54(4): 474–87.

Sampson, R. and Laub, J. (2003), 'Life-course desisters? Trajectories of crime among delinquent boys followed to age 70', *Criminology* 41: 555–92.

Schumpeter, J. A. (1942), *Capitalism, socialism and democracy*, London: Harper & Brothers.

Schütz, A. (1972), 'Der Fremde', in A. Schütz (ed.), *Gesammelte Aufsätze. Bd. 2: Studien zur soziologischen Theorie*, Dordrecht: Springer, pp. 53–69.

Simmel, G. (1906), 'Zur Soziologie der Armut', *Archiv für Sozialwissenschaft und Sozialpolitik* 1: 1–3.

Simmel, G. (1908), 'Der Arme', in G. Simmel (ed.), *Soziologie – Untersuchungen über die Formen der Vergesellschaftung*, Berlin: Duncker & Humblot, pp. 454–93.

Spini, D., Hanappi, D., Bernardi, L., Oris, M. and Bickel, J.-F. (2013), *Vulnerability across the life course: A theoretical framework and research directions*, Geneva: LIVES Working Paper 2013/27.

Stensrud, A. (2017), 'Precarious entrepreneurship: Mobile phones, work and kinship in neoliberal Peru', *Social Anthropology* 25(2), 159–73.

Stinchcombe, A. L. (1965), 'Social structure and organizations', in J. P. March (ed.), *Handbook of Organizations*, Chicago: Rand McNally, pp. 142–93.

Tönnies, F. (1957[1887]), *Gemeinschaft und Gesellschaft*, Leipzig: Fues.

Valkonen, T. and Vihriälä, V. (2014), *The Nordic model – challenged but capable of reform*, Denmark: Norden.

Van Gennep, A. (2013[1909]), *The rites of passage*, Chicago: University of Chicago Press.

Vuojala-Magga, T. (2009), 'Simple things but complicated skills: Sámi skills and tacit knowledge in the context of climatic change', in V. K. Oy (ed.), *Máttut Máddagat: The roots of Sámi ethnicities, societies and spaces/places*, Sastamala, Oulu: Publications of the Giellagas Institute, pp. 164–73.

Wallace, C. (2002), 'Household strategies: Their conceptual relevance and analytical scope in social research', *Sociology* 36(2): 275–92.

Warde, A. (1990), 'Household work strategies and forms of labour: Conceptual and empirical issues', *Work, Employment and Society* 4(4): 495–515.

Weber, M. (1914), *Wirtschaft und Gesellschaft*, Tübingen: J. C. B. Mohr.

Werner, E. (1992), 'The children of Kauai: Resiliency and recovery in adolescence and adulthood', *Journal of Adolescent Health* 13(4): 262–68.

Whyte, W. H. (2013), *The organization man*, Philadelphia: University of Pennsylvania Press.

Williams, C. C. and Windebank, J. (2000), 'Helping each other out? Community exchange in deprived neighbourhoods', *Community Development Journal* 35(2): 146–56.

15. Strategies of resilience and the welfare state in Southern Europe

Nelli Kambouri, Soula Marinoudi and Georgia Petraki

THE SOUTHERN EUROPEAN WELFARE MODEL IN TIMES OF CRISIS

Greece, Portugal and Spain are three of the four states that were originally 'excluded' from Esping-Andersen's typology of the three worlds of welfare because they were considered as underdeveloped versions of more advanced European models (Esping-Andersen 1996, 1997; Arts and Gelissen 2002). According to this linear theoretical framework, these three welfare systems have been characterized as delayed or primitive variants of conservative corporatist welfare regimes (Andreotti et al. 2001; Katrougalos 1996; Katrougalos and Lazaridis 2003). Contrary to this classification, there are also scholars who proposed that an additional ideal type should be added to the typology, a distinct 'fourth world' or a 'Southern European Welfare Model' (SEM) (Leibfried 1992; Petmesidou 1996; Ferrera 1996). This model is distinct because it is characterized by specific elements and traits that include: (a) the centrality of the Church and the family as welfare providers and a tradition of familialism (Leibfried 1992; Petmesidou 1996; Gal 2010); (b) high inequality and polarization of income maintenance systems (pensions, healthcare, social assistance) between privileged and under-privileged sectors of employment; (c) reliance on private–public alliances and networks; (d) the establishment of unified national health systems rather than corporatist ones; and (e) clientalism and reliance on political party patronage (Ferrera 1996).

Although the debates on ideal types of welfare regime may be useful in some academic and policy contexts, they often assume a rather static, homogenizing and ethno-centric conception of welfare institutions and processes. Scholars have stressed the need to overcome the methodological nationalism that characterizes typologies of welfare in Europe, acknowledging that while there are differences within and between welfare systems depending on the perspective from which one analyses them and the historical context, there are also common trends and dynamics that create a 'welfare mix' (Oosterlynck et al. 2013). Most welfare regimes can, thus, be seen as what Petmesidou and Guillén termed hybrid welfare states (2014).

In this chapter, we examine these three welfare states in Southern Europe in relation to household resilience. We argue that, despite differences in their historical development, during the period of the economic crisis there are common policies, dynamics and trajectories that transform welfare across Southern Europe. Although some of the characteristics that scholars have used in the past to describe the Southern European model remain dominant and are strengthened, as, for example, familialism, there are also trends that indicate convergence with the liberal model. These transformations, which are mostly the product of supranational and national decision-making, have a negative impact on the ability of vulnerable households to become resilient as they consist mainly of austerity cuts on welfare budgets and services combined with increased taxation and rises in the prices of utility services as well as the utilization of welfare as a form of social control. Narratives of household resilience in Southern Europe are characterized by negative perceptions of national welfare states as institutions that are failing to provide care and protection to vulnerable citizens and an increasing reliance on informal and non-governmental local institutions that are often in conflict with central governments.

LOCALIZATION AND CENTRALIZATION OF WELFARE IN SOUTH EUROPE: THE EXAMPLES OF GREECE, PORTUGAL AND SPAIN

Since the 1990s, the adoption of the European Union (EU) principle of subsidiarity has brought to the forefront of policy making the question of the localization of welfare regimes in member states (Kazepov 2008). While historical traditions of localization or centralization continue to play an important role in shaping different types of welfare state,[1] the aim of contemporary EU policies and processes of subsidiarity is not so much to dispense with national-level decision-making or to return to a charity-based approach on welfare, but rather to identify the appropriate policy level. In this context, emphasis is placed on encouraging the involvement of local institutions in areas where they may have a more positive, innovative, communal, participatory and ultimately low-cost impact on local communities (Evers et al. 2014; Moulaert et al. 2010; Andreotti et al. 2012). Nevertheless, as Purcell has argued, the localization discourse entails what he terms the 'local trap', the presupposition that there is something inherently more democratic and innovative at the local level – a presupposition that may be refuted if we consider how clientalist networks flourish and undemocratic forces, including ultra right-wing ones, have taken over the local level in several EU member states (Purcell 2006). Moreover, while formal processes of localization may be effective in reducing the financial costs and bureaucratic complexity in the face of the rising heterogeneity and diversity of welfare claimants, decision-making is still in the hands of national governments (Brenner 2004; Ferrera 2005; Moulaert et al. 1988).

There are two dimensions in the localization of welfare, which we examine separately in this section although they are interrelated: (a) vertical subsidiarity: the shifting of welfare responsibilities from the national to the local level; and (b) horizontal subsidiarity: the multiplication of welfare actors (Andreotti et al. 2012).

Vertical Subsidiarity

With regards to the transfer of responsibilities from the national to the local level in Southern Europe, the Greek, Portuguese and Spanish welfare systems share a structure based on three distinct but interdependent levels: the supra-national, the national, and the local (regional, municipal, parish). The degree of centralization, however, varies according to historical developments and EU-wide processes.

In Greece, although decisions about welfare are taken primarily at the national level, since the 1990s, some responsibilities – mainly bureaucratic and administrative ones – have been transferred from the central government to the regions and the municipalities. In 2010, at a period when austerity reductions in the personnel of regions and municipalities and severe budget cuts were imposed, the so-called 'Kallikratis' merger reform reduced the number of local authorities while at the same time transferring more competences to local institutions without corresponding transfers of funds (Chardas and Skamnakis 2016). These tasks included mainly the elderly and children, as well as administrative aspects of education and social policy. Although the localization of welfare in Greece mostly began as an attempt to follow top-down EU-wide processes and funding priorities, when the economic crisis began, more responsibilities were transferred to municipalities, including programmes for the poor, for the unemployed and the homeless. Although municipalities have acquired an active role in administrative, bureaucratic and implementation procedures, they continue to face severe obstacles in influencing national welfare policies, as they still depend overwhelmingly on national and supranational (EU) decision-making and sources of funding (Chardas 2014; Skamnakis and Pantazopoulos 2015).

While in Greece, localization was mostly triggered by the EU drive of the 1990s, in Portugal and Spain it was embedded into post-dictatorship historical developments. The Portuguese welfare system was constituted on the basis of a historical tradition of partnerships between the state and local public and private institutions, including social economy institutions often linked to the Catholic Church (see Chapter 12 of this volume). Contrary to Greece, these were established before the EU-wide localization turn of the 1990s and were deeply entrenched into local politics and traditions. The municipal councils and the parishes enjoy authority and perform specific state-funded work on poverty, food distribution and social housing in collaboration with non-governmental organizations (NGOs). In 1995, a programme for the Local Social Action Committees of the so-called social network was inaugurated in order to manage and coordinate different governmental and non-governmental actors specializing in anti-poverty and social development actions (Capucha et al. 2016). In 2013, however, a merger reform was introduced, which was part of the Memorandum of Understanding (MOU),[2] whose aim was to reduce the number of local authorities, in this case parishes only, in order to achieve an overall decrease in the costs of local administration. Similarly to the case of Greece after the economic crisis began, a rising number of state-funded programmes against poverty were assigned to local authorities without corresponding funds. Against the Portuguese tradition of decentralization and autonomy, the role of local institutions was undermined during the economic crisis as financial centralism increased especially in the sectors with impact on public deficit after the 2011 MOU (Nunes 2017; Nunes and Buček, 2014).

Finally, the Spanish welfare system is more decentralized as it grants important federal responsibilities and decision-making capabilities to local (especially regional) authorities in several areas, including social housing, welfare benefits and allowances, education, health, childcare and unemployment programmes (Martín and de Castro 2016). Both the state and regional authorities have local branches, which provide assistance, guidance and information to citizens. Compared to Greece and Portugal, public local welfare institutions in Spain have a stronger impact on decision-making processes, while the municipalities are mostly responsible for the implementation of programmes decided at the state and regional levels. Nevertheless, in Spain, as in Greece and Portugal, after the economic crisis began, rising centralization of decision-making and funds in the hands of national governments has been underway under the influence of the increasing Europeanization, which subordinated welfare policies to fiscal consolidation imperatives (González Begega and del Pino 2014). Local institutions in Spain were, thus, subject to much more severe austerity cuts in welfare expenditure than national institutions, although there were reductions in both (Del Pino and Pavolini 2015). These changes impacted negatively on local welfare. Scarcity of funding has made local institutions even more dependent on transfers from the national and EU budgets than in the past, delimiting their ability to influence decision-making on welfare policies (Martín and de Castro 2016).

The examples of Greece, Portugal and Spain illustrate that the impact of decentralization on welfare systems depends on the historical context

(Kazepov 2008). Despite differences in the structure of local governance and the degrees of centralization/localization and public–private coordination of welfare, Greece, Portugal and Spain have undergone profound political and socioeconomic transformations that have obstructed the development of their welfare regimes and increased socioeconomic inequalities (Karamessini and Rubery 2013; Petmesidou and Guillén 2015; Matsaganis and Leventi 2014). Supranational institutions, such as the EU Commission, the World Bank or the International Monetary Fund, acquired a much more active role in imposing welfare policy choices, outcomes and objectives that increased inequalities in the name of fiscal consolidation. In order to pass unpopular reforms enshrined in the MOUs in Greece and Portugal, the role of the central governments and executive structures has been reinforced, while parliaments and local governments have lost their ability to influence decision-making on welfare (Guillén and Pavolini 2015). For example, Sotiropoulos has coined the term 'legislating through fiat' to describe the increasing number of cases in which unpopular policy changes dictated by supranational institutions became laws through ministerial or presidential fiat, rather than through voting in Parliament, in Greece (Sotiropoulos 2015).

As welfare policies are increasingly decided in negotiations between national governments, European institutions and international organizations, local actors are displaced and become powerless. Thus, the notion of localization of welfare in times of crisis is rearticulated to serve micro-political purposes rather than innovative goals (Featherstone et al. 2012). According to critics, the turn to the local in times of crisis consists mainly of transfers of administrative and bureaucratic responsibilities for unpopular measures without the adoption of substantial and sustainable processes of decentralization or democratization (Andreotti et al. 2012).

Horizontal Subsidiarity

With regards to the multiplication of welfare actors in South Europe, there are divergences, but also convergences between the three welfare systems. In Greece, historically the main charitable organization was the Greek Orthodox Church, which has maintained a considerable influence on the distribution of welfare to the poor and destitute before and after the economic crisis, especially in rural areas (Fokas 2013).[3] NGO voluntarism and public fund-raising, however, has very weak foundations in Greek society, as state and political party clientalism were dominant forces at least in the pre-crisis period. According to Huliaras, this is mostly because of lack of trust in these organizations, which are often criticized for blocking bottom-up charity and in some cases of corruption involving public funds too. With the exception of a limited number of large-scale private foundations, NGOs in Greece are entirely dependent on state and the EU funding (Huliaras 2014).[4] It is, however, clear that, as the crisis deepened, the demand for the welfare services that the Church and some of these NGOs offered (including food, shelter, and medical and social services) rose[5] at the same time as budget cuts in government funding for civil society was severely curtailed rendering them more dependent on EU funding, objectives and policy priorities.

In Portugal, as mentioned above, 4,000 Private Social Solidarity Institutions (IPSSs) comprise social networks that have considerable influence on local social welfare.[6] The social networks are mostly headed by the council and, besides the IPSS, are comprised of municipal services, local welfare services (social security, job centres, and schools), local associations and companies (to a lesser extent). These social networks have achieved low or no cost social services for the poor, employment opportunities for groups deprived of access to the labour market, and avenues for representing the interests and discourses of vulnerable social groups in public debate (Capucha et al. 2016, p. 12). Nonetheless, beneficiaries contribute to IPSSs' social services according to their income: while services offered to those at the lower income levels are subsidized by the state through a system of per capita reimbursements, those with higher incomes pay part or the total cost. After 2009, the IPSSs came under scrutiny for losing some of their poorest recipients, who were no longer able to pay for the services provided because of a drop in income and wages (Capucha et al. 2016). Especially households that were forced to withdraw their children from day care centres, or their relatives from elderly care facilities, are suffering from a sharp deterioration of their living conditions. In response, the IPSSs have acquired new tasks to support deprived social groups, such as the creation of a network of social canteens or social kitchens that distribute free food to the poor.

In Spain, private NGO networks often play an active role as pressure groups. These networks include a variety of actors, from large religious NGOs like Caritas and the Red Cross to cultural, neighbourhood and parents' associations. Nonetheless, NGOs in Spain are in an ambivalent relationship with the central and regional governments since they depend and rely heavily on state and regional funding, but are often very critical and sometimes even in an adversarial relationship with them (Martín and de Castro 2016, p. 10). Overall, the NGO sector was deeply affected by budget cuts, which, as in Greece, increased their dependency on EU funding. However, NGOs in Spain stand out from those of Portugal and Greece because they have become very critical and often militant against austerity policies. As Martín and Serrano (2014) argued, on the one hand, there are often conflicts of legitimacy as NGO activities 'make visible gaps in the social service system' and, on the other, they are able to negotiate and cooperate with local governments because they have a more widespread popular basis than the authorities (Martín and Serrano 2014).

Unlike Greece, NGOs, especially in the anti-eviction movement, were able to voice critical demands of vulnerable social groups and to put pressure on the state and regional authorities. Spanish NGOs were positioned at the threshold 'both inside and outside the system' making 'visible some gaps in the social service system', but also reaching 'collective agreements, which the formal administration cannot achieve' (Martín and de Castro 2016).

NARRATIVES OF RESILIENCE AND THE FAILED WELFARE STATE IN SOUTH EUROPE

Despite national and regional differences, the Greek, Portuguese and Spanish welfare states were discussed by several interviewees as failing institutions that were unprepared to deal with recession, rising unemployment, increased numbers of citizens resorting to public services and the intensification of social inequalities. The unpreparedness and/or inability of national welfare states to cope with urgent social problems contributed to a climate of distrust and dissatisfaction, which on some occasions tended to become open animosity and hatred towards the political elites that controlled the government and democratic institutions. As an interviewee from the rural case study in Spain mentioned, expecting citizens to adapt to austerity while they themselves make no effort to adjust and tone down their affluent ways of living is unacceptable:

'At the moment in Spain we cannot get by, we cannot get by. There are things, things that I've adapted to, well the politicians should adapt too. Why do they have to have such high salaries, if I have to live on five or six hundred euros? They should adapt too! And they think that I can get by and that they can't. I'd like to see more than one of them in my situation, you know?' (Spain/F/Rural)

'And if not, then they (the politicians) should try it, they should try it, they'd have four hundred and twenty six [euros] to pay for the flat, and to last the month, let's see if they can do it too. And they'd have to do without many things, the same as we have to do without. Well that's the way I see it, right, things are going from bad to worse and I don't know how we're going to end up.' (Spain/F/Urban)

Statements of this kind are characteristic of an affective discourse questioning contemporary democracies and their main actors that were consolidated after recent historical experiences of dictatorship in all three of the states examined here. This affective discourse consists mainly of left-wing contestations of representative politics through non-representative grassroots alliances, protest and solidarity (Azzelini and Sitrin 2014). In some cases, especially in Greece, the same affective characteristics (anger, resentment, outrage) could be found in directly antagonistic practices of resilience that questioned the post-dictatorship regime in favour of ultra-right-wing ethnonationalist condemnations of the same elites and institutions.

In addition to the inability to cope with the economic crisis, the state was criticized in several narratives for increasing taxation. During our fieldwork, we often encountered individuals who were angry over the exceedingly unfair and unequal rises in taxation imposed by national governments and commented upon the lack of reciprocity. For several interviewees, the failing and indebted welfare state became a burden hindering resilience, rather than a protective and supportive mechanism. The following passage from a household located in rural Spain is characteristic:

> 'You're charging me a tax, and I haven't got a cent and I pay my electricity, water and rent every month, all these expenses are on me. And those people that are loaded … well because, those who earn more should pay more and those who earn less should pay less.' (Spain/F/Rural)

Narratives like the one above confirmed analysis that criticizes the prioritizing of fiscal discipline over welfare without any counterbalancing measures of social protection. National and supranational institutional involvement in decision-making and funding has persistently increased citizens' obligations, augmenting further social inequalities (Adam and Papatheodorou 2016).

In the narratives of resilient households, anger and resentment were directed equally against elites from national governments, local institutions and some civil society actors (Church, NGOs, labour unions) as they were all considered culpable of failure and corruption. An interviewee from Portugal also highlights his anger with the treatment he received from welfare institutions:

> 'I've been doing community service here in the parish council … But I never thought I could be exploited in such a way as I am going to, right? … They put us there, we do not have equipment … I had to be the one who bought the boots and they don't want to give me back my money. I have no right to holidays, I have no right to holiday pay, and I have no right to unemployment benefit.' (Portugal/M/ Urban)

In this context, citizens who were angry with the welfare state did not recognize different levels of governance, and did not shift the blame for austerity measures from the national to the local levels. From the perspective of household resilience, what the relevant literature identifies as localization of welfare was not widely perceived as a process that guarantees effectiveness, democratization or innovation in times of crisis as it was stained by austerity and systemic failure.

A common theme in the interviews was that households had to make strategic choices in order to cope with medical expenses given the limited resources that they had. Such choices undermined their resilience as they threatened their bodily integrity and well-being. Several interviewees, who were parents, for example, narrated how they decided to stop taking medication necessary for their own health in order to cover the expenses of their children. A participant from Portugal describes how these choices were made:

'Yes, he prescribed an antidepressant. I don't take it always, I only take it when I feel that I'm really falling, because I don't even have money for medicine ... I have to make these choices every month. Either I buy medicine for myself or I put food on the table [cries] for me and my sons. There aren't many options for me.' (Portugal/F/Urban)

In the same vein, an interviewee from Greece says:

'So I didn't buy medicine, so that the baby can have diapers; Yes ... that's difficult. ... The welfare card provides medical treatment just for one person in the family. The others don't have medical insurance ....' (Greece/F/Rural)

The structural reforms and cuts in the healthcare sector affected crucially the commitment to universal coverage, as those who were pushed outside the labour market often found themselves lacking access to healthcare (Karanikolos et al. 2013; Samikou 2014).

Dependency on public welfare became an expression of downward mobility and social failure. Interviewees often narrated nostalgically a past of wealth and affluence and were regretful of the times when they were able to secure high-quality services in education, housing, health, or social insurance by private means. A woman from Portugal was reminiscent of her job in the 1980s:

'At that time, they didn't check. They hired us, they told us to do one hairstyling or one haircut or whatever, well, they hired us immediately. It was so easy ... One day I left one hairdresser, and the next day I was in another one.' (Portugal/F/Urban)

In the Greek semi-rural case, a female interviewee told a story of economic decline, from a profitable family construction business to bankruptcy, indebtedness and unemployment.

'We don't have medical insurance at present ... and my husband was diagnosed with cancer. And fortunately, thanks to ... [an employee in the local insurance office] he helped us acquire a welfare card. We had nothing ... Our situation was ... I mean ... Nobody has medical insurance now. I have to take medicine, but I don't.' (Greece/F/Rural)

Such narratives are emblematic of the ways in which resilience becomes implicated into the stigmatization of the 'new poor', those who have lost their ability to cover basic needs only after the economic crisis. In the Portuguese case, for example, interviewees criticized the NGO social canteens programme, which was heavily subsidized and publicized by the government, as they argued that these were palliative measures which made them feel ashamed and avoided them (Capucha et al. 2016). Narratives and feelings of guilt and shame discouraged households who sought access to public welfare. As the following passage from an interview in rural Spain illustrates, stigma was internalized to such an extent that searching for support from the welfare system was considered to jeopardize one's self-image and social relations with friends and next of kin. 'There are people who ... take advantage [of the system] and then there are those who are ashamed and they don't go. I mean, sincerely, I'm quite embarrassed. I get embarrassed ...' (Spain/F/Rural).

In most cases, stigma and bureaucratic problems pushed interviewees to seek assistance from their extended families. A Spanish interviewee, for example, declared that she would rather ask for assistance from her family than undergo the humiliating treatment that she received from social services – 'I'd almost prefer to go to my mother and say to her, "please, go shopping for me" than to go there [to the, the social services] and talk to her ... ' (Spain/F/Rural). The quote not only illustrates a gap between citizens and the state with all its political and affective/emotional implications, but also reveals how bureaucratic procedures incorporate these forms of discouragement and shame to reduce numbers of claimants.

Narratives of return to the family as a provider of welfare manifested, on the contrary, the continuous importance of familialism in strategies of resilience in Southern Europe. Especially for younger interviewees, who were more deprived than older ones, such returns enabled intergenerational distribution of scarce resources, such as salaries or pensions. A woman in Greece explained the emotionally charged return of her son:

> 'My son has tried several times to leave home, he rents a house, then he realizes he cannot afford it and he comes back ... What else can he do? We won't leave him homeless ... he's in a very bad mood ... and depression ... and he gained weight and even smoked ... he never smoked before. He feels sad, he doesn't speak too much, but I see it. I can see it.' (Greece/F/Urban)

Interviewees in Portugal also stressed the help provided by their parents:

> 'I rely a lot on my parents' help. Although I work long hours – the business isn't good ... we eat at their house, me and my daughter ... They don't let us go without things. She has swimming classes; presently they pay for her swimming classes. If she needs shoes, if she needs clothes, they buy them.' (Portugal/F/Rural)

> 'Every month they [parents in law] bring us potatoes, vegetables, fruit, onions. The things that they grow on their kitchen garden – pumpkins and I don't know what – they send to us. Every month they come to Lisbon.' (Portugal/F/Urban)

Welfare entitlements, intended to cover the needs of a single recipient became distributed to children and grandchildren. Instead of common family practices that prevailed in the past (elderly relatives moving in with their offspring to be taken care of by younger women in the family) during the economic crisis it became more common for adult children to return back to the family home to live with their parents. The redistributive role of the family compensated for problematic areas in welfare systems including the lack of generosity in regards to unemployment, family or child benefits and allowances, often as well as increased feelings of guilt, powerlessness and dependency.

In parallel with the stigmatization of public welfare and the return to the family, we encountered cases in which the hegemonic narratives of austerity were assimilated into the criticisms that citizens mounted against the welfare state. So, in the narratives of interviewees in Spain, critical discourses often co-existed with the sharing and internalization of the guilt for the debt. In these narratives, austerity was presented as a necessary punishment for having lived in a period of 'waste without control' (Martín and de Castro 2016). In a similar way in Portugal, some interviewees adopted the highly moralistic rhetoric referring to the pre-crisis profligacy of households living beyond their means as the main causes for the crisis (Capucha et al. 2016). These percep-tions, however, were in complete contrast to the everyday realities of those who uttered them who worked long hours for low salaries and low welfare provision before the crisis too. As Douzinas has argued about Greece, although during the previous decade citizens were encouraged to live their lives to the full, to consume and most importantly to achieve success through excessive borrowing, during the crisis they were asked to feel guilty for their previous excesses and economize in order to 'pay back' what they had so recklessly borrowed. Collective feelings of guilt and remorse legitimized and normalized austerity for all, although it was mainly the political and economic elites that were responsible for these phenomena (Douzinas 2011).

LOCAL WELFARE AS SOCIAL CONTROL AND THE ENACTMENT OF SOCIAL RIGHTS

At the beginning of the economic crisis, local authorities in Greece, Spain and Portugal undertook new emergency tasks and responsibilities. One area in which local authorities became more active in Greece and Spain was the implementation of public employment programmes and programmes of acti-vation, including vocational training, which were implemented by municipal and/or regional authorities in collaboration with NGOs. Some unemployed interviewees, especially in the rural areas, said that such programmes were vital for household resilience. One interviewee from an area with high long-term unemployment observed:

> 'Since I became unemployed, I am doing nothing, just working as a waiter in a local coffee shop once or twice per week ... And my wife helps in another shop. Whenever he [the owner] needs me, he calls me ... without insurance. In the winter I worked for five months in the Kinofelis (the Greek public employment programme) of the Municipality ... and I am waiting for the next phase to work there again ... It's my only chance to work because here there are no jobs ....' (Greece/M/Urban)

The localization of welfare of public employment involved a closer and more direct relationship between beneficiaries and municipal officials, especially in rural or semi-rural areas. Even if on occasions this created clientalism, close-ness and intimacy between bureaucrats and beneficiaries, welfare was considered by many interviewees as a positive aspect of localization. Nonetheless, it also became apparent that so-called conditionalities, i.e. formal criteria that establish entitlements and access restrictions to welfare, had become the norm in Southern Europe bringing it closer to the liberal welfare model. As Loïc Wacquant argued, Western welfare states go through a process of 'gradual replacement of a (semi) welfare state by a police and penal state for which the criminalization of marginality and the punitive containment of dispossessed categories serve as social policy at the lower end of the class and ethnic order' (Wacquant 2009, p. 41). Ironically, thus, in the EU context, it seems that the same EU-wide processes of policy making and funding that push localization and subsidiarity of welfare forward may also be pushing towards liberalization and the imposition of control through welfare that Wacquant criticizes.

The comparative study included some informal processes of resilience that emerged out of the grassroots mass mobilizations, demonstrations and protest against austerity across Southern Europe. Especially through the mobilizations of the *aganaktismenoi* in Greece, and the *indignados* in Spain (Da Paz Campos Lima and Artiles 2013), alternative structures of welfare emerged.

In Greece, following the November 2008 mass protest that began as a reaction to police violence and moved on to become a movement of local assemblies, new structures developed, including citizen-run health clinics, cooperative food centres, food distribution without middlemen, educational classes, and legal aid centres that were run autonomously and without funding by local activists (see Vradis and Dalakoglou 2011). When the austerity measures were launched, these provided emergency welfare for households deprived of social ties and entitlements. What distinguished these solidarity centres from other local institutions was their lack of funding other than the contributions of their members, and their bottom-up, collective decision-making processes, in which some poor and deprived beneficiaries could participate and voice their demands. An example was an unemployed Kurdish–Syrian migrant, who explained in his interview that the solidarity space in question had become part of his everyday life as it provided welfare as well as a sense of identity, belonging and political identity. 'This is how it works, you give something and you take something ... Those who take without giving ... do you understand? They miss a lot and they are not worth the effort' (Greece/M/Urban).

In those solidarity initiatives, welfare was not as stigmatized as in other state or NGO run welfare providers, arming beneficiaries with a sense of agency that was lacking from state-funded welfare.[7]

In Portugal and Spain, on the contrary, similar mobilizations and protest movement did not lead to the creation of informal welfare structures.[8] Nevertheless, the NGOs played a different role in those societies, becoming spaces where poor, vulnerable groups and communities were able to participate actively. In Spain, the same dynamics as in Greece can be observed in the activist movement for the right to social housing that was supported by an alliance of NGOs and activist groups. The following passage from an interviewee argues that practices normally considered illegal were in fact legitimized by the failure of the welfare state to protect its citizens:

> 'Well of course, then there are those that say that if people are stealing to feed their kids, it's because they don't have a choice. Or those that say, "kick in a door and go in [to occupy the flat as squatter]". Because, look, you do that when you can't pay for a flat, you have to be in that situation to say to yourself, "well I'm going to break into this flat because no one is living here".' (Spain/F/Urban)

As long as states failed to guarantee their social rights, citizens had no choice – arguably – but to enact these social rights themselves, even if this meant that they had to turn against the state.[9] Another similar example was that of the civil disobedience movement 'Can't pay, won't pay' in Greece, which consisted of activists who refused to pay tickets, transport tolls or the special property tax. As the penalty for this tax was disconnection of electricity supply, reconnecting household electricity became an act of welfare. These enactments became part of a process through which citizenship was redefined as active participation in the production of welfare.

The failure of formal welfare structures to accept and support such enactments of rights transformed them into institutions promoting welfare through policing and control. In fact, informal welfare initiatives were often in conflict with established structures of welfare. While left-wing political parties, such as SYRIZA in Greece or PODEMOS in Spain, attempted and often succeeded in appropriating or co-opting those movements and structures,[10] they were attacked by the state with the support of municipal authorities, as they were considered 'dangerous' for public health, hygiene and damaging for social cohesion. Such conflicts between informal welfare institutions and the state

were coupled with emergency plans by more conventional NGOs and municipalities to mimic successful initiatives and create similar structures within the
official welfare system.

In general, cases of resilience that relied on local informal structures
challenged top-down representational politics and philanthropy/charity-based
institutions through practices that relied on the enactment of social rights (see
Chapter 11 of this volume). Although their sustainability is in question given
the fact that a lot of their activities were illegal, they enabled a critical political
response that brings to the forefront aspects of resilience that are neglected in
the literature.

CONCLUSION

Contemplating welfare state structures and institutions from the perspective of
households who have engaged in resilient practices in adverse circumstances
challenges the limits of existing typologies of welfare in Europe. This is
mainly because such typologies tend to focus overwhelmingly on formal institutions, including the family, and state policies silencing the often-invisible
web of formal and informal processes, practices and discourses that effectively constitute welfare in Southern Europe. The wide-scale emergence of
grassroots welfare structures and the direct enactment of welfare rights from
citizens groups in Southern Europe challenges existing models and tools to
analyse welfare in Europe.

As explained above, one of the main findings of our study is that, in order
to become resilient, households in Southern Europe increasingly resorted
to non-state and informal local structures that substituted for the state as
a provider of welfare. Local institutions such as solidarity centres and some
NGOs have shown that it is possible to offer welfare services run by collective
decision-making and deliberation. These examples illustrated that in order to
effectively transfer responsibility from the national to the local level a democratization of decision-making on welfare is required as well as greater participation of local residents, dispossessed communities, groups and individuals.
Moreover, initiatives like the anti-eviction NGOs in Spain or social solidarity
centres in Greece adopted practices that were devoid of stigmatization because
they relied on mutual support and self-organization. In that sense, rather
than examples of 'primitive' or regressive welfare regime types, the current
Southern European experiences of localization from below can be studied as
viable alternatives to the prevailing Europe-wide proliferation of the neoliberal
paradigm of austerity.

NOTES

1. The 1990s EU turn towards 'localization' has similarities to the pre-Second World War periods of European welfare, during which local religious ethnic and labour organizations played the pivotal role in distributing welfare to the most deprived segments of society (Evers et al. 2014). After the Second World War, however, there was a transfer of power from the local to the national level that also signified a shift from a charitable towards a citizenship and rights-based approach to welfare (Oosterlynck et al. 2013).
2. The MOU was signed between the Government of Portugal, the EU Commission, the European Central Bank and the International Monetary Fund.
3. The distinction between the Greek state and the Orthodox church, however, is not a very clear one as state remuneration of clergy and dependence of religious charities on state funding make the Church inextricably interconnected with secular governance. During the 1980s and especially the 1990s, other NGOs began to multiply through a mainly a top-down response to the funding opportunities that were offered by the EU (Huliaras 2014).
4. The main foundations are the Latsis Foundation, the Onassis Foundation and the Bodosakis Foundation, which have acquired an increasingly important role in welfare funding after the economic crisis started.
5. This was mainly due to two factors: (a) a rising number of Greek citizens lost their access to both public and private welfare as they became poor and unemployed and could no longer afford to pay contributions to public or private security funds (Petmesidou and Glatzer 2015); and (b) the number of asylum seekers and immigrants without access to social security increased, culminating in the so called 'refugee crisis'.
6. According to Almeida, IPSSs constitute 80 per cent of non-profit enterprises in the social and family services (Almeida 2016).
7. Beneficiaries who received assistance from the Greek Orthodox Church in the semi-rural area also expressed feelings of belonging and identity, being part of a congregation of faithful.
8. In Portugal, the mobilization of the '15-M' or the '15 October movement' of 2012 was loosely organized around an informal network of groups protesting against precarization and voiced the demands of the unemployed or those working under precarious conditions (Carvalho 2013; Fonseca 2013). The title 'Geração à Rasca' ('Precarious generation') was used during the coverage of the first mass demonstrations that took place in different cities in order to emphasize the young age of the majority of participants who identified as precarious workers (Da Paz Campos Lima and Artiles 2013).
9. For an understanding of the notion of enactment of rights, see Isin and Nielsen (2006).
10. An example of the efforts to appropriate such social movements was Douzinas' (2011) book, which made the argument that Syriza's electoral rise was effectively produced within these movements, a claim that is highly contested by some of the activists who were interviewed during the RESCuE project.

BIBLIOGRAPHY

Adam, S. and Papatheodorou, C. (2016), 'Dismantling the feeble social protection system of Greece: Consequences of the crisis and austerity measures', in K. Schubert, P. Villota and G. Kuhlmann (eds.), *Challenges to European welfare systems*, London: Springer, pp. 271–300.

Almeida, V. (2016), 'Portuguese private institutions for social solidarity in the context of austerity: The case of social canteens', *Interações: Sociedade e as Novas Modernidades* 30: 5–23.

Andreotti, A., García, S., Gómez, A., Hespanha, P. K. and Mingione, E. (2001), 'Does a Southern European model exist?', *Journal of European Area Studies* 9(1): 43–62.

Andreotti, A., Mingione, E. and Polizzi, E. (2012), 'Local welfare systems: A challenge for social cohesion', *Urban Studies,* 49(9): 1925–40.

Arts, W. A. and Gelissen, J. (2002), 'Three worlds of welfare capitalism or more? A state-of-the-art report', *Journal of European Social Policy* 12(2): 137–58.

Azzelini, M. and Sitrin, D. (eds.) (2014), *Reinventing democracy: From Greece to Occupy*, London: Verso.

Brenner, N. (2004), *New state spaces: Urban governance and the rescaling of statehood*, Oxford: Oxford University Press.

Capucha, L., Calado, A. and Estêvão, P. (2016), *Portugal: Resilient households and welfare state institutions*, unpublished RESCuE project report.

Carvalho, T. (2013), 'Ethnographic case studies of youth activism: Popular Assembly Bareiro', Unpublished Report for MY SPACE project. Available at: https://myplaceresearch.wordpress.com/ (accessed 7 October 2020).

Chardas, A. (2014), 'The interplay between austerity, domestic territorial reform and the European Union Cohesion Policy: Multi-level governance and the application of the partnership principle in Greece', *European Urban and Regional Studies* 21(4): 432–44.

Chardas, A. and Skamnakis, C. (2016), 'The social policy of municipalities in a period of crisis: Embeded autonomy of local policy services at the local level', *AEIchoros* 24: 125–50.

Da Paz Campos Lima, M. and Artiles, A. M. (2013), 'Youth voice(s) in EU countries and social movements in Southern Europe', *Transfer* 19(3): 345–63.

Dafermos, Y. and Papatheodorou, C. (2013), 'What drives inequality and poverty in the EU? Exploring the impact of macroeconomic and institutional factors', *International Review of Applied Economics* 27(1): 1–22.

Del Pino, E. and Pavolini, E. (2015), 'Decentralisation in a time of harsh austerity: Multilevel governance and the welfare state in Spain and Italy facing crisis', *European Journal of Social Security* 17(2): 158–81.

Douzinas, K. (2011), *Resistance and philosophy during the crisis: Politics, ethnics and the Syntagma Stasis*, Athens: Alexandreia.

Esping-Andersen, G. (ed.) (1996), *Welfare states in transition, national adaptations in global economies*, London: Sage.

Esping-Andersen, G. (1997), 'Hybrid or unique? The Japanese welfare state between Europe and America', *Journal of European Social Policy* 7(3): 179–89.

Evers, A., Ewert, B. and Brandsen, T. (eds.) (2014), *Social innovations and social cohesion: Transnational patterns and approaches from 20 European cities*, Liege: EMES European Research Network.

Evers, A., Ewert, B. and Brandsen, T. (eds.) (2014), 'Social innovations for social cohesion: Transnational patterns and approaches from 20 European cities', Liège: EMES European Research Network. Available at: http://www.wilcoproject.eu/ ereader-wilco/ (accessed 3 September 2020).

Featherstone, D., Ince, A., Mackinnon, D., Strauss, K. and Cumbers A. (2012), 'Progressive localism and the construction of political alternatives', *Transactions of the Institute of British Geographers* 37: 177–82.

Ferrera, M. (2005), *The boundaries of welfare: European integration and the new spatial politics of social protection*, Oxford, New York: Oxford University Press.

Ferrera, M. (1996), 'The "Southern Model" of welfare in social Europe', *Journal of European Social Policy* 6(1): 17–37.

Fokas, E. (2013), 'Immigrant welfare in Greece: portrait of a town', *Southeast European and Black Sea Studies* 13(4): 575–94.

Fonseca, D. (2013), 'Precarious but Inflexible: The rise of new social movements in Portugal', *Global Dialogue: The Newsletter of the International Sociological Association* 3(2). Available at: https://globaldialogue.isa-sociology.org/precarious -but-inflexible-the-rise-of-a-new-social-movement-in-portugal/ (accessed 3 September 2020).

Gal, J. (2010), 'Is there an extended family of Mediterranean welfare states?', *Journal of European Social Policy* 20(4): 283–300.

González Begega, S. and del Pino, E. (2014), *From letting Europe in to policy conditionality: Welfare reform in Spain under austerity*, Instituto de Políticas y Bienes Públicos (IPP) CSIC, Working Paper: 2017–01.

Guillén, A. M. and Pavolini, E. (2015), 'Welfare states under strain in Southern Europe', *European Journal of Social Security* 17(2): 147–57.

Huliaras A. (2014), 'The dynamics of civil society in Greece. Creating civic engagement from the top', *The Jean Monet Papers on Political Economy* 10/2014. Available at: https://jmonneteuldcs.files.wordpress.com/2013/11/huliaras.pdf (accessed 3 September 2020).

Isin, E. and Nielsen, G. (eds.) (2006), *Acts of citizenship*, London: Zed Books.

Johansson, H. and Panican, A. (ed.), *Combating poverty in local welfare systems: Active inclusion strategies in European Cities*, London: Palgrave.

Kambouri, N., Marinoudi, S. and Petraki, G. (2016), *Greece: Resilient Households and Welfare State Institutions*, unpublished RESCuE project report.

Karamessini, M. and Rubery, J. (eds.) (2013), *Women and austerity: The economic crisis and the future of gender equality*, Abingdon: Routledge.

Karanikolos, M., Mladovsky, P., Cylus, J., Thomson, S., Basu, S., Stuckler, D., Mackenbach, J. P. and McKee, M. (2013), 'Financial crisis, austerity and health in Europe', *Lancet* 13: 1323–31.

Katrougalos, G. (1996), 'The South European welfare model: The Greek welfare state in search of an identity', *Journal of European Social Policy* 6(1): 39–60.

Katrougalos, G. and Lazaridis, G. (2003), *Southern European welfare states: Problems, challenges and prospects*, Basingstoke: Palgrave Macmillan.

Kazepov, Y. (2008), 'The subsidiarisation of social policies: Actors, processes and impacts', *European Societies* 10(2): 247–73.

Leibfried, S. (1992), 'Towards a European welfare state? On integrating poverty regimes in the European Community', in Z. Ferge and J. E. Kolberg (eds.), *Social policy in a changing Europe*, Frankfurt am Main: European Centre for Social Welfare Policy and Research, pp. 245–80.

Martín, P. and de Castro, C. (2016), *Spain: Resilient households and welfare state institutions*, unpublished RESCuE project report.

Martín, P. and Serrano, A. (2014), 'Reinventando el Gobierno del Desempleo en un Entorno Flexiguro', in C. J. Fernández, A. y Serrano (eds.), *El Paradigma de la Flexiguridad en las Políticas de Empleo Españolas*, Madrid: CIS: 373–410.

Matsaganis, M. and Leventi, C. (2014), 'The distributional impact of austerity and recession in Southern Europe', *South European Society and Politics* 19(3): 393–412.

Moulaert, F., Swyngedouw, E. and Wilson, P. (1988), 'The geography of Fordist and Post-Fordist accumulation and regulation', *Papers of the Regional Science Association* 64: 11–23.

Moulaert, F., Martinelli, F., Swyngedouw, E. and Gonzalez, S. (2010), *Can Neighbourhoods Save the City?*, Abingdon: Routledge.

Nunes, S. C. (2017), ' Political and administrative decentralization in Portugal: Four decades of democratic local government', in S. C. Nunes and J. Buček (eds.) *Local government and urban governance in Europe*, The Urban Book Series, Cham: Springer, pp. 9–32.

Nunes, S. C. and Buček, J. (eds.) (2014), *Fiscal austerity and innovation in local governance in Europe*, Farnham: Ashgate.

Oosterlynck, S., Kazepov, Y., Novy, A., Cools, P., Wukovitsch, F., Saruis, T., Barberis, E. and Leubolt, B. (2013), *Exploring the multi-level governance of welfare provision and social innovation: Welfare mix, welfare models and rescaling*, ImPRovE Working Papers 13/12. Antwerp: Herman Deleeck Centre for Social Policy, University of Antwerp. Available at: https://ideas.repec.org/p/hdl/improv/1312.html (accessed 3 September 2020).

Petmesidou, M. (1996), 'Social protection in Southern Europe: Trends and prospects', *Journal of Area Studies* 9: 95–125.

Petmesidou, M. and Guillén, A. M. (2014), 'Can the welfare state as we know it survive? A crisis from the crisis ridden European periphery', *Southern European Society and Politics* 19(3): 295–307.

Petmesidou, M. and Guillén, A. M. (2015), *Economic crisis and austerity in Southern Europe: Threat or opportunity for a sustainable welfare state?*, OSE Paper Series 18, Brussels: Observatoire sociale européen.

Petmesidou, M. and Glatzer, M. (2015), 'The crisis imperative, reform dynamics and rescaling in Greece and Portugal', *European Journal of Social Security* 17(2), 158–181.

Purcell, M. (2006), 'Urban democracy and the local trap', *Urban Studies* 43(11): 1921–41.

Samikou, E. (2014), *The bureaucratisatisation of pain: An example of a public health service in Greece*, unpublished doctoral dissertation, Panteion University of Social and Political Sciences, Athens.

Skamnakis, C. and Pantazopoulos, S. (2015), 'Social protection and local government: The evolution of a double deficit', *Region and Periphery* (special issue) 3: 89–116.

Sotiropoulos, D. A. (2015), 'Southern European governments and public bureaucracies in the context of economic crisis', *European Journal of Social Security* 17(2): 226–45.

Vradis, A. and Dalakoglou, D. (eds.) (2011), *Revolt and crisis in Greece: Between a present yet to pass and a future still to come*, London: AK Press.

Wacquant, L. (2009), *Punishing the poor: The neoliberal government of social insecurity*, Durham, NC: Duke University Press.

16. Household resilience as an enhanced European policy discourse

Monica Tennberg and Joonas Vola

INTRODUCTION

Resilience has become a key concept for European Union (EU) policies in recent years. For example, the global strategy for the EU's foreign affairs and security (European Commission 2016) states that: 'Building resilience at home and abroad means creating a more responsive union. The EU will focus on enhancing both state and societal resilience, which includes supporting governance-building, accountability, and enhancing links with civil society.'

The origins of resilience thinking are in the natural sciences, to study the reactions and recovery of species, habitats and ecosystems after a shock, such as a natural hazard (Manyena 2006; Davidson 2010; Lorenz 2013; and Chapters 3 and 4 of this volume). The transfer of this idea, 'bouncing back after a shock', via social psychology into social sciences with different versions have brought some doubts about its relevance, applicability and policy implications. The resilience concept is also criticized, among other things, for the naturalization of risks and threats in everyday life; legitimizing the governance of uncertainty and unpredictability; promoting individual and institutional responsibilization as a governance response; and stressing more on preparedness and adaptation than prevention and transformation (Larner 2011; Joseph 2013; Welsh 2014). The success of the concept is explained by its fuzziness, while being politically neutral but still critical of some negative, unsustainable societal practices, and offering a set of rather simple technocratic solutions inside the same governmental frame that those harmful practices and related problems result from (Welsh 2014).

Despite these doubts and challenges, the social science discourses about resilience have become allied with contemporary governmental, national and international discourses with a new biopolitical object, resilient populations. The relationship between resilience, neoliberalism and governance continues to be discussed. Chris Zebrowski (2013) situates resilience of populations as a conceptual object and as a governmental concern to a specific power/

knowledge constellation, not as a socio-historical constant, but a result of broader restructuring of rationalities and practices of neoliberal governing. In contrast, Philip Bourbeau (2018) stresses multiple genealogies of resilience suggesting several paths of resilience thinking and points of contestation in its development. This more flexible understanding of resilience, beyond neoliberal governance, does not require the rejection of the concept completely while being critical of its neoliberal application. Finally, for some, resilience is not a neoliberal tool of governance, but a social response to neoliberal policies. The response draws on social resources, human and social capital, and their multilevel contexts (Hall and Lamont 2013).

In the EU context, resilience as a policy concept has developed within humanitarian and development assistance (European Commission 2013a), cybersecurity (European Commission 2013b) and global foreign policy and security strategy (European Commission 2016). The 'resilience turn' of the EU (Joseph 2014) has been explained in two ways: first, it is seen as a policy response to the complex, interlinked changes in the EU and close to considerable threats and risks; and, second, by the EU's diminishing role and capacity to deal with contemporary political and economic transformations and their consequences. Nevertheless, explicit bridges to social policy are rare so far, as most EU approaches are focused on public security issues, natural disasters and terrorism or global financial crises and their nexus to the 'real economy'. These threats to resilience often come from 'outside' Europe, as external threats, in the form of refugees, natural hazards and cyberattacks. Connecting households, economic and other hardships to resilience suggests that the threat to resilience may come from inside, due to the EU's own policies. Resilience from this perspective is the measure of one's fitness to survive in the turbulent order of things (Walker and Cooper 2011, p. 156).

According to Joseph (2014), resilience is a policy concept for the EU to provide a far more coordinated strategy in different, but often more complex fields of governance compared to previous efforts. Resilience-based EU policies also fit with the ways it sees itself in terms of both its identity and role. The resilience turn supports the idea that the EU should function with a more facilitative, advisory and normative role instead of an actor in the implementation of policies and change (See also Pawlak 2015, 2016; Möttölä 2016). In a sense, resilience is 'a half-way response' to an old, reoccurring dilemma of the EU's actorness, or more precisely, lack of it, which is called for in a number of cases (see for example Kratochvil 2013; Kristensen and Jovanovich 2015). In 2002, Tony Atkinson (2002, p. 639) discussed the EU's social cohesion model after the developments in Lisbon, complimenting the EU for the 'significant progress in the past two years towards European *integration* along the social dimension' with national policies and common social indicators. He recognized the challenges in the integration of national policies and the involvement of other actors at local and sub-regional levels with European priorities. In his view, social inclusion should be developed not only 'within Member States but at the level of the European Union as an *integrated* whole'. He called for further integration between social and economic policies and argued that policies for social inclusion may complement economic policies and performance. Atkinson (2002) called for the EU's global responsibility, especially in regard to immigration, and in development assistance, extending the concerns over social cohesion beyond the region. Our findings suggest that social cohesion in Europe is still under development. The question remains whether resilience could develop into an integrative concept for local, national and regional measures to support households at risks inside Europe and beyond.

Our approach of social resilience (Promberger et al. 2014, see Chapter 1 of this volume) complements the current EU resilience policies and their basic assumptions. Poverty is a complex, socially produced problem with many linkages to economic development, employment, labor rights, civil and property rights (see Chapter 6, this volume), gendered and age-related divisions in family and work lives (see Chapter 9, this volume), different forms of discrimination in society referring to ethnicity, citizenship and residency with many possible implications for societal security in Europe. Societal security refers to 'the ability of a society to persist in its essential character under changing conditions and possible or actual threats' (Waever 1993, p. 23). These concerns are not outside the influence of the EU's space for action and influence: the reaction of the EU to the economic crises in 2008 and measures to respond to it have led to a situation of cuts in social policy and infrastructure, and further intensified the problems for households to deal with their situation. The core issue is the future of European welfare statehood in and after the 2010s, and the question of how an alternative approach to resilience could possibly revitalize European social thinking with practical implications.

We will present and discuss the social resilience approach to household resilience as an enhanced policy discourse for the EU, and compare it to those discourses in the fields of humanitarian and development assistance and cybersecurity. The approach of social resilience to household resilience needs to respond to the critique of individualization and naturalization of risks and threats, legitimizing the governance of uncertainty and unpredictability, practices of responsibilization of individuals and institutions, and stressing more preparedness and adaptation than prevention and transformation. Similar kinds of discussions have been conducted in connection to academic discourses on interactive employability (Peck and Theodore 2000; de Bruin and Dupuis 2008). These discussions expand the issue of individual employability in terms of compulsory training and job-seeking activities to acknowledge the geography of labor markets, demand within local economies and other contextual factors. This approach calls for policy makers to target long-term unemployed people and disadvantaged groups, and to focus activation policies to prevent long-term unemployment and labor market disadvantage (McQuaid and Lindsay 2005, pp. 201, 205).

The analysis of contemporary resilience discourses of the EU helps us to identify what new, innovative elements the sociological thinking on resilience might bring to EU policies. The social resilience approach focuses on social, economic and cultural aspects of household resilience, the importance of social protection measures by the EU and the rejection of individual heroism often found central in the alternative resilience thinking. The results within this book emphasize the importance of common and public goods for household resilience, stressing the importance of the EU's role in social protection, and the need to maintain and develop welfare services and infrastructure in the EU (See also Hermann 2014; Pintelon et al. 2013).

RESILIENCE IN POLICY DISCOURSES

Language is a powerful tool in the world of policy making. Political discourse, often understood as simply talk in different political fora, is the way for politicians to argue their views and make an impact in terms of concrete practices of governance such as policies, programs and action plans that follow. Discourses, even the most technical and empirical ones, contain metaphors. One typical everyday metaphor to describe resilience is a rubber band (see Morgan 2013) as 'the ability of something to rebound or resume its original shape following exposure to a stressor' (Welsh 2014, p. 16). Metaphors establish what are considered to be natural parts of people's lives such as traumas, shocks and catastrophes even in the generally successful European countries compared to many other places in the world. Such metaphors also provide the boundaries of what can be said about resilience. The focus is on critical, short-term events and their consequences to people and assumes also their capacity to cope with, adapt to and transcend difficult circumstances (Keck and Sakdapolrak 2013, p. 14). According to this worldview, people live under constant threats and dangers.

Metaphors are highly political: they establish actors, either as individuals or collectives, for example, in the field of resilience-building and their responsibilities to support and maintain resilience. Discourses and practices of governance are closely connected. The question of whose responsibility it is to maintain and support resilience is a controversial question. A powerful discourse never emerges out of a vacuum. Discourses are the result of a constellation of power relations (Foucault 1972, p. 44f.) that regulate the conditions under which something like resilience as a societal concern can emerge as an object of political discourse and the way in which it is formulated as part of the European political agenda. The meaning of resilience, its relationships and political implications shifts depending on the context and the purpose it is used for. Resilience as a word as such is not 'bad', 'wrong' or 'misleading', but the political use of it might be.

In recent years, resilience, especially in the fields of humanitarian and development assistance, cybersecurity and global foreign policy and security, has become a popular European policy discourse which has been adopted, discussed and criticized widely (Walker and Cooper 2011; Hannigan 2012). In the following, we will analyze contemporary EU discourses on resilience to study their ontological, hierarchical and agent-related assumptions (Dryzek 1997; Rogers 2017). The approach is a rather simple methodology to analyze EU discourses about resilience in which a discourse is understood as a shared way of apprehending the world (Dryzek 1997). Discourses are enabling, limiting and constraining societal debates and practices, but they are not impenetrable. There are always cracks in the use of policy language which form the basis of eventual transformations of governance. However, it might be difficult to accomplish with the existing policy frame. According to Walker and Cooper (2011, p. 156), 'resilience thinking cannot be challenged from within the terms of complex systems theory but must be contested, if at all, on completely different terms, by a movement of thought that is truly counter-systemic'. In practice, the concept and its applications, however, seem rather open and flexible in current policy discourses. Critics complain that resilience is a rather 'shallow concept, it is also a shifting concept' (Joseph 2013, p. 51), but this ambiguity may explain its popularity, like another concept receiving the same kind of criticism such as sustainable development. Its meaning varies depending on the place and the level where this occurs as well as the aims and objects of governance (Joseph 2013).

The following analysis is based on EU documents on the so-called 'Resilience Paradigm' of humanitarian aid and disaster relief strategy (European Council 2013), and documents concerning cybersecurity (European Commission 2013b) and the digital single market (European Commission 2015). These EU discourses try to identify an issue as a problem, whether it refers to human casualties in connection to reoccurring natural hazards, cybercrime causing economic damages, or global insecurity threatening Europe. They also aim to attract political attention and foster political will to solve or at least to manage the problem by the EU's and other's actions using resilience-based policy measures. The chapter continues to reflect on the main elements of the analysis of EU discourses on resilience based on the approach and findings within this book. We will present the social resilience approach and the project results as an enhanced discourse on resilience while taking into account the major criticisms from the critical resilience research which has emerged in the last few years, especially in terms of accepting risk and crisis as a part of everyday life; the governance of contingency, unpredictability and uncertainty at a distance; and the focus on preparedness and adaptation instead of prevention and transformation.

EU RESPONSES TO AN UNSTABLE AND INSECURE WORLD OF GLOBAL THREATS

Current resilience policies formulated in the EU create order in the world, they make certain connections manageable and form expectations for action, not necessarily for the EU itself but for others, inside and outside the EU. The main principles of EU resilience thinking are systemic thinking, taking risks and threats as given, and dividing the responsibility of action between itself and others. While the fields of humanitarian and development assistance and cybersecurity are quite different from each other, the same EU logic seems to be at play: the definition of systemic problems, causing reoccurring problems with relevance for the EU, and managed by coordination and collaboration between EU and other relevant actors.

Systems thinking is the ordering principle in current EU resilience policies. Resilience in that term treats social and ecological systems as a fully integrated whole made of complex, multiple agents which interact with other agents and artefacts, including technology in different forms. This systemic view can be detected in the EU's action plan for resilience in developing countries which aims to manage and prevent crisis as well as risks while supporting long-term resilience. In this context, resilience is the ability of an individual, a community or a country to cope, adapt and quickly recover from stress and shocks caused by a disaster, violence or conflict without compromising long-term development. This kind of policy approach fits the socio-ecological tradition of resilience thinking. It considers that system-wide approaches are needed because the causes of vulnerability and poverty are multifaceted and inter-linked. A complex field of risks implies a need to confront uncertainty, and hence requires constant adaptation. Threats and risks, such as natural hazards, droughts, floods and storms in developing countries with human and material casualties are a result of complex challenges and trends of climate change, protracted displacements, pandemics, extremism, population movement and growth (European Commission 2013a, 2013b).

Another example of the EU's resilience thinking comes from a totally other kind of field, cybersecurity, but with a similar kind of logic. While 'digitalisation is often approached as an uninterrogatable external force of nature which turns structures, practices and processes around', according to Salminen (2016, p. 1), 'those to excel in the turmoil are those willing to adapt to its conditions and requirements'. For cybersecurity in the EU, the main concerns are protection of free and secured flow of information, and safety of the critical infrastructures due to the increasing number of harmful attacks and incidents causing economic damages to European companies. There is a recognized need to develop a resilient cybersecurity system. In order to keep track of cybercrime, a new directive imposes obligations on companies and member states to disclose information related to cyberattacks and incidents. It also suggests cyber defense as a collaboration between EU member states and between NATO and the EU, which is still in its early stages of tackling hostile, often foreign attacks on important national security infrastructure (European Commission 2013b, 2015). According to Christou (2015), the global cybersecurity ecosystem consists of a capacity to adapt to new structures and operating assumptions, the acceptance of complexity in governance logics, the development of trust-based partnerships between main actors, the shared acceptance of common understandings of key concepts, the adoption of a culture of cybersecurity among all stakeholders and, finally, the existence of coherence and consistency across levels and actors.

Resilience, as the EU mostly propagates it, is seen as a policy response to complex, interlinked changes which make the world contingent, unstable and insecure, and dealing with the consequences of changes might also prove to be expensive for the EU. For humanitarian and development assistance, resilience is a response to the threat of global migration. The 'migratory challenge' in Europe shows that 'distance or the natural borders inherent in seas, mountains and deserts are of little significance when people are confronted with challenges like conflict, fragility, and failure of governance' (Pawlak 2015, p. 2). The EU is motivated by the economic costs of dealing with migration and migrants: 'The costs of humanitarian crises are escalating, as climate change generates more severe weather-related disasters and as the world faces new pressures from population growth, urbanization, land and ecosystems' degradation, scarcity of natural resources, fragility of states and complex conflicts' (European Commission 2013c, p. 2). Economic reasoning explains the choice of resilience approach. Resilience is a cheaper option in terms of EU action. The EU's own assessment concludes that investment in resilience is cost effective and that preparedness and planning is not only more effective than disaster response but also more economically sensible.

Salminen (2016, p. 1) points out that the resilience of digitalized societies is 'an outcome of multifaceted human policies, negotiations, bargaining and calculations'. While economic reasoning here is important, another kind of reasoning can be found in the case of resilience thinking in European cybersecurity logic:

'Without trust and security, there can be no Digital Single Market and no digital economy. Europe has to be ready to tackle cyber-threats that are increasingly sophisticated and do not recognize borders. Europe needs high quality, affordable and interoperable cybersecurity products and services. There is a major opportu-

nity for our cybersecurity industry to compete in a fast-growing global market.'
(European Commission 2015)

Here the logic is to secure the major role of the EU in global digital markets
and its share in future, potential profits. The EU's cybersecurity resilience is
an example of the increasing popularity of security-based reasoning connected
to resilience policies.

Resilience governance aims to facilitate capacities in complex systems to
adapt and maintain an acceptable level of functioning and structure in the wake
of uncertainty. A shock, trauma or an emergency establishes 'a moment and
site of profound "opportunity" for societies to transform themselves so that
they might be governed differently' (Reid 2010, p. 404). Resilience is in that
view a capacity that can be 'built' with EU support. Resilience is therefore
fundamentally concerned with identifying particular subjectivities that are
in need of 'more resilience', such as vulnerable people, fragile infrastructure
and sensitive environments, or as in the cases of this book, households at risk.
For humanitarian and development assistance this means more investment to
'unlock peoples' potential and to improve their livelihoods' (see also Maxwell
2013). In the case of cybersecurity, cybersecurity maturity differs among the
EU member states greatly requiring special measures by the EU (Christou
2015).

The objective of resilience policies is to enable individuals, institutions and
economies to transform themselves or their natural and social environments
despite contemporary contingency, unpredictability and uncertainty, and,
in addition, to increase their resilience to exogenous and internal shocks by
limiting the potential for profound changes. While the so-called engineering
approach to resilience stresses an ability to withstand shocks to the system,
the more adaptive (and flexible) systems version of resilience emphasizes that
rigidity and centralized command and control systems lead to the brittleness
of systems themselves. Therefore, a system of self-organizing is highly recommended by advocates of resilience thinking. For example, vulnerable communities in developing countries need to organize themselves, primarily in the
context of sustaining economic growth. Or in the case of cybersecurity, 'there
is no overarching framework but rather a series of legal and regulatory instruments that overlap' (Christou 2015, p. 102), which calls for coordination and
self-organization of the cyber community and digital market. Thus, the resilience approach is part of 'a scaled-back, less interventionist strategy' (Joseph
2014, p. 1). Resilience gives the impression of being part of an integrated and
holistic strategy without there actually being one. The EU resilience discourse
is, thus, 'paradoxically more holistic and less engaged' (Joseph 2014, p. 1).

Poverty-related threats are widely recognized in the EU: social unrest and
terrorism is connected to poverty, social exclusion and discrimination of

Table 16.1   *An overview of main characteristics of EU discourses on resilience*

	Humanitarian development assistance	Cybersecurity	Household resilience
Resilience	A capacity to cope with a shock, a capacity to be built for the long term	A capacity to keep the digital environment secure; to endure crime and attacks; avoid brittleness	A resilient household can cope with, adapt to and transcend difficult circumstances
The system	Social–ecological systems with reoccurring hazards and disasters with human casualties and economic damages	European digital society and infrastructure	The degradation of the European welfare state system and the economic crisis
The problem	Natural hazards leading to the problem of migration and refugees; disasters disturbing development, trade and growth	Economic damages due to cybercrime, cyberattacks, vulnerable digital infrastructure	Poverty as a social problem; households at risk; household resilience is vulnerable and changing
The EU response	Support to resilience-building measures in developing countries	Coordinated national and international measures; clarifying company responsibilities	Securing welfare state services, public infrastructure and common goods to support household resilience, enable knowledge, skills and practices both of people and institutions
EU agency	Economic support to resilience-building measures with other actors, both governmental and non-governmental, in developing countries through projects	Regulation and coordination in the EU; collaboration with other stakeholders, such as NATO	In addition to national measures to invest in social welfare, employment opportunities, ensure labor rights, social participation and anti-discriminatory policies, foster learning and change in welfare institutions, spread knowledge on resilience, keep up the classical welfare state as a faultline
EU motivation	Economic costs; uncontrolled migration, security	Securing the digital market and profits; economic development and growth	The fulfillment of obligations made in Lisbon Strategy 2000;[a] Europe 2020[b] (European Commission 2010); societal security and well-being

Notes:
[a] https://portal.cor.europa.eu/europe2020/Profiles/Pages/TheLisbonStrategyinshort.aspx (accessed 3 September 2020).
[b] https://portal.cor.europa.eu/europe2020/Profiles/Pages/welcome.aspx (accessed 3 September 2020).

different kinds both inside and outside the EU. Poverty is a social problem in the EU that is reflected in the everyday struggles of households to secure a decent income and work as well as negotiate access to basic services, but it is also a question of identity, belonging and participation. Social resilience emphasizes the social nature of household resilience in terms of supportive family, neighborhood and community networks, and their role in sharing resources to support household resilience as well as their capacity to distribute poverty-related risks (problems with housing, income and unemployment, for example) to other actors and environments. These household practices involve problems, and may challenge resilience in the long term due to burnout, health issues and social problems. Welfare state – services and infrastructure – plays a key role in supporting household resilience in terms of public access to common goods and services such as healthcare and childcare, libraries, reasonable housing and public transportation, as well as private assets, such as gardens, tools and debt-free homes. This book voices concern over the degradation of the European welfare system and services, over an increase in poverty, declining labor and human rights and an increase in discrimination (based on age, ethnicity, citizenship and gender) due to the economic crises of 2008 and its aftermath in the studied countries (Capucha et al. 2014).

In Table 16.1, the three fields of resilience thinking and their differences are presented.

THE RESCUE RESULTS[1]

The economic crisis of 2008 and its consequences were among the many other difficulties that vulnerable, low-income households had to deal with in combination with divorce, sickness, housing problems, discrimination of different forms based on ethnicity, gender and citizenship, and social exclusion. Although it was nothing new that some of the participants in the research were poor and coping with different kinds of adversities, there were people who were hit hard by the 2008 crisis and its aftermath. For them, the situation was traumatic, new and frustrating, not only because of the economic difficulties but also due to the loss and re-configuration of social identity and status as the story of Larry (anonymized) in Box 16.1 suggests (Dagdeviren et al. 2017; Gray and Dagg 2016).

BOX 16.1 LARRY'S STORY: CRISIS, FAILED PLANS, ADAPTATIONS AND THE WELFARE STATE

Larry was born in the mid-1950s and was in his mid-50s when he participated in the RESCuE project. Larry took the option of retiring during the recession after 30 years of employment in the public service. However, he initi-ated his retirement plan in the early 2000s based on a projected income. By the mid-2000s Larry had secured a mortgage and built his retirement home in the countryside. He subsequently remarried and began to raise a young family. From 2008, he experienced a change in his finances as cuts to public sector wages were implemented as part of Ireland's bailout conditions. As a result, Larry's income declined dramatically, to the extent that by the time he retired he found he was no longer able to meet his financial obligations, was accruing debt and struggling to make ends meet.

Larry sought and secured occasional work, but due to his pension status he paid high taxes on additional income. Larry's wife was not working and as a result of her husband's retirement status she received no social welfare support. Larry sought help from financial advisory services but ultimately felt adrift with no prior knowledge of hardship, of what to do and how to access resources. Although Larry and his wife used rural resources such as chickens, peat and local woodlands to meet everyday challenges, they also accessed the services of local charities in order to assist with celebratory events such as birthdays and Christmas. Ultimately, Larry, his wife and her parents have pooled their extended family resources – selling both their homes in order to build one shared family home, enabling them to share financial obligations and caring duties between generations and under one roof. (Ireland/Father of 2 young children from a second marriage/part-time worker)

Households' resilience includes a combination of economic and social prac-tices including saving, subsistence economy, gift exchange and sharing, small entrepreneurship and informal work, good networks and community relations beyond the nuclear family, as well as cultural patterns of skills and education, norms and values on social reciprocity and solidarity outside the market-logic. Resilient households employ a broad range of resources comprising also common goods like access to nature, public infrastructure like transport, water and energy supply, information, subsidized or affordable housing, education, training and job creation schemes. These socio-economic practices help families to prevent greater deterioration in their living standards and to get by comparably better than non-resilient households (Dagdeviren and Donoghue 2015). Although such strategies can often be found among resilient households, other households with younger people may arrange their lives differently, with a different solution to a similar problem – as the case of Eleni in Box 16.2 illustrates.

BOX 16.2 ELENI'S STORY: ALTERNATIVE LIVING ARRANGEMENTS

Eleni is 24 years old, and an academic working as a waitress in a big Greek city. She participates in various civil society activities and wishes to establish an alternative way of life, based on mutual and equal social relations. She lives in a collective household shared by herself and two more people, also academics unemployed or in precarious non-academic jobs. Their shared flat is in one of the neoclassical buildings which are characteristic of the interesting architectural tradition of the neighborhood. This merges with the preferences of many young academics not to cope in the crisis by returning to traditional home patterns. As all their expenses are managed collectively, the flatmates share the costs and they have even made an agreement of mutual support, according to which if one of them cannot pay the rent or the bills the others will cover for him/her as long as it takes. (Greek/F/living in a collective arrangement)

Few low-income households in the study showed resilience. From Finland, Maija and her family, and other similar households, identified strands for a certain type of resilience (Box 16.3). This resilience entailed combining multiple sources of income and plurifunctional everyday practices. It entailed a skilled background, using manifold networks embedded in communities with a culture of sharing, gift exchange and mutual support, with some interfaces with civil society, subsidized labor and access to public goods, resulting in a high degree of resilience and autonomy.

BOX 16.3 MAIJA'S STORY: RETURNING AND REDEFINING

Maija, in her late 20s, returned to her childhood home in northern Finland and interrupted her studies in another city. She did not have the social and economic support networks there as a single mother. At home, Maija entered the local reindeer herding livelihood and community. Despite her gender and her lack of family connection to this traditional livelihood, Maija was accepted as a member of this social network, built around the herding practice. This was due to curiosity towards the newcomer and her skills to learn and perform in the demanding reindeer herder way of life. Her livelihood was supported by other farming practices, such as building a hen house, and by other forms of subsistence economy, such as picking berries and mushrooms, and by processing them further as household goods for her own use. Furthermore, the herding attracted Maija's siblings, so her decision to move back engaged also other members of her family to give a new direction to their lives. Her parenting was supported by a new partner and by her family of origin. Strong economic support to start reindeer herding came from Maija's father who worked abroad for several weeks at a time, and brought money home. (Finland/Mother of two children/late 20s/rural area)

The study also confirms that welfare states still continue to provide important resources to resilient households. For those few vulnerable yet resilient, low-income households identified in the project, the welfare state plays an important role either directly or indirectly, such as by income transfer, job creation schemes or other subsidized labor, counselling, affordable public services, healthcare, infrastructure, and access to public space and nature (see Chapters 6–12, this volume). It is notable that stronger forms of resilience among these households rely more on indirect support and infrastructure than on direct transfer income. Household resilience is, however, vulnerable: any strategies and practices of resilience may fail or become invalid when circumstances change. In such a case, direct transfers may be needed and have to be available, together with other kinds of support, in order to stabilize the situation. For such households, the resilience approach stresses the importance of still maintaining basic financial and other support from the welfare state when needed, and additionally puts the availability of common goods into the policy focus (Box 16.4).

BOX 16.4 FERNANDO'S STORY: COPING WITH ECONOMIC PROBLEMS AND HEALTH CONCERNS

Born in Cape Verde in 1954, Fernando emigrated to Portugal in the late 1970s. Abandoning a life of working the land with his mother, he found work in Portugal in construction. It is in this sector that he worked throughout his career. He eventually bought a shack to live in, located in an urban slum that was being demolished at the time of our interviews. The crisis and its effects had a strong impact on Fernando. He was fired and wasn't able to find a new job. This is related to lack of job opportunities, his age and accumulated work injuries. Social transfers – notably basic income support – constitute his main source of income. Also, extreme hardship has forced Fernando to transform a hobby – the cultivation of vegetables and fruit in the surroundings of the house – into a central strategy of survival and resilience. Taking advantage of unoccupied municipal lands in the area around his home, he cultivates a wide variety of vegetables and fruit, which play a key role in his food consumption. While the council does not assign other uses to the land, he will continue to use the land, sharing tools and cultivated goods with his neighbors. The practice of farming vacant public and abandoned private land is rather common in Lugarão and all over the Metropolitan Area of Lisbon. (Portugal/M/no formal education)

Household resilience is closely connected to the historical development of welfare statehood in Europe, which has resulted in different welfare state structures across the region (see Chapter 13, this volume). The welfare state as we know it could foster households' resilience by supporting mutual support and self-help, providing free and accessible knowledge, starting from good housekeeping, do-it-yourself and subsistence labor, strengthening everyday social and psychological competencies, to providing space, knots and crystallization points for network and community building. Analysis reveals that it is not just social networks, ties, and respective norms and values, but also skills and education that are part of the cultural resources mobilized by resilient households. Interestingly, this not only comprises formal and certified education and training, but also informal, practical and embodied knowledge, skills and competencies, ranging from good housekeeping, gardening and do-it-yourself to small agriculture, everyday psychology, learning abilities and knowledge of institutions and civil society (Box 16.5) (see Chapter 7, this volume).

BOX 16.5 ANDRZEJ'S STORY: EDUCATION AND SOCIAL TIES

Education is an important cultural resource for household resilience. Thus, Andrzej, a young man from Poland, was able to improve his situation despite a difficult family situation, gaining respect and support from wider kin in his village and among friends. His studies have become an impetus for self-development. His reputation as a good and diligent student helped him to gain support from his social environment in different ways: 'All people in our village know that we are in a bad financial situation. And for example … after training … I went to a supper to my friends or they helped me in a different way.' His extended family also helped him: 'I didn't even ask them for help, they simply helped me.' The crisis stimulated him to pull together and establish good, reciprocal social relationships, and motivated him to self-development. This also translates into plans for the future: 'over the next 10 years, I would like to have financial stability and start a family, help my club and of course establish a football school […] and I would like to finish my studies. Or maybe another major yet … my father worked as a welder all his life … to change something and to have better future. I don't want to complain in the future like other people … it would give me satisfaction.' (Poland/M/rural area)

Maintaining resilience also may have harmful effects in households, in terms of nutritional intake, balancing work and life, physical and mental health and so forth (see Chapter 6, this volume). Therefore, policy measures to support household resilience should also reflect and avoid any harmful transfers of risks to other social actors, along the lines of gender, age, ethnicity, citizenship or to the natural environment.

POLICY IMPLICATIONS FOR THE EU

The results turn attention within the EU to a question of societal security, and stress the activities of the EU itself in terms of assessing the effects of its own financial and social policies on households at risk, and opportunities to support household resilience. It also reminds us of earlier and current EU commitments (European Commission 2017) to social development in this area. Eventually, household resilience is a question of the EU's own resilience in terms of the well-being and societal security of its inhabitants. Developing an enhanced policy discourse about resilience for the EU requires looking at poverty as a socially produced problem, recognizing the social nature of household resilience and appreciating the role of low-threshold public and common goods in terms of welfare state services, while also considering the natural, technical and social infrastructure within household resilience.

Three proposals from the RESCuE project and its results may be drawn:

1. Integrate household resilience into the EU's 'Resilience Paradigm'.
2. Strengthen the EU's investment in societal security and welfare.
3. Increase the resilience of households at risk by securing decent labor and improving human rights, and access to information, education and employment, and by advancing their possibilities for participation and inclusion.

The EU's Resilience Paradigm should include the concerns raised in this book. The concept of resilience outlined here should be adopted in EU policy frameworks and action plans, not as a substitute but as a top-up to present EU anti-poverty and social Europe strategies. At the European level, as well as on national and local levels, there is a need for a structurally sustainable and responsive system to support household resilience in times of socio-economic crises and pressure on welfare structures.

Resilient practices of households can take place only in the presence of local, national and European policy instruments, such as intervention of instances of distribution of poverty-related risks and resilience-building resources. There are structural, systemic causes for the increase of poor, vulnerable households in Europe, and they are results of political and economic decisions and ideologies put in place in recent years, many of those made at the EU level with significant effects on the lives of the households in different parts of the region.

Household resilience is clearly an issue beyond European social policy. It is an intersectional issue (Hankivsky and Cormier 2011), across sectors and levels of policy action, requiring a multidimensional response, including local and national policies. EU actions and policies matter in supporting household resilience. Post-crisis social investment policies should include re-investment into the welfare state and public infrastructure that are needed to support household resilience. EU actions could include introducing empowerment and enabling concepts into activation policies, or making active self-inclusion into social networks and communities a target of activation policies – making them social, so to speak. It could also act to support skill and education acquirement, as well as alternative patterns of culture to maintain and develop the richness of humanistic European values, including those seemingly outside standard patterns of commodified life.

Poverty is a structural and social issue. Thus, it should not be taken for granted as a risk for individuals and families to be prepared for and ready to adapt to. Resilience emphasizes resources, skills and practices for households coping with adversity, but without making them victims, guilty or heroes because of the difficult circumstances they may find themselves in. Common and public goods, such as healthcare, reasonable housing, good public transport, libraries and counselling, are central for household resilience as well as above average assets like a car, animals, self-owned debt-free homes, tools, gardens and land. In addition to material support, sharing, exchanging, participation and inclusion are important non-material practices for household resilience as demonstrated in Chapters 6 to 13 of this book.

Social resilience calls for the reorientation of EU governance and institutional resources of the welfare state towards greater holistic, multidimensional and systemic understanding of household resilience and mobilization of collective household resources for resilience practices. It combines both macro- and micro-level mobilization of multiple, collective resources.

This chapter has discussed the problems seen in the contemporary EU discourses about resilience and argued for another kind of resilience approach to deal with the increasing number of poor, vulnerable households. Resilience here means a positive, transformative capacity to be supported and strengthened among the households. While there are many doubts about usability and applicability of resilience thinking for EU policies, its added value lies in its power as a convening concept, opening up different societal actors to new ways of thinking amongst the EU and providing a common ground for engagement in building household resilience among the European countries (cf. Wagner and Anholt 2016).

NOTE

1.   This section has been developed in collaboration with Markus Promberger.

REFERENCES

Atkinson, T. (2002), 'Social inclusion and the European Union', *JCMS* 40(4): 625–43.
Bourbeau, P. (2018), 'A genealogy of resilience', *International Political Sociology* 2(1): 19–35.
Capucha, L., Calado, A. and Estêvão, P. (2014), *International state of the art. Work package 2: International report*, unpublished RESCuE project report.
Christou, G. (2015), *Cybersecurity in the European Union: Resilience and adaptability in governance policy*, London: Palgrave.
Dagdeviren, H. and Donoghue, M. (2015), *Socio-economic practices of households. Work package 4: International report*, unpublished RESCuE project report.
Dagdeviren, H., Donoghue, M. and Meier, L. (2017), 'The narratives of hardship: The new and the old poor in the aftermath of the 2008 crisis in Europe', *The Sociological Review* 65(2): 369–385.
Davidson, D. J. (2010), 'The applicability of the concept of resilience to social systems: Some sources of optimism and nagging doubt', *Society and Natural Resources* 23(12): 1135–49.
de Bruin, A. and Dupuis, A. (2008), 'Making employability "work"', *The Journal of Interdisciplinary Economics* 19(4): 399–419.
Dryzek, J. (1997), *The politics of the Earth: Environmental discourses*, Oxford: Oxford University Press.
European Commission (2010), *Europe 2020*. Available at: http://ec.europa.eu/europe2020/index_en.htm (accessed 15 March 2019).
European Commission (2013a), *Action plan for resilience in crisis prone countries 2013–2020*. Available at: http://ec.europa.eu/echo/files/policies/resilience/com_2013_227_ap_crisis_prone_countries_en.pdf (accessed 3 September 2020).
European Commission (2013b), *Cybersecurity strategy of the European Union: An open, safe and secure cyberspace*. Available at: https://ec.europa.eu/digital-single-market/en/news/eu-cybersecurity-plan-protect-open-internet-and-online-freedom-and-opportunity-cyber-security (accessed 3 September 2020).
European Commission (2013c), *Building resilience – the EU's approach*, fact sheet. Available at: http://ec.europa.eu/echo/files/aid/countries/factsheets/thematic/resilience_en.pdf (accessed 3 September 2020).

European Commission (2015), *A digital single market strategy for Europe – COM(2015) final*. Available at: https://ec.europa.eu/digital-single-market/en/news/digital-single-market-strategy-europe-com2015-192-final (accessed 3 September 2020).

European Commission (2016), *Global foreign policy and security strategy*. Available at: https://europa.eu/globalstrategy/en/state-and-societal-resilience (accessed 3 September 2020).

European Commission (2017), *European pillar of social rights*. Available at: https://ec.europa.eu/commission/priorities/deeper-and-fairer-economic-and -monetary-union/european-pillar-social-rights_en (accessed 3 September 2020).

European Council (2013), *Council conclusions on EU approach to resilience, Brussels: European Council*. Available at: https://eucivcap.files.wordpress.com/2017/03/20130528-council_conclusions_eu_approach_resilience.pdf (accessed 3 September 2020).

Foucault, M. (1972), *The archaeology of knowledge & the discourse on language*, New York: Pantheon Books.

Gray, J. and Dagg, J. (2016), *Longitudinal and biographical aspects of household resilience. Work package 6: International report*, unpublished RESCuE project report.

Hall, P. A. and Lamont, M. (2013), *Social resilience in the neoliberal era*, Cambridge: Cambridge University Press.

Hankivsky, O. and Cormier, R. (2011), 'Intersectionality and public policy: Some lessons from existing models', *Political Research Quarterly* 64(1): 217–29.

Hannigan, J. (2012), *Disasters without borders: The international politics of natural disasters*, Cambridge: Polity.

Hermann, C. (2014), 'Structural adjustment and neo-liberal convergence in labour markets and welfare: The impact of the crisis and austerity measures on European economic and social models', *Competition and Change* 18(2): 111–30.

Joseph, J. (2013), 'Resilience as embedded neoliberalism: A governmentality approach', *Resilience: International Policies Discourses, Practices* 1(1): 38–52.

Joseph, J. (2014), *Explaining the EU's resilience turn: A not so special tool of a somewhat special actor*. Available at: https://kclrcir.org/2014/05/26/explaining-the-eus-resilience-turn-a-not-so-special-tool-of-a-somewhat-special -actor/ (accessed 3 September 2020).

Keck, M. and Sakdapolrak, P. (2013), 'What is social resilience? Lessons learned and ways forward', *Erdkunde* 67(1): 5–19.

Kratochvil, P. (2013), *The EU as a political actor: Analysis of the four dimensions of EU actorness*. Available at: https://www.nomos-elibrary.de/10.5771/9783845235585/the-eu-as-a-political-actor (accessed 3 September 2020).

Kristensen, S. B. and Jovanovich, T. H. (2015), 'Introduction – understanding EU actorness today: The role of crisis on the division between EU's internal and external actions and practices', *International Journal of Public Administration* 38(12): 833–37.

Larner, W. (2011), 'C-change? Geographies of crisis', *Dialogues in Human Geography* 1(3): 319–35.

Lorenz, D. F. (2013), 'The diversity of resilience: Contributions from a social science perspective', *Natural Hazards* 67: 7–24.

Manyena, S. B. (2006), 'The concept of resilience revisited', *Disasters* 30(4): 434–50.

Maxwell, S. (2013), *How can the EU take forward the resilience agenda: A ten point plan.* Available at: http://www.simonmaxwell.eu/blog/how-can -the-eu-take-forward-the-resilience-agenda-a-ten-point-plan.html (accessed 3 September 2020).

McQuaid, R. W. and Lindsay, C. (2005), 'The concept of employability', *Urban Studies* 42(2): 197–219.

Morgan, P. (2013), *How resilience is like a rubber band.* Available at: https://www .solutionsforresilience.com/resilience-is/ (accessed 3 September 2020).

Möttölä, K. (2016), 'EU asettuu sopeutettuun kokoon ja uuteen muottiin', *Politiikasta.* Available at: http://politiikasta.fi/eu-asettuu-sopeutettuun-kokoon -uuteen-muottiin/ (accessed 3 September).

Pawlak, P. (2015), 'Risk and resilience in foreign policy', *EPRS, European Parliamentary Research Service. Briefing.* Available at: http://www.europarl .europa.eu/RegData/etudes/BRIE/2015/568349/EPRS_BRI(2015)568349_EN .pdf (accessed 3 September 2020).

Pawlak, P. (2016), 'Resilience in the EU's foreign and security policy', EPRS, European Parliamentary Research Service. Briefing. Available at: http:// www.europarl.europa.eu/RegData/etudes/BRIE/2016/583828/EPRS _BRI(2016)583828_EN.pdf (accessed 3 September 2020).

Peck, J. and Theodore, N. (2000), 'Beyond employability', *Cambridge Journal of Economics* 24(6): 729–49.

Pintelon, O., Cantillon, B., Van den Bosch, K. and Whelan, C. T. (2013), 'The social stratification of social risks: the relevance of class for social investment strategies', *Journal of European Social Policy* 23(1): 52–67.

Promberger, M., Huws, U., Dagdeviren, H., Meier, L., Sowa, F., Boost, M., Athanasiou, A., Aytekin, A., Arnal, M., Capucha, L., Castro, C., Faliszek, K., Gray, J., Łęcki, K., Mandrysz, W., Petraki, G., Revilla, J. C., Şengül, T., Słania, B., Tennberg, M., Vuojala-Magga, T. and Wódz, K. (2014), *Patterns of resilience during socioeconomic crises among households in Europe (RESCuE). Concept, objectives and work packages of an EU FP 7 project*, Nuremberg: IAB research report 05/2014.

Reid, J. (2010), 'The biopoliticization of humanitarianism: From saving bare life to securing the biohuman in postinterventionary societies', *Journal of Intervention and State-building* 4: 391–411.

Rogers, P. (2017), 'The etymology and genealogy of the contested concept', in D. Chandler and J. Coaffee (eds.), *The Routledge handbook of international resilience*, London and New York: Routledge, pp. 13–25.

Salminen, M. (2016), *Digitalising high north – on whose benefit?* Available at: http://www.arcticcentre.org/blogs/Digitalising-High-North-%E2%80%93-On -Whose-Benefit/ne2t4glg/0b5995a9-5c8c-4894-98ff-ca78711ab13e (accessed 3 September 2020).

Waever, O. (1993), *Identity, migration and the new security agenda in Europe*, New York: St. Martin's Press.

Wagner, W. and Anholt, R. (2016), 'Resilience as the EU Global Strategy's new leitmotif: Pragmatic, problematic or promising?', *Contemporary Security Policy* 37(3): 414–30.

Walker, J. and Cooper, M. (2011), 'Genealogies of resilience: From systems ecology to the political economy of crisis adaptation', *Security Dialogue* 42(2): 143–60.

Welsh, M. (2014), 'Resilience and responsibility: Governing uncertainty in a complex world', *The Geographical Journal* 180(1): 15–26.
Zebrowski, C. (2013), 'The nature of resilience', *Resilience: International Policies, Practices and Discourses* 1(3): 159–73.

17. Crisis and resilience in poor European households: core findings and conclusions

Jennifer Dagg, Markus Promberger, Marie Boost and Jane Gray

CONCEPTUAL DEVELOPMENT OF RESILIENCE

Resilience is an increasingly popular framework when linking development and wellbeing in social and ecological research and in recent years has been effective in drawing the attention of agencies, policymakers and practitioners (Walsh-Dilley et al. 2016; Joseph 2013). The significant challenge in the conceptual development of resilience for poverty research was to address previous definitions, particularly the individualistic and 'heroic' understanding of resilience as a set of individual qualities – personal traits – allowing someone to bounce back. Instead, the work in this volume focused on developing a more critical sociological understanding of the concept that endeavoured to explain how individuals and families can withstand or overcome hardship, and in some cases even thrive despite the adversity they face (Hoggett 2001; Mitchell 2013; Dagdeviren et al. 2016; Estêvão et al. 2017; Promberger et al. 2019). Exploring resilience as a social phenomenon operating within specific cultural, socioeconomic and welfare contexts, that is, across nine European countries post-recession, enabled us to embrace resilience as a complex multidimensional and dynamic process that is shaped and embedded in structures, processes and institutions. Social resilience refers to practices by which people overcome adversity through certain capacities or actions that, while individual in observation, are clearly conditioned by the social context and subjects' social position as well as being embodied in their personal histories (Dagdeviren et al. 2016; Estêvão et al. 2017).

Resilience within the poverty literature challenges the traditional deficit model that considers individuals as passive victims of circumstance, powerless to engage with structural forces that constrain or enable their opportunities. Instead resilience revives focus on people's capacities and agency; however,

301

this focus has often overemphasized individuals' strategies and practices in their use of resources rather than the material and structural conditions required for the positive use of these resources. Thus, resilience within the poverty perspective highlights the role of society, the state and the socioeconomic model that conditions social structures to operate in the way that they do. Accounting for the social and structural conditions that mitigate poverty spotlights, and may challenge, the mechanisms and instruments of the welfare state that redistribute resources to those most in need. After this book and the underlying research, it seems clear that the scope of resources provided by the welfare state should certainly provide sufficient transfer income, employment and social services, but should also go beyond toward guaranteeing a broader range of common goods to enable poverty alleviation. Moreover, it is clear that a welfare state that supports households' resilience should not confine itself to just direct monetary distribution in a strict sense or looking after and supervising dependent clients with a deficit, but should enable them to care for themselves, be it in terms of leaving poverty, in reducing dependency or improving their daily life.

The chapters of this book have attempted to reveal the ways in which households and families facing or enduring adversity or crisis managed to cope, adapt, or transform their everyday lives in order to sustain their wellbeing. In what way can it be said that they exert or engage social resilience, if at all? For many households experiencing continued hardship there is a day-to-day monotony and primacy of survival as all available resources seem to already be extended to their maximum. The central theme of social resilience is the ability to take control of one's circumstance and excel with limited resources, moving beyond simply surviving. For a select few households, the capacity to access new resources or mobilize alternative resources enabled these resilient households to gradually improve their circumstances in either the short or long term. As Estêvão et al. (2017, p. 17) argued, social resilience implies the exercise of reflexive agency to mobilize available resources and to shift risks in time and space within changing social structural contexts. Using the household as a basic economic unit enabled us to explore the ways in which families seek out different ways to develop and practice social resilience. To this end, our chapters concentrated on investigating the various dimensions of resilience such as economic, cultural and social aspects and their intersection with scale, time, gender and biography.

Since the research underlying this book started in early 2014, the literature on resilience has increased. Development economists have started to integrate social, economic and ecological aspects into a resilience framework of studying rural poverty (Lade et al. 2017), interestingly with a concept of 'capitals' similar to the Bourdieu-inspired concept of resources common to many of the chapters in this book. Planning sciences have adopted the resilience concept in a cautious way (Davoudi and Porter 2012). Studies on disaster recovery, which had adopted a socioecological 'holistic' approach as well as the resilience concept earlier, are increasingly pointing at communities' social capital and its role in resilience formation, showing a broad variety of measurement concepts to depict what we call social resources (Aldrich and Meyer 2015). In the UK, criticisms of the concept have been ongoing (Harrison 2013; Joseph 2013), and the authors of this volume have contributed new scholarship emphasizing the importance of including social structures within the investigation of resilience (Dagdeviren et al. 2016), as well as confronting UK political rhetoric about households' reactions to the crisis of 2008 and after (Dagdeviren et al. 2017, 2019). The chapter authors from Spain and Portugal have similarly challenged 'heroic' constructions of resilience, contributing new substantive and conceptual perspectives on resilience as a structural and collective phenomenon (Estêvão et al. 2017; Revilla et al. 2018). The relations between household situations and consumption practices in resilient households have been explored by Arnal Sarasa et al. (2019) and Boost and Meier (2017), and so have the interactions between resilient households, civil society organizations (Promberger et al. 2016) and certain forms of social economy (Mandrysz and Klimek 2018; Mandrysz and Wódz 2019). Gray and Dagg (2019a, 2019b) have contributed new analytical approaches and substantive findings to the growing scholarship on vulnerability and resilience within the life course. Last but not least, the topic of resilience has found a way into relevant scholars' and practitioners' handbooks on poverty and poverty research (Promberger et al. 2018; Gray et al. 2019).

Thus, the concept of resilience is on its way. Nevertheless, this way is a contested one. As Amparo Serrano pointed out,[1] there are two threads of the European policy discourse on resilience: one is the scientific discourse most of the contributions in this volume are following, investigating the capacities of members of a population getting by better in terms of wellbeing and available use-values, within given social and political contexts, in order to learn and improve social and economic support interventions. But the other one is using the term of resilience in the context of a political discourse on downsizing state responsibilities and shifting them to municipalities, neighbourhoods, families and individuals, diminishing the state's role as a guarantor of good living conditions when facing crises in economy, political or public safety. We think the concept of resilience is well worth defending against misuse by neoliberal political agendas. The research results compiled in this book clearly point towards the need to maintain and enhance social investment, not only in direct transfer incomes but also in social, educational, informational and other infrastructure as common goods (see also Chapters 14 and 16 of this volume).

RESILIENCE AND ITS RESOURCES

Resilience among poor households is a comparatively rare phenomenon, especially when focusing on a short timeframe (see the discussion in Chapter 1, this volume, about differences in the editors' perspectives on this point) and when looking at households living below or around the poverty line, registered poor or not, and if we define resilience roughly as getting by better than others under similar circumstances. Partly, this rareness of resilience is associated with poverty itself. Being in poverty usually means that mainstream strategies of sustaining or improving circumstances have failed, or have not been available for long enough, such as selling capital assets or finding a new decently paid job. Such strategies could be considered the standard forms of resilience for the propertied or working classes. The few resilient cases we actually could observe were able to identify and mobilize alternative resources which comparable non-resilient cases could not, in the latter case mostly because those resources simply were not there, or were restricted, underestimated, seemingly obsolete or forgotten, insufficient or not accessible at all. Now what are these resources, available and used by a few, and unavailable for many? In analogy to Pierre Bourdieu's sorts of capital, we can classify the resources as economic, social and cultural – but before we come to that, we must take a look at what might be called personal resources.

Personal traits are the key sources of physical and psychological resilience. They are astonishingly strong in description but somehow less powerful in explanation – like a person being strong due to his or her strength, or being able to solve problems according to an extraordinarily high personal problem-solving capacity. This might be one explanation why an important part of the research on resilience has been turning towards protective or salutogenetic factors (Lösel and Bliesener 1990; Antonovsky 1987), which can encompass not only physical properties, psychological factors and close personal relations, but also epidemiologic, social, cultural and economic factors, paralleling the concept of resources utilized in this book. However, in the next step, from a sociological perspective it is hard to distinguish personal characteristics from social factors, because 'the social' is everywhere, in nourishment, body habits, health culture formed by social stratification or socially asymmetric histories. This might lead us to the conclusion that the social and the personal are just two different aspects of observing the same phenomenon, and not two different phenomena. But there is also good reason to reject this, and to regard personal characteristics as a separate phenomenon. Humans are tied to temporality and live in history, and their life is a complex longitudinal path of events, sensemaking and practice (see Dilthey 2010[1927]; Schütz 2013; Abbott 2016 and Chapter 8 in this volume). As a condition of a certain life path, history comes into play twice: first as the conditions of an individual's socialization in the formative period, not completely determining but influencing the personality and its further development strongly, and, second, as an external challenge in the present (Dagdeviren et al. 2016). Both are not the same – as the social structures who influenced us in our formative period are not those we encounter today. History has its own path of change and development, which in turn is connected to the aggregated life nexuses (Dilthey 2010[1927]) of individuals, as they take a linked developmental form within the life courses (and bodies) of historical individuals (see also Gray and Dagg 2019b). Again, this connection is not a deterministic one, as the development of social structures involves contradictions and open-ended conflicts (Giddens 1984), information loss or structural oblivion (Mannheim 1928) and other unintended consequences.

This indeterminateness and contradictoriness of histories and historical influences on the personal identity is one of the sources where individual degrees of freedom come from (Dagdeviren et al. 2016). Thus, we can roughly define freedom at least as the distance between the historical conditions of an individual's socialization period, and the present social conditions. Individuals' identities include or comprise patterns of culture and practice learned and incorporated earlier in life, and individuals utilize those patterns for coping with the present historical conditions of social structures. Thus, the personality or individual with a biography is a fundamental dimension for resilience, aside from the actual environment of resources and risks. The trajectories and life paths of individuals can suffer or gain physically and psychologically from crises, or positive developments in their social and cultural environment, which form an important bridge between sociological and psychological research on resilience. The most impressive connection can be found in the 'healing' type of resilience in Chapter 14 of this volume, where the 'crisis' is less the economic crisis alone, and more a painful family event or process that coincides with the challenges presented by the crisis. In that case, the use of social resources manifested as resilience practices that transformed the negative downward trajectory of the interviewee's life path to recover a sense of physical, psychological and social stability. Apart from this, psychological resilience plays a certain role in most of the resilient poor families but, given our disciplinary backgrounds, we decided not to focus on this well-researched issue, looking instead at the under-regarded environmental resources of resilient poor families – economic, cultural and social.

Economic resources relevant for resilience are manifold. First, they may include small private productive assets, like a self-owned home, a car (however old), a garden, tools and premises, all of which allow participation in several forms of formal and informal economic activity, be it for self-subsistence, gift exchange, wages in kind or money, as labour or small business or indiscernible mixtures of both. Moreover, there are resources which could be called natural, including access to public land, entitlements and rights (formal or informal), allowing for foraging, fishery or hunting, secondary harvesting or other use of natural conditions, but there is also appropriation of leftovers, abandoned stuff, be it formally redistributed through foodbanks and charity shops or just found on the street, by rummaging in waste sites or in open nature. Other economic resources comprise small informal jobs, informal entrepreneurship or self-employment. As Pahl (1988, p. 250) noted with respect to an earlier recessionary period, participation in informal economic activity requires 'in addition to free time, tools, transport and social contacts', all of which are more scarcely available to those in poverty.

A third category of economic resources is common goods, some public in the strict sense such as public education and information, public transport and infrastructure, be they directly or indirectly funded by the state or not, enabled or supported by law, or not. Some are accessible through restricted collectives, like cooperatives or clubs – such as housing, fishing or hunting grounds, non-commercial banking, mutual help societies like non-private healthcare services, community centres, housing cooperatives and the like, some of it organized through various forms of social economy (see Chapter 12 of this volume). It has to be noted that the public character of such resources, where they exist, has a double effect: the first is quite simple – they offer affordances, goods and services without or with little monetary price as the costs are shared by all citizens and/or members, benefits go to members or people in need, and profits, where occurring, can be socialized through different means. They are de-commercialized, non- or less-commercialized, and they do or do not fully function as a commodity, thus the term de-commodification applies (Esping-Andersen 1990). The second effect is that such public or common goods – at least if existing at a larger scale – may also put market prices under pressure or keep them at bay. This is the main function of neoliberalism, to put public goods under political pressure, and for private suppliers to transfer their competitive fight into the political sphere, at all levels.

One open question is how to consider welfare benefits in this respect? The operational answer is that welfare certainly is a public good, usually coupled with restricted entitlements (such as means tested benefits), but it differs from the other mentioned public goods in a sense that receiving income transfers is the standard case for non-resilient situations in developed welfare states. Welfare benefits have been created precisely for exactly those situations and households where all other means have failed, and thus they are the point of comparison for resilience, meaning not only to survive but to get by better than others under similar circumstances. This means a triple role of the welfare state in relation to resilience: guaranteeing the existence and accessibility of all or specific public goods in general, creating special public goods for poor households (from subsidized jobs to a counselling infrastructure) and producing a safety net of transfer incomes for those whose other activities fail – which of course is also crucial for resilient poor households, as their resilience is fragile.

Cultural resources include two rather different types. The first is what we might call cultural capital (Bourdieu 2002[1986]), which may be converted to human capital (Becker 2009), whether we deem these terms appropriate or not (see Promberger 2017 for the latter position). It consists of knowledge, skills and practical capabilities, whether acquired through education and training and/or by practical experience, ranging from certified primary, secondary and tertiary education, vocational training, through fragmentary or non-certified versions, to learning by doing and training on the job. Findings indicate that these kinds of resources appear in resilient families a bit more often than in non-resilient ones. Without the final word spoken yet – still being in the qualitative world – we can justifiably hypothesize that practical labour or craft skills as well as fragmentary academic education strengthen resilience. Access to a society's cultural resources and practical knowledge is a crucial common good for transferring those resources from societies and communities to individuals and families.

The second type of cultural resources relevant for resilience are the value systems or cultural frames (see Lamont and Small 2008) that allow persons and families concerned to maintain positive self-esteem and make sense of their lives even under the condition of being less successful, or of being outsiders from the point of view of competitive personal careers and economic success. We have encountered religious and other 'traditional' ethical frameworks, valuing solidarity, community, traditional spirituality, trust or charity over economic success, but also post-traditional value frameworks based on creativity, spirituality, mutual help and tolerance, in some cases manifesting themselves in a certain aesthetic self-expression (see Chapter 13, this volume) or community related ritual practice (see Chapter 11, this volume), but all of them supporting the respective resilient households in leading a life at least some way apart from the constraints of careers, consumerism and commodification.

Social resources have been shown to be extremely important for the resilience of poor or close-to-poverty households. The term 'networks' might seem familiar yet not sufficiently complex to describe what case studies reveal as sophisticated layers of social tissue, or social capital. (There is a very substantial body of research on social networks, social capital and poverty. For recent authoritative discussions see Nast and Blokland 2014; Curley 2010; Desmond 2012.) Complex networks and layers include tissues of the immediate family or circle of intimate relationships, the wider kin of nephews, brothers, sisters, ex-partners, uncles and aunts, cousins, nephews, in-laws, step- or grandparents or grandchildren, relationships that often stretch out across several generations

and long spatial distances. Neighbours, schoolmates, co-students, fellows of
the trade, church parish, prayer brotherhood or non-governmental organization
(NGO) members, colleagues, bosses, all also with an 'ex-', party comrades,
army pals, club mates constitute the third layer, while well-running contacts
to decision makers in formal or semiformal organizations as well as good
customer relations form the fourth layer.

An informal job offer, a business opportunity, a small loan, a hot meal,
a basket of potatoes, a room for a couple of days or relevant information might
come from anywhere among the layers and within the network. Gift exchange,
or social exchange in various ways, could be observed as a dominant mode of
keeping up those social relations which circulate goods and opportunities that
enable households to do better than expected. Three hypotheses can be derived
from these observations: (i) Good intimate relations may support resilience
– which is in line with long standing psychological findings (Werner 1993).
(ii) Unemployment and impoverishment have usually been considered to be
associated with a reduction of network involvement since Jahoda et al. (1933).
But a substantial part of the observed resilient households seems to break this
rule, showing comparably high participation in networks. (iii) Social relations
serve a dual purpose, as transfer and mobilization channels for other resources,
as well as reproducing themselves, not only as being practically useful, but for
the life satisfaction and sense of belonging of the participants.

Solely identifying above-average resources beyond money or decent jobs
would not do justice to what we found among resilient households. Much
of the impact of becoming resilient rests with identifying and utilizing these
resources and combining them in an efficient way. Being unemployed means
not having to use one's time for paid work, and lots of literature claims detrimental effects on the unemployed by simply having too much time and too
little structure in everyday life (as early as Jahoda et al. 1933). First recorded
of men in Marienthal, an Austrian working-class neighbourhood doomed by
unemployment, this probably does not count for the poor in general, as organizing a life around the poverty line can be extremely time consuming – often
for female household members. Considering the case studies underlying the
book chapters, it seems as if leading a resilient life in a low-income situation
requires long hours and huge efforts – going for bargains, walking to a food
bank and queuing up, doing extended housework, extensive do-it-yourself,
subsistence work, informal jobs or engaging in struggles with welfare authorities, on top of the usual care, housekeeping, supply and consumption work.
Low monetary budget and extensive hours create a pressure of efficiency on
the decisions on household practices. The regular answer of economics is
that efficiency comes from division, specialization and/or standardization of
labour, and an economy of scale. A plumber in the early twenty-first century
does his job efficiently not only because he knows his trade, but also as he does

not have to produce the tubes, joints and sinks himself, not to mention having to do agriculture, fishing or forestry to supply his household with basic goods. A bank accountant neither has to print the banknotes nor set the bank building up, nor does she have to raise chickens or grow wine to have good food on her table – it was Emile Durkheim (2014[1893]) who emphasized the role of this 'organic' division of labour between specialized workers for the formation of society.

The surprising finding, for the authors of Chapters 2, 4 and 14 of this volume, was that resilient families have to step out of this efficiency pattern to a certain degree – to extend their scope of action and reintegrate practices into their daily life which are outside their profession, or outside the scope of what a normal twenty-first century working-class household normally is expected to do. And they have to combine instead of specializing, in two substantial ways. First, in **combining effects**, they seem to select practices which do not maximize just one kind of outcome, but create different outcomes at satisfying levels at the same time. The higher the diversity of outcomes per activity the better – as in the case of the Finnish woman in Chapter 2, collecting berries with her children: knowledge transfer, improving the family diet, releasing the leisure budget and investing time into family relations by spending monetarily cheap but valuable family time. Or, like the García family, in Chapter 14, meeting with other families from the parish to share a meal where everyone contributes what they can, with the yield of strengthening inter-family and community ties, reproducing religious culture in terms of a holy ritual, feeding those who have less and enjoying community. Second, by **combining sources**: a garden gives a better yield when the gardener has better knowledge and skills, thus combining soil and knowledge. Informal jobs come easier and are better paid when one is better qualified and more involved in professional net-works. A skilled person combines an old car with tools to be a mobile informal craftswoman – like the travelling brides' dressmaker in one of the East German case studies.

Such processes so far happen mostly below the radar of poverty research in present-day developed countries. Development economics and labour history sometimes speak of mixed economy (Malcolmson 1988) or multi-source livelihoods (Gladwin et al. 2001), but rarely talk about synergies between such sources or a plurifunctionality of practices, which Promberger et al. (see Chapter 4, this volume) suggest as an important analytical concept. Nevertheless, the basic idea is in the world since Mauss' (2002[1923/24]) analysis of the gift exchange (see below). And there is a small but relevant handful of theoretical and empirical sources we drew upon, first, when specifying and designing the project and trying to align our first empirical suspicion with theory and previous results (see Chapter 2), second, when connecting the – sometimes surprising – findings to the previous state of the art. Promberger et al.'s discovery started with Robert Malcolmson's paper on the mixed economy of seventeenth-century rural English working-class households (1988), of which working for wages was just a part, with Marcel Mauss' famous essay on the gift discovering the unity of economic exchange and social relations (2002[1923/24]), Anthony P. Cohen's paper on the Whalsay islanders still keeping up ancient forms of agriculture for cultural and social reasons (Cohen 1979), and Wilfried Deppe's observation (1982) that the urbanization of the German working class went relatively slowly, with rural roots and cultural patterns continuing far into the second half of the twentieth century, as well as observations among East German households, informal labour or the datcha economy, family traditions and transferred narratives about bad times (Kreher 2012), case study reports on rationality in poverty situations (Jordan et al. 1992), Massimiliano Mollona's reports from Sheffield after Deindustrialization (2017) and some findings on persisting working-class identities and practices through economic change (Kirk et al. 2011) in which many authors of this book had been involved earlier. Despite these scattered works, there was hardly any international comparative case study research on household-level practices around the poverty line in developed countries before the research for this book was undertaken.

There is also an existing literature on the everyday presence and relevance of informal economy, not only in developing countries but in the heart of metropolitan capitalism (for example Portes et al. 1989) and the observation that seemingly obsolete cultural patterns were moving on through biographies and through time with the sheer function of contributing to identity confirmations (see Kirk et al. 2012), but being ready to become activated if necessary – Raymond Williams' (1977) idea of residual cultural patterns was originally formulated for working-class cultural patterns in literature and other forms of self-expression, but easily transferred into the analysis of household economy. This fitted well into the more general findings of the 'ecology of life' approach in anthropology: human–animal–plant relations, ecosystems, human economic endeavour, human identities and psyche in Arctic (and other indigenous) life – many of them still existing and active – enskilment and embodiment of knowledge and practice (Nergård 2004, 2006; Ingold 2002; Pálsson 1994). Quite soon, then, connections were made to the economy of common goods (Ostrom 1990; Dietz et al. 2003), a number of which we observed to be used more extensively in resilient households than in others. Chapter 2 in this volume gives an impression of how this process of combined empirical and theoretical discovery worked, while Chapter 14 shows the relevance of common goods for particular types of household resilience. It turned out that people under pressure, at least some of them, the resilient ones, can fall back into different, sometimes older layers of economic behaviour, utilize social, economic and cultural resources forgotten or undiscovered, and create stability not by scaling up their core activity, but by diversification of sources, giving preference to plurifunctional practices.

Now, what does this utilization of – non-monetary – resources do for the resilient households observed compared to the non-resilient, or what is the outcome? First of all, it improves the livelihood, not always necessarily in monetary terms, but in terms of available use-value or practical value. Second, it improves the subjective quality of life. Third, it may reduce the need for transfer income, but, fourth, it does not reduce the need for the welfare state, its infrastructure and capacity as a lender of last resort, as resilience turned out to be a gradual and vulnerable phenomenon. Fifth, it does not come for free but needs investment of time and energy – and requires reinvestment of gained yields, like garden fruit spent in gift exchange, or the self-repaired car allowing a person to drive to a small job, or meet a city official to arrange a stage play for and with poor inhabitants. Sixth, the time and energy spent may well exceed that of an employed mid-level working-class family, may be unevenly distributed within the household, and – in some cases – may overburden household members and/or cause problematic effects on their health. And, seventh, where it improves the actual living conditions, it may reduce transfer incomes required but does not necessarily bring people out of a poverty or close-to-poverty situation. Cases actually returning into paid sustainable and decent employment seem to be a minority among the resilient cases, which themselves are a minority among the poor, which are again a minority among the working classes. As a last remark on this, we have to keep in mind that these are findings for the case studies of the RESCuE project, namely about 250 households scattered across nine European and neighbour countries – certainly more than anecdotal evidence, but not representative in a statistical sense – thus functioning as a hypothesis for further investigation. Furthermore, additional research on welfare state variations in households' capabilities to access and mobilize such non-monetary resources is needed.

CRISIS, RESILIENCE AND INTERSECTIONS

For low-income households, the importance of sustained paid employment is crucial to ensure that the needs of family members are provided for. For many households across the nine countries, the Financial Crisis and Recession resulted in a loss of employment opportunities, particularly stable and secure paid employment. It also affected men and women differently, in that, unemployment as a result of the crisis had a more pronounced direct effect on men, while austerity policies following the crisis affected women (see Chapter 9, this volume). For example, Barry and Conroy (2013) highlighted the phased nature of the crisis in Ireland and how this affected men and women differently. They found that men, particularly young men, were more affected by the crisis during the years 2008–2010, while the second phase of the crisis during 2011–2012 affected women. They suggest that these differences highlight the transition of the crisis from the male-dominated construction sector to the more female-dominated service industry. As a result, precarious and informal employment prevailed with many households combining different forms of formal, informal and precarious employment opportunities. In some of the observed cases, this deterioration in working conditions and insecurity within the working environment in terms of access to sufficient working hours, employment rights and social protection can prevent households from anticipating their future, as so much effort is concentrated upon prioritizing present needs. Additionally, this external change of working environment can impact upon the internal domestic dynamics or 'gender regime' of households in terms of labour market participation, household duties and care work. The findings in Chapter 9 of this volume revealed how households' prior gender organization was found to affect their capacity to overcome hardship during the recession. Single parent households and households with traditional and inflexible gender regimes proved rigid in their capacity to manoeuvre assigned identities, shift caring and domestic duties, and alternate engagement in the labour market.

Unemployment, low wages and insecure employment conditions resulted in few participants having savings to guard against additional unexpected developments, or ill-timed transitions in their lives, such as illness or relationship breakdown. Turning points, such as loss of employment, can trigger critical moments when such ill-timed transitions collide with wider socioeconomic effects creating a 'perfect storm' of challenges that often contributed to overwhelming economic and emotional strain (see Chapter 8, this volume). Despite such adverse circumstances and experiences, families engaged in practices to try to stabilize their incomes, including combining different forms of work, for example taking up insecure jobs like cash-in-hand to complement other sources of income, zero contract hours, engaging in successive short-term contracts, or periods of short-term emigration. Arguably, these practices do not generate long-term resilience but do act as short-term measures to stabilize income generation, particularly when combined with in-work benefits and child benefits. In many countries, such as Finland, Germany, the UK and Ireland, state transfers supported households in remaining above the poverty line despite austerity policies. This can be contrasted with Greece where austerity policies ravaged social protection measures. Additionally, reverse migration from urban to rural locations in Greece raised the chances of economic opportunities and reduced the cost of living.

While some families focused on stabilising their income, many also endeavoured to lower their cost of living (see Chapters 6 and 14, this volume). Material deprivation or 'going without' ranged from essential consumption to non-essential consumption depending on the severity of hardship they experienced. Essential consumption included heating, food and medical necessities while curtailing non-essential expenses such as holidays and leisure activities directly affected children. Instead of paid activities for children, families sought free public spaces and resources to entertain children, particularly during school holidays. Economizing activities such as bargain hunting, strict budgeting, self-provision, family support and reconfiguring living conditions contributed to enabling households to adapt to their new circumstances. Within these economizing narratives, the prominence of the protective woman/mother figure emerged in terms of direct material care, orchestrating care through the activation of networks and relationships beyond the household, and emotional care (see Chapter 9). In general, although men who faced unemployment took up greater caring roles within the household, these were temporary as some were unable to rectify their subjective identity with its current objective status as unemployed; for many they remained workers. As such, these shifts of internal household dynamics did not lead to greater gender equality, but did provide opportunities for women to assert their ability to enter the work force, or become the main breadwinner of the household, albeit often precarious and short lived. In some cases, it was only the fact that women could delegate care tasks to other members of their extended family (mainly grandmothers) that made it 'worthwhile' or even possible for them to go out to work.

At the same time, families not only improved their livelihood, but also maintained their self-esteem and sense of dignity by participating in practices of informal exchange, group solidarity and acts of reciprocity. Sharing cars, tools and magazine subscriptions, providing repair skills, giving or taking home-made or home-grown foodstuffs, as well as providing financial support enabled families and individuals to stimulate and transfer their knowledge and skills into resilient practices that provided benefit for themselves and others. Additionally, this behaviour of proactively mobilizing cultural resources served to stymie social isolation triggered by a loss of social status and financial resources. Engaging in cultural activities that required persistent and conscious participation in the cultural life of the community ensured a break from the normal daily routine (see Chapter 11, this volume). As such, linking in with local community groups and activities instilled confidence in the creative use of existing cultural resources and enabled the implementation of possessed knowledge and experience to transfer into cultural elements. In fact, cultural activities that supported values transformed into durable resilience practices that over time were transmitted through generations and were gradually assimilated as tacit knowledge. For example, self-help bricolage, such as car repairs or sewing, functioned as a shared activity intergenerationally within families, or between families, enabling individuals to cope with crisis through the creative use of shared knowledge. Norms, values and behaviour models available to individuals and groups through cultural transmission constitute the foundations of daily practices, and knowing how to go on (Promberger 2017; see also Chapters 7 and 14, this volume).

In this sense, resilient households were those that managed to move beyond the physical trappings of the home and connect to networks of solidarity within their neighbourhood or community. While social participation at the local scale was most important in terms of bolstering the opportunities of household resilience, it also posed the possibility of seriously hindering household resilience in instances where a reactionary sense of place presented itself and excluded certain groups and collectives, particularly along cultural, ethnic or religious lines (see Chapters 10 and 11, this volume). Under globalization, social relations have expanded spatially leading to translocal connections, that is, between people living in different places, with residents of a locality increasingly affected by processes that operate at scales higher than the local. Consequently, a progressive sense of place is related to networks that link a particular place to other localities as well as higher scales, with their success determined by the degree of inclusiveness of those networks. The successful operation of community organizations and networks that function to provide spaces of communication, solidarity and support for families facing difficulties can be used to rationalize a retreat of the welfare state and justify neoliberal policies. At the same time, high functioning networks or organizations can evolve to become part of the social economy. Social economy enterprises operate as alternative forms of employment and support local development as they are often active in areas of social protection, social services, healthcare, consumer issues, neighbourhood services, education and training, or sport, culture and recreation. Undoubtedly, the social economy contributes to satisfying certain needs of citizens, often particularly those who are struggling (see Chapter 12, this volume). However, the transfer of responsibility for the provision of such services from state to civil society arguably serves to reduce the cost of policy measures that are the responsibility of the state. Through exploitation of the social economy, workers are generally paid less than their peers who are in the public sector doing equivalent work (Capucha et al. 2016, p. 6).

WHAT DOES THIS MEAN FOR RESEARCH AND PRACTICE OF SOCIAL POLICY?

Concerning social policy research, the findings of this book demonstrate the relevance and fruitfulness of two approaches that until recently have been neglected. First, a bottom-up approach can be supplementary to others, providing deeper insights and clarity about the actual ways of living in and around poverty. It can add to the rationalities of living in hardship which might be quite different from the rationalities of living from a decent working- or middle-class perspective. A diversity of livelihood practices that does focus less on optimizing the utility of a single resource and more on multisource livelihoods or multi-use sources allows for a broader scope of use-values to be achieved (the sense of 'don't put all your eggs in one basket'). Choosing the most plurifunctional practices is a striking example of alternative rationalities that enable people to live a bit better on little money. This would not have come to light without a broad set of qualitative case studies. Second, it is possible and beneficial to do international comparison based on qualitative case studies across different countries, despite different economic situations and welfare state types. Many of the resilient practices observed were quite ubiquitous – parsimoniousness, bargain hunting, informal economic activities, extended household labour, increased relevance of family ties. Others were at least loosely associated with different cultural patterns. For example, grassroots self-organization was observed more in some Mediterranean countries, although the authors of Chapter 11 reject the idea of an increased sense of community in Southern Europe. The authors of Chapter 15 diagnose a retrenchment of the welfare state, with self-organization and civil society insufficiently filling the gap. Subsistence labour based on available natural resources was observed almost everywhere, in different forms, with a loose association to rural settings – but also in huge cities like Lisbon. The most extensive examples were in Northern and Eastern Europe – including East Germany, and more seldomly in the UK, although so far there has been no quantitative measurement of the intensity or extent of these practices. For the theory of the welfare state, this indicates that the Esping-Andersen (1990) 'three worlds of welfare capitalism' model first has to be extended by a Mediterranean type, suggested by Esping-Andersen himself due to the higher meaning of familialism and clientelism, but also by a Post-Socialist type. This is because the absorption of Eastern European countries into the Anglo-Saxon, continental or social-democratic types neglects, among others, issues like the high relevance of particular patterns of informal economy, the low level of trust in state institutions, and the relatively low level of welfare state provisions in all of those countries. Therefore, the Esping-Andersen model should be downgraded a bit from an assumed truth to a starting heuristic device, in need of further testing and refinement or indeed partly replaced by other heuristics, if not by statistical data.

Moreover, the findings displayed in this book bring culture, rationalities, identity, participation, enablement, social networks and civil society into the foreground of analysis. If we want to understand poverty, we need to understand life in poverty through the means of qualitative social research. Since the early twentieth century valuable research has given voice to the poor and reconstructed the suffering of hardship and adversity, but it is not sufficient. It has to be supplemented by studies which do not treat 'the poor' as a homogeneous aggregate, but as a group with large differences and a lot of capabilities, which could be brought forward within a better framework of support. Such a framework needs to include research into those who manage to beat the odds while also looking at the conditions, side effects and necessary baselines to do so.

As well as social policy research the findings of this book have implications for practical social policy. The research results call for the rebalancing of EU governance and the institutional architecture of the welfare state towards a more holistic, multidimensional and systemic understanding of household resilience and the mobilization of collective resources. Chapter 16 discussed resilience as a policy objective in order to enable actors at all social levels to cope with contingency, unpredictability and uncertainty. Poverty continues to be a challenging social phenomenon within the EU, as reflected in the everyday struggles of households within this book to secure a decent and stable income as well as negotiate access to basic services. They provide lived experience of the erosion of the European welfare states, where austerity policies and economic restructuring of the early 2000s met the Great Recession of 2008 and after, with strong impact on welfare services, stagnation or increase in poverty (see Chapter 3), declining economic chances, and eroding social and labour rights, enabling a rise of right-wing votership and parties with openly discriminatory policy programmes in terms of age, ethnicity, citizenship and gender (Capucha et al. 2014). Resilience emphasizes resources, skills and practices for households coping with adversity, but without making them victims, guilty or heroes, because of the difficult circumstances they may find themselves. Common and public goods, such as healthcare, reasonable housing, good public transport, libraries and counselling could be shown as central for household resilience as well as above-average assets like a car, animals, self-owned debt-free homes, tools, gardens and land. In addition to material support and efforts, sharing, various levels of exchange, participation and inclusion are important non-material practices for household resilience.

De la Porte and Heins' (2015, p. 24) examination of the multiple new instruments and policy aims of the EU post-crisis that affected welfare reform revealed that those instruments designed to develop the European Social Model were comparatively weak in comparison to those seeking fiscal discipline resulting in tight budgetary criteria that restricted social investment. Patterns of response to the global financial crisis included institutional welfare change such as 'the development of employment at the margins, which re-enforces patterns of labour market dualization, toughening of access to unemployment and other benefits, as well as curtailing public expenditure in the areas of healthcare, pensions and education' (De La Porte and Heins 2015, p. 2). While the EU supported investing in a highly skilled labour force to boost economic growth, it did not balance this impetus with sustained social investment (De la Porte and Heins 2015, p. 24).

Our results reveal that households across Europe not only struggled with material demands, but also grappled with questions of identity, belonging and participation. The chapters within this book have emphasized the social nature of household resilience as families support one another, and access neighbourhood and community networks. We emphasized their role in sharing resources to support social resilience and, in doing so, their capacity to redistribute poverty-related risks to other actors and environments. At the same time, we highlighted the crucial role of the welfare state as a key provider of services and infrastructure that support social resilience. Public assets such as access to common goods, to healthcare and childcare services, the provision of reasonable accommodation, public transportation and community facilities all serve to reinforce, support and sustain household practices of resilience. The welfare state plays a crucial role in enabling income transfer through networks, job creation schemes or other subsidized labour, counselling, affordable public services, healthcare, infrastructure, and the maintenance of access to public spaces and nature that matter for households at risk. While income transfer enabled some households to remain on or above the poverty line, long-term practices of resilience were sustained by indirect support and infrastructure. Household resilience is, however, vulnerable: any strategies and practices of resilience may fail or become invalid when circumstances change. In such a case, direct transfers may be needed, together with other kinds of support, to stabilize the situation. For such households the resilience approach stresses the importance of still maintaining basic financial and other support by the welfare state when needed (Gray and Dagg 2016). Maintaining resilience also may have harmful effects in households, in terms of nutritional intake, balancing work and life, physical and mental health, and so forth. Therefore, policy measures to support household resilience should also reflect and avoid any harmful transfers of risks to other social actors, along the lines of gender, age, ethnicity, citizenship or to the natural environment.

The welfare state as we know it could foster households' resilience by supporting mutual support and self-help, providing free and accessible knowledge, starting from good housekeeping, do-it-yourself and subsistence labour, strengthening everyday social and psychological competencies, to providing space, knots and crystallization points for network and community building. Analysis reveals that it is not just social networks, ties, and respective norms and values, but also skills and education that are part of the cultural resources mobilized by resilient households. Interestingly, this not only comprises formal and certified education and training, but also informal, practical and embodied knowledge, skills and competencies ranging from gardening, small agriculture, everyday psychology, learning abilities, and knowledge of institutions and civil society.

Post-crisis social investment policies should include re-investments into the welfare state and public infrastructure that are needed to support household resilience. Common, collective and public goods beyond social services deserve more attention than in the recent past. And the cutting down and/ or privatization of formerly public services should be more thoroughly discussed in terms of their side effects on poor (including non-registered poor) or low-income groups at least from now on, and should be avoided where they are likely to cause harm, if not reversed. There is lots of evidence that privatization of services can be associated with rising prices and a decrease in coverage and availability, and often can't even keep promises of efficiency increase. Social investments in common or public goods increase social resilience in at least three ways: (i) They make institutional provisions for crises. They are broad in coverage, while marketized services emerge or continue only where there is enough substance for profit. (ii) They generate public employment and they do not target the registered poor alone, but low-income groups in a broader way, if we consider that welfare non-uptakes range above 40 per cent of the eligible population in Germany and other European countries, and there is a certain number of persons and households in low-income situations above but close to the poverty line. (iii) Moreover, there is a hard to measure but positive side effect of public social investments on social integration and social cohesion, the neglect of which has been contributing to right-wing populism and other corrosive impacts on Europe and the EU member states' political climate. The contrary narrative of overburdening public budgets by social policy, which has become so familiar to us in times of austerity policies, is a naïve fallacy, as it completely neglects the social and economic costs of issues like social exclusion, persistent poverty, malfunctioning social integration and deficient conditions for social stability and socially inclusive development. As abstract as this may sound, it is as palpable as a £10 train fare for the 29 km Hatfield to London distance, the closing down of a public library in Duisburg, evictions in Madrid, unaffordable flat rents in Munich, increasingly visible homelessness in Athens and Paris, just to name a few.

Based on analysing the lives, practices and circumstances of resilient and non-resilient households living around the poverty line, we suggest that expanding social investment, understood as public investment in common and public goods, could create a solid basis for other EU anti-poverty actions, such as introducing empowerment and enabling concepts into activation policies, make active self-inclusion into social networks and communities a target of activation policies – to make them social, so to speak. Additionally, we suggest supporting skill and education attainment, as well as alternative patterns of culture to maintain and develop the richness of humanistic European values, including those seemingly outside standard patterns of commodified life. The European welfare states have to keep up their role as lender of last resort and step in with transfer incomes where everything else fails, but also accept their role for guaranteeing, maintaining, developing and managing public goods, not just for the registered poor but for everyone who needs them. As we know now, in a period of right-wing voting, dissolutive tendencies of the implicit social contracts and increasing social fragmentation within and between the European member states, social peace and societal inclusion are at stake.

At the time of finalizing this book for publication in early 2020, we find ourselves in a crisis that exceeds the Great Recession of 2008 and beyond: the Covid-19 pandemic. In responding to this crisis, the question of resilience has arisen loudly. The resilience of cities and regions, healthcare provision and infrastructure, decision-making procedures, and critical infrastructure in our communities and countries are determining the level of suffering and loss we are encountering. The Covid-19 pandemic is capturing the escalation of precarity and inequality that has been statistically evident for the majority of people for some time. We dare say that some of the findings of this book on poor households can be transferred to social aggregates confronted with and acting against Covid-19. Leaving aside salutogenetic factors for individuals, of which we know little so far, it seems that solidarity as one expression of a non- or less-commodified system of social values helps to cope with this crisis as well, be it households exchanging mutual support, or people volunteering to help the sick or quarantined. We can also say that diversity enhances resilience – be it household practices in poverty, or supply chains in a constrained economy for health equipment or goods of daily life. It also turns out that the classical welfare state and its transfer systems have not only to work properly, but also need to expand to include minorities, immigrants and other disadvantaged groups not previously supported in order to protect the daily livelihood of millions of people in Europe. There is also the question of common goods, which under most circumstances enhance the resilience of individuals, families, cities and societies – from public libraries in poor neighbourhoods providing information and supporting education of the underprivileged to the unprofitable reserve capacities in hospitals which are extremely valuable in a pandemic situation, to a vaccine that has yet to be found and distributed quickly to all who need it through international cooperation instead of being captured by national governments. Across Europe, the Covid-19 crisis is playing out differently depending on the level of social investment and robustness of the public sector. Nevertheless, there is one difference to this crisis – virtual social networks. Direct and personal social networks supported poor families during and after the Great Recession. For the Covid-19 pandemic, virtual social networks are providing key links of support across generations and between groups and communities. It seems resilience can be one key perspective on crises of many kinds.

NOTE

1. Written correspondence between Amparo Serrano Pascual and Markus Promberger, September 2019.

REFERENCES

Abbott, A. (2016), *Processual sociology*, Chicago, IL: University of Chicago Press.

Aldrich, D. P., and Meyer, M. A. (2015), 'Social capital and community resilience', *American Behavioral Scientist* 59(2): 254–69.

Antonovsky, A. (1987), *Unraveling the mystery of health: How people manage stress and stay well*, San Francisco: Jossey-Bass.

Arnal Sarasa, M., de Castro Pericacho, C. and Martín Martín, M. P. (2019), 'Consumption as a social integration strategy in times of crisis: The case of vulnerable households', *International Journal of Consumer Studies* 44(2):111–121.

Barry, U. and Conroy, P. (2013), *Ireland in crisis 2008–2012: Women, austerity and inequality*. Available at: http://hdl.handle.net/10197/4820 (accessed 3 September 2020).

Becker, G. S. (2009), *Human capital: A theoretical and empirical analysis, with special reference to education*, Chicago: University of Chicago Press.

Boost, M. and Meier, L. (2017), 'Resilient practices of consumption in times of crisis – Biographical interviews with members of vulnerable households in Germany', *International Journal of Consumer Studies* 41(4): 371–78.

Bourdieu, P. (2002[1986]), 'The forms of capital', in N. Biggart (ed.), *Readings in Economic Sociology*, London: Wiley, pp. 280–91.

Capucha, L., Calado, A. and Estêvão, P. (2014), *International state of the art. Work package 2: International report*, unpublished RESCuE project report.

Capucha, L., Calado, A. and Estêvão, P. (2016), *National case study. Report on the social economy and household resilience. Portugal, national report*, unpublished RESCuE project report.

Cohen, A. P. (1979), 'The Whalsay Croft: Traditional work and customary identity in modern times', *Social Anthropology of Work*, New York: Academic Press, pp. 249–67.

Curley, A. M. (2010), 'Relocating the poor: Social capital and neighborhood resources', *Journal of Urban Affairs* 32(1): 79–103.

Dagdeviren, H., Donoghue, M. and Promberger, M. (2016), 'Resilience, hardship and social conditions', *Journal of Social Policy* 45: 1–20.

Dagdeviren, H., Donoghue, M. and Meier, L. (2017), 'The narratives of hardship: The new and the old poor in the aftermath of the 2008 crisis in Europe', *The Sociological Review* 65(2): 369–85.

Dagdeviren, H., Donoghue, M. and Wearmouth, A. (2019), 'When rhetoric does not translate to reality: Hardship, empowerment and the third sector in austerity localism', *The Sociological Review* 67(1): 143–60.

Davoudi, S. and Porter, L. (2012), 'Applying the resilience perspective to planning: Critical thoughts from theory and practice', *Planning Theory & Practice* 13(2): 299–333.

De la Porte, C. and Heins, E. (2015), 'A new era of European integration? Governance of labour market and social policy since the sovereign debt crisis', *Comparative European Politics* 13(8): 8–28.

Deppe, W. (1982), *Drei Generationen Arbeiterleben: eine sozio-biographische Darstellung*, Frankfurt: Campus.

Desmond, M. (2012), 'Disposable ties and the urban poor', *American Journal of Sociology* 117(5), 1295–335.

Dietz, T., Ostrom, E. and Stern, P. C. (2003), 'The struggle to govern the commons', *Science* 302(5652): 1907–12.

Dilthey, W. (2010[1927]), *The formation of the historical world in the human sciences* (Selected Works Vol. 3), Princeton, NJ: Princeton University Press. [First published in Germany in 1927 as: *Der Aufbau der geschichtlichen Welt in den Geisteswissenschaften*, Göttingen: Vandenhoeck and Ruprecht.]

Durkheim, E. (2014[1893]), *The division of labor in society*, Simon and Schuster. [First published in France as: *De la division du travail social: Étude sur l'organisation des sociétés supérieures*, 1893, Paris: Félix Alcan].

Esping-Andersen, G. (1990), *The three worlds of welfare capitalism*, Princeton, NJ: Princeton University Press.

Estêvão, P., Calado, A. and Capucha, L. (2017), 'Resilience. Moving from a "heroic" notion to a sociological concept', *Sociologia, problemas e practicas* 85: 9–25.

Giddens, A. (1984), *The constitution of society*, Oakland, CA: University of California Press.

Gladwin, C. H., Thomson, A. M., Peterson, J. S. and Anderson, A. S. (2001), 'Addressing food security in Africa via multiple livelihood strategies of women farmers', *Food Policy* 26(2): 177–207.

Gray, J. and Dagg. J. (2016), *Longitudinal and biographical aspects of household resilience. Work package 6: International report*, unpublished RESCuE project report.

Gray, J. and Dagg, J. (2019a), 'Using reflexive lifelines in biographical interviews to aid the collection, visualisation and analysis of resilience', *Contemporary Social Science* 14(3–4): 407–22.

Gray, J. and Dagg, J. (2019b), 'Crisis, recession and social resilience: A biographical life course analysis', *Advances in Life Course Research* 42: 100293.

Gray, J., Dagg, J. and Rooney, C. (2019), 'Coping with poverty in everyday life', in B. Greve (ed.), *International handbook of poverty*, Abingdon: Routledge.

Hacker, J. S. (2004), 'Privatizing risk without privatizing the welfare state: The hidden politics of social policy retrenchment in the United States', *American Political Science Review* 98(2): 243–60.

Harrison, E. (2013), 'Bouncing back? Recession, resilience and everyday lives', *Critical Social Policy* 33(1): 97–113.

Hoggett, P. (2001), 'Agency, rationality and social policy', *Journal of Social Policy* 30: 37–56.

Ingold, T. (2002), *The perception of the environment: Essays on livelihood, dwelling and skill*, Abingdon: Routledge.

Jahoda, M., Lazarsfeld, P. F. and Zeisel, H. (1933), *Die Arbeitslosen von Marienthal. Ein soziographischer Versuch über die Wirkungen langandauernder Arbeitslosigkeit*, Psychologische Monographien, 5, Leipzig: Hirzel.

Jordan, B., James, S., Kay, H. and Redley, M. (1992), *Trapped in poverty? Labour market decisions in low-income households*, London: Routledge.

Joseph, J. (2013), 'Resilience as embedded neoliberalism: a governmentality approach', *Resilience* 1(1): 38–52.

Kirk, J., Contrepois, S. and Jefferys, S. (2011), *Changing work and community identities in European regions*, London: Palgrave Macmillan.

Kirk, J., Jefferys, S. and Wall, C. (2012), 'Representing identity and work in transition: The case of South Yorkshire coal-mining communities in the UK', in J. Kirk, S. Contrepois and S. Jefferys (eds.), *Changing work and community identities in European regions*, London: Palgrave Macmillan, pp. 184–216.

Kreher, S. (2012), *Von der 'Leutenot' und der 'Not der Leute*', Leipzig: Bohlau.

Lade, S. J., Haider, L. J., Engström, G., and Schlüter, M. (2017), 'Resilience offers escape from trapped thinking on poverty alleviation', *Science Advances* 3(5): e1603043.

Lamont, M. and Small, M. L. (2008), 'How culture matters: Enriching our understanding of poverty', in D. Harris and A. Linn (eds.), *The colors of poverty: Why racial and ethnic disparities persist*, New York: Russell Sage Foundation, pp. 76–102.

Lösel, F., and Bliesener, T. (1990), 'Resilience in adolescence: A study on the generalizability of protective factors', in K. Hurrelmann and F. Lösel (eds.), *Health hazards in adolescence*, Berlin, New York: De Gruyter, pp. 299–320.

Malcolmson, R. W. (1988), 'Ways of getting a living in eighteenth-century England', in R. Pahl (ed.), *On work: Historical, comparative and theoretical approaches*, Oxford: Blackwell, pp. 48–60.

Mandrysz, W. and Klimek, M. (2018), 'Social economy and household resilience', *Problemy Polityki Społecznej. Studia i Dyskusje* 41(2): 55–72.

Mandrysz, W. and Wódz, K. (2019), 'Social economy entities and its eco-system in different European countries', *Review of Applied Socio-Economic Research* 18(2): 58–72.

Mannheim, K. (1928), 'Das Problem der Generationen', *Kölner Vierteljahreshefte für Soziologie* 7(2): 157–185, 309–33.

Mauss, M. (2002[1923/24]), *The gift: The form and reason for exchange in archaic societies*, Routledge. [First published as: 'Essai sur le don. Forme et raison de l'échange dans les sociétés archaïques', in *L'Année Sociologique* 1 (1923/24), Paris: Alcan, 1925, pp. 30–186.]

Mitchell, A. (2013), *Risk and resilience: From good idea to good practice*, OECD Development Co-operation Working Papers No. 13, Paris: OECD.

Mollona, M. (2017), 'Factory, family and neighbourhood: The political economy of informal labour in Sheffield', *Journal of the Royal Anthropological Institute* 11(3): 527–48.

Nast, J. and Blokland, T. (2014), 'Social mix revisited: Neighbourhood institutions as setting for boundary work and social capital', *Sociology*, 48(3): 482–99.

Nergård, J. I. (2004), 'The sacred landscape', in M. Jones, and A. Schanche (eds.), *Landscape, law and customary rights: Report from a symposium in Guovdageaidnu-Kautokeino 26–28. March 2003*, Guovdageaidnu: Sámi Instituhtta, pp. 85–92.

Nergård, J. I. (2006), *Den levende erfaring: en studie i samisk kunnskapstradisjon*, Oslo: Cappelen akademisk.

Ostrom, E. (1990), *Governing the commons: The evolution of institutions for collective action*, Cambridge: Cambridge University Press.

Pahl, R. E. (1988), *On work: Historical, comparative and theoretical approaches*, New York, NY: Basil Blackwell.

Pálsson, G. (1994), 'Enskilment at sea', *Man* 29(4): 901–27.

Portes, A., Castells, M. and Benton, L. A. (1989), *The informal economy: Studies in advanced and less developed countries*, Baltimore, MD: Johns Hopkins University Press.

Promberger, M., Marinoudi, T. and Martin, M. P. (2016), 'Unter der erschütterten Oberfläche: Sozioökonomische Praktiken, Zivilgesellschaft und Resilienz in der europäischen Krise', *Forschungsjournal Soziale Bewegungen* 29(3): 86–97.

Promberger, M. (2017), *Resilience among vulnerable households in Europe: Questions, concept, findings and implications*, Nuremberg: Institute for Employment Research, IAB Discussion Paper No 12/2017.

Promberger, M., Meier, L., Sowa, F. and Boost, M. (2018), 'Armut und Resilienz', in P. Böhnke, J. Dittmann and J. Goebel (eds.), *Handbuch Armut. Ursachen, Trends, Maßnahmen*, Opladen: Budrich, pp. 341–51.

Promberger, M., Meier, L., Sowa, F. and Boost, M. (2019), 'Chances of 'Resilience' as a concept for sociological poverty research', in B. Rampp, M. Endreß and M. Naumann (eds.), *Resilience in Social, Cultural and Political Spheres*, Wiesbaden: VS Verlag, pp. 249–78.

Revilla, J. C., Martín, P. and de Castro, C. (2018), 'The reconstruction of resilience as a social and collective phenomenon: Poverty and coping capacity during the economic crisis', *European Societies* 20(1): 89–110.

Schütz, A. (2013), *Der sinnhafte Aufbau der sozialen Welt: Eine Einleitung in die verstehende Soziologie*, New York: Springer-Verlag.

Walsh-Dilley, M., Wolford, W. and McCarthy, J. (2016), 'Rights for resilience: Food sovereignty, power, and resilience in development practice', *Ecology and Society* 21(1): 11.

Werner, E. (1993), 'Risk, resilience, and recovery: Perspectives from the Kauai Longitudinal Study', *Development and Psychopathology* 5(4): 503–15.

Williams, R. (1977), 'Dominant, residual, and emergent', *Marxism and Literature* (1): 121–27.

Index

organizations, criticism against 212
patterns of 209
practices in individual households
214
responsibility of 201
'traditional' activities of 215
units 213
vulnerable households with 210
social economy and household resilience
198, 203
charity economy 203–5
collective/community-based
economy 207–8
concepts of 199–202
labour market (re-)integration
entities 206–7
mixed non-state social service and
support providers 205–6
role of 208–13
social embeddedness 221
social entrepreneurship 203
conceptual framework of 198
social exchange 97, 193–4, 308
social exclusion 59, 75–6, 201, 290
social expenditure per inhabitant 45
social fragmentation 180, 183
social grouping 114
social identity, transformation of 124–5
social inclusion, form of 206–7
social infrastructure 66
social innovation initiatives 180
social insurance benefits 235
social integration 24, 68, 180–81, 215
social interaction 183–4
social isolation 116, 182–5
social movements 180
emergence of 181
social networks 187–8, 222
research on 307
social norms 149–50
social participation
forms of 185–6
spaces for 185
social policy 67–8, 214–15, 282
perspectives 59
practical 316
research 314–16
social practice 76, 107, 192, 234, 291
social projects 244
social protection 101

lack of contribution to 93
measures 312
policies 211
social realities 107
social reciprocity 291
social relations 116, 187–8, 310
personal dimensions of 184–5
social relationships 211
social resilience 62–3, 236, 290, 301–2,
317–18
approach of 283–4
capacities of 60
social resources 65, 303, 307
social rights, enactment of 273–6
social sciences, embryonic in 73
social security 249
institutions 204–5
social services
suppliers of 201
system 269
social space 80
social stability 318
social stratification 81, 304
social structures
historical conditions of 305
reconfiguration of 82
social systems, cohesion of 82
social transfers 50
evolution of 44
social welfare centres 112
social welfare mechanisms 77
social workers 220
socieconomic resilience, forms of 234
societal security, implications for 283
socio-cultural environment 129
socioecological 'holistic' approach 303
socio-ecological systems 30–31
socio-economic development 202
socioeconomic inequalities 267
socio-economic practices 88–92, 99–100
forms of 89
socio-economic responses 90
socio-economic situation 189, 191
socioeconomic vulnerability 6
socio-spatial infrastructure 183–4
solidarity 181, 188–9, 193–4, 291
Southern Europe
enactment of social rights 273–6
localization and centralization of
welfare in 264–5